THE FINANCIAL TIMES

GUIDE TO

USING THE FINANCIAL PAGES

THE FINANCIAL TIMES

GUIDE TO
USING THE
FINANCIAL
PAGES

THIRD EDITION

ROMESH VAITILINGAM

FT
PITMAN
PUBLISHING

London · Hong Kong · Johannesburg · Melbourne
Singapore · Washington DC

PITMAN PUBLISHING
128 Long Acre, London WC2E 9AN
Tel: +44 (0)171 447 2000
Fax: +44 (0)171 240 5771

A Division of Pearson Professional Limited

First published in Great Britain 1993
Second edition published 1994
Third edition published 1996

© Pearson Professional Limited 1996

British Library Cataloguing in Publication Data
A CIP catalogue record for this book can be obtained
from the British Library.

ISBN 0 273 62201 3

1 3 5 7 9 10 8 6 4 2

Typeset by PanTek Arts, Maidstone, Kent
Printed and bound in Great Britain by
Bell and Bain Ltd, Glasgow

*The Publishers' policy is to use paper manufactured
from sustainable forests.*

CONTENTS

Part II
INTERPRETING THE MARKETS

Part III
UNDERSTANDING THE ECONOMIES

Part IV
BEYOND THE FINANCIAL PAGES

FOREWORD

'I don't read the financial pages,' friends sometimes tell me. 'I'm not interested in stocks and shares.'

They don't know what they are missing. Information carried each day in the business press sheds light on – and helps to explain – issues which range far beyond the stock exchange. Movements in bond and commodity prices provide sensitive indicators to trends in business activity. Economic statistics give a whole series of snapshots of the health of nations. They do not only show what has happened in the past: they also provide early signals of what is likely to happen in the future.

The markets have developed enormous political importance as well. They have become global in character, and in the process have imposed severe curbs on individual governments' freedom of action. A finance minister who behaves in what the international financial markets believe to be an imprudent way will find it very difficult to manage his national budget, and to sustain his currency.

The French found this to their cost in the early 1980s, and had to reverse their policies as a consequence.

As one of President Clinton's aides famously observed: 'I used to think that if there was reincarnation, I wanted to come back as the president or the pope. But now I want to be the bond market: you can intimidate everybody.'

But it is true that financial pages all too often have an uninviting appearance: great slabs of numbers, impenetrable columns of jargon ridden prose. Business editors have tried hard in recent years to make their pages more accessible, but the results can still look daunting to the uninitiated.

This is why I welcome the *Financial Times Guide to Using the Financial Pages*. It will certainly be of practical help to stock market investors. But it also provides a valuable service to a much wider group of readers, by explaining the way in which information

published in the financial pages can provide insights into the workings of the economy as a whole.

Why publish a new edition? There are two main reasons. The first is that the financial pages themselves are changing, as a result of competition and technological development. Business sections have expanded considerably over the past decade, as rival titles have tried to capture a larger share of readers and advertisers. Newspapers have also had to face competition from electronic news services and a whole host of specialist newsletters. The result is that financial editors have given a lot of time to refining and improving their pages. Many of the tables in the FT have been enhanced for this reason in recent years. Moreover, technology makes it possible to be much more ambitious than in the past. In the old days, the FT managed to calculate a price index for a group of 30 leading shares just once a day. Now, the power of the computer makes it possible for us to work out an index for 600 companies on a minute-by-minute basis.

The second reason for producing a new edition is that markets themselves are changing, and so are the ways of reporting on them. Features appearing for the first time in this third edition include sections dealing with new financial markets and electronically delivered financial information, plus a chapter on how to analyse company news and commentary.

The Internet offers especially exciting opportunities for publishers of financial information. It can offer limitless capacity for data, and the information which it provides can be updated during the course of the day. The *Financial Times* site on the Word Wide Web is www.com. Watch this space. For obvious reasons, I read the FT carefully every day. But I have still managed to learn new things from this guide. It will stay within arm's reach of my desk.

Richard Lambert,
Editor, *Financial Times*

INTRODUCTION

Money and the financial markets, as reflected in the television or radio news or the financial pages of a newspaper like the *Financial Times*, may often seem to be a different world, something well beyond the experience of most people. But the global movement of capital, the constant shifting of what are often vast amounts of money, does have a connection with our daily lives. Everyone has some contact with the financial system: through having a bank account; through contributing to a pension fund; through buying an insurance or life assurance policy; or through taking out a mortgage or running up an overdraft. And despite its appearance as a foreign country accessible to only a favoured few, and dealing in a baffling language of numbers and jargon, its basic workings are fairly simple to grasp.

The markets are simply a huge clearing house where the different financial needs of individuals, companies and governments can be brought together and matched through appropriate pricing mechanisms. They might be actual places or they might be networks of computer screens and telephones. Either way, they address two fundamental needs: what is variously known as saving, lending or investing – the use of funds excess to spending requirements to secure a return; and borrowing – the demand for funds over and above those already owned, to put to work in various ways.

The players in the financial markets and in the wider economy can be classified into four broad groups:

- **Investors** who have money to spare to spend on assets and, indirectly, lend it to the issuers of those assets. This includes individual investors, though nowadays the bulk of investment is done by large investing institutions such as pension funds and insurance companies.

- **Companies** which want to borrow money in order to buy capital goods or increase the scale of their business.

- **Financial institutions** (banks, building societies, brokers, dealers,

marketmakers, etc.) which act as intermediaries, bringing together the borrowers and lenders in various marketplaces.

- **Governments** which act as both borrowers and lenders, but which, in addition, regulate the markets and attempt to monitor and influence the state of the economy through fiscal and monetary policy.

The role and behaviour of each of these players are examined in the first four chapters of this book. The second part of the book looks at the different markets in which they operate: the stock markets, bond markets, international capital markets, foreign exchange and money markets, futures and options markets, and commodity markets. Each chapter takes the relevant charts and tables from the *Financial Times* and explains how they work, what their significance is, and how they might be read and employed by private individuals or business managers. The third part broadens the picture, examining the UK, European and world economies, and the effects that key economic indicators have on the financial markets.

The final chapters of the book, newly added for the third edition, move beyond the financial pages to explore other sources of financial information: the variety of newspapers, magazines, newsletters and other publications, and how to read between the lines of their financial reporting; the new electronic markets and online datafeeds, including the internet; and how to use company reports to find the key performance ratios. Readers who are very unfamiliar with the *Financial Times* may want to start here: chapter 18 gives a brief synopsis of the newspaper's contents. Lastly, two new appendices reiterate the key ratios for easy reference and list the constituent companies of the leading market indices in the United Kingdom and the United States.

This book is intended for anyone who reads or needs to read the financial pages of a newspaper. It aims to provide a simple guide to understanding the statistics and the language of modern finance. Right from the first chapter, tables of figures with explanations are introduced to accustom the reader to the ease with which the numbers (as well as the reports and comments) can be interpreted and used with just a little background.

Much of the importance of the statistics lies in the ratios between numbers rather than in the actual numbers themselves. It is the

relationship between the figures, both across companies, industries, sectors and economies, and over time that is critical. It is these ratios that investors, companies and the finance types that "make" the markets pore over to identify past patterns, future trends, and present opportunities and dangers.

The tables and charts of the financial pages are reference points, published every day as a snapshot of the state of the markets. But the markets themselves are dynamic, constantly in flux and, in some cases, trading twenty-four hours and across the globe. For readers needing immediate, real-time data, there are the more sophisticated sources of financial information of the computer age, screen-based data and telephone services. These are discussed in chapter 17.

Nevertheless, FT figures are a globally used reference point and the newspaper plays an important institutional role in the financial markets. It has pioneered such industry standards as the FT-SE (known as the 'footsie') 100 index, used widely as an indicator of the state of the UK stock market, and as a benchmark for the performance of investors' asset portfolios. Furthermore, its pages fulfil the obligation of unit trusts to publish data on the value of their funds.

Although this is the *Financial Times* guide to using the financial pages, the map it provides to understanding that newspaper's financial and economic reports, comments, tables and charts is equally applicable to other papers, and even to other media. The newspaper is merely the most detailed and widely used of the non-specialised media. Indeed, other papers frequently provide information on many of the leading indicators that the *Financial Times* has developed, such as the Footsie and its derivative products.

Before turning to the markets and their statistical analysis, some basic and recurring mathematical concepts might be valuable:

- **Average:** a single number used to represent a set of numbers. It can be calculated variously as: a mode, the number that occurs most frequently in a set of numbers; a median, the number with 50 per cent of the rest lying below it and 50 per cent above, or if there is an even quantity of numbers, the average of the middle two; the arithmetic mean, the total sum of the numbers divided by the quantity of them; and the geometric mean, the figure that derives

from multiplying the numbers together and taking their *n*th root, where *n* is the quantity of numbers.

- **Percentage:** the proportion that one number represents of another or the change in a number from one period to another. To calculate the proportion or percentage of y that x represents (whether x is another number or the difference between one number over two periods), x is divided by y. The result will be a fraction of 1, and to convert it into a percentage figure, it is simply multiplied by 100. Movements of a percentage figure might be mentioned in terms of points (one point is one per cent) or basis points (one basis point is one hundredth of one per cent). Percentage points or basis points are different from percentage changes.

- **Inverse and positive relationship:** the connection between two numbers. Numbers with an inverse relationship move in opposite directions; those with a positive relationship move together. This is the mathematical explanation of why, for example, bond prices and yields move in opposite ways; if x is equal to y divided by z, and y is constant, then as x rises, z falls or *vice versa*. But if x or z is constant, x and y or z and y will rise or fall together. The two pairs are in a positive relationship.

- **Index:** a number used to represent the changes in a set of values between a base year and the present. Index numbers blend many different ingredients into a single index, and measure changes in it by changes in its parts. This involves giving appropriate weighting to the components according to their importance in what is being measured. A weighted average is usually calculated as an arithmetic mean, either using the same weights throughout (a base-weighted index) or adjusting the weights as the relative importance of different components changes (a current-weighted index). Base-weighted indices may have the base shifted periodically.

With these simple tools and developments of them explained in the text, the reader should be well equipped to negotiate the figures of the *Financial Times'* financial pages, analysed in what follows.

All tables and figures are reproduced by kind permission of the *Financial Times*. Reproduced computer screens are courtesy of

Reuters and thanks go to *Private Eye* for permission to reproduce the Nick Whitmore cartoon on p. xvi. I would like to thank those members of staff at the *Financial Times* who have contributed their time and assistance in the preparation of this book over its three editions, particularly Adrian Dicks, Emma Tucker and Keith Fray. I would also like to thank all the staff (past and present) who have worked on the book at Pitman Publishing, notably Mark Allin, Sally Green, Helen Pilgrim and Richard Stagg. Thanks also to Stephen Eckett of Numa for advice, and especially to Annemarie Caracciolo and Skanda Vaitilingam.

"Heard the latest?"

Part I

IDENTIFYING THE PLAYERS

"To avoid having all your eggs in the wrong basket at the wrong time, every investor should diversify."

SIR JOHN TEMPLETON

"Remember that time is money."

BENJAMIN FRANKLIN

1

INVESTORS

- **Buying assets** – the important considerations: risk and return; liquidity and time; portfolio diversification; and hedging and speculation

- **Comparing investments** – how to make comparisons between the prospects for different assets: the markets on which they are traded; asset prices and the role of interest rates

- **Using the financial pages** – how to navigate through the markets: stock markets; bond markets; commodity markets; derivative markets; foreign exchange markets; money markets; and managed funds

Most people have a weekly or monthly income – remuneration for the work they put in at their job. Once their basic needs (food, drink, clothing, accommodation) are taken care of, the choices for what they do with what is left over, if anything, are essentially two. They can spend it on more "luxurious" items, such as holidays, music and books. This, together with the basic needs expenditure, is known as consumption. Alternatively, they can save it for future spending by them or their heirs, as a precaution against unanticipated future needs, or to generate future income.

Investors are people who have a surplus of money from their income that they want to save for any of these reasons. They can do this by keeping it in cash, or by putting it in a bank account or building society, the traditional meaning of savings. Alternatively, they can buy something that they expect at least to maintain its value, that might provide a flow of income, and that can be resold when needed. Any of these is an asset. How investors decide on the assets that they buy and own is the subject of this chapter.

BUYING ASSETS

Assets come in many shapes and forms: cash, bank and building society deposits, premium bonds, securities (that is, ordinary shares in a company or gilt-edged stocks, bonds issued by the government), life assurance policies, works of art and antiques, gold or foreign currencies, and houses and flats. Each type of asset has different characteristics, and the investor's preferences between those characteristics will determine which assets are bought.

The first characteristic of an asset that an investor might consider is its annual return: does ownership of it entitle the investor to receive any further income and, if so, how much? Obviously, for hard cash, the answer is no, but if that cash is placed in a building society account, the investor will earn monthly, quarterly or annual interest

at a specified rate. Similarly, a premium bond does not pay its owner any interest (though it offers the regular chance of winning a prize), but a gilt-edged bond will pay a guaranteed fixed amount each year. And ownership of ordinary shares (equities) will generally mean that the investor gets a dividend, a slice of the profits made by the company over a six or twelve-month period.

Investors typically consider the return on an asset as an annual percentage of its value. This is the rate of return or yield, and is calculated by dividing the return by the asset's value. For example, if a building society adds £5 to every £100 deposited with it for a year, the return is that £5 and the rate of return is 5 per cent. In this case, of course, it is known as the interest rate. Similarly, the yield on fixed interest securities like gilts is the fixed amount each pays, known as the coupon, as a percentage of the current price quoted in the bond market.

> **The basic rate of RETURN on an asset is the income received as a percentage of the price paid for it**

The basic rate of return on a share, the dividend yield, is calculated in a similar way: the dividend paid by the company is divided by the price of the share as quoted on the stock market. Of course, unlike bonds or indeed bank deposits, the dividend payment is by no means guaranteed. The company may, for whatever reason, decide not to pay out a dividend. But with shares, there is another way of receiving a return and that is the second important characteristic of an asset, its potential for capital appreciation.

Capital appreciation or capital growth is an increase in the value of invested money. For example, money in building society and some bank accounts earns interest, but that is the only way in which it can gain in value. In fact, if inflation is high, higher than the rate of interest, money will lose value in terms of its purchasing power, that is, how many goods can be bought with it. Gold and houses, in contrast, do not earn interest, but they can appreciate in value, their prices can rise. When inflation strikes, gold has often been a good asset to protect or hedge against loss of purchasing power. Houses too generally maintain their real value at these times (though not in the United Kingdom in recent years!).

Ordinary shares possess both characteristics: they can earn a dividend as well as appreciate in value. A share bought at a price of 100 pence might receive a dividend of 5 pence for a year, and it might also increase in price to 110 pence. In this case, the profit or capital gain is 10 pence, the total return on the asset is 15 pence and the overall rate of return is 15 per cent. Of course, the share might also fall in price in which case the return might be negative. In this example, if the price dropped to 90 pence, the capital loss is 10 pence, and the share is said to have depreciated in value by 10 per cent. Because of the dividend, the overall loss is only 5 pence, but this still means that the overall rate of return is negative at minus 5 per cent.

> The TOTAL RETURN on an asset comprises income plus capital growth; for a share, TOTAL RETURN is the dividend yield plus any change in its market price

Risk and return

The possibility of loss on an asset is the third characteristic an investor will look at. Different assets have different degrees of risk, and these usually relate to their potential for appreciation or depreciation. Bank deposits, for example, cannot appreciate or depreciate in price and, hence, are virtually risk-free: their level remains the same apart from the periodic addition of interest. Unless the bank goes under, a rather rare occurrence nowadays, the investor's money is safe. The interest rate may drop so that the annual return is lower, but the basic capital is protected from any loss except for the loss of value caused by inflation.

Gilt-edged securities, in contrast, can fall in value. However, since they are sold and therefore backed by the government, they do still guarantee to pay that fixed amount, the coupon. But ordinary shares carry the risks of both falling prices and falling yields. Not only might declining profits lead to share prices declining in the market, but they might also lead to a company deciding it cannot afford to pay as big a dividend as a proportion of the share price, or even to pay one at all. Thus, while equities offer attractive potential rewards and often a relatively safe haven from inflation, the uncertainty over the future movements of their prices makes them a risky proposition.

Clearly, some assets are riskier than others, and some offer potentially better returns, both in terms of yield and capital growth. These characteristics of risk and return that all assets possess are intimately related, and this relationship is the foundation of investment decision-making. Portfolio theory, the body of ideas that attempts to explain why investors select and organise their assets in portfolios in the way they do, has at its core the connection between risk and return, between safety and yield. And all investors should ask themselves the question: how much of my capital am I prepared to risk on an uncertain future, and how much should I ensure gets a safe, solid return?

Portfolio theory can provide a guide to making these kinds of decision, suggesting that the greater the riskiness of an asset, the greater the potential return. If an asset like a bank deposit earns a fairly certain yield, that yield will be lower than the uncertain return on an asset like an ordinary share. The owner of the riskier asset is compensated for taking on greater risk by the possibility of much higher rewards. The appropriate aphorism to encapsulate this concept might be "nothing ventured, nothing gained"!

In practice, this risk/return relationship appears to be true: the yield on a government bond is usually more than the interest rate on a bank deposit while the return on a share can be far more than both. While the dividend yield on shares is usually low compared to gilt yields, the potential for capital gain can more than make up for it. At the same time, the risk of loss is higher than for either the bond or the bank deposit. Thus, there is a trade-off between risk and return, and the investor will choose assets on the basis of his or her attitude to risk. Risk-aversion means that the primary consideration is safety: the investor will prefer owning assets that cannot fall in price. Ideally, these assets should also avoid the possibility of falling in value, but, unfortunately the assets that best do that, gold and shares, run the risk of price falls. It is also desirable for the safer assets to offer a reasonable rate of return, but again a relatively poor yield may be the cost of safety. The investor can merely select the best return among the assets that carry the maximum level of risk he or she is prepared to take on.

Different assets have different degrees of RISK; generally, the more RISK of loss, the higher the potential return

Liquidity and time

Having weighed up the risk/return trade-off, the investor will probably want to consider how easy it will be to convert an asset into ready money in the event that it is needed. This is known as the liquidity of an asset, its fourth characteristic, and it too relates to the return on an asset. Generally, the more liquid an asset is, the lower its return. The easier it is for an investor to give up ownership of an asset without undue loss, the higher the price paid in terms of foregone return. Notes and coins, for example, the most liquid of assets, earn no interest and do not appreciate in value.

Liquidity is also used in a slightly different sense as a term to describe the nature of the markets in which assets are bought and sold. An asset that is in a liquid market can be bought or sold in a substantial quantity without the transaction itself affecting its price. The most liquid markets are those with a large amount of trading, a high turnover of assets. These generally include the currency and gilt markets, discussed in detail in chapters 9 and 10.

> **LIQUIDITY is the ease with which an asset can be converted into cash; the more LIQUID an asset, the lower its return**

Asset liquidity and asset values are also affected by time, and this time value might be called an asset's fifth characteristic. For example, the longer money is tied up in a bank account, the more illiquid it is, and the higher the return it earns. Because of uncertainty about the future, especially about inflation, money today is worth more than money tomorrow. To bring their values into balance, and to encourage saving/investing rather than spending, the longer money is unavailable in the present, the more it needs to be rewarded. In addition, since the returns on other assets might change for the better over that period of time, the investor receives compensation for being unable to enjoy them. This is the second aphorism of portfolio theory: "time is money".

Another example in which time value affects asset value is the time to maturity of an asset with a finite life, such as a gilt. The nearer a gilt is to its redemption date (the time that the government will redeem it for its face value), the more likely it is to be priced at

or close to its redemption value; the further out it is, the more uncertainty and time value come into play and the further the price can be from the gilt's redemption value. In the latter case, depending on investor expectations about the future, the price might be at a premium to (above) the redemption price or at a discount (below).

With other assets as well as gilts, uncertainty, expectations, and time all combine to influence their risk/return characteristics. The interaction of these factors can have dramatic effects on asset prices, and it is important for investors to understand them when evaluating an asset's prospects for yield and capital appreciation.

> **TIME has an important effect on asset values: because of uncertainty, money today is worth more than money tomorrow**

Portfolio diversification

In selecting an asset, an investor will look at not only its own various characteristics, but also those of other assets he or she owns or intends to purchase. The whole collection of assets an investor owns is known as a portfolio, and the risk/return relationship of any given asset can be tempered by adding assets with different risk/return characteristics to the total portfolio of assets. For example, a portfolio comprising only cash in a bank account offers a safe but unspectacular return, while a portfolio made up solely of shares might perform very well but may also fall dramatically in value.

A portfolio that contains a combination of stock and cash, say with money allocated 50/50 between the two, provides a risk/return trade-off somewhere in between. In the extreme case where share values fall to zero, the total portfolio still maintains half of its value, in contrast with both an all-stock portfolio which becomes worthless, and an all-cash portfolio which holds its value. At the same time, if shares double in price, the total portfolio only makes half the profits of the all-stock portfolio, but still significantly outperforms the all-cash portfolio.

With investment objectives that seek a certain degree of safety, but also some potential of higher rewards, it makes sense to own a balanced portfolio, a range of different assets with varying degrees of

risk and potential returns. These might include shares, gilts, gold and cash plus some of the more exotic assets discussed in later chapters, such as options and Eurobonds. This is the principle of portfolio diversification, and the third aphorism of investment decision-making: "Don't put all your eggs in one basket".

> The different risk/return profiles of assets in a portfolio combine to generate its overall risk and potential return; the principle of **PORTFOLIO DIVERSIFICATION** demands a balance of stocks, bonds, cash and/or other assets

Hedging and speculation

When weighing up which assets to buy or which to hold, investors will keep returning to the degree of risk involved. The more risk-averse ones will want as much protection of their assets' value as possible, and once they have taken the first step into the unknown of investing in assets more uncertain and riskier than a building society deposit, there are various means of achieving that.

The basic strategy is called hedging, and it is a version of the strategy of portfolio diversification: the investor holds two or more assets whose risk/return characteristics to some degree offset one another. One example might be simply to hold a low risk and low but solid return asset for every high risk and high potential reward asset. A more precise way to hedge is to use derivatives, the range of securities whose price depends on or derives from the price of an underlying security. A put option, for example, gives its owner the right but not the obligation to sell a share at a fixed price (the striking price) on or by a certain date. Owning one with the share itself means that the investor's potential capital loss is limited to the loss implied should the share fall to the striking price. If it falls further, the investor can use the option and sell the share at the striking price.

On the other side of the hedger's trading is the speculator, someone who is prepared to take on the extra risk that the hedger wants to avoid. Speculators are in the markets for the express purpose of making as large a profit as possible. They typically believe that they know the future prospects for asset prices better than the majority of

investors, and hence are prepared to take bigger risks. The key characteristics of speculators are that they are prepared to leave themselves unprotected from possibly adverse market moves, and that they like to trade often and in substantial amounts. This behaviour is beneficial to other investors since it allows the more efficient management and transference of risk, and it gives the market greater liquidity.

With a put option, the speculator aims to make a profit from the premium paid by the hedger. He or she anticipates that the price of the underlying share will not fall to its striking price, and hence that the hedger will not need to exercise it. Of course, the risk taken on is substantial since, if the share price does fall below the striking price, the potential loss is unlimited: the speculator is obliged to buy the share at the striking price and can sell it only at whatever price it has fallen to.

The nature of the derivatives, or futures and options markets is discussed in more detail in chapters 11 and 12. For the moment, it is merely important to note that these derivatives can be used for the complementary aims of hedging and speculation across a wide range of markets, including future movements of interest rates, exchange rates, commodity prices and securities' prices.

Both hedgers and speculators "go long" in the assets they expect to increase in value, that is, quite simply, that they invest in them. But they can also "go short": this means that they expect an asset to fall in value, and hence sell it on the expectation of buying it back in the future and realising a capital gain. It is quite possible for investors to short assets they do not own by borrowing them with the intention of returning them once the expected profits have been made. Of course, this is usually a highly speculative activity since the shorted assets may rise in value. It may be used by hedgers when the shorted asset offsets a long asset, for example, where selling a future (a contract to buy a certain asset at a fixed price on a fixed future date) protects against a fall in the price of the underlying asset over that period.

Investors, whether hedgers or speculators, who expect a rise in a particular asset price or in the market as a whole are known as bulls, while those who are pessimistic about future price prospects are known as bears. And it is quite possible to be bullish and bearish at the same time if contemplating contrasting assets or markets. For example, risk-averse investors wary of UK stock market prospects

might view gilts as good buys, while ambitious speculators might short the pound or the franc and go long in gold or property.

COMPARING INVESTMENTS

It is important to clarify one potential source of confusion early on and that is the use of the words "investor" and "investment". Popularly, and especially in financial markets, an investment is an asset purchased by an investor with a view to making money, either through its yield or its appreciation in price. But this kind of investment involves only a transfer of ownership. No new spending has taken place: in the language of economics, the "investor" is actually saving! It might be better called financial investment.

Economists, on the other hand, define investment as spending by companies or the government on capital goods: new factories or machinery or housing or roads. This is capital investment. Generally, it is funded by borrowing from savers, perhaps through the issue of stocks or bonds. Thus, investment in this sense is the other side of the market from saving; it is borrowing rather than lending, spending rather than saving.

The financial pages of a newspaper may well use the words in both senses, though generally they will mean financial investment. Usually, though, the context will make it quite clear which is intended. In each case, the cost of the investment is determined in the markets for assets. The price of a stock or bond is on the one hand what an investor will have to pay to own it; on the other hand, it is what a company or government can expect to receive for the issue of a similar security.

Markets

Assets are bought and sold in markets, but what are these markets exactly? Essentially, they are institutions that allow buyers and sellers to trade assets with one another through the discovery of prices with which both parties are satisfied. They might be physical places where

traders meet to bargain, but in an age of technology, they do not need to be: often, nowadays, they operate through computer screens and telephones. Open outcry is the term for an actual gathering of traders offering prices at which they are prepared to buy and sell. But a very similar process is happening when they list their desired prices over the telephone or on a screen.

In each case, what is taking place is a form of auction. For example, a trader might have ten lots of an asset to sell. If there are too many or too few buyers at his or her suggested price (more or less than ten), the trader will lower or raise the price until there are exactly ten buyers. In effect, investors wishing to buy an asset are looking for sellers offering it at a price they find acceptable; sellers are doing the reverse. If neither side finds a counterparty willing to trade at that price, the buyers will raise the price they are prepared to pay, while the sellers will lower their acceptable price. Eventually, a compromise price is reached, and that becomes the current market price.

In the language of economics, this process is the balancing of demand and supply. The price of an asset moves to the level where demand and supply are equal. And since demand and supply continually shift with the changing patterns of investors' objectives and expectations, the price is continually moving to keep them in balance. In this environment of constant flux, it should, in principle, be possible for a seller to extract an excessive price from an unwary buyer if that buyer is kept unaware of the market price. Hence, another angle on the nature of a market is that it is a means for providing information. The more widely available that information, the better that market will operate.

Aggregating from the market for an individual asset produces a market in the recognised sense, an institution providing and generating prices for a range of assets with similar properties, and typically with an aggregate indication of which way prices are moving. In much financial reporting, this market is personified as having an opinion or sentiment. What this means is that the bulk of the traders in a market consider it to be moving in a particular direction: if buyers overwhelm sellers, it will be up, while if more traders are trying to leave the market than to come in, it will be down.

Financial markets can be classified in different ways. One basic distinction is between primary and secondary markets: in the former, new money flows from lenders to borrowers as companies and

governments seek more funds; in the latter, investors buy and sell existing assets among themselves. The existence of the secondary market is generally considered to be essential for a good primary market. The more liquid the secondary market, the easier it should be to raise capital in the primary market by persuading investors to take on new assets. The secondary market allows them to sell it should they decide it is not an asset they want to hold.

Markets may also be classified by whether or not they are organised, that is, whether or not there is an overarching institution setting a framework of rules and ready to honour the contracts of a failed counterparty. For example, London's Stock Exchange is an organised market while the over-the-counter derivatives market is not. Similarly, markets might be physical places like the New York Stock Exchange, screen-based computer systems like London's Stock Exchange Automated Quotation, or networks of telephones and electronic communication, such as those between the speculators and traders of foreign currencies.

And, of course, markets can be classified by the assets that are traded on them: stocks, bonds, derivatives, currencies, commodities and so on. Although these are all distinct markets, and the analysis in later chapters examines them each separately, there are very strong connections between them, connections that grow stronger as increasing globalisation and improved technology allow better flows of information. Investors do not simply choose one category of asset – they can select a mix. This means they can constantly compare the potential returns (yields and price changes) on a variety of assets. Hence, the markets are all linked by the relative prices of assets traded on them, and by the most important price of all, the rate of interest.

Prices and interest rates

Interest rates are prices for the use of money. An investor holding cash rather than depositing it in an interest-bearing bank account is paying a price, the foregone interest. Once the money is deposited, it is the bank that pays the price for the funds it can now use, again the interest payable on that account. Lastly, when the bank lends the money to a company, the company is paying a price for being able to

borrow – the interest the bank charges for loans which is normally higher than the rate it pays the investor so it can make a profit.

At any one time, there are different rates of interest payable on different forms of money. For example, money deposited long-term receives more interest than a short-term deposit. Similarly, money loaned to a risky enterprise earns more than that in a risk-free loan. Thus, an alternative view of the rate of interest is as the price of risk: the greater the risk, the higher the price.

All of these rates are intimately related: if one changes, they all do. This works by the same process as the changing prices of assets, that is, the rebalancing of demand and supply. If, for example, the rate of interest payable on short-term deposits were to rise, money in long-term deposits would flow into short-term deposits. The sellers or suppliers of long-term deposits would decline, and to attract them back, the price, the interest rate would need to rise in line with the short-term rate.

A rise in interest rates has a beneficial effect on investors with cash deposits in interest-bearing accounts. On the other side of the market though, the buyers of money or the borrowers face increased costs since the price has gone up. This would be the experience of companies borrowing to finance new investment, or of homeowners with monthly mortgage payments to make. But a change in interest rates also has effects on the prices of other assets, notably bond and gilt prices, equity prices and the prices of currencies.

The relationship between bond prices and interest rates is an inverse one: as one goes up, the other goes down. This is because a bond pays a fixed amount which, when calculated as a percentage of its market price, is the yield, equivalent to the rate of interest. If rates go up, the relative attractiveness of a deposit account over a bond increases. Since the coupon is fixed, for the yield on the bond to rise to offer an interest return once again comparable to that on the deposit account, the price of the bond must fall.

The relationship between bond prices and interest rates is simple and certain; that between equity prices and interest rates is more complicated and less predictable. As with bonds, the relative dividend yield of shares will be less attractive than the interest rate on a deposit account if interest rates rise. The yield will also be less attractive than that on the bond with its adjusted price. Furthermore, the yield may become even less desirable because the rate rise will raise the company's interest

costs, reduce its profitability and perhaps lead it to cut the dividend. However, much of the return sought on shares is from their potential for capital growth and an interest rate rise need not affect that.

Interest rates tend to rise and fall in line with the level of economic activity. In a recession and the early stages of a recovery, they will generally be low and falling to encourage borrowing, while in the subsequent boom, they will rise as the demand for money exceeds the supply. Thus, a recession should be good for bond prices and a boom less positive. For shares, the rising interest rates of a boom might be bad, but the rising economy should be advantageous because of its opportunities for enhanced profitability. In the long term, the prospects for the latter are far more of an influence on share prices than interest rates.

The last significant market influenced by interest rates is that for currencies. Exchange rates are in part determined by the relative rates across countries. If these change, by one country perhaps raising its rates, deposits in that country will become more attractive. To make the deposits, its currency will be bought and others sold, pushing up its price in terms of the other currencies. The higher value of a country's currency might also make its stocks and bonds more attractive relative to other international assets. On the other hand, a higher currency value makes exports more expensive, weakening the country's competitive position and potentially reducing exporters' profits. This may lead to equity price declines.

Each of these effects of changed interest rates could conceivably come before the change is actually implemented. This is because of the expectations of investors: if a rate rise is anticipated, bond owners will probably sell in the expectation of being able to buy the bonds back at the new lower price. This will cause prices to fall automatically because of surplus supply. Markets often discount the future in this way, building into the prices of the assets traded on them all past, present, and prospective information on their future values. Expectations of company profits can influence the current price of a share just as much as actual announced profits, sometimes more so.

USING THE FINANCIAL PAGES

How do all these concepts work out in practice in the financial pages of a newspaper? And how does the investor check on the prices of assets

owned or considered for purchase? The second part of this book covers the entire range of market information carried by the *Financial Times*, providing details on the background and operations of the various markets as well as a guide to how to read the daily charts and tables.

Saturday's newspaper is the issue that focuses most on the interests of the individual investor in its personal finance pages. One table is titled "Best deposit rates", and it provides details on the best options available for depositing money in various kinds of accounts at major banks and building societies. The table lists the names of the financial institutions and accounts, telephone numbers, the notice periods for withdrawing funds from the account, the minimum deposits, and the interest rates and frequency at which they are paid.

A neighbouring table is titled "Best borrowing rates", and it covers details for a variety of mortgages, personal loans, overdrafts and credit and store cards: the lenders, their telephone numbers, and such key features as the period the quoted rate will last for and the maximum amount that will be lent in the case of mortgages. In a sense, the deposit rates table gives an indication of what is called the opportunity cost of an investment, the benefits lost by not employing the money in its most profitable alternative use. These rates of return represent the best alternative use of money invested elsewhere, and, of course, they are relatively risk-free investments as well. When making selections of assets, they serve as valuable benchmarks.

The concept of benchmarks is one that is repeated throughout this book: many of the figures provided by the *Financial Times* fulfil this purpose of enabling both investors and borrowers to make comparisons. This is particularly the case with indices which provide investors with the guidelines for passive portfolio management. If the objective is to perform as well as, and no worse or better than the overall stock or bond market, the investor can simply buy the relevant index or mimic it by buying the equities or gilts whose values it measures. The converse of the passive approach is active management where the investor attempts to beat the market by following his or her personal philosophy of what moves asset prices.

Money markets

The money markets are the markets where highly liquid assets like money are traded. The term usually refers to the short-term markets

in which financial institutions borrow from and lend to one another, as well as the foreign exchange markets. They are the short-term counterpart of the Stock Exchange's long-term investment market.

These markets are, for the most part, limited to a small number of institutional participants but they have the potential for enormous effects on the whole financial and economic system, and hence will be of interest to most investors and companies (see chapter 10). They directly involve the individual investor in a more simple way, through their provision of places to deposit money safely and with a reasonable rate of return, the interest rate.

The *Financial Times* produces a daily table listing these money market bank accounts as part of its managed funds service, of which Figure 1.1 is a sample extract. Tables and charts with annotations, commentary and explanation like this appear frequently throughout the rest of the book, as a guide to financial pages everywhere, and particularly the *Financial Times*. They are intended to show how easy the interpretation and use of the financial pages really are once the basic principles and jargon have been understood:

- **Account name and amounts:** the first column lists the name of the account and/or the minimum/maximum that needs to be deposited in it to earn the interest rates indicated.

- **Gross:** the second column shows the gross interest rate currently payable on money deposited in the account. Gross simply means the amount payable before deductions, in this case not allowing for deduction of income tax at the basic rate. As with all income, the interest received on an asset of this kind is liable to taxation and tax considerations will have an impact on all of the features of investment decision-making discussed above.

- **Net:** the third column indicates the interest rate payable on the account net of income tax at the basic rate. Net is the converse of gross, the amount payable after deductions. Some accounts are tax exempt (for example, Tax Exempt Special Savings Accounts or TESSAs) under particular rules designed to shelter relatively modest savings. For these accounts, the gross and net rates are naturally the same.

Money Market Bank Accounts

	Gross	Net	Gross CAR	Int Cr

Allied Trust Bank Ltd
25 Dowgate Hill, London, EC4R 2AT — 0171–626 0879

	Gross	Net	Gross CAR	Int Cr
SIMNA (£2,001–£9,999)	6.96	5.22	6.96	Yearly
SIMNA (£10,000–£24,999)	7.50	5.62	7.50	Yearly
SIMNA (£25,000+)	7.76	5.82	7.76	Yearly
FOMNA (£2,001+)	6.96	5.22	6.96	Yearly
TREMNA (£2,001+)	6.70	5.02	6.70	Yearly
TOMNA (£2,001+)	6.54	4.90	6.54	Yearly
OMNA (£2,001+)	6.33	4.74	6.33	Yearly
HICA 5000 (£2,001–£4,999)	4.50	3.38	4.59	Mth
HICA 5000 (£5,000+)	6.00	4.50	6.17	Mth
HICA (£2,001+)	4.50	3.38	4.59	Mth
HIBCA (£2001+)	4.00	3.00	4.07	Mth
Premier TESSA	7.50	5.62	7.50	Yearly

American Express Bank Ltd
Sussex House, Burgess Hil RH15 9AQ — 01444 232444
High Performance Cheque Account

	Gross	Net	Gross CAR	Int Cr
£500–£999.99	1.00	0.75	1.00	Mth
£1,000–£4,999.99	3.50	2.63	3.56	Mth
£5,000–£9,999.99	3.75	2.81	3.82	Mth
£10,000–£24,999.99	4.00	3.00	4.07	Mth
£25,000–£49,999.99	4.25	3.19	4.33	Mth
£50,000+	4.75	3.56	4.85	Mth

Arbuthnot Latham & Co Ltd
Royex Hse, Aldermanbury Sq, London EC2 0171–418 7200
Treasury Account – for professional advisers

	Gross	Net	Gross CAR	Int Cr
£25,000–£49,999	5.25	3.9375	5.38	Mth
£50,000 or more	5.50	4.125	5.64	Mth

Mnthly Inc Acc – for personal and business clients

	Gross	Net	Gross CAR	Int Cr
Up to £9,999	3.25	2.4375	3.30	Mth
£10,000–£24,999	4.50	3.375	4.59	Mth
£25,000–£49,999	5.00	3.75	5.12	Mth
£50,000 or more	5.25	3.9375	5.375	Mth

Money Market quotations – please telephone

Bank of Ireland High Interest Cheque Acc
36–40 High St, Slough SL1 1EL — 01753 516516

	Gross	Net	Gross CAR	Int Cr
£2,000–£9,999	4.500	3.375	4.577	Qtr
£10,000+	5.250	3.938	5.354	Qtr

Bank of Scotland
38 Threadneedle St, EC2P 2EH — 0500 828888

	Gross	Net	Gross CAR	Int Cr
MM Chq Acc (Pers) £2,500–£24,999	4.50	3.38	4.59	Mth
£25,000–£99,999	5.00	3.75	5.12	Mth
£100,000–£249,999	5.25	3.94	5.38	Mth
£250,000+	6.25	4.68	6.43	Mth

Bank of Scotland
38 Threadneedle St, EC2 2EH — 0500 828000

	Gross	Net	Gross CAR	Int Cr
MM Chq Acc (Bus.) £2,500–£24,999	4.00	3.00	4.07	Mth
£25,000–£99,999	4.50	3.37	4.59	Mth
£100,000–£249,999	5.25	3.93	5.38	Mth
£250,000+	6.25	4.68	6.43	Mth

Barclays Select
PO Box 120, Westwood Bs Pk, Coventry — 0800 400100

	Gross	Net	Gross CAR	Int Cr
£2,000–£9,999	5.20	3.90	5.20	Yearly
£10,000–£24,999	5.25	3.94	5.25	Yearly
£25,000–£49,999	5.30	3.98	5.30	Yearly
£50,000–£99,999	5.40	4.05	5.40	Yearly
£100,000+	5.50	4.13	5.50	Yearly

Barclays Prime Account H.I.C.A.
Wavertree Boulevard, Liverpool — 0151–254 6236

	Gross	Net	Gross CAR	Int Cr
£1,000–£2,499	2.80	2.10	2.83	Qtr
£2,500–£9,999	3.60	2.70	3.65	Qtr
£10,000–£24,999	3.70	2.78	3.75	Qtr
£25,000+	4.10	3.08	4.16	Qtr

Brown Shipley & Co Ltd
Founders Court, Lothbury, London EC2 — 0171–606 9833

	Gross	Net	Gross CAR	Int Cr
HICA/Prof Demand A/c	5.375	4.031	5.484	Qtr
£50,000–£100,000 1 Mth Depo	6.500	4.875	6.697	Mth
£100,000 + 1 Mth Depo	6.625	4.969	6.830	Mth
£100,000 + 3 Mth Depo	6.625	4.969	6.791	Qtr

Caledonian Bank Plc
8 St Andrew Square, Edinburgh EH2 2PP — 0131 556 8235

	Gross	Net	Gross CAR	Int Cr
HICA £5,000+	6.25	4.6875	–	Yearly

Cater Allen Ltd
20 Birchin Lane, London EC3V 9DJ — 0171–623 2070

	Gross	Net	Gross CAR	Int Cr
HICA/HIMA	4.62	3.47	4.72	Mth
CHICA/MASTER PLUS	4.50	3.37	4.59	
Fixed £50,000+ 1 Mth	6.25	–	6.43	Mth
Overnight £50,000+	6.06	–	6.23	Mth

Charterhouse Bank Limited
1 Paternoster Row, EC4M 7DH. — 0171–248 4000

	Gross	Net	Gross CAR	Int Cr
£2,500–£19,999	5.00	3.75	5.12	Mth
£20,000–£49,999	5.25	3.94	5.38	Mth
£50,000–£99,999	5.50	4.13	5.64	Mth
£100,000+	5.75	4.31	5.90	Mth
$5,000–$49,999	4.00	3.00	4.07	Mth
$50,000–$99,999	4.50	3.38	4.59	Mth
$100,000–$199,999	4.75	3.56	4.85	Mth
$200,000+	5.00	3.75	5.12	Mth

Many other currencies are available – for rates please telephone ex 2166

Labels (left): Account type · Gross interest rate payable · Gross compounded annual rate

Labels (right): Interest rate net of income tax · Frequency at which interest is credited

Fig. 1.1 Money market bank accounts

- **Gross CAR:** the fourth column represents the gross compounded annualised rate. This applies to accounts where the interest is credited in periods more often than once a year. What happens here is that interest earned on the basic amount in the first period itself earns interest in succeeding periods, and so on. Hence the annualised rate is more than the sum of the interest paid in each period. It is instead said to be compounded.

- **Interest credited:** the last column supplies the detail on the frequency at which interest is credited to the account.

The early part of this chapter explained how the degree of risk affects the yield, with higher risk indicating higher potential return. Similarly, the time it takes to release money from an account, the notice period, affects its return. For example, savings accounts where the saver/investor is required to give thirty days' notice before withdrawing funds (or be penalised for early withdrawal) pay a higher rate of interest than those that allow immediate access. These tables indicate a third factor that affects return, namely the amount of money put into an asset. Generally, the more money an investor is prepared to tie up, the greater the return.

Major markets

The front page of the *Financial Times* carries a summary of values and changes in a number of key indicators across the broad range of markets (see Figure 1.2):

- **Stock market indices:** equity performance indicators for the London, Tokyo and New York exchanges, as well as broad indices for Europe and the world. These are explored in more detail in chapters 6 and 7.

- **US rates:** principal US interest rates and bond yields. These are explored in more detail in chapters 9 and 11.

- **London money:** the London interbank market rate and the price of a future on the long UK government bond. These are examined further in chapters 10 and 11.

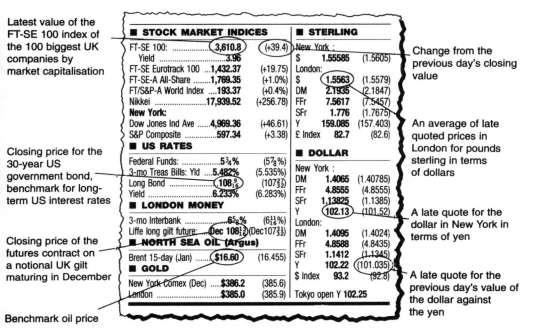

Latest value of the FT-SE 100 index of the 100 biggest UK companies by market capitalisation

Closing price for the 30-year US government bond, benchmark for long-term US interest rates

Closing price of the futures contract on a notional UK gilt maturing in December

Benchmark oil price

Change from the previous day's closing value

An average of late quoted prices in London for pounds sterling in terms of dollars

A late quote for the dollar in New York in terms of yen

A late quote for the previous day's value of the dollar against the yen

Fig. 1.2 Key market statistics

- **North Sea oil and gold:** prices of these two key commodities in New York and London. These are examined further in chapter 12.

- **Sterling and dollar:** rates for these two currencies in New York and London in terms of each other and D-Marks, French and Swiss francs, and yen, as well as the value of sterling and dollar trade-weighted indices. These are the focus of chapter 10.

Saturday's newspaper also features a summary table designed to provide a snapshot of the previous week. Labelled "Money watch", it is carried on the back page of the Weekend Money section (see Figure 1.3). The table includes the latest values (plus comparable values for six months and a year previously) for a range of key economic and investment indicators: inflation rates, interest rates, yields, exchange rates and the price of gold. The significance of each of these indicators is discussed in the ensuing chapters.

The Weekend Money section provides an extensive range of articles, tables and charts relating to issues of personal finance and

■ Money watch			
	Latest value	6 mths ago	Year ago
Retail Prices Index ♣ †	3.2	3.3	2.4
Halifax House Price Indx ✖ †-1.8		-1.4	-0.9
Halifax mortgage rate (%)	7.99	8.35	8.10
Base lending rate (%)	6¾	6¾	5¾
3-mth interbank mid rate (%)	6⅝	6⅝	6₁₆
10-year gilt yield	7.63	7.92	8.44
Long gilt/equity yld ratio (%)	2.08	2.00	2.08
$/£ exchange rate	1.5608	1.6069	1.5631
Dm/£ exchange rate	2.2108	2.2221	2.4366
Gold price ($ per oz)	383.60	387.00	384.95

♣ RPI for Oct. ✖ All Houses index shown for Oct.
† Annual % change.

Fig. 1.3 Money watch

investment. Savers, borrowers and investors of all kinds can find valuable information in its coverage of companies, markets, saving and borrowing, investing for growth and for income, pensions, financial planning and unit trusts and investment trusts. A number of its key tables are examined in later chapters. Others include a table of top annuity rates (financial products that offer guaranteed income for life in return for a lump sum investment), a table of prices, coupons and yields for permanent interest-bearing shares (fixed interest securities in building societies) and a calculator for capital gains tax indexation allowances for assets sold in the current month.

Stock markets

Major share price movements around the world are highlighted in a feature on the front of the newspaper's second section. This gives chief price changes on the previous day for equities not only in London, but also in Frankfurt, New York, Paris and Tokyo (see Figure 1.4):

● **Market, stock, closing price in the local currency and change on the previous trading day:** the prices shown are not necessarily those involving the greatest percentage change in the various markets since this

often applies to relatively small companies with only a narrow market in their shares. The *Financial Times* table generally concentrates on the most interesting price movements among large companies.

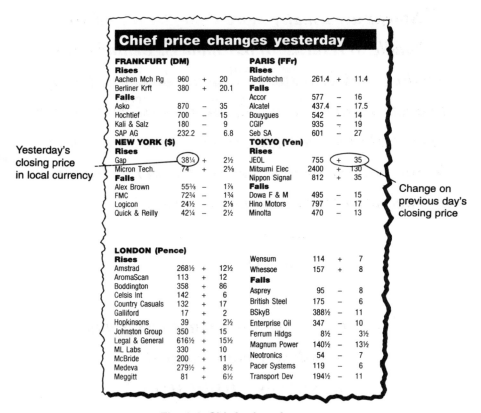

Yesterday's closing price in local currency

Change on previous day's closing price

Fig. 1.4 Chief price changes

The information is a valuable checklist for the key moves in the major markets of the world. Much more detailed data, as well as reports on the markets and commentary on the main forces influencing them, are available throughout the rest of the newspaper. Explanations of how these work, and further background on the markets appear in chapters 5, 6 and 7. First, chapter 2 turns to the other side of the markets for capital, the companies who come to borrow and whose share prices are quoted on the stock markets.

"Stocks are usually more than just the abstract 'bundle of returns' of our models. Behind each holding may be a story of family business, family quarrels, legacies received, divorce settlements, and a host of other considerations. These stories may be too interesting and thereby distract us from the pervasive market forces that should be our principal concern."

MERTON MILLER

"I would rather see finance less proud and industry more content."

WINSTON CHURCHILL

2

COMPANIES

- **Presenting figures** – how to understand companies' key financial statements: profit and loss; balance sheets and cash flows; investment ratios; and company financial news

- **Rewarding shareholders** – when companies issue information on their performance: results; and dividends

- **Raising finance** – where companies find their sources of capital: equity; and debt

- **Contesting corporate control** – the importance of bidders and targets: UK mergers and acquisitions; cross border M&A activity

Companies are organisations established for some kind of commerce and with a legal identity separate from their owners. The owners are the shareholders who have rights to part of the company's profits, and who usually have limited liability. This means that the liability of the owners for company debts is limited to the amount paid for their shares. They can only lose what they invested.

Companies are often run by people other than the owners, although in theory at least the ordinary shareholders control the company. Management is expected to act in the best interests of the owners. Nonetheless, the ordinary shareholders are the last in the queue of claimants on a company: before they can receive anything, the demands of basic operating costs, interest payments and taxation must be met. This is especially evident when a business is wound up, and the owners become the final creditors to receive their stake.

Since this book is concerned with financial markets covered in the *Financial Times*, and in which, in principle, anyone can participate, the companies considered are typically public: this means that their shares are traded in a market, usually the Stock Exchange for UK companies and, for the most part, there are no dominant owners. The focus on companies in this chapter is on the features of corporate life over which the company has some direct control: its profitability, its dividend payments, its methods of raising new capital in the primary market, and its means of offence and survival in contests for corporate control. Chapter 5 focuses more on the secondary market, and the interplay of companies and investors in the context of the market for UK equities.

PRESENTING FIGURES

The primary source for data and analysis of a company is its annual report and accounts. These give all the information on its business and financial affairs, and their publication is one of a company's legal

obligations to its shareholders. They describe the current trading conditions of the company, what it has sold (its turnover, sales or revenues) and what it has paid out in wages and salaries, rent, raw materials and other inputs to the production of the goods or services it sells (its costs). They also indicate the company's profits or losses, the state of its assets and liabilities at the start and end of the financial year, and its cash flow.

Detailed explanations of the various financial statements published by a company and the ratios that can be used to analyse and interpret them can be found in numerous publications. This book aims merely to outline some of the relevant figures and ratios. Readers seeking greater depth of analysis are referred to Ciaran Walsh's *Key Management Ratios: How to Analyse, Compare and Control the Figures that Drive Company Value* (*Financial Times* Pitman Publishing, 1996) for a management perspective, and to Michael Stead's *The Investor's Guide to How to Use Company Accounts for Successful Investment Decisions* (*Financial Times* Pitman Publishing, 1995) for an investor's perspective. They should also turn to chapter 16 which explores some of the key ratios from the perspective of both manager and investor over the course of a company's history as well as providing some worked examples.

There are essentially three financial statements in a company's annual report: the profit and loss account, the balance sheet, and the cash flow statement. From these three can be calculated all the significant ratios needed for companies to practice sound financial management of their business, and for investors to interpret corporate performance relative to the share price and the market more generally.

Profit and loss

A company's profit and loss account is a statement of the final outcome of all its transactions, all revenues and costs during a given period, usually a year. It shows whether the company made any money in the previous year, how it did it, and what it did with the profits, if any. It also allows comparison with previous years' performances and with other companies.

The total value of all goods sold by the company is known as its sales or turnover. Deducting from that figure the cost of achieving those sales either directly or indirectly (for example, either the raw materials in the sold products, or staff salaries paid for work on these and other products) gives the company's operating or trading profit. Deducting from that figure, in turn, the cost of interest payments made on loans from banks or in the form of corporate bonds, gives the company's pre-tax profit. This is the most widely quoted figure in financial reporting on company results and profitability.

The next deduction is tax: first, corporation tax is paid by the company on profits after all costs have been met except for dividends paid out to ordinary shareholders; and second, advance corporation tax, income tax paid on behalf of shareholders on their dividend income, is paid. The latter is paid at the lowest rate of income tax and can be reclaimed or supplemented by the shareholders depending on their tax bracket. Companies can also partially offset tax payable on dividend distributions against mainstream corporation tax.

Money left once taxation demands have been met is known as after tax profit or equity earnings. This is now at the disposal of the company for distribution as dividends or ploughing back into the business as retained earnings. The allocation will depend on the conflicting aims of maintaining the level of dividends so that investor confidence in the share price remains solid, and having access to the least expensive source of funds for investment in further developing the business. The conflict corresponds to the dichotomy an investor faces between income and capital gain. The two do not preclude one another, but an appropriate balance needs to be struck.

The basic profit and loss account:

Sales or turnover or revenue
minus cost of sales
minus overheads
= operating/trading profit or profit before interest and tax
minus net interest paid
= pre-tax profit
minus tax (corporation tax and advance corporation tax)
= after tax profit, net profit or equity earnings
minus dividends
= retained earnings

The profit and loss account quantifies revenue and cost flows over a given period of time. In a sense, it links two versions of the second key financial statement, the balance sheet, one at the beginning of the year and the other at year end. The third document is the cash flow statement, which depends on a combination of the two balance sheets and the profit and loss account.

Balance sheets and cash flows

The balance sheet is a snapshot of a company's capital position at an instant in time. It details everything it owns (its assets) and everything it owes (its liabilities) at year end. The two sides of a balance sheet, by definition, balance. They are merely two different aspects of the same sum of money: where it came from and where it went. Essentially, liabilities are sources of funds while assets are the uses to which those funds are put.

A company's assets are made up of two items: fixed or long-term assets, such as land, buildings, and equipment; and current or short-term assets, such as stocks of goods available for sale, debtors or accounts receivable, and cash in the bank. Its liabilities are made up of three items, the first two being current or short-term liabilities, such as trade credit or accounts payable, tax, dividends, and overdrafts at the bank; and longer term debt, such as term loans, mortgages and bonds.

The third form of liability is that of ordinary funds, and this in turn divides into three forms: revenue reserves or retained earnings – the company's trading profits that have not been distributed as dividends; capital reserves – surpluses from sources other than normal trading such as revaluation of fixed assets or gains due to advantageous currency fluctuations; and issued ordinary shares.

Ordinary shares have three different values: their nominal value, the face or par value at which they were issued and which may have no relation to the issue price or current trading price; their book value, the total of ordinary funds divided by the number of shares in issue; and their market value, the price quoted on a stock exchange. For the purpose of reading the financial pages, the last value is the one of primary significance.

> **The basic balance sheet:**
>
> **Assets (fixed or long-term assets + current or short-term assets)**
> **= Liabilities (long-term debt + current or short-term liabilities**
> **+ ordinary funds)**
> **Ordinary funds or shareholders' funds = retained earnings**
> **+ capital reserves + issued ordinary shares**

The cash flow statement details the amount of money that flows in and out of a company in a given period of time. Cash flows into a company when a cheque is received and out when one is issued. This statement tracks the flow of the funds in those cheques: how much has flowed through the accounts, where the funds have gone to and where they have come from.

The balance sheet is a check of a company's financial health, and the profit and loss account an indicator of its current success or failure. Together they can be used to calculate a number of valuable ratios, and the cash flow statement can be used to understand what lies behind short-term movements in these ratios.

Financial ratios

Numerous ratios can be calculated from a company's financial statements, many of which are covered in detail in the Ciaran Walsh and Michael Stead books, and in chapter 16. For the purposes of a reader of the financial pages, some of the most useful are pre-tax profit margins, net asset values and the return on capital employed. Each of these allows valuable insights into corporate value and performance from the point of view of both investor and company manager.

The pre-tax profit margin is simply the pre-tax profit divided by the turnover for the period. Profit margins vary considerably between industrial sectors but can certainly be used to compare company performance within an industry. There are often rule-of-thumb industry standards.

> $$\text{Pre-tax profit margin (per cent)} = \frac{\text{pre-tax profit} \times 100}{\text{turnover}}$$

Net asset value (NAV) is the total assets of a company minus its liabilities, debentures and loan stocks. This is the amount that the

ordinary shareholders will receive if the business is wound up, the sum left for the last claimants on a defunct company's assets. It is also known as shareholders' interests or shareholders' funds, and is effectively the total par value of the shares in issue plus all historic retained earnings.

Net asset value per share is calculated by dividing net assets by the number of shares in issue. This has varying degrees of significance depending on the nature of the business. For example, the net asset value of a company whose performance depends primarily on its employees will not be important since its tangible assets are few. In contrast, a business heavily built on assets, such as investment trusts or property companies, will find its share price considerably influenced by its net asset value per share. The share price might be at a premium or a discount to the net asset value per share (see chapter 8).

Return on capital employed (ROCE) is a ratio that indicates the efficiency of a business by showing to what effect its assets are used. It is calculated as the pre-tax profit divided by the shareholders' funds and any long-term loans. The resulting figures enable comparison between one company and another within the same sector; for the investor, they can also be used to compare across different sectors.

> Capital employed = ordinary funds + long-term debt
>
> Return on capital employed (per cent) = $\dfrac{\text{pre-tax profit} \times 100}{\text{capital employed}}$

Some other important ratios, including earnings per share, dividends per share and the debt/equity ratio, are explained below. First, though, it is important to see how all these results and ratios feature in the pages of the *Financial Times*.

Company financial news

The Company News: UK pages of the newspaper contain details of the financial results of all quoted UK companies, and a handful of those without quotations. There may only be space for a sentence or two on the results of the smaller companies, but larger ones will be given a substantial news story as well as a separate comment in the Lex column on the results. The comment, clearly separated from the

news, gives the newspaper's views on why the results are as they are, what the company's prospects might be, and whether its shares are rated appropriately by the market. These pages also report fully on rights and other share issues and large takeover bids. They include briefer items on many smaller acquisitions.

A typical news report on a company's results looks like this, with remarks on the underlying determinants of a company's performance and prospects, and the sometimes unpredictable impact on the share price:

> A strong first-time contribution from the Chef & Brewer pub acquisition helped Scottish and Newcastle, the drinks and leisure group, to a 22 per cent rise in pre-tax profit for the year to May 1 to £222m. However, earnings per share rose only 1.2 per cent, as a result of the rights issue which helped finance the £700m deal. The shares fell 3p to 501p.
> (*Financial Times*, 5 July 1994)

In addition to the day-to-day reporting, the *Financial Times* publishes an annual list of the top 500 UK companies, a ranking of companies quoted on the Stock Exchange as measured by market capitalisation (the number of a company's shares in issue multiplied by their market price). This analyses a range of key figures on the companies, including their turnover, profits, return on capital employed and employee numbers. It also ranks and analyses the top 500 European companies.

REWARDING SHAREHOLDERS

Saturday's newspaper contains a table of company results due in its Weekend Money section. This includes all the companies expected to announce results in the following week, their sectors and announcement dates, the interim and final dividends paid the previous year and any interim dividend this year.

Results

Saturday's newspaper also lists recently announced statements of interim results and preliminary results (see Figure 2.1). The latter are

actually the full year's results made to the Stock Exchange, to be fleshed out in the annual report a little later.

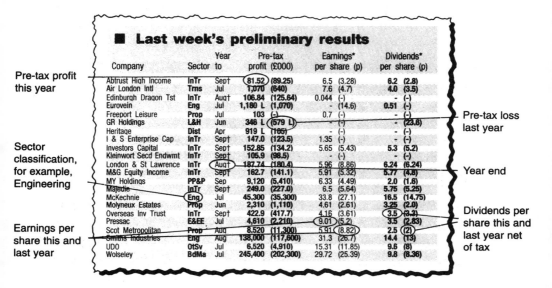

Pre-tax profit this year

Sector classification, for example, Engineering

Earnings per share this and last year

Pre-tax loss last year

Year end

Dividends per share this and last year net of tax

■ Last week's preliminary results

Company	Sector	Year to	Pre-tax profit (£000)	Earnings* per share (p)	Dividends* per share (p)
Abtrust High Income	InTr	Sept	81.52 (89.25)	6.5 (3.28)	6.2 (2.8)
Air London Intl	Trns	Jul	1,070 (640)	7.6 (4.7)	4.0 (3.5)
Edinburgh Dragon Tst	InTr	Augt	106.84 (125.64)	0.044 (-)	- (-)
Eurovein	Eng	Jul	1,180 L (1,070)	- (14.6)	0.51 (-)
Freeport Leisure	Prop	Jul	103 (-)	0.7 (-)	- (-)
GR Holdings	L&H	Jun	348 L (579 L)	- (-)	- (23.8)
Heritage	Dist	Apr	919 L (185)	- (-)	- (-)
I & S Enterprise Cap	InTr	Sept	147.0 (123.5)	1.35 (-)	- (-)
Investors Capital	InTr	Sept	152.85 (134.2)	5.65 (5.43)	5.3 (5.2)
Kleinwort Secd Endwmt	InTr	Sept	105.9 (98.5)	- (-)	- (-)
London & St Lawrence	InTr	Augt	187.74 (180.4)	5.96 (8.86)	6.24 (6.24)
M&G Equity Income	InTr	Sept	162.7 (141.1)	5.91 (5.32)	5.77 (4.8)
MY Holdings	PP&P	Sep	9,120 (5,410)	6.33 (4.49)	2.0 (1.6)
Majedie	InTr	Sept	249.0 (227.0)	6.5 (5.64)	5.75 (5.25)
McKechnie	Eng	Jul	45,300 (35,300)	33.8 (27.1)	16.5 (14.75)
Molyneux Estates	Prop	Jun	2,310 (1,110)	4.61 (2.61)	3.25 (2.0)
Overseas Inv Trust	InTr	Sept	422.9 (417.7)	4.16 (3.61)	3.5 (3.3)
Pressac	E&EE	Jul	4,610 (2,210)	9.01 (5.2)	3.5 (2.83)
Scot Metropolitan	Prop	Aug	8,520 (11,300)	5.91 (8.82)	2.5 (2)
Smiths Industries	Eng	Aug	138,000 (117,600)	31.3 (26.7)	14.4 (13)
UDO	OtSv	Jul	6,520 (4,910)	15.31 (11.85)	9.6 (8)
Wolseley	BdMa	Jul	245,400 (202,300)	29.72 (25.39)	9.8 (8.36)

Fig. 2.1 Last week's preliminary results

- **Name, sector and year to:** company details and the period covered by the results (half or full year) are given.

- **Pre-tax profits:** these are figures both for this year and the same period of last year (the figure in brackets) in thousands of pounds. The letter L indicates a loss.

- **Earnings per share (eps):** this measures a company's total net return earned on ordinary share capital. It is calculated by first deducting tax, depreciation, interest and payments to preference shareholders (leaving after tax profit), and then dividing by the number of ordinary shares in issue. The figures given allow a comparison with the previous year.

- **Dividends per share:** the total dividend net of tax divided by the number of shares in issue. Again, the figures allow a comparison with the previous year.

The value of earnings per share is one of the most widely quoted statistics in discussion of a company's performance and share value. The growth and stability of this ratio are a good indicator of how much a company is increasing profits for its shareholders. But it is difficult to make comparisons across companies because of different methods of calculating earnings. The ability to offset advance corporation tax leads the *Financial Times* to use two methods: one based on nil distribution of profits, the other on net distribution.

$$\text{Earnings per share} = \frac{\text{after tax profit}}{\text{number of shares}}$$

Dividends

In Monday's newspaper, The Week Ahead page lists the dates of forthcoming company meetings that have been notified to the Stock Exchange. These board meetings are usually to consider the company's results and approve the level of the dividend, with an announcement on the figure coming either the same day or the following day. The page also lists the dividend and interest payments due to be made in the week ahead. A daily chart lists all results announced on the previous day, particularly focusing on dividends (see Figure 2.2):

- **Company, dates, turnover, pre-tax profits and earnings per share:** details of the companies that announced results and dividends the previous day, the periods covered and three key indicators of size and profitability.

- **Dividends:** the current payment; the date of the payment; the corresponding dividend the previous year; and the totals for the current and previous year.

Companies usually announce their dividends net of tax since they calculate them on the figure for after tax profit. The amount of the dividend paid as advance corporation tax (say, a 20 per cent deduction for the lowest rate of income tax) has already figured in the profit calculation. The gross dividend, the basis for estimating the gross yield (examined in chapter 5), is calculated by "grossing up", in this case the net dividend multiplied by 100 and divided by 80.

RESULTS

		Turnover (£m)	Pre-tax profit (£m)	EPS (p)	Current payment (p)	Dividends			
						Date of payment	Corresponding dividend	Total for year	Total last year
Capital & Regional	6 mths to June 24	4.9□ (3.5□)	2.04 (1.24)	3.66† (2.85)	0.8	Nov 24	0.6	-	2.1
Cobham	6 mths to June 30	111.4 (100.8)	14.1 (12.3)	12.39 (11.01)	3.05	Dec 11	2.7	-	8.32
Cohen (A)	6 mths to June 30	49.5 (35.5)	1.8 (0.764)	72.6 (27)	6★	Feb 2	nil	-	7.5
Development Secs	6 mths to June 30	11.9 (9.7)	0.6 (1)	2 (4)	0.8	Nov 23	0.8◆	-	2.4◆
Five Oaks Invs	Yr to June 30	6.13 (9.13)	2.33 (2.28◆)	2.1 (2.54)	0.4	Dec 9	0.3	0.7	0.5
JJB Sports	6 mths to July 31	37.5 (25.6)	4.82 (2.55)	10.36 (6.55)	2.75	Dec 11	-	-	2
Lendu	Yr to June 30	0.897 (0.636)	0.043L (0.087L)	0.01 (0.29)	0.25	Nov 22	0.25	0.25	0.25
Lloyds Chemists	Yr to June 30	1,082 (940)	42.2◆ (58.3◆)	22.26 (33.67)	7.3	Dec 14	6.8	10.2	9.5
QSP	6 mths to June 30	10.1 (7.27)	0.805 (0.604)	9.2 (7.2)	1.5	Jan 15	1	-	4.5
St Ives	Yr to July 28	264.2 (237)	35.5 (22.3◆)	25.36 (13.48)	6	Dec 4	4.5	8.5	6.4
Sinclair (Wm)	Yr to Aug 31	44.4 (41.3)	4.73 (4.17)	14.7 (13)	5.8	Nov 16	5.45	7.6	7.15
Thorntons	Yr to June 24	95.6 (96.6)	10.5◆ (12.1)	10.36 (12.19)	3.8	Nov 30	3.45	5.3	4.9
Trafficmaster	6 mths to June 30	1.25 (0.571)	1.12L (0.541L)	5.1L† (2.9L)	-	-	-	-	-
Walker Greenbank	6 mths to July 31	45 (36.3)	4.24 (4.14)	2.51† (2.88)	1.3	Dec 12	1.3	-	3.6

Investment Trusts		NAV (p)	Attributable Earnings (£m)	EPS (p)	Current payment (p)	Date of payment	Corresponding dividend	Total for year	Total last year
European Smaller	Yr to June 30	137.3 (135.3)	0.215 (0.277)	0.6 (0.78)	0.56	Nov 30	0.56	0.56	0.56
Henderson Highland	6 mths to Aug 31 ★	129.5 (126.1)	0.903 (0.835)	3.46 (3.2)	1.45‡	Nov 17	1.4	-	5.7
HTR Inc & Growth	37 wks to Aug 31	110.3 (-)	0.965 (-)	3.9 (-)	1.5†‡	Nov 10	-	-	-
Intl Biotechnology	Yr to Aug 31	127.37 (96.24)	0.329 (0.191)	0.87 (0.51)	1	-	-	1	-
NB Smaller Cos	6 mths to Aug 31	151.4 (145.2)	0.902 (0.479)	3.34 (1.78)	0.94#	Dec 5	0.94	-	3.68

Dividends shown net. Earnings shown basic. Figures in brackets are for corresponding period. □ Rental income. †On increased capital. ✷Foreign income dividend. ◆Restated for share consolidation. ♥After exceptional charge. ◆After exceptional credit. ★ Comparatives restated. ‡Second interim. ‡‡Second interim; makes 3p to date. ‡Second interim; makes 2.9p to date. #Special of 0.74p also declared.

Fig. 2.2 Results

Dividends are paid only out of earnings, but in order for companies to maintain some consistency in their payments, these need not necessarily fall into the same year as the dividends. Where there has been a loss, a company might choose to make dividend payments out of retained earnings. Dividends are typically reported like this:

Vodaphone, the UK mobile communications group, announced a 13 per cent rise in pre-tax profits. Earnings per share rose 10 per cent to 24.34p (22.07p). A final dividend of 4.23p makes a total of 8.35p, up 20 per cent.

(*Financial Times*, 8 June 1994)

RAISING FINANCE

From a company perspective, the financial markets exist to raise money through various financial instruments. The sources of capital are basically three: the permanent capital of shareholders (also known as equity capital, ordinary shares or, in the United States, common stock); ploughed back profits (equity funds or shareholders' reserves); and various forms of debt or loan capital.

Corporate finance, the subject of how companies arrange their capital structure, tends to focus on the relative benefits of financing via debt or equity. The relationship between the two elements in a company's capital structure is known as its gearing, balance sheet gearing or debt/equity ratio (or leverage in the United States), and is commonly calculated as total debt (current plus long-term debt liabilities) divided by ordinary funds (shareholder's equity plus retained earnings). The more highly geared or leveraged a company is, the higher are its borrowings relative to its share capital or turnover.

Total debt liabilities = long-term debt + current or short-term liabilities

$$\text{Balance sheet gearing or debt/equity ratio (per cent)} = \frac{\text{total debt liabilities} \times 100}{\text{ordinary funds}}$$

Gearing, in a general sense, is any situation where swings between profits and losses can be caused by quite small changes in underlying conditions. In the case of gearing with debt and equity, a small change in interest rates can have a dramatic effect: with an increase in the rate of interest, a highly geared company suffers much more from

the increased payments necessary to service its debt. The small change can have a substantial effect on profits.

Another prominent gearing ratio is income gearing, which indicates a company's ability to service its debt, that is, how much room there is between the interest payments it has to make on its debt and the operating profit it is earning. The ratio is calculated as total interest expense divided by operating profit. An alternative way to express this ratio is what is known as interest cover, the number of times interest could be paid out of operating profit. In this case, the calculation is the reciprocal, operating profit divided by interest expense.

$$\text{Income gearing (per cent)} = \frac{\text{interest expense} \times 100}{\text{operating profit}}$$

$$\text{Interest cover} = \frac{\text{operating profit}}{\text{interest expense}}$$

Equity

Equity finance is the capital that allows companies to take the risks inherent in business, embarking on risky new investment programs. It is limited in a private company, and this is the main reason why such a company would want to "go public". In "coming to the market", getting quoted on the Stock Exchange, the Unlisted Securities Market (USM) or the Alternative Investment Market (AIM), through a new issue, a company has access to significantly more money for investment in the business. The means by which this is done, and *Financial Times* reporting of new issues, are discussed in chapter 5.

There are two common classes of equity capital: ordinary shares, which have no guaranteed amount of dividend payments, but which carry voting rights; and preference shares, which usually carry a fixed dividend and have preference over ordinary shareholders if the company is wound up, but which have no voting rights. There are also a number of variations, including cumulative preference shares and part-paid shares. These are also discussed in more detail in chapter 5.

Companies already listed on the exchange and wishing to raise new equity capital would normally do so by a pre-emption rights issue. This means that existing shareholders have first option on the new shares or the right to sell that option. An increase in the number

of ordinary shares in a company without a corresponding increase in its assets or profitability results in a fall in their value – what is known as a dilution of the equity.

To avoid immediate dilution of the shares in issue, a company might use an alternative financial instrument to raise capital, a convertible (also known as a convertible loan stock or a convertible bond). These are debt instruments that can be converted into ordinary or preference shares at a fixed date in the future, and at a fixed price. Their value to a company, besides avoiding dilution, is that, in exchange for their potential conversion value, they will carry a lower rate of interest than standard debt.

Another form of financial instrument that companies use to raise capital is the equity warrant. This is a security that gives the owner the right, though not the obligation, to subscribe cash for new shares at a fixed price on a fixed date. Warrants are themselves traded on stock markets and work in a way similar to options, which are discussed in detail in chapter 11. Since the subscription price on a new warrant will exceed the current market price of the underlying stock, the warrant is a speculative asset, gambling on a price rise. They are popular with companies since they can be issued without including them in the balance sheet.

Debt

The alternative to share capital as a source of finance is loan capital. Debt finance is attractive to companies since it allows the business to be developed without giving up a stake in the ownership, and the consequent loss of a share of the profits and a degree of control. It is also often more readily available than new equity capital other than that from retained profits, and it can be built into a company's capital structure as both short-term and long-term debt.

Like equity capital, corporate debt takes a number of different forms. Long-term loans are usually raised by issuing securities: the most common form in the United Kingdom is the debenture. Most debentures offer a fixed rate of interest payable ahead of dividends in the queue of claimants; and they are often secured on specific company assets. They usually trade on the Stock Exchange, involve less risk than equities, but pay a lower rate of interest than other kinds of debt.

Other forms of industrial or corporate loans include fixed and floating rate notes, and deep discount and zero coupon bonds. These differ in how the interest or coupon is determined and paid. Fixed notes pay a specified amount whatever happens to interest rates generally, and hence their price in the secondary market varies inversely with interest rates in the same way as gilts. Bonds of this kind have been a central part of corporate finance in the United States for many years, but became more significant in the United Kingdom only when the temporary surplus in the government's budget between 1989–91 led to a shortage of gilts.

Floating rate notes are more prevalent in the Euromarkets, the markets in which players lend and borrow Eurocurrencies (currencies deposited and available for use outside their country of origin). These instruments pay a rate of interest determined by some standard rate such as the LIBOR, an agreed rate for short-term loans between banks, discussed in chapter 10. Deep discount and zero coupon bonds, in contrast, pay little or no interest. Instead, the issuer offers them at a significant discount to their redemption value so that the investor makes most of the return from a capital gain rather than periodic interest payments. Each of these kinds of debt is discussed in more detail in chapter 9.

The most common form of short-term loan is the overdraft at the bank, where companies can borrow up to an agreed limit and only pay interest on the amount actually borrowed at any given point in time. Another form is the commercial bill, the short-term counterpart of bonds, where the issuer promises to pay a fixed amount on a given date a short time in the future, usually three months. The bills are generally "accepted" (guaranteed) by a financial institution, and sold at a discount ("discounted") to their face value to provide the buyer with an appropriate return and the issuer with immediate cash.

The most recent innovation in debt instruments is the junk bond, a form of finance developed and used primarily in the United States. This is a bond that offers a higher rate of interest in return for a higher than usual risk of default by the issuer. In the 1980s, junk bonds were used as a means of generating substantial amounts of finance for the takeover of large companies by relatively small ones. They became a focal point of controversies over leveraged buyouts and other supposedly unwelcome or undesirable takeover bids.

CONTESTING CORPORATE CONTROL

One of the aspects of corporate life that features prominently in reporting on companies and the financial markets is the contest for corporate control. Mergers and acquisitions (M&A), bidders and targets, corporate control and corporate governance are issues that frequently make the headlines, and ones that often have an impact on the market far beyond the individual companies or sectors they involve. An extract from the *Financial Times* illustrates the excitement that surrounds them:

> As the City takes stock of Lasmo's victory over the bid from Enterprise Oil last week, merchant bankers have been reaching for sporting metaphors. 'If you'd asked me at the start, I'd have put more money on a Briton winning Wimbledon,' said one. All agreed it was one of the most unexpected results to a big takeover battle for years.
>
> (*Financial Times*, 5 July 1994)

In this example, Enterprise Oil's bid for Lasmo Oil was successfully repulsed by the target company. The bidder failed to win control of enough of the target's shares, either through direct ownership or by persuading the actual owners that they would benefit from the takeover, and that they should therefore vote in favour of it. Hostile bids of this kind are normally settled through what are known as proxy contests, where shareholders appoint proxies to vote on their behalf, either for or against accepting the bid.

The primary argument in favour of acquisitions is that they are good for industrial efficiency: without the threat of their company being taken over and, in all likelihood, the loss of their jobs, managers would act more in their own interests than those of the owners. In particular, this might imply an inefficient use of company resources and a lack of concern about the share price, the value of which is often a sign of a company's vulnerability to takeover. Certainly, a bid is frequently beneficial to the shareholders of the target company in terms of immediate rises in the share price. On the other hand, it is argued that the threat of takeover means that management takes too short-term a view: bolstering the share price where possible, investing inadequately for the future, and, where a company has been taken over in a leveraged buyout, perhaps burdening it with too high

a debt/equity ratio. The demands of making enough profits to meet interest payments might mean it is managed solely for the short term.

Bids and mergers

Saturday's newspaper has a list of the takeover bids and mergers announced in the previous week and involving bidder and target companies primarily based in the United Kingdom (see Figure 2.3):

■ Current takeover bids and mergers

Company bid for	Value of bid per share**	Market price**	Price before bid	Value of bid £ms**	Bidder
Atkins ‡	110*	109	92	3.70	Coats Viyella
Aran Energy	77.7	76	76	203.00	Statoil
Beckman	60*	59	40	7.20	Directors
Boddington	412	401	358	518.00	Greenalls
Chiltern Radio‡	318	395	300	21.10	GWR
Copymore	214*	208	170	23.50	Alco Standard
Country Casuals	140*	140	130½	26.80	Ciro
Dobson Park	130*	132	113	203.60	Harnischfeger
Eastern ‡	975*	974	700	2500.00	Hanson
Fine Decor	172*	168	175	21.50	IntWallcoverings
Fisons ‡	265*	264	193	1800.00	Rhone-Poulenc
Magnolia	27	29	40	1.55	Northern Acq
Manweb ‡	1019	1009	730	1100.00	Scottish Power
Midlands Electric	£10 ✗	963	938½	1950.00	PowerGen
NORWEB	1105	1134	975	1723.00	North West Water
SWEB✗ ‡	965*	900	912	1072.11	Sthn.Elec.Intl.
Scantronic	10.54	9½	10	10.50	Menvier Swain
Southern Electric	1010	952	897	2800.00	National Power
TSB	352½ §	369	350	13.60bn	Lloyds
Taunton Cider	237	238	217½	271.00	Matthew Clark
Vistec	17½	20½	16	22.00	Lynx

Prices in pence unless otherwise indicated. *All cash offer. §For capital not already held. ‡ Unconditional. **Based on lunchtime prices 27/10/95 §§Shares and cash. ✗ Value of bid per share includes £2 special dividend. §Value of bid per share includes 68.3p special dividend.

Fig. 2.3 Current takeover bids and mergers

- **Bids:** details of current takeover bids for publicly quoted companies, naming the bidder and target, the value of the bid per share, the current market price of the target's shares, the price before the bid, and the total value of the bid in millions of pounds.

Bids might be made in the form of a cash offer for all the shares in issue (the value of the bid per share), a paper offer where shares in the bidder are offered in exchange for those of the target (as in the case of Lasmo and Enterprise), or a combination of the two. The bids might be agreed to by the management of the target, or they might be defended or contested. The battles over corporate control have generated a new vocabulary of company life: white knights (alternative bidders who are preferred by the existing management of the target) and poison pill defences (tactics that mean a successful takeover triggers something deleterious to the target company's value) are just two of the most popular. For example:

> Mattel yesterday snatched victory from rival US toy group Hasbro in the battle for JW Spear, the British company which owns the rights to the Scrabble board game outside North America. Mattel, the maker of Barbie dolls, raised its offer for shares in Spear from £10 to £11.50, valuing the company at £62m. Mattel entered the battle for Spear as a white knight after Hasbro launched a surprise bid in late May.
> (*Financial Times*, 12 July 1994)

Cross border deals

Monday's newspaper extends the coverage of M&A deals to international bids made in the previous week (see Figure 2.4):

- **Deals:** details of the bidder/investor, the target company, the industrial sector and the value of the bid in pounds (how much the bidder is offering to pay).

- **Comment:** a phrase analysing the essential feature of the deal. Figure 2.4 includes the background on various deals, for example, one company disposing of non-core businesses, another seeking to expand overseas by acquisition, and a third looking for potential white knights.

Throughout the 1980s, the market for corporate control was the source of considerable financial innovation as well as a significant degree of controversy, notably in the United States. A new kind

CROSS BORDER M&A DEALS

BIDDER/INVESTOR	TARGET	SECTOR	VALUE	COMMENT
Rhône-Poulenc Rorer (France/US)	Fisons (UK)	Pharmaceuticals	£1.83bn	Fisons rejecting higher offer
Houston Industries (US)/ Central & South West (US)	Norweb (UK)	Power	£1.7bn	Long struggle looks likely
Investor group (Germany/ Switzerland)	Postbank (Germany)	Banking	£1.36bn	White knights wanted
Aegon (Netherlands)	Seguros Banamex (Mexico)	Insurance	£158m	High-growth stake
Ceridian Corp (US)	Unit of NatWest (UK)	Computer services	£33.1m	Non-core disposal
Arjo Wiggins Appleton (UK/France)	Graphtec (S Africa)	Paper distribution	£23m	AWA continues sector growth
English China Clay (UK)	Genstar Stone Products (US)	Building materials	£22.5m	Redland non-core disposal
Northumbrian Water (UK)	Gema (Mexico)	Water	£15.4m	NW's third overseas move
Hicking Pentecost (UK)	Blue Mountain (US)	Textiles	£14.5m	Buy from US Industries
Banca Commerciale Italiana (Italy)	Banco de Lima (Peru)	Banking distribution	n/a	Extends LatAm presence

Fig. 2.4 Cross border M&A deals

of arbitrage also became prevalent at this time. Arbitrage is the technique of buying an asset at one price in a market, and almost simultaneously, selling it in another market for a profit.

Risk arbitrage dealt in the shares of companies targeted for takeover, buying before the announcement of a bid and selling when the usual price rise after announcement followed. At times it relied on inside information and the practice of insider trading, compounded with other financial scandals, undoubtedly earned financial institutions a dubious reputation. The next chapter presents the much more positive side of these institutions, first, their provision of a marketplace for lenders and borrowers of money, and second, their advice and assistance to these two sides of the market.

"Some collective nouns: a gleam of bulls; a gloom of bears; a roller-coaster of stock markets; a commission of brokers."

JAMES LIPTON

"The market – whether stock, bond or super – is a barometer of civilisation."

JASON ALEXANDER,

PHILOSOPHY OF INVESTORS

3

FINANCIAL INSTITUTIONS

- **Managing money** – how assets are distributed into the portfolios of investors: investing institutions and money managers; and clearing banks

- **Financing industry** – how new securities are created to provide funds for borrowers: merchant banks; securitisation

- **Making markets** – the provision of facilities for assets to be priced and traded: marketmakers and broker-dealers; stock exchanges; money, currency, and derivative markets

- **Moving prices** – demand, supply, and other key economic forces: short- and long-term determinants of share price movements; overall market movements

The most basic financial institution is a market – a place, not necessarily physical, where buyers and sellers can come together to trade. There are essentially four kinds of market in the financial system. The first type is the securities market where new capital is raised (the primary market) and where trading in existing shares and bonds takes place (the secondary market). Such markets include stock exchanges around the world, as well as the international capital markets. The other three kinds of market are: the money markets where highly liquid financial instruments are traded; the foreign exchange markets where currencies are bought and sold; and the futures and options markets where these derivatives can be used to hedge or speculate in future interest rate, exchange rate, commodity price and security price movements.

All of these markets are organised in the sense that they operate on well-established custom and practice, and direct access to them is limited to professional participants. Investors and borrowers usually gain access to the markets through intermediaries. Beyond the organised markets are the over-the-counter (OTC) markets – places or, more often, computer screen-based or telephone networks where securities are traded outside the recognised exchange. The biggest of them all is the foreign exchange market, although the OTC derivatives market is also growing dramatically.

There are three basic functions that have to be performed in a financial market: distribution of assets into the portfolios of investors who want to own them; creation of new ones in order to provide funds for borrowers; and "making" the markets, providing the means by which all of these assets can be easily traded. The first function relates more to investors, the second to companies, and the third is the central facilitating role to which all financial institutions contribute in one way or another.

One single financial institution might perform all three of these functions and do them across a broad range of markets. For example, some UK merchant banks and US investment banks are involved in

portfolio management of clients' investments as well as corporate finance, arranging deals, helping clients raise money through flotations, rights issues and bond issues, and advising them on takeovers. Furthermore, they often act as marketmakers, trading on their own behalf, especially in the foreign exchange, Eurobond and derivatives markets.

The performance of a range of different roles, and the contrast between acting as a principal on one's own behalf or as an agent on behalf of a client, throw up a number of conflicts of interest. Such devices as Chinese walls, notional barriers intended to deter valuable market information from being shared between parts of a company with conflicting interests, aim to prevent abuses. But this is still an area of considerable controversy. Apart from the benefits of specialisation, it is one of the reasons companies might focus on working different sectors and functions of the market.

MANAGING MONEY

Chapter 1 explained the principles of investment on the premise that an individual investor is the dominant player on the saving/lending/investing side of the capital markets, making and implementing his or her own investment decisions. In reality, individual investors acting alone form only a small part of the investment community. Nowadays the bulk of investment is done by large investing institutions such as pension funds and insurance companies, operating on behalf of the millions of people who put money into them. Furthermore, such individual investors as there are rely on the services of a range of market professionals, intermediaries who offer advice on, and management of, their asset portfolios.

Investing institutions and fund managers

Many people save in occupational pension schemes. These savings are administered by pension funds which have become the major players in equity and other markets, operating vast portfolios of assets on some of the basic principles outlined in chapter 1. Annually, the

Financial Times publishes a survey of pension fund management. This lists leading pension fund managers, the value of the funds under their management, and the number of clients for whom they provide these services, with comparative figures for previous years. This is a valuable guide to the performance of these institutions, and their relative weight in the investment community.

Life assurance and general insurance companies are also key players in securities markets. In common with pension funds, they manage their funds on the principle of matching the nature of the assets they hold with that of their liabilities. Thus, pension funds and life assurance companies often have liabilities that will only fall due in the long term. Hence, they typically have a preference for long-term assets, such as ordinary shares with good growth and capital gain potential. Insurance companies, whose liabilities might fall due much sooner, tend to prefer a portfolio containing some more liquid assets. In either case, the fund managers are bound to act prudently under their fiduciary obligations to the people who placed money in their care.

Unit trusts (known in the United States as mutual funds) are another form of managed investment. Investors buy units in a trust, and the trust manager invests the money in shares or any other assets laid down by the trust's investment objectives and its guidelines for decision-making. The advantage for investors is that relatively small amounts of money can be spread between a range of assets, securing the benefits of portfolio diversification: if invested well, the trust's capital grows and so does the price of its units. Unit trusts generally specialise in particular types of asset, such as equities of a certain industrial sector or a specific country or region.

Investment trusts are similar to unit trusts except that they have a limited size. Like unit trusts, they invest in equities and other assets, but whereas unit trusts are open-ended, with no limit on the amount of units that can be bought, investment trusts are closed-ended. In a sense, they are more like a regular company with a set number of shares in issue, and in fact their shares are usually listed on the stock markets. Shareholders receive their income on investment trusts from dividends as well as any capital gains. Both unit and investment trusts are examined in more detail in chapter 8.

Investing institutions will generally manage their asset portfolios themselves, but at times they will use the services of companies specifically set up to manage the portfolios of large institutional investors or wealthy individuals with substantial holdings. These are variously known as fund, asset, equity, capital or money management companies, and they will distinguish themselves both by the kinds of markets in which they operate, and by their investment philosophies. For example, certain companies may deal only in equity markets, others on such diverse principles as passive indexation, a preference for growth stocks, or the exploitation of market inefficiencies.

Pension funds and other investors, large and small, may also use the services of stockbrokers and other investment advisers. These brokers provide research to institutional and large individual investors for which they are paid by commission on business placed through them. They also provide market access for smaller retail clients, supplying a range of different services: relatively low-cost trading; and advice on portfolio allocation, on particular transactions, and on tax issues. Stockbroking is often just one of the activities of a large diversified securities house or investment bank.

Clearing banks

The clearing banks' role in the management of money is very varied. Their key activity is as deposit-taking and loan-making institutions that make their money by borrowing (usually taking deposits, but also using wholesale funds from the money markets) at one rate of interest and lending at a higher one. Building societies operate in a similar way except that they specialise in lending for the purchase of property. But banks differ in that they also provide a range of other financial services, dealing directly with the public over matters from investment advice (both financial and capital) to foreign exchange needs for holidays or business trips abroad.

Banks also "create" money through what is known as the money multiplier. What happens is that a bank receives a deposit, some of which is kept in liquid form as a safeguard in case the depositor needs it back, with the rest being lent on. The borrower will then spend the money on an item, the seller of which will deposit it in a bank. Again, part of the

deposit will be kept liquid with the rest lent on, and so the cycle continues. If it were not for the fact that the banks do not lend all that they receive in deposits, the process would continue indefinitely with the amount of money in the economy, the money supply, ballooning.

In fact, the proportion of their deposits not lent determines how much a given deposit eventually becomes within the whole banking system. If, for example, all banks keep back 10 per cent of their deposits, an initial deposit can expand tenfold: of a £100 deposit, £90 is lent and deposited, of which £81 is lent and deposited, and so on. The eventual total of bank deposits is £1,000.

As a result of the money multiplier, banks are highly geared companies, with a substantial proportion of their capital made up of borrowed funds. Since high gearing implies that small changes can have major effects, it is critical that they lend soundly or a large credit failure by one of their borrowers could have devastating consequences. This is why the monetary authorities attempt to influence, at times by decree, the various ratios (such as cash, liquidity and reserve assets ratios) banks employ to manage their finances. The other reason they do so is to control the expansion of the money supply, one of the most important determinants of inflation and the overall level of economic activity. Alternative means by which this might be done are discussed in the next chapter.

FINANCING INDUSTRY

The provision of funds for industry is the role of the primary markets where new securities are issued on behalf of clients. The aim of the financial institutions that perform this service on behalf of client companies is to attract cash for new capital investment, in the form of either equity or debt finance, from individual and institutional investors, banks and, in some cases, the Euromarkets.

Merchant banks

When a company wants to raise new equity or debt finance, it will usually approach a merchant bank for advice and assistance, and a

broker to sponsor the issue. The bank is responsible for advising on the terms of the issue and, in particular, designing its key features. This is one of the most fertile areas for innovation as banks create the new and more exotic financial instruments discussed in chapters 2 and 9. The bank will also arrange the mechanics of the issue, such as the various techniques for making new issues and rights issues discussed in chapter 5.

New issues of equity capital require the publication of a prospectus to satisfy the regulations of the Stock Exchange, which is naturally concerned to protect its reputation and the interests of its investors. The issues also require underwriting by the issuing house, the merchant bank. It must agree to subscribe for any shares not taken up by investors once the offer period has expired. The role of the sponsoring broker, which will be a member of the Stock Exchange, is to ensure that the Exchange's legal requirements are met, to pass on, if necessary, some of the risk of underwriting to sub-underwriters and to distribute the shares into the portfolios of willing investors.

As well as raising new capital, merchant banks will usually be involved on one side or the other of the market for corporate control, advising on strategies. Annually, the *Financial Times* publishes a survey of corporate finance. This ranks merchant bank corporate advisers by the value of their work in three areas: takeover bids, flotation of companies, and issues of shares by companies already with quotations. It is a valuable guide to how well the banks are performing against one another.

Securitisation

Of course, many companies might raise new capital through borrowing directly from a bank in the form of a loan. Nowadays, this has become less common owing to a process known as securitisation. This is the process that enables bank borrowing and lending to be replaced with the issue of some of the debt securities mentioned in chapter 2: commercial bills, bonds, and floating rate notes. It creates attractive new securities for investors, and it has significant benefits for the companies. In particular, bank charges are reduced, and the cost of raising funds may be even less expensive if the markets turn

out to be more efficient judges of the creditworthiness of companies than banks. Of course, merchant banks will normally arrange the issue of these debt securities.

Securitisation also refers to the conversion of previously untradeable assets into securities that can be bought and sold. For example, an innovation of the 1980s was the mortgage-backed security. This is produced by converting the assets of a building society, the stream of payments due on its mortgages, into a tradeable security. Closer to the interests of the small investor is the certificate of deposit (CD), a very liquid, almost risk-free asset which pays a relatively low rate of return. It is analogous to an interest-bearing bank account, but it has the advantage that it can be traded; it is effectively a bank account that has been securitised.

MAKING MARKETS

Marketmaking is the central function of financial institutions in the secondary markets where existing securities are traded. The role of the marketmakers is to determine security prices and to ensure that buyers and sellers can trade without having a significant impact on prices. Efficient marketmaking avoids substantial price shifts or undue volatility in response to individual buy or sell orders, providing liquidity and allowing dealing to take place on a large scale. It also ensures that the costs of trading are not too high.

Marketmakers and broker-dealers

The companies or branches of companies that are marketmakers buy and sell securities on their own account, acting as a principal. With the right to trade in this way goes the obligation to make the market. Hence, it is conceivable that at the end of a day's trading a marketmaker will be left with unwanted stocks or an undesirable shortage of stocks. They will therefore always be seeking to find a price that "balances their books". Their activities are an important influence on stock price movements.

When quoting prices at which they will buy or sell securities, marketmakers list bid (buying) prices and offer (selling) prices. The

difference between the two figures is known as the spread. Since marketmakers naturally aim to profit from their transactions, the bid price is invariably lower than the offer price. This is comparable to a bank that takes deposits (borrows or "buys" money) at one rate of interest, and loans (sells) it at a higher price. Although the spread for the marketmaker or the rate differential for the bank may seem small, totalled over the huge amount of transactions they make, they are often able to make very considerable profits.

Stockbrokers or, as they are more commonly known nowadays, broker-dealers, are companies that act both as an agent for the investor, and as a principal, trading on their own behalf. Such companies face especially difficult conflicts of interest. But for the existence of Chinese walls, their marketmaking arm might be inclined to encourage their broking arm to advise client investors to take on securities the former is keen to unload. Similarly, they may also be inclined to the practice of "front running", buying promising securities or selling dubious ones ahead of clients, and potentially affecting the price adversely prior to the clients' trades.

Marketmakers and broker-dealers both thrive on activity: the more transactions they make or facilitate, the better their opportunities for profit or commission. Obviously, the benefit of the marketmakers' activity is to enhance market liquidity, but that of the brokers might not be so valuable. Again, there is a conflict of interest: the investor is aiming for return on assets; the broker is aiming partly for this (even if simply to ensure his or her services are retained), but also for commission on trades. The process of making trades frequently just to earn commission rather than for any long-term investment objective is known as churning.

Stock exchanges

The London Stock Exchange is the main securities market in the United Kingdom. This is the market for listed shares and gilts plus debentures, convertibles and warrants. For all of these securities, it is both a primary and secondary market. The second tier of the Stock Exchange is known as the Unlisted Securities Market (USM). This market was established in 1980 to trade in shares not suitable for the

main market. It enables smaller companies to "come to the market" to raise capital without having to satisfy the more onerous listing and disclosure requirements of the Stock Exchange. However, as of the end of 1996, the USM will be closed. Its effective replacement is the Alternative Investment Market (AIM), launched in June 1995 by the Stock Exchange as a more regulated but still "unquoted" market for small, growing, companies. Its listing and disclosure requirements are considerably less than for the USM. The equities listed on all of these markets and the indices that measure their overall performance are the focus of chapters 5 and 6.

The most significant stock exchanges elsewhere in the world are in New York, Tokyo, Frankfurt and Paris. These are explored further in chapter 7. In terms of total market capitalisation, the sum of the "market cap" (the share price multiplied by the number of shares in issue) of all the securities listed on them, the two that outrank the London Stock Exchange are the New York Stock Exchange and the Tokyo Stock Exchange. The indices that evaluate them (in the United States, the Dow Jones Industrial Average and the Standard and Poor's 500, and in Japan, the Nikkei) are some of the most important indicators of the state of the world's financial markets.

Until quite recently, trading on world stock exchanges was conducted in a physical setting, such as the City of London or Wall Street. The impact of technology has been that there are now fewer actual marketplaces. Instead, much trading is conducted through computer screen-based systems, such as London's Stock Exchange Automated Quotation (SEAQ) system and the National Association of Securities Dealers Automated Quotation (NASDAQ) system in the United States. These electronic trading systems tend to be quote-driven, with marketmakers and dealers quoting bid and offer prices on screen for other traders to select from. This contrasts with the older, order-driven, system of trading where dealers listed their orders to buy and sell shares with the aim of finding a counterparty wanting to buy or sell that quantity at a price on which both parties could agree. These issues are discussed in more detail in chapter 17.

On top of technological advances, stock markets have also seen considerable deregulation in recent years – an easing of the restrictions on their operating methods. In the United Kingdom, the most

notable event of this kind was the Big Bang of 1986. Prior to this deregulation, the two key institutions in the market were jobbers and brokers, each of whom operated in a single capacity. The jobbers were marketmakers who did not deal directly with customers, but only with brokers; the brokers placed their orders only through jobbers, and worked on behalf of customers but never dealt with them for their own account. The system protected investors from abuses of some of the conflicts of interest that arise from the principal/agent relationship, but it had a number of weaknesses.

The main problems of the pre-Big Bang Stock Exchange were that it operated as a cartel with fixed commissions on trades, it limited access to capital and new technology, and it constrained liquidity and the ability to make substantial trades without unduly influencing prices. The radical changes of Big Bang led to far more competition between financial institutions, a significant influx of outside capital as banks bought into the market, and the adoption of the screen-based trading system. Between them, these developments created a much more fluid market with information flowing more freely, liquidity enhanced, more and larger transactions made more feasible, and the costs of doing business, at least for the major players, notably reduced.

Money, currency and derivative markets

The money markets are markets where money and any other liquid assets such as Treasury bills and bills of exchange can be lent and borrowed for periods ranging from a few hours to a few months. Their primary function is to enable banks, building societies and companies to manage their cash and other short-term assets and liabilities, the short-term counterparts of the long-term capital markets. The main participants in these markets in the United Kingdom are: the banks; companies that issue short-term debt instruments; money market brokers; and the discount houses, which act as the marketmakers for most of these assets. Discount houses are discussed in the next chapter.

The foreign exchange markets deal in currencies, for the most part the leading currencies of the developed world: the dollar, the yen, the pound, the Swiss franc, the lira and the currencies of the European

Monetary System (EMS). The main players are the marketmakers, primarily banks, who buy and sell currencies on their own account and deal with customers and other banks, and brokers who try to find trading counterparties for their clients. This is an over-the-counter market with business transactions conducted almost exclusively through a telephone network. Both the money and currency markets are explored in more detail in chapter 10, while the EMS and its exchange rate mechanism form part of the subject of chapter 14.

The derivatives markets deal in futures and options, and increasingly in more exotic financial instruments such as interest rate and currency swaps. Futures and options originated in the commodities markets, the markets for raw materials and primary products, as a means of protecting against seriously adverse price swings. They are still used today in such markets as the London Metal Exchange and the London Commodity Exchange, but contracts and markets have also now evolved for a range of other securities, debt instruments and indices. In the United Kingdom, the focal point for this activity is the London International Financial Futures and Options Exchange, the LIFFE. There is also a growing market in over-the-counter derivatives, custom-built contracts between very large investors and borrowers usually created by the investment banks. The markets for futures and options other than those traded over-the-counter are discussed in chapter 11, while the commodities markets feature in chapter 12.

MOVING PRICES

Chapter 1 examined how changes in interest rates might affect the prices of equities, bonds and currencies, but what other factors move the prices of individual assets and of whole markets? Obviously, supply and demand are the basic influences for an individual asset, but what are the underlying determinants of these economic forces, and what causes substantial broad market moves? These are questions surrounded in controversy, especially related to the stock market, and it is important to differentiate between various kinds of price movement.

In the stock market, there are essentially three kinds of moves: the long-term trend of the overall market as reflected in various indices; short-term moves around the trend; and the movements of individual shares and sectors. For the most part, individual sectors broadly follow overall market trends, though some may be growth industries, some may be mature or declining industries, or some may simply be the beneficiary or victim of a particular event with ramifications peculiar to that industry (for example, the oil industry and the Gulf War, or the computer, media and telecommunications industries and the hype surrounding the "information superhighway"). In those cases, sector values can diverge from the market trend.

The price movements of individual stocks are influenced by a range of factors specific to the business. Most of these are explored in chapters 5, 6, and 7, but the more common include company profits, the growth of those profits, dividends, and takeover bids. These are the fundamentals of corporate life and fundamental analysis aims to uncover the truths about a company behind the figures to determine whether its shares are over- or underpriced. The way changes in company fundamentals actually cause price movements is not always obvious because of the market's capacity to discount future events. These are news events, the core of the forces that move individual stock prices, but expectations of future news events can be just as powerful.

The fact that prices move on account of expectations of the future, as well as being determined by historic and current knowledge of a company's performance, suggests that they incorporate all known information about the value of shares. This is the foundation of one of the most powerful theories of asset valuation, the efficient market hypothesis. The predictions of this theory are that no one can forecast future price moves consistently and that, over the long term, without inside information, no one can beat the market. The corollary is that stock prices follow what is called a random walk: at any point in an equity's price history, it is impossible to predict whether its next move will be up or down. Hence, investment strategies based on chartism or technical analysis, the study of past price trends, will not perform dependably.

Market movements

As well as causing individual equity price movements, news about particular companies can also have an impact on the whole market. This is especially the case with blue chip companies, the most highly regarded companies in the market and usually ones with substantial assets, a strong record of growth, and a well-known name. The following extract illustrates their importance:

> The FT-SE 100 Index closed 18.3 down at 2,946.7. Around 4 points of the Footsie fall reflected the heavy setback in GEC, which was among the most actively traded shares after severely disappointing City analysts with virtually unchanged profits. A market now looking for growth of around 6 per cent overall in UK corporate earnings this year is no longer prepared to be forgiving of slow progress. The reaction to GEC's figures helped to upset equities in early trading.
> (*Financial Times,* 7 July 1994)

There is much dispute about what causes market moves like this. In this case, it is partly a short-term move and these tend to be affected by such intangibles as sentiment, investor psychology and how the market is "feeling"! Medium-term moves seem to be influenced by supply and demand factors, such as the weight of money moving into or out of stocks: there is also an element of that in this case as the market expects a certain level of growth in overall corporate earnings.

It is probable that long-term moves depend on fundamental economic and political factors. The market often follows the broad patterns of economic activity, and certainly news about inflation, productivity, growth and the government's fiscal and monetary stance can have major effects on the level of the market. Hence the importance of understanding what the economic indicators mean and how they relate to the markets. These are the subjects of chapters 4, 13, 14, and 15.

On occasion, stock prices can plummet in a way that appears to bear no relation to fundamentals, supply and demand or even, at least in its early stages, to market sentiment. Such an occasion was Black Monday and the stock market crash of 1987, when prices fell by record amounts in markets throughout the world. Much analysis of this event has been conducted and there is still no agreement on its root causes. Certainly, fundamental economic forces do not appear to

have been critical, since most economies continued to grow reasonably well in its aftermath, and the downturn did not come until the very end of the decade. Part of this was due to the prudent economic policies of key governments, which avoided some of the disastrous policy mistakes made after the last major market meltdown, the crash of 1929. The central role of governments in financial markets and economic policy more broadly is the subject of the next chapter.

"The important thing for government is not to do things which individuals are doing already, and do them a little better or a little worse, but to do those things which at present are not done at all."

JOHN MAYNARD KEYNES

"There have been three great inventions since the beginning of time: fire, the wheel and central banking."

WILL ROGERS

4

GOVERNMENTS

- **Balancing the budget** – what the government gives and gets: fiscal policy; taxation and the budget deficit

- **Controlling the money supply** – government intervention in the money markets: Treasury bills and open market operations; interest rates and monetary control; central bank independence

- **Forecasting the economy** – the basis for government action: economic policy; credibility and the political business cycle

- **Regulating the markets** – government's goals of preserving financial stability, promoting competition and protecting investors and depositors

Lenders/investors and borrowers/companies are the two sides of the interactions that meet in the financial markets, with financial institutions the third party, facilitating these transactions. The government is the fourth player in this picture. It typically acts as both borrower and lender but, in addition, it will frequently intervene, directly, through legislation or by persuasion, to regulate the markets.

Overarching all of these roles, is the government's position as primary economic agent, attempting to monitor and influence the state of the economy. The principal means by which it does this are: fiscal policy, the budgetary balance between public spending and taxation; and monetary policy, essentially control of the money supply and manipulation of interest rates. Forecasting the future direction of the economy plays an important role in determining these policies. How they all impinge on the financial markets is the subject of this chapter. Further details on the economy feature in the third part of the book.

BALANCING THE BUDGET

Governments spend money on a range of different goods, services, salaries, subsidies, and other payments. These include defence, education, health, public transport, public infrastructure, public housing, the pay of public sector employees, social security, and interest on government borrowings. To help pay for the services this spending provides and, to some extent, to redistribute incomes from the wealthier to the poorer, the government raises money, primarily through taxation. Some taxes are direct, levied on personal and corporate income; some are indirect, levied on sales, value-added, imports, and certain products such as petrol, cigarettes and alcohol.

The difference between public spending and taxation is known as the budget balance, the budget being the collective term for the government's annual decisions on how its tax and spending plans will be designed and implemented. It might be a balanced budget where rev-

enues equal expenditure, a budget surplus where revenues exceed expenditure, or, most typically for the UK government, a budget deficit, where expenditure exceeds revenues. Net income is known as the public sector debt repayment (PSDR) since the surplus allows repayment of debts from previous years. This was the UK government's position for a brief period in the late 1980s. More commonly, there is a net outflow, the public sector borrowing requirement or PSBR. The cumulative total of all PSBRs and PSDRs is known as the national debt.

Through the 1980s and 1990s, the UK government has had one other source of revenue, namely the receipts from the sale to the public of nationalised industries, the process of privatisation. The influx of cash from "selling the family silver" had a very positive effect on government finances, and, naturally enough, through the issue of a significant amount of new equities, aroused considerable interest in the financial markets. Many new investors were tempted to participate in the stock market, particularly with its "stag" opportunities, buying the privatised stocks in the primary market and selling them shortly afterwards at a premium in the secondary market. These matters are examined further in the next chapter.

Fiscal policy

Fiscal policy is used by the government in a variety of ways: to provide services, such as education, health, defence, and infrastructure, that might not be so well provided by the free market; to meet social goals of alleviating poverty and assisting the disadvantaged; to influence the behaviour of individuals and companies, encouraging desirable activities like investment and discouraging undesirable ones like smoking; and to manage the overall level of demand for goods and services in the economy, and hence the degree of economic activity and the rate of inflation. The government goal that may affect financial markets most significantly is that of influencing behaviour. For example, different tax treatment of different categories of assets will influence investment decision-making. Similarly, the tax treatment of corporate earnings will affect a company's dividend policy and its choice between raising capital through debt or equity. More broadly,

government spending policy, perhaps in public procurement, might mean increased turnover and profitability for companies in the relevant industries. This might have a positive effect on their share prices. On the other hand, excessive borrowing might drive up the costs of funds for all borrowers, perhaps resulting in a crowding out of private capital investment.

Achievement of the government ambition of demand management is generally attempted through countercyclical policy: the government aims to smooth out the more extreme patterns of the business cycle, damping demand in a boom and boosting it in a recession. This can be done in a boom either through raising taxes or cutting spending; in a recession, it may try lowering taxes or increasing spending. To some extent, there are built-in stabilisers, and this is what is meant by the cyclical effects of the business cycle. For example, in a recession, people are earning and spending less which means that the government's tax revenues fall. Of course, if the budget is already in deficit at that point, the deficit will expand even further. The government's problem then is to decide between raising taxes and cutting spending to ease the deficit or the reverse to help pull the economy out of recession. At such a point, it may turn to monetary policy.

Taxation and the budget deficit

There is considerable controversy about the use of taxation and budget deficits to influence aggregate demand and incentives to work. The pursuit of higher output and lower unemployment, without overheating the economy and causing inflation, is Keynesian economic policy. Growth is pursued through increasing government spending or cutting taxes, creating or raising the budget deficit, and increasing the PSBR. Tax cuts, for example, increase demand through their beneficial effects on personal disposable income.

The question is, though, how far can the government manage demand in this way before running into inflationary bottlenecks. Furthermore, it is not clear that governments can make accurate enough assessments to judge exactly how much "pump-priming" or "deficit financing" is needed to "fine-tune" the economy to a non-inflationary growth path. Indeed, when demand should be restrained to avoid

overheating, there are political reasons why governments might avoid raising taxes.

Increased spending or lower taxes as a means of demand management in times of recession are typically a politically centre-left policy. But tax cuts may also be advocated by centre-right politicians who view them as having a different economic effect. These politicians and the economists who advise them, focus on the incentive and disincentive effects of taxation, arguing that lower taxes have a strong incentive effect, encouraging people to work harder, and thereby raising national output.

Certainly, taxation does affect incentives to some extent, but extreme believers in this position, who gained political power in the United States in the 1980s, took it a little too far. These supply side economists claimed that cutting the tax rate significantly would have such powerful incentive effects that the level of tax revenues would actually rise. In reality, the result was a series of massive budget deficits.

Debates about taxation also focus on the appropriate form it should take. For example, progressive income tax is a way of redistributing income from richer to poorer sections of the population, creating a more equitable society. Supply siders prefer the use of indirect taxes, such as value added tax. These, they argue, are easier to enforce, and reduce the incentive to work by less than equivalent levels of income tax. The claim is that taxpayers experience "money illusion": if they pay taxes concealed in product prices, they notice it less than taxes taken out of their pay, and are thus prepared to pay more tax on goods than on income. This might have a number of political and economic benefits: if people feel less heavily taxed, they will behave accordingly.

CONTROLLING THE MONEY SUPPLY

In order to finance their frequent budget deficits, and in common with any other individual or organisation that wants to live beyond their means, the government has to borrow in the financial markets. This it does by issuing securities with a range of different maturities, from the short, medium, long and irredeemable gilt-edged stocks

traded on the Stock Exchange to three-month Treasury bills issued weekly in the money markets.

The government's agent for the sale of its debt instruments is the Bank of England, often known simply as the Bank. The stocks are first created by the Treasury and then the Bank arranges their sales, purchases and redemptions. New issues replace the ones that have matured in order to meet the government's continuing financing needs and the market's demand for a balance of differently dated stocks. Most are redeemable at some specified date, although a few, such as War Loan and Consols, are irredeemable.

Longer term government debt takes the form of gilts. These are examined in detail in chapter 9. For the present, it is merely important to distinguish gilts from fixed interest stocks generally. Not all gilts are fixed interest, nor are all fixed interest stocks gilts. For example, some of the corporate debt instruments discussed in chapter 2 are fixed interest while some gilts are index-linked with their interest payments determined by the prevailing rate of inflation.

For a period in the late 1980s, the government's budget surplus meant that there were no new issues of gilts, whether fixed interest or index-linked. However, as the budget returned to deficit, the Bank of England resumed issuing new ones early in 1991. The means by which this is done, the public offering of stocks where a minimum price is set and tenders invited, is most easily illustrated through the way the government's shortest term debt securities are issued, the Treasury bills.

Treasury bills and open market operations

Treasury bills are bills of exchange, short-term debt instruments issued by the Bank of England on behalf of the UK government. They have a three-month maturity but carry no interest, the total yield being the difference between the purchase and redemption prices. The bills are issued by tender each week to the discount houses in units of between £5,000 and £100,000, and every Monday the *Financial Times* contains a table with details of the tender (see Figure 4.1):

- **Bills on offer, total of applications and total allocated:** the value of the bills on offer is £1500 million and the value of the total applications to buy those bills is a measure of market enthusiasm for them.

In this example, the earlier tender was much more oversubscribed than the later one. The factor by which an issue is oversubscribed is known as the auction's cover. Since there is almost invariably over-subscription, naturally the total allocated is the same as that offered.

- **Minimum accepted bid and allotment at minimum level:** the former is the lowest bid price accepted, in these cases £98,355 and £98,365 for every bill with a face value of £100,000. The bid is lower than the redemption price so that the purchaser can make money on the difference. The allotment is simply the proportion of the bills sold at the minimum price; the rest would have been sold for higher prices (lower discounts).

- **Rates of discount and yield:** the top accepted discount rate is the other side of the minimum accepted bid, with the average rate calculating in the discount on the bills sold for higher prices. The discount rates do not correspond exactly to the actual discount since they are presented as annual rates even though the bills mature in three months. Loosely speaking, these are the rates a buyer would earn for purchasing four consecutive bills. The discount rate is calculated as the difference between the purchase and redemption prices as a percentage of the latter. In contrast, the yield is the difference as a percentage of the former. Thus, it corresponds to any other current yield, that is, annual return divided by current market price.

BANK OF ENGLAND TREASURY BILL TENDER					
	Oct 6	Sep 29		Oct 6	Sep 29
Bills on offer	£1500m	£1500m	Top accepted rate	6.5981%	6.5580%
Total of applications	£3795m	£6998m	Ave. rate of discount	6.5775%	6.5378%
Total allocated	£1500m	£1500m	Average yield	6.6872%	6.6461%
Min. accepted bid	£98.355	£98.365	Offer at next tender	£1500m	£1500m
Allotment at min. level	27%	88%	Min. accept. bid 182 days	-	-

Fig. 4.1 Bank of England Treasury bill tender

The discount houses have a special relationship with the Bank of England that is central to the implementation of the government's monetary policy. First of all, they act as marketmakers in the money markets and, as such, they are obliged to cover the amount of bills on

offer in a Treasury bill tender as well as having a bid price for other bills of exchange and certificates of deposit. These then are their assets; their liabilities are deposits by banks of what is known as call money. This is money borrowed at interest rates lower than the discount houses earn on bills (again, as marketmakers, they are obliged to take the deposits), but which can be withdrawn at very short notice.

Discount houses can take on these obligations because the Bank stands behind them as the "lender of last resort". If they run short of funds, either because banks have withdrawn money or because they have been obliged to purchase other money market instruments, perhaps the weekly Treasury bill tender, they can go to the Bank. Every day the Bank estimates the market's fund shortage and usually meets it by buying bills from the discount houses. In doing this they are injecting funds into the whole financial system; if instead they sell bills, they are withdrawing funds, effectively mopping up surplus money. This is known as open market operations and is one of the means by which the government controls the money supply.

Interest rates and monetary control

The extension of this control is how the Bank of England manipulates the level of interest rates. Since it deals actively in the bill markets through open market operations, it is in a position to create a shortage of cash when it wishes to. In that case, the discount houses are obliged to borrow, and as the lender of last resort, the level at which the Bank provides funds is an indication of the level of short-term rates of which it approves. These rates can then be used to influence rates across the whole economy.

As the previous three chapters made clear, the rate of interest, that is, the price of money, is one of the most powerful forces in the financial markets. Under the relatively free market approach of recent UK governments, interest rates have been allowed, for the most part, to be determined by market forces with the Bank's guidance. But with this system the Bank has to be careful to give only very subtle indications of where it wants rates to go: if it alerts the market to its intentions, the force of expectations will have immediate ramifications throughout the economy as traders discount the future.

An alternative method of controlling the money supply is using direct controls on bank lending, aiming to limit money multiplier effects. This might be achieved by changing banks' reserve asset ratios, that is, the proportions they keep liquid from any given deposit, by imposing limits on total bank lending or consumer credit, or simply by persuading bankers to restrict their lending. A further technique, which has been popular in the United Kingdom since the late 1970s, is setting targets for monetary growth. The most recent target in the United Kingdom was the monetary base: this consists of cash in circulation plus banks' deposits at the Bank of England.

The last way in which the Bank of England acts in the financial markets is with foreign exchange where it may intervene to try to raise or lower the value of sterling. This again can be done through short-term interest rates: usually raising them attracts investors into buying sterling, while lowering encourages selling. The Bank might also work on the currency by using its official reserves of foreign currencies to buy pounds and, through the weight of its intervention, push up its value or at least hold it steady. But, nowadays, with the vast speculative volume of transactions in the foreign exchange markets, a successful intervention may need international cooperation. A government acting alone is no longer able to manage the financial markets nor its national economy.

Central bank independence

Management of the economy through monetary policy used to be the preserve of monetarists, who focused on the importance of controlling the money supply as a way of keeping inflation in check. But monetary policy also affects growth: it is said to be neutral if the level of interest rates neither stimulates nor slows growth. If the interest rate rises, monetary policy might restrain consumer spending and encourage savings, hence reining in growth. Nowadays, the key roles of monetary policy in economic management of demand and inflation are almost universally acknowledged: the question is more one of who should control it, the government or independent monetary authorities.

The argument for central bank independence is that governments are poor at managing their economies, providing monetary accom-

modation not only for their own deficits, but also for wage claims, oil shocks and so on. This has caused inflation: since government control of the money supply is open to manipulation in response to political expediency, there is a built-in inflationary bias. The bias can only be removed by handing control over to the central bank, which will be free of political pressures. The central bank can then pursue its twin goals of monetary and financial stability, a sound money supply and a safe financial system.

Naïve monetarist versions of this view suggest that central banks can control inflation with interest rates without an intermediate effect on economic activity. This visualises a clear connection between interest rates, the money supply and inflation, that is separate from output and employment. This seems a rather unlikely scenario: given the powers over the whole economy an independent central bank would have, it is clearly important to make it democratically accountable.

The issue of central bank independence has become particularly important in the United Kingdom as a direct result of the failure of the UK government's monetary policy in 1992. This policy, discredited by circumstances, was to control inflation and pursue economic convergence with fellow members of the European Union, by keeping the pound in the exchange rate mechanism (ERM) of the European Monetary System (see chapter 14). After the collapse of this policy, the government aimed to restore its credibility in "the fight against inflation" by greater openness and an enhanced role for the Bank of England.

The UK government's post-ERM policy is something of a compromise response to this argument, going part of the way to bank independence, but still retaining substantial control. It is based on a specific inflation target of 1–4 per cent for retail price inflation excluding mortgage interest payments, and a promise to push inflation into the lower half of its target band by the end of the 1992–7 parliament.

The goal is to be achieved by the traditional means of using the interest rate to manage demand and the money supply. But in order to discourage a lax monetary policy (lowering or holding interest rates down too long to court political popularity), the goal is supplemented by the Treasury publishing a monthly monetary report, the Bank publishing a quarterly inflation report, and most importantly, the minutes of monthly policy meetings between the Bank governor and the Chancellor being published six weeks later. Making interest

rate policy more transparent in this way, it becomes harder for politicians to abandon the fight against inflation. It also strengthens the Bank's power, either to dictate policy or to discredit the government's economic policy if its policy recommendations are ignored.

FORECASTING THE ECONOMY

Forecasts play an important role in determining the policies of governments as well as companies and investors. These may be based on models of overall developments in the aggregate national or global economy: such models can be used to forecast shifts in demand across different markets, growth in total world trade, or changes in inflation, interest rates or unemployment. Or they might be models of parts of the economy: disaggregated forecasts may relate to developments in particular industrial sectors or regions of the world; while even more specific forecasts may relate to a single product or asset.

Basic approaches to forecasting simply extrapolate the past; they are merely a way of articulating present indications. More sophisticated models attempt to understand the source of past changes and build it into their forecasts. This requires a detailed knowledge of economic history and economic principles, though, even then, forecasting is by no means an exact science. But, while the accuracy of economists' predictions is frequently a target of jokes about the profession, forecasting remains an essential pursuit. As conducted at its most general level, by national governments and by global organisations on behalf of groups of countries, it drives all aspects of their economic policy.

Government forecasts are primarily concerned with forecasting the movement over time of key macroeconomic variables: output, inflation, unemployment, interest rates, and so on. They derive from large-scale macroeconomic models of the economy, and are usually produced every three to six months. In the United Kingdom, for example, the Treasury produces a central forecast at the time of its annual budget in November, which is then published again in revised form six months later.

Treasury forecasts include each component of the economy that contributes to overall growth: retail sales, manufacturing output and so on. But even models as detailed as that are more systems of manag-

ing information than accurate representations of real economies. Thus, while they can be expected to describe the present reasonably accurately, they cannot be relied upon to forecast the future and get it right. Nevertheless, government forecasts are very much tied to the levers of economic policy, as well as the government's underlying beliefs about the way the economy works, and there can often be conflict between the ideas on which forecasts and policy are based.

A country's monetary authorities also typically produce an economic forecast, though it is not always published. The Bank of England, for example, is currently barred from publishing its full forecast in case it clashes with that of the Treasury. However, its quarterly inflation report does contain prognostications on current and future inflationary pressures. The considerably more independent Federal Reserve ("the Fed") in the United States presents a half yearly report to the US Congress containing its economic projections.

Central bank forecasts may well derive from models of the economy that are a little biased towards the levers of monetary policy, those over which the banks hold most sway. Such forecasts are sometimes criticised for being based on a view of the economy that focuses on a symptom (inflation) of poor economic performance, rather than deeper structural weaknesses, and which relies on monetary policy alone as a cure.

Economic policy

Treasury and central bank forecasts represent governments' views of the future. In conjunction with their stated economic goals, these form the basis for the planning and execution of economic policy. For example, the essence of the UK government's ambitions can be encapsulated in the phrases "a low tax, low inflation economy", and "free markets, free trade and free enterprise". The macroeconomic means by which it pursues these goals are monetary, fiscal and exchange rate policy, while the actual levers used to intervene in the economy are interest rates and decisions on taxation and public spending. These policies can have as important implications for the private sector as the forecasts.

The budget and short-term economic forecasting are intimately related, forming a central plank of overall economic policy. The

macroeconomic task of the budget is to get the level of the PSBR right: first, in terms of its effects on demand (will reduced taxes or increased spending boost demand and output?); and second, in terms of its effects on real interest rates (will an excessive debt ratio raise rates, "crowding out" private investment?). The two sets of effects are closely linked: a high PSBR might tempt the government to tolerate high inflation to erode the real value of the debt, but it also might restrict the government's ability to use fiscal policy in a recession, making it difficult for taxes to be pushed lower or spending higher.

Monetary and exchange rate policy relate more to inflation and international competitiveness. They too are intimately related in that interest rates, the primary tool of both, can be used to target either the money supply or the exchange rate, but not both. From a manager's point of view, both goals are important, one in terms of the rate and predictability of inflation, the other in terms of the level and predictability of the exchange rate. An acceptable balance of inflation, interest and exchange rates may be pursued through a policy such as participation in the ERM, but this can easily come unstuck.

On the supply side of the economy, government policy can have direct effects on corporate and investor behaviour. For example, in the product markets, competition and regulatory policy, through government departments and such institutions of market regulation as the Monopolies and Mergers Commission (MMC) and the Securities and Investments Board (SIB), can be important in the provision of a stable business environment and the improvement of industrial performance. In the labour markets, tax incentives, education and training, and a host of other policies might boost productivity and competitiveness.

Credibility and the political business cycle

Economic policy is typically put together with a set of national objectives in mind: low inflation, full employment, no new taxes, and so on. Certainly, these goals are the slogans by which governments get themselves elected, or otherwise. For example, since 1979, the UK Conservatives have found that they can win elections by focusing on tax and inflation, and without a great deal of concern for unemployment. Elections have been won and lost on the basis of actual or distorted economics, such as the "Labour's tax bombshell" claim of the 1992 campaign.

But elections are also won and lost over the government's perceived management of the economy and its actual delivery on election pledges. Bill Clinton's 1992 campaign's frequent reminder, "it's the economy, stupid", for example, was a reflection of public perceptions of the failure of the Bush administration to ameliorate the recession, and the breaking of its promise not to raise taxes. Failure to deliver is often a result of politicians omitting to explain how difficult the fulfilment of economic ambitions might be when they are campaigning for office. This is most conspicuously the case in the former communist states where the fruits of market economic success will not be immediately shared by a large section of the population, as a result of which they often hanker for the old days.

Government economic credibility can also be strained when its policies are blown apart by events, as happened to the UK government with sterling's exit from the ERM. In this case, the government's primary objective was low inflation, and the means by which it was pursued, exchange rate policy through the ERM. Although inflation targets became a good alternative policy goal and relatively low inflation was maintained, Black Wednesday saw a sharp collapse in public confidence in the government's ability to handle the economy, a loss of credibility that is extremely damaging to its re-election prospects.

The importance of the economy to the electoral process has led to what is called the political business cycle, as governments attempt to achieve favourable economic circumstances at election time. For example, in engineering a boom before an election they might set the business cycle in motion, so that expansionary policies to boost incomes, reduce unemployment and maintain power, must be followed by contractionary policies to limit inflation. For the present UK government, lower taxes and continuing low interest rates might be the option, but these could cause longer term problems for the PSBR and inflation. Electoral success also requires the elusive "feel good" factor, and, most importantly, restoration of government credibility.

Credibility extends importantly to business and financial market confidence in the government's ability to achieve its objectives. For example, UK Treasury forecasts are often criticised for being as much an expression of what the government would like to see happen, as what they expect to happen; they are sometimes seen to be more akin

to some companies' annual budgets, incorporating desirable rather than necessarily achievable targets. There is an element here of using forecasts as means to the goal, perhaps trying to talk inflation down. Nevertheless, the Treasury's forecasting record in the late 1980s boom and the early 1990s recession is poor. In particular, it is often more optimistic about inflationary prospects than the City, something companies and investors should bear in mind.

REGULATING THE MARKETS

The overall objective of government economic policy is to secure sustainable economic growth and rising prosperity. This is primarily implemented through the macroeconomic policies outlined above, but the government also uses microeconomic policies, aiming to improve the efficiency of markets. In the context of the financial markets, this involves regulation through various measures to promote competition, to protect investors and depositors, and to preserve financial stability.

Financial services regulation plays a key role in securing market efficiency, but a competitive and versatile investment industry must be underpinned by adequate protection of investors and depositors. In setting the framework of regulatory rules, the government must aim to leave firms free to innovate and compete in an increasingly international market. At the same time, investor confidence requires open, free and fair markets in which all participants adhere to best practice.

The UK government, for example, encourages investors to follow five golden rules of investment to avoid being vulnerable to pressure selling of inappropriate financial products. These are that the buyer should always beware (*caveat emptor*); that investors should spread their investments; and that they should seek good advice; read the small print; and recognise that authorisation by a government agency is not a guarantee. For companies and financial institutions, the government emphasises the need to provide full disclosure of all relevant material and to follow the codes of business conduct directed by such regulatory bodies as the Securities and Investment Board (SIB) and the Monopolies and Mergers Commission (MMC).

There are essentially two approaches to regulation, statutory regulation via legislation, and self-regulation where industry participants

are encouraged to set their own rules and enforcement procedures. In the United States, the system of financial regulation is more orientated towards statutory regulation. It is primarily under the direction of the Securities and Exchange Commission (SEC), a government agency that closely monitors the activities of stockbrokers and traders in securities, and also monitors takeovers. If, for example, an individual or company acquires 5 per cent or more of the equity of another company, the SEC must be informed. There are also more specialised agencies such as the Commodity Futures Trading Commission which oversees derivatives trading.

In the United Kingdom, the bias is more towards self-regulation within the framework of the 1986 Financial Services Act. Under its provisions, anyone involved in investment business has to be authorised by the SIB. A private company with regulatory powers delegated by the President of the Board of Trade, the SIB consists of representatives from leading City institutions nominated by the President and the Governor of the Bank of England. Besides authorisation, it is also responsible for all monitoring, supervision and enforcement, demanding high standards of honesty and competence from all financial market participants.

Reporting to the SIB are three Self-Regulating Organisations (SROs): the Securities and Futures Authority (SFA), responsible for the conduct of brokers and dealers in securities, financial and commodity futures, and international bonds; the Investment Management Regulatory Organisation (IMRO), which regulates any institution that offers investment management (primarily such pooled investments as investment trusts, unit trusts and pension funds); and the Personal Investment Authority (PIA), created in 1994 to regulate investment business carried out with or for private investors. The PIA supersedes the Financial Intermediaries, Managers and Brokers Regulatory Organisation (FIMBRA, overseeing insurance brokers and independent investment advisers) and the Life Assurance and Unit Trust Regulatory Organisation (LAUTRO, overseeing the marketing of pooled investments by the companies that provide them).

The borrowing, asset-creating side of the market is also regulated by a combination of legislation and monitoring. Company behaviour falls under various Companies Acts enforced by the Department of

Trade and Industry; while the provision of figures (and the requirement that companies give a "true and fair view" of their status)
comes under the control of the Financial Reporting Council and the
Accounting Standards Board. In the market for corporate control,
the key institutions are the City Panel on Takeovers and Mergers, the
MMC and the Office of Fair Trading.

Banks are regulated under the Banking Act and supervised by
the Bank of England with the assistance of the Board of Banking
Supervision. The Bank has general responsibilities to protect the stability of the financial system and to be the lender of last resort in the
event of a liquidity crisis. But it also has this specific role as super-
visor of the UK banking sector with the power to regulate banks and
protect depositors.

Beyond the United Kingdom, the single market in financial services requires common access and minimum standards throughout
the European Union. This is achieved by vesting in member states
responsibility for authorisation of investment business participants,
and continuing prudential supervision. Providers of financial services
are entitled to do business across the Union solely on the basis of
their home authorisation.

Recent international scandals such as the collapses of Barings Bank
and of the Bank of Credit and Commerce International have raised an
important question about financial regulation: whether the globalisation of money, markets and information has put some companies and
financial institutions beyond the reach of regulation. It seems clear
that financial innovation, technology and the globalisation of investment have created a fragmented market for which the current rules
may no longer protect investors. In particular, regulators fear that
there may be gaps between the national and sectoral areas of supervision, and variations of standards which can give comparative advantage to one country's financial sector. Efforts to tackle the problem of
"regulatory arbitrage", where companies can take advantage of different rules and governments are tempted to loosen domestic rules to
gain advantage, focus on refining the rules on capital requirements
(the ability of institutions to meet their creditors' needs), on increasing
disclosure and on improving international cooperation.

Part II

INTERPRETING THE MARKETS

"Information is the key input to the market. In an efficient market, prices immediately reflect all the available information."

PETER BERNSTEIN

"Work the other side of the street! The nonpredictability of future prices from past and present prices is the sign, not of failure of economic law, but the triumph of economic law after competition has done its best."

PAUL SAMUELSON

5

STOCKS AND SHARES
The UK equity markets

- **The London share service** – reading the figures for the London stock market and using the information: evaluating weekly performance; other share dealings; trading volume; rises and falls, highs and lows; highlights; winners and losers

- **Issuing new securities** – how new companies are launched (offers for sale, placings, introductions, rights issues, popular privatisation issues); and how extra funds are raised for existing ones (rights offers)

- **Dealing and settlement** – the new system; and directors' share transactions

An equity is a stake in a company, a risk-sharing ownership of a part of a company's capital. The buyer of a share receives the rights to a probable flow of income in the form of dividends (which vary with the profitability of the company) and a potential capital gain.

The UK equity markets trade stocks across a wide spectrum of firms, ranging from established blue chip companies to higher risk ventures.

The *Financial Times'* coverage of UK equities, the shares in UK companies that have a stock market quotation, consists of four main interlocking components:

- A daily report of the most interesting trading features in the stock market.

- The share prices of individual companies and various financial ratios based on those prices.

- Detailed reports and comment in the news pages of the paper on events in company life.

- A number of stock market indices which chart the overall progress of equity share prices.

UK company news was explored in chapter 2 while indices are the subject of the next chapter. This chapter focuses on *Financial Times* reporting on the market for UK equities, as reflected in its stock market reports and the London share service.

FT coverage of the UK equities market begins with reports on the London Stock Exchange on the back page of the second section. This is headed with an overview of the movements in the stock market indices of the previous day and possible reasons for them, as well as highlights of individual sectors that have moved significantly or that have been particularly prominent in trading. It also examines the main share price movements of the day in individual stocks, and

suggests reasons for them. Particularly important movements are explored in separate stories further down the page.

THE LONDON SHARE SERVICE

This is the most complete record of UK stock market statistics readily available to the public and covers around 3,000 shares. That is practically all of those actively traded in the London stock market, together with gilt-edged stocks, already mentioned in chapter 4 and discussed in more detail in chapter 9.

The London share service is divided into various geographical and industrial classifications, derived from the groupings used in the FT-SE Actuaries All-Share Index discussed in detail in the next chapter (see Figure 6.3). Categorisation in this way allows easy comparison of companies within the same industrial sector.

The share service covers not only companies that have a full stock market listing, but also those quoted on the Unlisted Securities Market (USM) due for closure in 1996, and the new Alternative Investment Market (AIM). The USM and AIM have less onerous listing requirements than the main market and are designed to encourage smaller, fast-growing businesses to seek a quotation. Generally, there is less trading in USM and AIM stock, and hence shares may be less easy to buy and sell. In addition, the service incorporates many non-UK companies whose shares are traded in London, notably groups of shares classified as Americans, Canadians and South Africans.

The standard version of the share service is published on Tuesday to Saturday, just before the back page of the second section of the newspaper. Figure 5.1 features two sample industrial categories from the daily London share service, annotated with brief explanations of price, price change and year high and low, market capitalisation, yield and price/earnings ratio.

Reading the figures

- **Name and notes:** the first column lists the company name or its abbreviation, plus various symbols representing particular features of its shares. For example, a square indicates the most actively traded

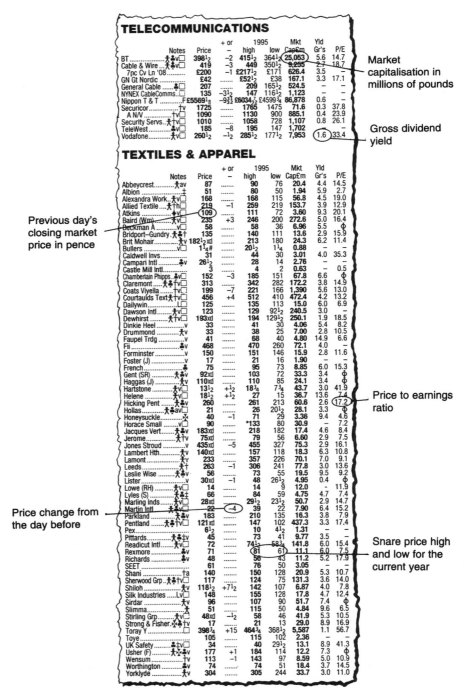

TELECOMMUNICATIONS

	Notes	Price	+ or –	1995 high	low	Mkt Cap£m	Yld Gr's	P/E
BT	★♣v□	398½	−2	415½	364½	25,053	5.6	14.7
Cable & Wire	★♣v□	419	−3	449	350½	9,255	2.7	18.7
7pc Cv Ln '08		£200	−1	£217½	£171	626.4	3.5	–
GN Gt Nordic		£42	......	£52½	£38	167.1	3.3	17.1
General Cable	♣□	207	......	209	165½	524.5	–	–
NYNEX CableComms	□	135	−3½	147	116½	1,123	–	–
Nippon T & T	F£5569⅛		−9¾⅛	£6034⁷₁₂	£4599¾	86,878	–	–
Securicor	†v	1725	......	1765	1475	71.6	0.3	37.8
A N/V	†v	1090	......	1130	900	885.1	0.4	23.9
Security Servs	★†v□	1010	......	1058	728	1,107	0.8	26.1
TeleWest	♣v□	185	−8	195	147	1,702	–	–
Vodafone	★v□	260½	−½	285½	177½	7,953	1.6	33.4

TEXTILES & APPAREL

	Notes	Price	+ or –	1995 high	low	Mkt Cap£m	Yld Gr's	P/E
Abbeycrest	★av	87	......	90	76	20.4	4.4	14.5
Albion	‡	51	......	80	50	1.94	5.9	2.7
Alexandra Work	★v□	168	......	168	115	56.8	4.5	19.0
Allied Textile	★†h□	219	−1	259	219	153.7	3.9	12.9
Atkins	♣v□	109	......	111	72	3.60	9.3	20.1
Baird (Wm)	★v□	235	+3	246	200	272.6	5.0	16.4
Beckman A	□	58	......	58	36	6.96	5.5	Φ
Bridport–Gundry	★♣†	135	......	140	111	13.6	2.9	15.9
Brit Mohair	★v 182½xd		......	213	180	24.3	6.2	11.4
Bullers	v□	1¼#	......	20½	1¼	0.88	–	–
Caldwell Invs		31	......	44	30	3.01	4.0	35.3
Campari Intl	♣v	26½	......	28	14	2.76	–	–
Castle Mill Intl		3	......	4	2	0.63	–	0.5
Chamberlain Phipps	♣v□	152	−3	185	151	67.8	6.6	Φ
Claremont	★♣†v□	313	......	342	282	172.2	3.8	14.9
Coats Viyella	†v□	199	−7	221	166	1,390	5.6	13.0
Courtaulds Text	★†v□	456	+4	512	410	472.4	4.2	13.2
Dailywin	□	125	......	135	113	15.0	6.0	6.9
Dawson Intl	★v	123	......	129	92½	240.5	3.0	–
Dewhirst	★†v□	193xd	......	194	129½	250.1	1.9	18.5
Dinkie Heel	v	33	......	41	30	4.06	5.4	8.2
Drummond	★v	33	......	38	25	7.00	2.8	10.5
Faupel Trdg	v	41	......	68	40	4.80	14.9	6.6
Fii	♣v	468	......	470	260	72.1	4.0	–
Forminster	v	150	......	151	146	15.9	2.8	11.6
Foster (J)	♣	17	......	21	16	1.90	–	–
French	♣	75	......	95	73	8.85	6.0	15.3
Gent (SR)	★♣av	92xd	......	103	72	33.3	3.4	Φ
Haggas (J)	★v□	110xd	......	110	85	24.1	3.4	Φ
Hartstone	★v□	13½	+½	18¾	7¾	43.7	3.0	41.9
Helene	★v□	18½	+½	27	15	36.7	13.6	7.4
Hicking Pent	★♣v	260	......	261	213	60.6	2.6	17.2
Hollas	★♣av□	21	......	26	20½	28.1	3.3	Φ
Honeysuckle	X	40	−1	71	29	3.36	9.4	4.6
Horace Small	v□	90	......	*133	80	30.9	–	7.2
Jacques Vert	★♣v	183xd	......	218	182	17.4	4.6	8.4
Jerome	★†v	75xd	......	79	56	6.60	2.9	7.5
Jones Stroud	★v	435xd	−5	455	327	75.3	2.9	16.1
Lambert Hth	★v	140xd	......	157	118	18.3	6.3	10.8
Lamont	★v	233	......	357	226	70.1	7.0	9.1
Leeds	★†	263	−1	306	241	77.8	3.0	13.6
Leslie Wise	★♣v	56	......	73	55	19.5	9.5	9.2
Lister	v	30xd	−1	48	26½	4.95	0.4	Φ
Lowe (RH)	v	14	......	14	9	12.0	–	11.9
Lyles (S)	★♣±	66	......	84	59	4.75	4.7	7.4
Marling Inds	★v□	28xd	......	29½	23½	50.7	2.9	14.7
Martin Intl	★♣v□	22	−4	39	22	7.90	6.4	15.2
Parkland	★♣av	183	......	210	135	16.3	3.8	7.9
Pentland	★♣†v□	121xd	......	147	102	437.3	3.3	17.4
Pex		6½	......	10	4½	1.31	–	–
Pittards	★♣‡v	45	......	73	41	9.77	3.5	–
Readicut Intl	★v	72	......	74½	58¾	141.8	6.0	15.4
Rexmore	♣v	71	......	81	61	11.1	6.0	7.5
Richards	♣v	48	......	76	43	11.2	5.2	17.9
SEET		61	......	76	50	3.05	–	–
Shani	†a	140	......	150	128	20.9	5.3	10.7
Sherwood Grp	★♣†v□	117	......	124	75	131.3	3.6	14.0
Shiloh	★v	118½	+7½	142	107	6.87	4.0	7.8
Silk Industries	Lv□	148	......	155	128	17.8	4.7	12.4
Sirdar	★v	96	......	107	90	51.7	7.4	Φ
Slimma	★	51	......	115	50	4.84	9.6	6.5
Stirling Grp	★v□	48xd	−½	58	46	41.9	5.3	10.5
Strong & Fisher	★♣†v	17	......	21	13	29.0	8.9	16.9
Toray Y	□	398¾	+15	464¼	368½	5,587	1.1	56.7
Toye		105	......	115	102	2.36	–	–
UK Safety	♣v□	34	......	40	29½	13.1	8.9	41.3
Usher (F)	★♣♣v	177	+1	184	114	12.2	7.3	Φ
Wensum	†v	113	−1	143	97	8.59	5.0	10.9
Worthington	♣v	74	......	74	51	18.4	3.7	14.5
Yorklyde	★v	304	......	305	244	33.7	3.0	11.0

Annotations:
- Market capitalisation in millions of pounds
- Gross dividend yield
- Previous day's closing market price in pence
- Price to earnings ratio
- Price change from the day before
- Snare price high and low for the current year

Fig. 5.1 London share service (daily): Telecoms and Textiles & Apparel

shares, including those UK stocks where transactions and prices are published continuously through the Stock Exchange Automated Quotation (SEAQ) system. A Maltese cross indicates shares traded on the USM. A heart symbol indicates a stock not officially listed in the UK, for example many shares of overseas mining companies.

- **Market price:** the second column shows the average (or mid-price) of the best buying and selling prices (in pence) quoted by market-makers at the 4.30pm close of the market on the previous trading day. Most prices are obtained from the Stock Exchange throughout the day via a direct computer link with the last transmission of data taking place at 4.45pm. If trading in a share has been suspended, perhaps because the company in question is involved in takeover negotiations, the figure shown is the price at suspension and this is indicated by a symbol. The letters "xd" following a price mean ex-dividend, and indicate that a dividend has been announced recently but that buyers of the shares will not be entitled to receive it.

- **Price change (plus or minus):** the third column gives the change in the closing price compared with the end of the previous trading day.

- **Previous price movements:** the fourth and fifth columns show the highest and lowest prices recorded for the stock during the current year.

- **Market capitalisation:** the sixth column is an indication of the stock market valuation of the company in millions of pounds sterling. It is calculated by multiplying the number of shares by their market price. In order to calculate the number of shares in issue from the figures listed here, the market capitalisation figure can be divided by the market price. If there are other classes of share capital in issue, their value would need to be added in order to calculate the company's total market capitalisation.

- **Gross dividend yield:** the seventh column shows the percentage return on the share before income tax is deducted. It is calculated by dividing the gross dividend by the current share price.

- **Price/earnings (p/e) ratio:** the last column is the market price of the share divided by the company's earnings (profits) per share in its latest twelve-month trading period. Yields and p/e ratios move

in opposite directions: if the share price rises, since tne gross dividend remains the same, the dividend yield falls; at the same time, since the earnings per share are constant, the p/e ratio increases.

Using the information

The first indicator to look at in a share is its price. This is a reflection of the discounted value of future dividend payments plus a premium for the risk that the company may not pay dividends in the future and/or go under. On its own, though, it conveys minimal information since it needs to be seen in the context of its history and possible future.

The figures for high and low provide some of the historical perspective on the share price. If, for example, the present price is a long way below its high point for the year, and performing against the market trend, the indications are that the market is expecting trouble. The reverse is true in the case of a share that is pushing up strongly to new points when the market or its sector is not. The difference between the high and low also gives an indication of the price volatility of the stock.

The prices quoted are mid-prices between the bid or buying price and the offer or selling price at which marketmakers will trade. The difference between bid and offer is known as the spread, and it represents marketmakers' profit on any given transaction, a reward for taking the risk of making the market. The implication of this spread is that investors will only be able to buy at a higher price and sell at a lower price than that printed in the newspaper. Of course, since the share service is in effect merely an historical record of prices the previous day, actual prices subsequently may be very different.

Market capitalisation is a measure of the size of a company. Since the total value of a company's shares will rise and fall according to its financial results, it is a good guide to performance over time. It also has other advantages over alternative yardsticks of size: it gives a proper weighting to banks and commodity groups which get distorted in lists based on turnover; and it takes account of loss-making companies which disappear from lists based on profits.

Market capitalisation = number of ordinary shares × share price

Dividends depend on profits which in turn depend on the quality of a company's management and the state of the economy. The dividend yield, though, since it is partly determined by the current share price, is a reflection of the way that the market values a share. If the company is thought to have a high growth rate and a secure business, then its current dividend yield will probably be relatively low, since the scope for increasing dividends in the future ought to be above average. Sales will be expanding, earnings growing, and often investment in new products and new capital goods will be substantial.

If, by contrast, the company is involved in a mature or dying industry or is exposed to high levels of business or political risk, its dividend yield will normally be high. Thus, the yield on a share can be a valuable indicator when an investor is deciding between income and capital growth from an investment. For example, a growth stock, perhaps in high-technology industries, suggests a preference for capital appreciation, while a share in a company in a mature industry like textiles would indicate a desire for income.

Of course, as seen in chapter 2, the dividend is, to some degree, an arbitrary figure, decided at the whim of the company. Hence the figure for yield is not always a good indicator of the value of a share. Price/earnings ratios are generally better since they are independent of possibly arbitrary corporate decisions.

$$\text{Dividend yield (per cent)} = \frac{\text{gross dividend per share} \times 100}{\text{share price}}$$

Price/earnings ratios are the most commonly used tool of stock market analysis. Essentially, they compare a company's share price to its annual earnings, indicating the number of years it would take it, at its current earning power, to earn an amount equal to its market value. Shares are often described as selling at a number times earnings or on a multiple. In general, the higher a company's ratio, the more highly rated it is by the market: investors expect the relative expense of the company's shares to be compensated for by higher than average earnings over the next few years. But high ratios can also mean that the market is expecting a poorly performing company to be on the receiving end of a takeover bid, with the predator being prepared to pay a premium for control.

High price/earnings ratios are usually associated with low yields, and certainly they move in opposite directions. Thus, a high ratio suggests a growth stock, and is, like a low yield, an indicator of an investment where capital growth might be more important than income.

Investors can use price/earnings ratios to gauge whether one company's share price is too high or too low compared with competitors with similar products and earnings performance, compared with the market as a whole, or compared with past ratios. If a p/e ratio is above average, investors expect profits to rise and hence, their prospective dividends: the higher a p/e ratio, the greater the confidence in the company. But high ratios are often viewed as overpriced, while low ones are viewed as bargains.

Since the methods of calculating the ratios can give significantly different results, the investor's prime concern should be to use ratios that are consistent (that is, from the same source) when making comparisons. It is also important to be aware of the difference between the historic ratios in the newspaper and what the market's expectations are for the future, expressed more through forecasts of prospective price/earnings ratios. Reports on companies might also distinguish historic and prospective yields. In addition, there is a distinction between nil and net ratios: the former ignores the distribution of dividends. Chapter 16 contains some examples of yield and p/e ratios.

$$\text{Price/earnings ratio} = \frac{\text{share price}}{\text{earnings per share}}$$

Evaluating weekly performance

Monday's edition of the *Financial Times* brings some important changes to the share information service, concentrating on changes that do not take place daily. Figure 5.2 shows an example. The special weekly columns provide information on the following:

- **Price change:** the weekly percentage change in the price of the stock.

- **Net dividend:** the after-tax dividends paid in the company's last full financial year. A double dagger sign shows that the interim dividend has been cut in the current financial year, while a single dagger indicates an increased interim dividend.

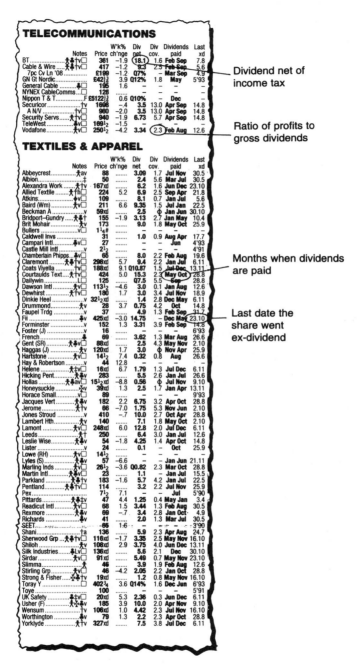

Dividend net of income tax

Ratio of profits to gross dividends

Months when dividends are paid

Last date the share went ex-dividend

Fig. 5.2 London share service (weekly): Telecoms and Textiles & Apparel

- **Dividend cover:** the ratio of profits to dividends, calculated by dividing the earnings per share by the gross dividend per share. This indicates how many times a company's dividend to ordinary shareholders could be paid out of its net profits. Another way of looking at dividend cover is as a percentage of profits: this is the way it is done in the United States where it is known as the payout ratio.

- **Dividend paid:** the months in which the dividends are actually paid, usually either twice or four times a year.

- **Ex-dividend date:** the last date on which a share went ex-dividend, expressed as a day and month unless a dividend has not been paid for some time in which case the date may be a month and year. On and after this date, the rights to the last announced dividend remain with the seller of the stock. What happens is that the share register is frozen on the xd date and the dividend will be paid to the people on the register at that time. Until it is paid, buyers of the share will not receive the next payment. The price is adjusted down a little to account for this.

- **Cityline:** the FT Cityline code by which real-time share prices are available over the telephone by calling 0336 43 or 0891 43 plus the four digit code for any given share. This telephone information service is designed primarily for investors wanting to keep track of their own investments or the activity of the UK and world stock markets at any point during the day or night.

The key information from this listing is the figure for dividend cover. This indicates how safe the dividend is from future cuts. The higher the figure, the better able the company will be to maintain its dividend if profits fall. Even at a time of losses, a company may decide to pay dividends out of its reserves, though this clearly could not continue indefinitely.

A relatively high dividend cover might also reflect a commitment to investment and growth, implying a substantial retention of earnings to be ploughed back into the business. On the other hand, if the dividend cover is too high, the shareholders may complain that the company should increase its payout. Chapter 16 contains some examples of dividend cover.

$$\text{Dividend cover} = \frac{\text{earnings per share}}{\text{gross dividend per share}}$$

LONDON STOCK EXCHANGE: Dealings

BTR PLC ADR (4:1) - $20 .2
Bank of Ireland(Governor & Co of) Units NCP Stk Srs A £1 & £9 Liquidation - £12⅜ (6Fe96)
Banner Homes Group PLC Ord 10p - 85 (6Fe96)
Barclays PLC ADR (4:1) - $48.8ϕ
Barclays Bank PLC 12% Uns Cap Ln Stk 2010 - £123¾ 4½
Barclays Bank PLC 16% Uns Cap Ln Stk 2002/07 - £140½ 1 (7Fe96)
Bardon Group PLC 7.25p (Net) Cnv Red Prf 25p - 93 (7Fe96)
Bardon Group PLC 11.25p Cum Red Prf 2005 10p - 112 3
Barnato Exploration Ld Ord R0.01 - 100 35
Barr & Wallace Arnold Trust PLC Ord 25p - 223 (7Fe96)
Bass PLC 10⅜% Deb Stk 2016 - £116 13/16 (6Fe96)
Bass PLC 4½% Uns Ln Stk 92/97 - £96¾
Bass PLC 7¾% Uns Ln Stk 92/97 - £100½
Bass Investments PLC 7⅜% Uns Ln Stk 92/97 - £99¾
Batleys PLC 10% Cum Prf £1 - 108 (2Fe96)
Bellway PLC 9.5% Cum Red Prf 2014 £1 - 111 (6Fe96)
Bergesen d-y AS "B" Non Vtg Shs NK2.5 - NK126 (6Fe96)
Birmingham Midshires Building Soc 9⅜% Perm Int Bearing Shs £1000 - £99 ¼
Blockleys PLC 6% Cum Prf 50p - 27 (5Fe96)
Blue Circle Industries PLC ADR (1:1) - $5.47
Blue Circle Industries PLC 6¼% Uns Ln Stk(1975 or aft) - £69ϕ
Boots Co PLC ADR (2:1) - $18.7
Bradford & Bingley Building Society11⅝% Perm Int Bearing Shs £10000 - £121¾
Bradford & Bingley Building Society13% Perm Int Bearing Shs £10000 - £134¾ 5 ¼ (6Fe96)
Brent Walker Group PLC Wts to Sub for Ord - 0¼ (7Fe96)
Brent Walker Group PLC 8.5% 3rd Non-Cum Cnv Red 2007/10 £1 - 0¾
Bridon PLC 7¾% Uns Ln Stk 2002/07 - £93 (5Fe96)
Bristol Water PLC 8¾% Cum Irrd Prf £1 - 119½ (7Fe96)
Bristol Water Hldgs PLC Ord £1 - £11.8 12.2 (7Fe96)
Bristol & West Building Society 13⅜% Perm Int Bearing Shs £1000 - £139¼ 40 ¼
Britannia Building Society 13% Perm Int Bearing Shs £1000 - £134 4 ¼ ½ ¾
British Airways PLC ADR (10:1) - $77⅝ .65 ⅞ 8
British Land Co PLC 6% Subord Irrd Cnv Bds(Reg) - £90½
British Land Co PLC 11⅜% First Mtg Deb Stk 2019/24 - £122 (7Fe96)
British Petroleum Co PLC 8% Cum 1st Prf £1 - 89½ (6Fe96)
British Steel PLC ADR (10:1) - $26⅝ ⅝ ⅞
Brixton Estate PLC 9.50% 1st Mtg Deb Stk 2026 - £108¼ (2Fe96)
Brixton Estate PLC 10⅝% 1st Mtg Deb Stk 2012 - £116¼ (6Fe96)
HSBC Hldgs PLC 11.69% Subord Bds 2002 (Br £Var) - £116½
Halifax Building Society 8¾% Perm Int Bearing Shs £50000 - £93¾ (6Fe96)
Halifax Building Society 12% Perm Int Bearing Shs £1 (Reg £50000) - £124¾ 5¼ ¾ 6 ¾
Hardys & Hansons PLC Ord 5p - 329 (7Fe96)
Hasbro Inc Shs of Com Stk $0.50 - £22.7305
Hercules Inc Shs of Com Stk of NPV - $56¼ (5Fe96)
Hillsdown Hldgs PLC ADR(4:1) - $11⅛ (6Fe96)
Hong Kong Land Hldgs Ld Ord $0.10 (Jersey Reg) - £1.3
Housing Finance Corporation Ld 11½% Deb Stk 2016 - £118¾ (6Fe96)
IS Himalayan Fund NV Ord FL0.01 - $13½
Iceland Group PLC Cnv Cum Red Prf 20p - 118 ½
Illingworth,Morris Ld 6½% Cum 2nd Prf Stk £1 - 56
Industrial Control Services Grp PLCOrd 10p - 113 ½
Irish Life PLC Ord Ir£0.10 - I£2.49 p 256 6 7 7 ½ 60
Jardine Strategic Hldgs Ld Ord $0.05(Bermuda Register) - $3.42367 (5Fe96)
Jersey Electricity Co Ld "A" Ord £1 - £17
Johnson Group Cleaners PLC 7.5p (Net) Cnv Cum Red Prf 10p - 134
Johnston Group PLC 10% Cum Prf £1 - 110 (6Fe96)
Jurys Hotel Group PLC Ord Ir£0.25 - I£2.22 p 228 32
Kingfisher PLC ADR (2:1) - $15.96
Korea-Europe Fund Ld SHS(IDR to Br) $0.10 (Cpn 8) - £4250ϕ 4442½ϕ
Kvaerner A.S. A Shs NK12.50 - NK216¼
Ladbroke Group PLC ADR (1:1) - $2.67
Lamont Hldgs PLC 10% 3rd Cum Prf £1 - 106
Land Securities PLC 9% 1st Mtg Deb Stk 96/2001 - £100½ (7Fe96)
Land Securities PLC 6⅞% Uns Ln Stk 92/97 - £99 (6Fe96)
LASMO PLC 10⅜% Deb Stk 2009 - £113¾ (7Fe96)
Lebowa Platinum Mines Ld Ord R0.01 - R3.8 (6Fe96)
Leeds & Holbeck Building Society 13⅜% Perm Int Bearing Shs £1000 - £139½
Lewis(John) PLC 5% 1st Cum Prf Stk £1 - 56 (5Fe96)
Lewis(John)Partnership PLC 5% Cum Prf Stk £1 - 58 (6Fe96)
Lewis(John)Partnership PLC 7½% Cum Prf Stk £1 - 71 (2Fe96)
London Cremation Co Ld 10% Cum Prf £1 - 137 (5Fe96)
London International Group PLC ADR (5:1) - $9.1 9.2 (6Fe96)
London Park Hotels PLC 10½% 1st Mtg Deb Stk 2000/05 - £102 (7Fe96)
Lonrho PLC ADR (1:1) - $3.15 .16 .24
Lonrho PLC 10¼% 1st Mtg Deb Stk 97/2002 - £104
Lookers PLC 8% Cnv Cum Red Prf £1 - 95
Marks & Spencer PLC ADR (6:1) - $40.32 (7Fe96)
Marshalls PLC 10% Cum Prf £1 - 107 (6Fe96)
Marston,Thompson & Evershed PLC 10¼% Deb Stk 2012 - £113¾ (6Fe96)
Medeva PLC ADR (4:1) - $14⅝ϕ ⅝ϕ .65ϕ ¾ϕ .775ϕ
Merchant Retail Group PLC 8¾% Uns Ln Stk 99/04 - £73 (7Fe96)
Merivale Moore PLC 10½% 1st Mtg Deb Stk 2020 - £106
Mersey Docks & Harbour Co 6⅝% Red Deb Stk 94/97 - £97½ (5Fe96)
Mersey Docks & Harbour Co 6¾% Red Deb Stk 96/99 - £95¾ (5Fe96)
Mersey Docks & Harbour Co 3⅝% Irrd Deb Stk - £38
NFC PLC 7¾% Cnv Bds 2007((Reg) - £89½ ¾
National Westminster Bank PLC 9% Non-Cum Stlg Prf Sers "A" £1 - 117¼ ¼ ⅜ ½ ½
National Westminster Bank PLC 12½% Subord Uns Ln Stk 2004 - £124¾ (7Fe96)
Newcastle Building Society 12⅝% Perm Interest Bearing Shs £1000 - £137¾ (7Fe96)
News International PLC 4.9% (Fmly 7%) 1st Cum Prf £1 - 64 (2Fe96)
Northchart Investments Ld R 0.10 - £0.29
Northern Foods PLC 6¾% Cnv Subord Bds 2008 (Reg) - £87
Northern Foods PLC 6¾% Cnv Subord Bds 2008 (Br £ Var) - £86¾ (6Fe96)
Northern Rock Building Society 12⅝% Perm Int Bearing Shs £1000 - £137 ¾ 8 9
Ontario & Quebec Railway Co 5% Perm Deb Stk(Int Gtd by C.P.) - £53
Orbis PLC Ord 10p - 43 4 5 ½ 6 7
Oryx International Growth Fund Ld Wts to sub for Ord - 43ϕ
PSIT PLC 8% Cum Prf £1 - 93 (7Fe96)
Pacific Gas & Electric Co Shs of Com Stk $5 - $27.45 ⅝
Parkland Group PLC Ord 25p - 190
Paterson Zochonis PLC 10% Cum Prf £1 - 119½
Pearson PLC 9.3% Uns Ln Stk 96/2001 - £101 (5Fe96)
Pearson PLC 13.625% Uns Ln Stk 2007 - £139½ (2Fe96)
Peel Hldgs PLC 9⅞% 1st Mtg Deb Stk 2011 - £104.825 ⅞ 5 1/32
Peel Hldgs PLC 5.25% (Net) Cnv Cum Non-Vtg Prf £1 - 127
Perkins Foods PLC 8p(Net) Cum Cnv Red Prf 10p - 97 (7Fe96)
Petrofina S.A. Ord Shs NPV (Br in Denom 1,5 & 10) - BF8622.66 35 6.36 41.35
Pittards PLC 9½% Cum Prf £1 - 90 (7Fe96)
Plantation & General Invs PLC 9½% Cum Red Prf £1 - 92
Plantation & General Invs PLC 9% Cnv Uns Ln Stk 1999 - £92 (6Fe96)
Pokphand (C.P.) Co Ld Shs $0.05 (Hong Kong Registered) - $H3.9531
Readicut International PLC 5¾% 2nd Cum Prf £1 - 59 (7Fe96)
Reckitt & Colman PLC 5% Cum Prf £1 - 55
Regis Property Hldgs PLC 8¾% Gtd Uns Ln Stk 1997 - £98 (6Fe96)
Republic Goldfields Inc Shs of NPV - $C0.97
Retail Corporation PLC 4.55% (Fmly 6½%) Cum Prf £1 - 60 (2Fe96)
Ronson PLC Ord 5p - 48 50
Ropner PLC 11½% Cum Prf £1 - 116 (6Fe96)
Royal Bank of Scotland Group PLC 11% Cum Prf £1 - 113 (2Fe96)
Royal Insurance Holdings PLC 7¼% Cnv Subord Bds 2007 (Br £ Var) - £127½ (7Fe96)
Rugby Group PLC 6% Uns Ln Stk 93/98 - £97¼ (7Fe96)
Sainsbury(J) PLC ADR (4:1) - $24.35 (7Fe96)
Savoy Hotel PLC "B" Ord 5p - £70 (6Fe96)
Scholl PLC 8⅞% Cum Red Prf 2001/05 £1 - 104ϕ
Schroder Japanese Warrant Fund Ld IDR (In Denom 100 Shs & 10000 Shs) - $65ϕ
Schroders PLC 8¾% Uns Ln Stk 97/2002 - £102¾ (7Fe96)
Scottish Metropolitan Property PLC 10¼% 1st Mtg Deb Stk 2016 - £110¼ (7Fe96)
Scottish & Newcastle PLC 6.425% Cum Prf £1 - 93½
Scottish & Newcastle PLC 7% Cnv Cum Prf £1 - 295 (7Fe96)
Seagram Distillers PLC 12⅜% Deb Stk 2012 - £132.4 (7Fe96)
Sears PLC 8.75% (Fmly 12½%) Cum Prf £1 - 109 (5Fe96)
Securicor Group PLC 4.55% Cum Ptg Prf £1 - £196 8 (5Fe96)
Severn River Crossing PLC 6% Index-Linked Deb Stk 2012 (6.702%) - £122¾
Shell Transport&TradingCo PLC Ord Shs 25p (Br)(Cpn 195) - 853 (5Fe96)
Shell Transport&TradingCo PLC 5½% 1st Prf(Cum)£1 - 64 9 (7Fe96)
Shield Group PLC Ord 5p - 4½ (5Fe96)
Shoprite Group PLC Ord 5p - 8¼ ½
Singapore Para Rubber Estates PLC Ord 5p - 135 3/16 (7Fe96)
Singer & Friedlander Group PLC 8.5% Cnv Subord Uns Ln Stk 2009/14 - £132 (7Fe96)
Skipton Building Society 12⅞% Perm Int Bearing Shs £1000 - £136¼
SmithKline Beecham PLC ADR (5:1) - $54.90509ϕ
SmithKline Beecham PLC/SmithKline ADR (5:1) - £36.2491 36.2958 36.339 $ 55⅝ ¾ .77 .85 ⅞ 6
Standard Chartered PLC 12⅞% Subord Uns Ln Stk 2002/07 - £121½ (7Fe96)
Sutcliffe Speakman PLC 9½% Red Cum Prf £1 - 95 (5Fe96)
Symonds Engineering PLC Ord 5p - 45 ¾ 6
THFC (Indexed) Ld 5.65% Index-Linked Stk 2020(6.9390%) - £128½
TSB Group PLC 10⅝% Subord Ln Stk 2008 - £115½ ¾
TT Group PLC 10.875% Cnv Cum Red Prf

Fig. 5.3 London Stock Exchange: dealings

TRADING VOLUME

■ Major Stocks Yesterday

	Vol. 000s	Closing price	Day's change
3i†	998	406	$-4\frac{1}{2}$
ASDA Group†	16,000	$103\frac{1}{2}$	$-1\frac{1}{2}$
Abbey National†	4,700	548	-8
Albert Fisher	83	$52\frac{1}{2}$	
Allied Domecq†	2,200	506	$-8\frac{1}{2}$
Anglian Water	2,000	589	-9
Argos	284	482	-5
Argyll Group†	3,500	335	$-4\frac{1}{2}$
Arjo Wiggins†	2,000	243	$-3\frac{1}{2}$
Assoc. Brit. Foods†	418	690	-4
Assoc. Brit. Ports	278	313	-2
BAA†	7,600	$465\frac{1}{2}$	$-9\frac{1}{2}$
BAT Inds.†	8,600	533	$+1$
BET	2,900	123	-4
BICC	1,300	280	-6
BOC†	3,300	833	$+3\frac{1}{2}$
BP†	6,700	459	$-9\frac{1}{2}$
BPB Inds.	1,100	291	-11
BSkyB†	4,100	$383\frac{1}{2}$	$+\frac{1}{2}$
BT†	11,000	$385\frac{1}{2}$	-8
BTR†	11,000	317	$-3\frac{1}{2}$
Bank of Scotland†	5,300	$243\frac{1}{2}$	$+3$
Barclays†	5,400	725	-19
Bass†	1,300	654	-4
Blue Circle†	3,000	296	-6
Booker	1,300	378	-3
Boots†	2,300	561	$-13\frac{1}{2}$
Brit. Aerospace†	2,400	728	-17
British Airways†	3,500	459	-7
British Gas†	12,000	$249\frac{1}{2}$	-6
British Land	736	392	-10
British Steel†	6,800	168	$+\frac{3}{4}$
Bunzl	5,000	196	-6
Burmah Castrol†	1,200	975	-6
Burton	2,000	$107\frac{1}{2}$	$-\frac{1}{2}$
Cable & Wire†	11,000	412	$-1\frac{1}{2}$
Cadbury Schweppes†	5,000	514	-13
Caradon	3,100	210	-4
Carlton Comms.†	1,100	974	-20
Coats Viyella	1,500	196	-2
Comm. Union†	2,700	565	-11
Compass	3,100	437	$+3$
Cookson†	3,800	277	-6
Courtaulds†	2,300	399	$+1$
Dalgety	289	431	-4
De La Rue†	617	910	-19
Dixons	7,200	365	-10
East Midland Elect.	385	861	-19
Electrocomps	654	308	-21
Eng China Clays	374	348	-11
Enterprise Oil†	3,100	$332\frac{1}{2}$	$-6\frac{1}{2}$
Eurotunnel Units	490	88	$+2$
FKI	1,500	164	-1
Fisons†	38,000	263	$-\frac{1}{2}$
Foreign & Col. I.T.	2,100	146	$-\frac{1}{2}$
Forte†	4,700	234	-5
Gen. Accident†	1,300	605	-14
General Elect.†	7,500	$329\frac{1}{2}$	-2
Glaxo Wellcome†	4,400	758	$-15\frac{1}{2}$
Glynwed	779	355	-2
Granada†	1,800	652	-7
Grand Met.†	4,400	423	-8
GUS†	1,600	560	-15
GRE†	2,800	209	-6
GKN†	717	781	-18
Guinness†	2,900	503	-9
HSBC (75p shs)†	1,300	891	-29
Hammerson	68	354	
Hanson†	5,300	$196\frac{3}{4}$	$-2\frac{3}{4}$
Harrisons Crosfield	133	154	-3
Hays	325	349	$+2$
Hillsdown	1,200	172	-2
IMI	61	326	-2
ICI†	3,800	791	-11

Fig. 5.4 Trading volume

Other share dealings

On Saturday, the newspaper expands its share price coverage to cover dealings in securities which are not included in the standard FT share information service (see Figure 5.3). It covers many fixed interest securities issued by companies, as well as dealings in some smaller company shares and securities where the principal market is outside the British Isles. The actual selection is variable according to whether a stock has been traded during the five trading days ending each Thursday. If it has not been traded it will generally not be included. Information is provided on:

- **Name and stock type:** chapter 2 detailed some of the different forms of corporate finance available, and these securities provide a number of examples. Marshalls' 10 per cent cumulative preference shares with a par value of £1, for instance, are shares that pay a fixed dividend, 10 pence. The payment can be suspended in the event of losses, but when the company returns to profit, all dividends in arrears are guaranteed to be paid ahead of dividends on ordinary shares.

- **Prices:** these are reproduced from Thursday's Stock Exchange official list. They show the prices at which business was done in the 24 hours up to 5pm on Thursday. For shares where no business was recorded during that period, the latest recorded business in the previous four days is listed with the relevant date.

Trading volume

The back page of the newspaper's second section includes a useful reference table with the trading volume and basic price information for a selection of the largest capitalised and most active stocks (see Figure 5.4). The information includes:

- **Volume, price and change:** the daily trading volume for these stocks (including all of the constituents of the FT-SE 100 index which are discussed in detail in the next chapter and listed in appendix 2) plus the day's closing price and change on the previous trading day. Trading volume figures count both the buying and the selling of a particular share, so that the number of shares actually changing hands is really half of the total.

Trading volume is an indication of the liquidity of a stock. The higher the figure, the easier it will be to buy or sell significant quantities of a stock without having a major impact on its price.

Rises and falls, highs and lows

The newspaper also carries two other lists for quick reference on share price movements. First, there is a list of rises and falls for broad share categories as in Figure 5.5:

RISES AND FALLS YESTERDAY

	Rises	Falls	Same
British Funds	19	41	12
Other Fixed Interest	0	0	14
Mineral Extraction	41	96	92
General Manufacturers	126	140	404
Consumer Goods	43	57	126
Services	113	118	318
Utilities	25	12	21
Financials	81	109	227
Investment Trusts	91	97	420
Others	40	60	34
Totals	579	730	1668

Data based on those companies listed on the London Share Service.

Fig. 5.5 Rises and falls yesterday

- **Rises and falls:** the daily version of this table, reproduced here, shows how many securities rose, fell and stayed at the same price level during the previous trading session. It is broken down into eight different categories of security and shows how movements in the main share price indices were reflected in trading across various broad market subdivisions. Saturday's version also lists rises and falls on the week as a whole.

The second list covers individual stocks that have recorded new highs and lows for the year (see Figure 5.6):

- **Highs and lows:** this table shows which shares have on the previous trading day reached new high or low points for the year. If space is limited, only the number of shares in each sector is listed and not their names.

NEW HIGHS AND LOWS FOR 1995

NEW HIGHS (59).
BANKS, RETAIL (3) Bank Ireland, Lloyds, TSB,
BREWERIES (1) Boddington, BLDG MATLS &
MCHTS (2) Atreus, Heiton, CHEMICALS (2)
Canning (W), Perstorp, DISTRIBUTORS (2) BMG
Charles Sidney, Perry, ELECTRICITY (1)
Norweb, ELECTRNC & ELECT EQUP (3)
Critchley, Druck, Oxford Instrs, ENGINEERING
(3) Manganese Bronze, Molins, Six Hundred,
EXTRACTIVE INDS (4) INSURANCE (1) London
Insc Mkt, INVESTMENT TRUSTS (8)
INVESTMENT COMPANIES (1) First Pacific,
LEISURE & HOTELS (1) Bluebird Toys, LIFE
ASSURANCE (1) London & Manchester, MEDIA
(1) HTV, OIL EXPLORATION & PROD (2) Aran
Energy, Dana Petroleum, OTHER FINANCIAL (1)
Gartmore, OTHER SERVS & BUSNS (1) Esselte,
PAPER , PACKG & PRNTG (1) API, PROPERTY
(1) TBI, RETAILERS, GENERAL (3) Arnotts,
Blacks Leisure, Hamleys, SUPPORT SERVS (5)
Cedardata, Coda, JBA, Kewill Systems, Parity,
TEXTILES & APPAREL (2) Alexandra Workwear,
Beckman (A), WATER (1) Welsh Water, AIM (1)
Dawson, AMERICANS (2) CANADIANS (4)
SOUTH AFRICANS (1).
NEW LOWS (61).
BANKS, RETAIL (3) Fuji, Sakura, Yasuda T & B,
BREWERIES (1) Gibbs Mew, BUILDING &
CNSTRN (1) Gleeson (MJ), BLDG MATLS &
MCHTS (5) Bardon, Cape, Lafarge Coppee,
Sharpe & Fisher, Titon, DISTRIBUTORS (1) Mid
–States, DIVERSIFIED INDLS (1) Barlo,
ELECTRICITY (1) ELECTRNC & ELECT EQUP
(2) ENGINEERING (1) Hopkinsons, ENG,
VEHICLES (1) ERF, EXTRACTIVE INDS (5) GAS
DISTRIBUTION (1) British Gas, HOUSEHOLD
GOODS (1) BLP, INSURANCE (2) Fenchurch,
Steel Burrill Jones, INVESTMENT TRUSTS (7)
MEDIA (7) Adscene, Carnell, Copyright Proms,
Golden Rose Comms, Holmes Marchant,
Phonelink, Sunset & Vine, OIL EXPLORATION &
PROD (1) Evergreen Res, OTHER FINANCIAL
(3) OTHER SERVS & BUSNS (1) Calderburn,
PAPER , PACKG & PRNTG (1) Norcor,
PROPERTY (2) Carlisle, Fiscal, RETAILERS,
GENERAL (1) Oliver, TEXTILES & APPAREL (3)
Allied Textile, Chamberlain Phipps, Faupel
Trading, TRANSPORT (1) Eurodollar, AIM (7)
AMERICANS (1).

Fig. 5.6 New highs and lows

This list helps to highlight companies that are moving against the trend of their sector. Warnings signs would start to flash if a company featured repeatedly in the "new lows" section when the sector as a whole was not moving in this direction. The list can be used in conjunction with the listing of rises and falls to compare individual share price movements with overall market sector moves.

Highlights

Saturday's newspaper features a table of highlights of the week in share price movements. This summarises the chief price changes of the week in the shares of fairly large companies, and adds a brief suggestion of the reasons for the moves (see Figure 5.7):

■ Highlights of the week					
	Price y'day	Change on week	1995 High	1995 Low	
FT-SE 100	3509.8	+42.3	3509.8	2954.2	Good economic news
FT-SE Mid 250	3897.2	+32.8	3897.2	3300.9	£1.7bn bid for Fisons
Airtours	379	+20	449	323	Oversold
BSkyB	347½	+17½	349	242	FT-SE 100 inclusion hopes
Cable & Wireless	431	+21	449	350½	Strong dollar
Cadbury Schweppes	500	+15	505	370	Talk of gains in market share
Fisons	264½	+67½	265½	103	Rhone-Poulenc Rorer bid
Grand Metropolitan	421	+23	423	352	Favourable presentations
Kwik-Fit	167	+6	168	142	Smith New Court recommendation
Northern Elec	920	+23	1138	715	Sharehldrs approve benefits package
Pearson	618	-22	667	539	Results
Reuters	577	+39½	577	404	Strong dollar
Securicor A	1113	+16	1113	900	Hopes for Cellnet
Vodafone	276	+14½	281½	177½	US Interest/Nat West Sec positive
Zeneca	1099	-25	1177	840	Bid talk evaporates

Fig. 5.7 Highlights of the week

- **Price, change and high and low:** an overview of the week's movements and how they compare with prices in the rest of the year to date.

- **Explanation:** in this example, the upward and downward moves are put down to a number of different factors, including economic news, positive or negative company news, and public evaluations by financial institutions.

Winners and losers

Saturday's Weekend Money section also includes a table of the FT-SE winners and losers (see Figure 5.8). This lists the top and bottom six performing companies over the previous week in three

sectors (the FT-SE 100, the FT-SE Mid 250 and the FT-SE SmallCap sector), including their latest price, percentage price change on the week and change on the start of the year. It also lists the top and bottom six performing market sectors.

■ **FT-SE winners and losers**			
TOP 100	Friday's price (p)	% change: 1 week	since 30/12/94
WINNERS			
Forte	346	32.1	44.2
Ladbroke	148	16.5	-13.5
Guardian Royal Exchange	258½	10.5	55.3
Cable & Wireless	452	8.4	20.2
Standard Chartered	587	7.5	109.3
British Aerospace	787	7.4	85.6
LOSERS			
De La Rue	713	-21.6	-24.2
Inchcape	245	-17.5	-42.8
Vodafone	217½	-13.2	2.6
REXAM	341	-8.3	-21.6
Powergen	524	-7.9	-2.1
National Power	464	-7.4	-5.1
MID 250	Friday's price (p)	% change: 1 week	since 30/12/94
WINNERS			
Savoy Hotel "A"	1025	16.1	12.3
Trafalgar House	24	11.6	-68.4
Sedgwick	126	7.7	-16.0
Storehouse	340	7.6	57.4
MIRROR GROUP NEWSPAPERS	187	6.9	45.0
DFS Furniture	378	6.8	39.0
LOSERS			
Powell Duffryn	467	-19.1	-6.0
Hazlewood Foods	96	-11.9	-16.5
Babcock International	147	-10.9	-1.2
British Vita	200	-8.7	-12.7
Smith (David S)	245	-7.7	-2.6
Kalon	101	-7.3	-13.7

SMALLCAP	Friday's price (p)	% change: 1 week	since 30/12/94
WINNERS			
AMEC	96	33.3	39.1
McAlpine (Alfred)	159	26.2	-7.0
Geest	142	21.4	-19.3
Betterware	80½	17.5	57.8
Signet	15	13.2	-36.2
Alpha Airports	114	12.9	-20.8
LOSERS			
Calderburn	65	-19.8	-68.0
MAID	243	-19.3	252.2
Sterling Publishing	25	-16.7	-74.5
Prospect Industries	4¼	-15.0	-71.2
Exco	120	-14.9	-24.5
Domino Printing Sciences	392	-12.1	-29.0
MARKET SECTORS*	Friday's index	% change: 1 week	since 30/12/94
WINNERS			
Leisure & Hotels	2572.09	4.6	20.8
Life Assurance	3531.25	3.5	50.1
Insurance	1437.59	3.2	25.2
Extractive Industries	4267.81	2.9	13.4
Retailers, General	1895.22	2.6	19.8
Tobacco	4807.23	2.5	33.1
LOSERS			
Paper, Pckg & Printing	2507.26	-7.4	-8.6
Distributors	2502.19	-4.7	0.3
Chemicals	2312.69	-3.7	2.2
Electricity	2784.69	-3.5	7.8
Textiles & Apparel	1467.22	-2.5	-2.9
Spirits, Wines & Ciders	2757.63	-2.2	0.9

Based on last week's performance.
*FT-SE Actuaries Industrial Sectors.

Fig. 5.8 FT-SE winners and losers

ISSUING NEW SECURITIES

The *Financial Times* provides detailed information on the secondary market for company securities. But the exchanges also have a vital

role as a primary market, providing new long-term capital for investment through the offering of new issues. These might be for companies entering their shares on the market for the first time or for companies already listed but requiring further capital. In each case, the newspaper offers extensive coverage.

There are three daily published tables for new securities: equities (ordinary shares issued by newly floated companies); fixed interest stocks (corporate bonds, such as convertible preference shares that yield a fixed rate of interest now and can be converted into ordinary shares at a later date); and rights offers (trading in the rights to issues of new shares in existing companies to which current shareholders are given the first right of refusal). In addition, Saturday's newspaper carries one list of forthcoming rights issues, and another of new companies coming to the market through what are known as offers for sale, placings and introductions as in Figure 5.9:

OFFERS FOR SALE, PLACINGS & INTRODUCTIONS

Amey Holdings is coming to the market via a placing of 8.07m shares
Bloomsbury Publishing is to raise £5m via a placing.
Gander is to raise £5m via a placing and open offer via a 1-4 basis of 71.6m shares @ 7p
Spargo Consulting is coming to the market via a placing of appx. £12m.
UPF Group is to raise £7.5m via a placing of 7.87m shares @ 108p.
VideoLogic is coming to the market via a flotation of appx. £25m.

Fig. 5.9 Offers for sale, placings and introductions

Launching companies

Companies can raise money by selling some of their shares to investors before getting them quoted on the stock market. Shares may be being sold by original owners/existing shareholders or by the company to raise new capital: so sometimes the money goes into the business, sometimes to the existing shareholders.

There are three ways of floating shares on the market:

- **Offers for sale:** these are shares offered to the public through advertising and the issue of prospectuses and application forms. The

most notable form in the 1980s and 1990s has been the privatisation issues, especially British Gas and British Telecom. These are the kinds of new issue likely to be of most interest to the small, private investor (see Figure 5.10).

- **Placings:** these are private sales of shares to a range of investors through a broker. The broker will typically go first to its clients, and subsequently shares may be available to a wider public through the stock market. This is a popular way for smaller companies to come to market, often through the USM or the AIM, and companies may combine a placing with an open offer for sale.

- **Introductions:** these take place when there is already a number of shareholders, and the company is simply seeking permission for the shares to trade on the market. Such issues do not raise new capital, but might allow a company to move up from the USM or the AIM to the main market, or a foreign company to trade in London as well as in its home market.

Offers for sale are the most prominent form of new issue. They can come in two forms. In the first, the company offers the public a fixed number of shares at a fixed price. The price is set by the sponsors of the issue, usually a merchant bank, based on forecasts of likely future profits. The sponsor will have two conflicting objectives in mind: a low enough price to ensure that the shares trade well in the secondary or aftermarket; and a high enough price for the client raising the money.

Since fixed price offers for sale often underprice the issue, they provide a good opportunity for stags. These are investors who buy in anticipation of an immediate price rise, and a quick profit right away. Prices often rise well above the sale price when dealings start, and the potential premiums encourage speculators seeking to benefit from the mistakes made by the issuers.

The alternative, and the way to avoid excessive stagging, is the tender offer. In this case, no price is set in advance but, instead, the price is determined by what investors are prepared to pay. Investors are invited to bid for shares and, if the issue is fully subscribed, the price will generally be set at a little below one at which all available shares can be sold.

With either the fixed price or tender offer, the shares might be oversubscribed, and a decision needs to be made on the appropriate allocation of shares. This might be done by ballot, by scaling down certain over-large applications, or by giving preferential treatment to certain investors, usually small, private ones. Alternatively, an issue might be undersubscribed, and this is why new issues are underwritten by big investors who guarantee to buy any unwanted shares. If underwriting is needed, shares will overhang the market as underwriters wait to sell when the price is rising. A result of this is that the share price will tend to stay flat until the majority of the shares are in firm hands, the portfolios of investors who want to hold them.

The timetable for a new issue is usually fairly standard: an early announcement is made without information on the intended share price, prospective yield and price/earnings ratio. This is followed by the publication of the full prospectus, incorporating price and yield details and with a cut-off date for applications and a date on which decisions on the allotment will be made. The Stock Exchange then decides on a date on which official dealings begin.

New issue launches are often affected by the overall state of the market, as in the following example, a launch that appeared to combine features of fixed price and tender offers:

> The flotation of £700m of equity in 3i, the largest European investor in unquoted companies, is to go ahead today despite the weakness of the London stock market. Shares will be priced at slightly more than a 13 per cent discount to their net asset value. Advisers have found strong demand for 3i shares in an informal 'bookbuilding' exercise over the past few weeks. Large funds were asked to submit informal 'bids' for equity at various prices.
>
> (*Financial Times*, 21 June 1994)

Because of the size of the issues and the desire to appeal to first-time investors in the markets, the privatisation issues follow a rather longer schedule. In the case of BT3, the third British Telecom offer in 1993, for example, the government and SG Warburg, the global co-ordinator of the issue, were keen to ensure that such a significant launch should not have a deleterious effect on the whole market, and that downward pressure on the issue price should be resisted with "stabilising" buying by the underwriters.

■ Popular shares

	Launch price (p)	Yesterday's price (p)	Change on week %
Abbey National	130	608	3.8
BAA	*122½	495*d	
British Airways	125	469	−0.6
British Gas	135	237	−0.2
British Steel	125	168½*d	3.4
BT	130	360½	−0.1
Eurotunnel units	350	98	2.1
Rolls-Royce	170	170	−0.6
TSB	100	404	−0.2
ELECTRICITY			
East Midlands	*272½	870	−4.0
Eastern	240	974	
London	240	906	−2.9
Manweb	240	1023	0.8
Midlands	240	933	−5.0
National Power	175	464	−7.4
Northern	*242½	953	2.7
Northern Ireland	220	445	−5.9
Norweb	240	1025	0.8
PowerGen	175	524	−7.9
Scottish Hydro	240	361	3.4
Scottish Power	240	385	3.8
Seeboard	*120	642	0.2
South Wales	240	1027	−0.3
South Western	240	900	
Southern	240	920	−5.3
Yorkshire	*272½	888	−3.2
WATER			
Anglian	240	578	0.5
North West	*220½	603*a	3.4
Northumbrian	240	1169*d	4.1
Severn Trent	240	662	2.6
South West	240	500½	0.3
Southern	240	675	0.6
Thames	240	558	−0.2
Welsh	*250½	699	−0.1
Wessex	*122	344	0.3
Yorkshire	240	609	0.8

* Adjusted for capital change.

Fig. 5.10 Popular shares

The privatisation issues tended to be markedly underpriced, some-times coming with incentives for the private investor, and positively dis-criminating against the institutions in terms of allocation and even price. In consequence, they have been among the most successful new issues of the past 15 years. Saturday's *Financial Times* includes a table of "Popular shares", listing all the major UK privatised companies with their launch price, their current price and their percentage increase over the previous week (see Figure 5.10). The table's regular appearance reflects the fact that for many investors, these are the only shares they own.

Like privatisations, private sector new issues are often viewed as a way to quick and easy profits, but for every ten or so successes, there is usually one that goes wrong or seriously fails to perform. As a result, private investors must always show great caution, being care-ful to study the prospectus, balance sheet, and profit and loss account of any potential investment. As with investing in any company share, it is critical to ask such questions as: where did the company's profits and growth come from in previous years? What markets does it operate in? Where is its customer base? And what is the quality of the management?

Once possible purchases have been highlighted, it should then be asked whether the price is fair? Does it reflect the assets? Is there too much emphasis on potential growth? And are market expectations for this type of business unrealistically high? Paradoxically, a com-pany that has recently reported very good results, or is in fashionable industries such as biotechnology or multimedia with its best results at an indeterminate point in the future, may be best avoided.

The *Financial Times* has a special table listing information on shares in newly floated companies (see Figure 5.11):

- **Issue price:** the price at which the security was issued.

- **Amount paid up:** the amount of the issue price that had to be paid up immediately by the investor. Most issues are fully paid but some, including many government privatisations, have only required the investor to pay in stages. These part-paid shares are highly geared since if, after issue, a premium or discount emerges on the full issue price, it will be a significantly higher percentage of the part-paid investment. A small movement in the full price will be a relatively big movement in the part-paid price.

LONDON RECENT ISSUES: EQUITIES

Issue price p	Amt paid up	Mkt. cap (£m.)	1995 High	Low	Stock	Close price p	+/-	Net div.	Div. cov.	Grs yld	P/E net
–	F.P.	32.2	93	92	Abtrust Asian Smllr	92		–	–	–	–
–	F.P.	2.27	33	32	Do Warrants	32½		–	–	–	–
–	F.P.	11.7	22	17	†Alpha Omikron	21	–1	–	–	–	–
–	F.P.	2.13	10	9	†Arion Props	9		v–	–	–	–
306	F.P.	48.6	301	285	BZW Eq Tesco WI	299	–1	v–	–	–	–
100	F.P.	8.32	96	95	Baronsmead VCT	96		v–	–	–	–
–	F.P.	61.2	102	101	Benfield & Rea	102	+1	–	–	–	–
–	F.P.	5.76	64	50	†Chartwell Intl	64	+4	v–	–	–	–
–	F.P.	43.8	139	102	†Creos Intl	122		–	–	–	–
60	F.P.	3.79	71	65	†David Glass	70		Rv2.88	2.4	5.1	10.0
145	F.P.	59.7	152	142½	Enterprise Inns	147½	+2½	Wv6.4	–	5.4	10.3
–	F.P.	91.0	95	90	Guinness Flight	91		–	–	–	–
–	F.P.	191.0	195	191	Do Units	191		–	–	–	–
–	F.P.	2.00	13	10	Do Warrants	10		–	–	–	–
125	F.P.	27.8	155	128	Heritage Bath	155		–	–	–	–
–	F.P.	11.2	119	112	†Indpt Radio	112		v–	–	–	–
–	F.P.	21.1	543	488	†Intl Greetings	503		–	–	–	–
45	F.P.	18.7	65	52	†MultiMedia	65		v–	–	–	–
–	F.P.	14.1	101	-97	Northern Venture	97		–	–	–	–
100	F.P.	24.8	102	99	Perpetual UK Smlr	99		–	–	–	–

† Alternative Investment Market. For a full explanation of all other symbols please refer to The London Share Service notes.

Fig. 5.11 London recent issues: Equities

- **Market capitalisation:** the total value of the new issue.

- **High and low:** figures representing the price highs and lows for the year.

- **Stock:** the name of the security.

- **Price and change:** the closing price the previous night, and the change on the day.

- **Dividend cover, yield and p/e ratio:** for new equity issues, details of the net dividend, cover, gross yield and p/e ratio are provided. In the case of newly floated companies, these figures are based on the figures given in the launch prospectus until the company issues audited financial reports.

- **Fixed interest stocks:** a periodic table lists recent issues of corporate bonds, generally issued by an existing company seeking extra funding and preferring debt to equity.

New equity issues remain in the table for around six weeks after the company comes to market depending on the volume of new issues, and most then choose to be transferred to the London share service.

Raising extra funds

Rights issues are the way in which companies raise additional equity finance for expansion or refinance if they are over-borrowed. They are issues of new shares in a company already on the market to which existing shareholders are given the right of first refusal. Shares are issued in proportion to existing holdings and at a discount to the current share price to give shareholders an incentive to take them up. The discount has the effect of depressing the price of existing shares and so shareholders will naturally want the rights to them. If they do not actually want to buy the shares, they can sell their rights.

Details of forthcoming rights issues are listed in a table in Saturday's newspaper (see Figure 5.12):

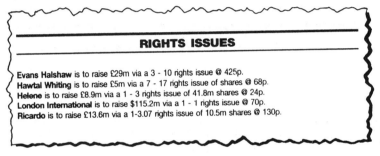

RIGHTS ISSUES

Evans Halshaw is to raise £29m via a 3 - 10 rights issue @ 425p.
Hawtal Whiting is to raise £5m via a 7 - 17 rights issue of shares @ 68p.
Helene is to raise £8.9m via a 1 - 3 rights issue of 41.8m shares @ 24p.
London International is to raise $115.2m via a 1 - 1 rights issue @ 70p.
Ricardo is to raise £13.6m via a 1-3.07 rights issue of 10.5m shares @ 130p.

Fig. 5.12 Rights issues

- **Rights issues:** the companies, the amount they are seeking to raise and the number of shares they are planning to issue at what price. A 1–3 issue means that a shareholder is entitled to buy one new share for every three currently held; a 7–17 issue indicates an offer of seven new shares for every seventeen held.

The Stock Exchange sets a cut-off date after which the shares go ex-rights ("xr" in the share service tables). After this date the buyer does not get rights, and clearly at this point the share price has to adjust. Shares with the rights are known as cum-rights.

Nil paid rights (that is, rights for which the subscription price has not yet been paid) can be bought and sold. Their value is the ex-rights price less the subscription price for the new shares. These too

are highly geared investments. The newspaper lists them in a table of rights offers, as in Figure 5.13:

Issue price p	Amount paid up	Latest Renun. date	1995 High	Low	Stock	Closing price p	+or-
320	Nil	14/11	102pm	93pm	Alumasc	100pm	
105	Nil	24/11	17pm	5pm	Anglo-Eastn Plants	13pm	−1
16	Nil	28/10	2pm	1pm	Baris	2pm	
275	Nil	13/10	51pm	25pm	Close Brothers	25pm	−3
490	Nil	13/11	103pm	50pm	Forth Ports	82pm	
950	Nil	8/11	152pm	113$\frac{1}{2}$pm	RMC	113$\frac{1}{2}$pm	−1

RIGHTS OFFERS

pm premium.

Fig. 5.13 Rights offers

- **Issue price and amount paid up:** as for the new issues, these are the price at which new shares are issued and the proportion of price already paid, if any.

- **Latest renunciation date:** the final date by which holders of rights can dispose of their allotments to purchasers who will not have to pay stamp duty. Before this date, all dealings are for cash rather than the account.

- **Closing price (as a premium), change and high and low:** the price quoted for rights to buy new shares, plus the change on the previous day and the highest and lowest points for the year. The price is actually a premium for the right to subscribe. Percentage swings in price can be large because of gearing.

Rights offers normally remain in the table until they are fully paid. The price of rights offers is pitched well below the market price to ensure maximum take-up of the issue although, as with new issues, the shares will be underwritten, usually by a merchant bank. A standard issue might aim to raise up to 30 per cent more equity capital with shares at about a 20 per cent discount to market price. Rarely, a company might do a deep discount rights issue that does not need to be underwritten. Once a century, a closely held firm might do a very unusual and highly priced issue:

Everton, one of the great names of British football, has announced the details of its first share issue for more than a century. The Merseyside club is to raise

£9.75m through a one-for-one rights issue. There is just one catch – each share-holder has to stump up £4,000 per share. A loyal band of supporters have between them 2,500 shares which change hands at more than £2,500 each. About 40 per cent of the shares are held by the Moores family. The remainder are largely owned by relatives of well-heeled fans who bought one or two shares when they were first issued in 1892 at £1 apiece.

(*Financial Times*, 7 July 1994)

The price at which the shares are pitched does not matter since the company already belongs to the shareholders. The only benefit they get is on the yield if the dividend per share remains the same amount. Because the equity is diluted, the price drops: naturally, if the dividend is static, the yield goes up.

Other techniques by which new issues in existing companies can be arranged include vendor placings, placings and bought deals and convertible loan stock sold through the Euromarkets.

There is also the scrip issue or capitalisation issue where a company turns part of its accumulated reserves into new shares. This is essentially an accounting transaction to convert the part of shareholders' funds that is not revealed by stock market capitalisation into stock. It keeps the number of shares in issue in line with the growth of the business, and keeps their prices down. It can also be a tax-efficient way of handing part of the company's added worth back to shareholders.

The Stock Exchange sets a date when shares go "xc" (ex-capitalisation), after which the price will go down. The only real effect is if the dividend remains the same, in which case the yield has gone up. It also makes it difficult to compare share prices over time unless calculations have made the appropriate adjustment. The term "xa" means a share is ex-all, not entitled to scrip issues, rights issues or dividends.

DEALING AND SETTLEMENT

For 173 years up until July 1994, the Stock Exchange year was divided into twenty-four share trading or accounting periods. These determined the payment dates for stocks bought and sold, each trading period normally lasting two weeks. Within that period, trans-actions were recorded but no money changed hands. On account or settlement day, all transactions had to be settled: buyers had to pay

for what they had bought during the period, while sellers received their cash. At settlement, share certificates passed on to the new owner and changes were made to the register of shareholders.

This account dealing system allowed scope for speculative behaviour with the minimum capital outlay, since for shares bought and sold within an account period, only differences had to be settled. In the course of an account dealing period, optimistic (or bullish) speculators could buy stocks intending to sell them at a higher price before settlement day. Similarly, pessimistic speculators (bears) could "short" sell a stock that they did not own in the hope of obtaining it for a lower price before settlement. The result of this system was that market movements could be affected by the account dealing periods: the market would often move up at the beginning of a period as bullish speculators started buying, and down at the end as profits were taken.

As of 18 July 1994, the Stock Exchange moved to a ten day rolling settlement system in which deals had to be settled within ten working days of being struck. Thus, the first settlement date of the new system was 1 August 1994 with every working day thereafter a potential settlement date. Following the successful implementation of the system, as of 26 June 1995, the Stock Exchange moved to five day rolling settlement, with 3 July 1995 as the first settlement date. The intention is to move to a three day system during 1996, and to same day settlement by the turn of the century.

Directors' share transactions

Saturday's newspaper lists details of the previous week's share transactions by directors in their own companies (see Figure 5.14):

- **Directors' share transactions:** sales or purchases listed by company, sector, number of shares bought or sold, their value in thousands of pounds, and the number of directors involved in the trading activity. The list contains all transactions with a value over £10,000, including the exercise of options if 100 per cent of the stock on which the options were granted is subsequently sold.

The information on directors' share transactions might give an indication of how company "insiders" feel about the prospects for

■ Directors' share transactions in their own companies

Company	Sector	Shares	Value £'000	No of directors
SALES				
Archer Group	Insu	50.000	27	1
Berkeley Group	BCon	200.000	800	1
Critchley	Elec	3.000	18	1
F&C Spec Utilities♦	InvT	80.000	49	1
First Technology	Eng	35.000	173	1
Formscan	SSer	25.000	21	1
Inspec Group	Chem	397.575	1240	3
Inspirations	L&HI	240.000	277	1
Osborne & Little	HGod	18.500	78	2
Porvair	Chem	6.000	22	1
Quality Care	Hlth	1.946.400	5061	1
RPS Group	SSe	54.000	51	3
Rolfe & Nolan	SSer	7.666	15	1
Seton Healthcare	Hlth	70.550	276	6
South Wales Elect	Elec	2.000	17	1
Trifast	Dist	66.000	205	3
Utility Cable	Elec	250.000	50	1
Waste Recycling	OS&B	9.090	11	1
Wyko Group	Dist	300.000	243	1
Yorkshire Elec	Elec	5.000	39	1
BPB Inds	BM&M	261.942	885	2 *
Caledonia Inv	OthF	232.999	1531	2 *
FKI	Eng	99.150	160	1 *
GKN	Eng	22.035	174	1 *
Hardy Oil & Gas	Oil	32.621	56	1 *
Trifast	Dist	52.000	161	1 *
PURCHASES				
Bostrom	Eng	3.000	10	1
Brown & Jackson	RetG	10.000	12	2
Coda	SSer	100.000	145	1
Coutts Consult	SSer	30.000	17	2
F&C Spec Utilities§§	InvT	75.000	50	1
Mercury Asset Mngmt	OthF	10.000	87	1
Quality Care	Hlth	13.300	36	1
Spargo Consulting	SSer	25.000	18	1
Unitech	Elec	5.000	22	1
Watson & Philip	RetF	5.000	24	1
Wholesale Fitg	Dist	40.000	116	1

Companies must notify the Stock Exchange within five working days of a share transaction by a director. This list contains all transactions (listed and USM), including exercise of options (*) if 100% subsequently sold, with a value over £10,000. Information released by the StocAugust 7-11 1995. Shares traded are ordinary unless otherwise stated: §§=Capital Shares. ♦=Income Shares

Source: The Inside Track, Edinburgh, 0131-538 7070

Fig. 5.14 Directors' share transactions

their company's share price both in terms of its relationship to the company's prospective performance and relative to broader market movements. For example, directors frequently buy against the trend of a market fall, perhaps feeling secure in the longer term prospects for their company's share price. On the other hand, sales of stock on which directors have been granted an option as part of their remuneration package might indicate a lack of confidence in market prospects for the stock, at least for the immediate future; of course, it might also indicate that the director simply needs to free up some cash. For example:

> Body Shop fell $2^1/_2$ to 243p after announcing that Mrs Anita Roddick and Mr Gordon Roddick had sold 3.m shares at 240p each reducing their stake to 25.4 per cent. The sale raised £8.4m which is targeted at charity and company projects. (*Financial Times*, 9/10 July 1994)

The attraction to an investor of following directors' transactions is obvious, but scholarly research in both the United Kingdom and the United States reveals mixed results. On average, it appears that directors are good at deciding when to sell, but not significantly above average at knowing when to buy. The latter result may be because they have too insular a view about their companies' prospects, believing their own propaganda and not taking sufficient account of their competition or the overall economic situation.

"We live in the Age of Performance. Performance means, quite simply, that your portfolio does better than others."

GEORGE J W GOODMAN

("ADAM SMITH")

"The past history of the series (of stock price changes) cannot be used to predict the future in any meaningful way. The future price of the price level or a security is no more predictable than the path of a series of cumulated random numbers."

EUGENE FAMA

6

INDICES AND AGGREGATES
Market indicators

- *Financial Times* **equity indices** – the original investment statistics: the FT Ordinary Share Index (FT-30); and the FT Gold Mines Index

- **FT-SE Actuaries share indices** – reading the figures and using the information on the key market indicators: evaluating quarterly performance; key indicators; hourly movements and industry baskets; highs, lows and base dates; and leaders and laggards

The fundamental data of the equities markets are the prices of shares and the various ratios that can be calculated from them. But while this information is highly valuable for understanding both the performance of individual companies and investors' evaluation of their prospects, it does not indicate the state of the market as a whole nor a given company's relative performance. This question of share price measurement for the stock market as a whole led to the development of figures for baskets of shares, or indices. An index is purely a number to compare the value of companies now with their value at the starting date.

All indices are an attempt to create order and direction out of diversity. Stock market indices are designed to pull together the disparate movements of different share prices, each responding to a myriad of individual pressures, to find out whether the market, or a subsection of it, is moving up or down, in a bullish or bearish direction. There are numerous ways of composing equity indices, each with advantages and disadvantages, and the one selected will depend on just what it is that is being tracked. Indices are important benchmarks for measuring the performance of the fund managers who put money into the stock market on behalf of investors. Most will try to outperform the various benchmarks, though some will passively aim merely to "track" the rise and fall of the indices. In its simplest form, this could be attempted by buying the stocks that constitute the index.

For managers too, such benchmark information is highly valuable for understanding both the performance of their individual companies and investors' evaluation of their prospects. For example, it is important to ensure that the company's share price is not underperforming the overall market, perhaps making the management vulnerable to a hostile bid. Indeed, increasing numbers of companies are making the share price a key management target through programmes of corporate value creation and value-based management.

FINANCIAL TIMES EQUITY INDICES

Perhaps the *Financial Times*' greatest contribution to investment statistics has been its pioneering of stock market indices. The oldest and most familiar of these is the FT Ordinary Share Index, also known as the FT-30 share index, or simply the FT index. It is the longest standing continuous index covering UK equities: started in 1935 with a base 100, it is compiled from the share prices of thirty leading UK companies, chosen to be representative of UK industry and is calculated as a geometric mean. It is biased towards major industrial and retailing companies, the traditional blue chips, but now includes financial and oil stocks which have become more important (see Figure 6.1):

FINANCIAL TIMES EQUITY INDICES

	Oct 9	Oct 6	Oct 5	Oct 4	Oct 3	Yr ago	*High	*Low
Ordinary Share	2596.2	2612.9	2625.4	2627.3	2613.7	2338.9	**2666.5**	2238.3
Ord. div. yield	4.13	4.10	4.08	4.08	4.10	4.41	**4.73**	4.02
P/E ratio net	15.61	15.73	15.81	15.82	15.73	17.86	**21.33**	15.47
P/E ratio nil	15.43	15.54	15.62	15.63	15.55	18.32	**22.21**	15.25

*For 1995. Ordinary Share index since compilation: high 2713.6 2/02/94; low 49.4 26/6/40
FT Ordinary Share index base date 1/7/35.

Ordinary Share hourly changes

Open	9.00	10.00	11.00	12.00	13.00	14.00	15.00	16.00	High	Low
2617.9	2609.0	2605.9	2599.7	2598.8	2599.2	2595.2	2593.7	2593.3	2618.1	2591.0

	Oct 9	Oct 6	Oct 5	Oct 4	Oct 3	Yr ago
SEAQ bargains	33,133	28,058	28,244	27,769	29,461	22,921
Equity turnover (£m)†	-	1563.6	1944.5	1931.1	2033.2	1022.0
Equity bargains†	-	34,012	33,251	33,675	35,784	26,909
Shares traded (ml)†	-	648.7	776.8	775.3	580.4	440.7

†Excluding intra-market business and overseas turnover.

Fig. 6.1 *Financial Times* equity indices

- **Ordinary share:** the movements of the FT index over the past five trading days, together with its level a year ago, and the values and dates of its highs and lows for this year. The basis of 100 dates from the index's inception on 1 July 1935.

- **Yields and ratios:** ordinary dividend yield and price/earnings ratios on a net and nil basis. In the same way that the index reflects prices of the component shares, so these reflect the dividends and earnings of the relevant companies.

- **Ordinary share hourly changes:** the hourly movements of the FT index through the previous trading day plus the day's high and low point of the index. Originally calculated daily, it is now available as a real-time index like the Footsie (see below).

- **Trading volume:** the figures for SEAQ bargains are the number of transactions of equities and gilts on the Stock Exchange's SEAQ trading system by 4.30pm on the five most recent trading days, as well as a year earlier. Equity turnover is the value of the volume of equities traded in millions of pounds. Equity bargains is the number of transactions, while shares traded is the actual number of shares to have changed hands in millions. As with trading volume on individual shares, all volume figures should be divided by two since each share is recorded twice as being both bought and sold.

The FT-30 was for decades the standard barometer of investor sentiment in the City, quoted in the press and on radio and television as regularly as the FT-SE 100 index is today. Although in terms of public attention the FT-30 has now been superseded by the Footsie, it still has a role to play. As the oldest surviving stock market index, it represents an important part of financial history and may be used by analysts to compare the impact of great events, such as the outbreak of wars or surprise election results, on the market. Its list of constituents is also used by followers of the O'Higgins method of share selection, which involves finding the ten stocks in the index with the highest dividend yield and selecting the five of those with the lowest price.

The mathematical structure of the index and the fact that all shares count equally regardless of their market capitalisation (the index is unweighted) make it a sensitive short-term indicator of the mood of the market. But it has a downward bias over the long term, and so is not suitable for measuring market levels or the performance of an investment portfolio over time.

In contrast to the Footsie where the components are selected purely on size (see below), judgement has always been important in choosing companies for the FT-30. The aim has been to include a representative cross-section of UK industry. Companies have been removed from the index because they have been taken over, their fortunes have declined, or to make room for more dynamic or market-

sensitive shares. For example, British Telecom and British Gas were brought into the index immediately on privatisation. It is a measure of the dynamics of the stock market that only six of the original components remain in the index today (see appendix 2).

FT Gold Mines Index

A subsidiary FT equity index tracks the performance of thirty-four international gold mining companies in Africa (primarily South Africa but also Ashanti in Ghana), Australasia and North America (see Figure 6.2). The base value for the Gold Mines Index is 1,000 set on the last day of 1992, and the currency basis for the value calculations is US dollars.

FT GOLD MINES INDEX

	Oct 9	% chg on day	Oct 6	Year ago	Gross div yield %	P/E ratio	52 week High	Low
Gold Mines Index†(34)	1957.56	+0.2	1953.07	2248.25	1.92	–	2304.73	1637.91
■ Regional Indices								
Africa (16)	2702.38	+0.5	2687.81	3547.06	4.02	24.86	3711.87	2428.19
Australasia (6)	2382.43	+0.9	2362.12	2793.52	2.14	26.10	2951.49	1788.20
North America (12)	1683.65	–0.1	1684.69	1783.07	0.80	48.29	1831.00	1348.18

Copyright, The Financial Times Limited 1995. "FT Gold Mines Index" is a trademark of The Financial Times Limited. Figures in brackets show number of companies. Basis US Dollars. Base Values: 1000.00 31/12/92. † Partial. Market closed 9/10/95: Canada.

Fig. 6.2 FT Gold Mines Index

- **Gold Mines:** the value of the index at the end of the last two days' trading in London as well as one year ago and the high and low point of the previous fifty-two weeks. In addition, this index shows the current gross dividend yield.

- **Regional indices:** similar values and yields for the three regional components of the overall gold mines index, plus their p/e ratios.

There are three categories of gold mining companies: the "majors" with production of one million ounces of gold per year (around fifteen companies); the "independents" with production of over 100,000 ounces a year (around fifty companies); and the "juniors",

companies with little or no production but determination to discover some. But while the universe of mining stocks worldwide is quite extensive, the total capitalisation of the FT Gold Mines Index (which includes only companies with production of over 300,000 ounces a year) is roughly equivalent to the combined market capitalisation of British Telecom and Guinness. Broad criteria for valuing mining companies include the quality, quantity and overall status of a company's production, reserves, management and exploration programme, as well as the political risk of the country in which it is based.

FT-SE ACTUARIES SHARE INDICES

More widely based indices have been developed by the *Financial Times*, the Stock Exchange and the Institute and Faculty of Actuaries. As of November 1995, these have been managed by a new joint company, FT-SE International. These indices are arithmetically weighted by market capitalisation rather than being based on crude price movements. In other words, the larger a company, the bigger the effect its price movements will have on the index.

The FT-SE Actuaries share indices (see Figure 6.3), and notably the All-Share index, are the professional investor's yardstick for the whole UK equity market, for use in analysing investment strategies and as a measure of portfolio performance. There are thirty-eight component indices in the All-Share index relating to different industrial sectors of the market, and eight component indices relating to different levels of capitalisation (including the well known Footsie). Beyond the All-Share are the new fledgling indices, incorporating companies with a market capitalisation below around £40 million.

Reading the figures

- **FT-SE 100:** the Footsie index was started with a base of 1,000, in January 1984 to fill a gap in the market. At that time, the FT-30 index was calculated only hourly, and there was demand for a constantly updated – or real-time – index in view of both the competition from overseas and the needs of the new traded options and financial futures markets. For most purposes, the Footsie has replaced the FT-30. The index, amended quarterly, includes the 100

FT - SE Actuaries Share Indices   The UK Series

	Oct 16	Day's chge%	Oct 13	Oct 12	Oct 11	Year ago	Div. yield%	Net cover	P/E ratio	Xd adj. ytd	Total Return
FT-SE 100	3557.3	−0.3	3568.0	3523.8	3474.3	3120.2	3.97	2.07	15.22	125.35	1410.99
FT-SE Mid 250	3939.0	−0.2	3945.3	3936.4	3919.8	3548.0	3.46	1.84	19.57	117.81	1532.83
FT-SE Mid 250 ex Inv Trusts	3960.2	−0.1	3966.1	3960.2	3945.5	3541.9	3.60	1.90	18.28	123.31	1541.03
FT-SE-A 350	1771.3	−0.3	1776.0	1758.0	1737.3	1563.0	3.85	2.02	16.02	60.30	1435.81
FT-SE-A 350 Higher Yield	1764.8	−0.3	1770.9	1753.2	1732.3	1566.4	4.91	1.82	13.96	75.98	1186.62
FT-SE-A 350 Lower Yield	1782.5	−0.2	1785.9	1767.6	1746.8	1520.7	2.77	2.39	18.87	43.33	1206.82
FT-SE SmallCap	1964.12	......	1964.73	1960.69	1958.68	1800.15	3.30	1.67	22.68	53.11	1580.58
FT-SE SmallCap ex Inv Trusts	1949.37	......	1949.80	1947.03	1946.17	1767.86	3.52	1.74	20.37	55.79	1576.85
FT-SE-A ALL-SHARE	1749.74	−0.3	1754.15	1737.42	1718.30	1548.45	3.81	2.00	16.38	58.62	1441.55

■ FT-SE Actuaries All-Share

	Oct 16	Day's chge%	Oct 13	Oct 12	Oct 11	Year ago	Div. yield%	Net cover	P/E ratio	Xd adj. ytd	Total Return
10 MINERAL EXTRACTION(23)	2921.72	......	2922.78	2908.40	2878.04	2753.36	3.86	2.09	15.52	105.02	1224.54
12 Extractive Industries(7)	4168.84	−0.4	4187.63	4173.66	4081.05	4013.97	3.55	2.51	14.02	143.77	1195.30
15 Oil, Integrated(3)	2894.04	......	2894.26	2882.80	2860.63	2707.47	4.06	2.04	15.12	107.92	1241.85
16 Oil Exploration & Prod(13)	1965.26	+0.7	1952.54	1915.80	1894.54	1904.00	2.56	1.48	32.98	49.88	1166.51
20 GEN INDUSTRIALS(278)	1969.65	−0.2	1973.98	1967.63	1955.62	1903.74	4.18	1.83	16.33	70.36	1051.10
21 Building & Construction(38)	917.10	−0.3	919.44	915.52	913.36	1071.57	4.44	1.87	15.07	36.51	752.65
22 Building Matls & Merchs(31)	1709.44	−0.5	1717.29	1712.30	1698.40	1859.42	4.32	2.02	14.35	65.12	844.25
23 Chemicals(23)	2447.80	−0.2	2451.60	2454.27	2429.61	2367.05	3.93	1.82	17.41	80.65	1132.67
24 Diversified Industrials(20)	1768.37	−0.2	1771.85	1763.60	1748.94	1819.90	5.61	1.58	14.14	87.22	960.89
25 Electronic & Elect Equip(36)	2178.29	−0.7	2192.95	2167.77	2146.84	1924.82	3.44	1.93	18.83	61.51	1110.02
26 Engineering(69)	2161.26	......	2160.71	2156.89	2153.20	1830.80	3.36	1.99	18.67	58.48	1284.20
27 Engineering, Vehicles(13)	2581.87	−0.6	2596.19	2615.73	2614.22	2260.72	3.63	1.39	24.85	89.48	1313.30
28 Paper, Pckg & Printing(27)	2888.70	+0.4	2877.41	2862.89	2845.81	2802.66	3.46	2.48	14.56	86.90	1178.82
29 Textiles & Apparel(21)	1577.61	−0.5	1585.18	1583.26	1592.32	1631.77	4.58	1.78	15.34	51.24	932.90
30 CONSUMER GOODS(92)	3458.19	−0.4	3472.00	3430.23	3389.64	2790.25	3.86	1.76	18.38	117.55	1248.60
31 Breweries(18)	2680.93	......	2679.82	2640.76	2608.23	2228.28	3.71	1.99	16.89	62.79	1254.08
32 Spirits, Wines & Ciders(10)	2985.89	+0.1	2983.28	2930.63	2877.62	2877.20	4.00	1.84	16.94	106.86	1049.87
33 Food Producers(24)	2539.63	−0.7	2557.66	2560.81	2515.12	2317.01	3.99	1.76	17.83	80.34	1116.98
34 Household Goods(11)	2643.69	+0.6	2626.90	2572.28	2556.24	2416.12	3.60	2.05	16.89	59.15	980.68
36 Health Care(17)	2011.40	−1.2	2036.62	2034.60	2019.80	1639.93	2.59	1.82	26.50	48.10	1206.42
37 Pharmaceuticals(11)	4550.71	−0.4	4566.90	4501.52	4459.50	3081.89	3.55	1.57	22.36	153.87	1517.33
38 Tobacco(1)	4646.28	−1.2	4701.34	4620.87	4608.16	3854.79	5.16	1.90	12.77	229.23	1124.07
40 SERVICES(226)	2182.57	−0.5	2193.35	2165.35	2138.84	1919.34	3.05	2.07	19.81	58.07	1113.42
41 Distributors(30)	2708.14	−0.5	2721.68	2713.91	2705.45	2562.90	3.66	1.75	19.50	73.32	975.15
42 Leisure & Hotels(29)	2525.46	+0.5	2512.07	2466.69	2424.39	2082.28	3.17	1.85	21.31	73.28	1293.41
43 Media(43)	3388.94	−0.5	3405.43	3355.78	3315.36	2826.74	2.15	2.40	24.26	77.51	1211.47
44 Retailers, Food(16)	2100.99	−1.5	2132.70	2110.63	2090.51	1713.49	3.43	2.41	15.14	58.55	1306.13
45 Retailers, General(44)	1795.50	−0.9	1811.62	1788.41	1760.78	1655.46	3.26	2.17	17.71	48.43	1005.90
48 Support Services(37)	1858.15	+0.1	1855.55	1833.41	1825.22	1509.63	2.46	2.44	20.87	34.98	1163.17
49 Transport(20)	2202.28	+0.1	2199.84	2176.63	2150.54	2272.42	3.91	1.29	24.84	72.68	898.78
51 Other Services & Business(7)	1204.46	+0.1	1203.48	1202.33	1202.72	1252.76	4.22	1.43	20.70	38.30	1078.33
60 UTILITIES(36)	2527.94	+0.1	2525.03	2523.70	2498.25	2425.70	4.51	2.01	13.80	95.19	1032.59
62 Electricity(14)	2797.16	+0.2	2792.23	2778.16	2751.84	2459.45	3.98	2.92	10.75	116.18	1244.61
64 Gas Distribution(2)	1618.89	−3.2	1672.90	1656.42	1634.02	1934.57	7.40	0.65	26.03	119.82	812.22
66 Telecommunications(7)	2125.14	+1.1	2102.81	2106.81	2078.09	2083.30	3.86	1.71	18.96	51.48	945.22
68 Water(13)	2088.55	−0.3	2095.85	2114.04	2119.81	1890.33	5.49	2.75	8.29	85.07	1110.06
69 NON-FINANCIALS(655)	1858.90	−0.3	1863.81	1849.58	1830.76	1674.42	3.83	1.92	16.99	62.01	1375.72
70 FINANCIALS(113)	2726.70	−0.2	2732.20	2681.43	2639.46	2182.13	4.08	2.45	12.49	101.82	1137.78
71 Banks, Retail(9)	3827.58	−0.4	3843.87	3748.32	3679.75	2851.96	3.80	2.82	11.67	140.81	1207.22
72 Banks, Merchant(6)	3640.31	−0.1	3645.37	3494.03	3485.91	2749.04	2.55	2.74	17.90	91.76	1136.98
73 Insurance(25)	1360.61	+0.5	1353.46	1331.40	1299.69	1270.88	5.42	2.69	8.59	64.55	990.85
74 Life Assurance(6)	3111.60	......	3111.29	3086.51	3023.82	2364.50	4.48	1.53	18.17	136.72	1267.67
77 Other Financial(22)	2394.10	+0.3	2386.14	2370.49	2348.86	1834.70	3.69	1.95	17.43	62.49	1333.68
79 Property(45)	1388.96	−0.4	1394.39	1400.53	1409.71	1480.35	4.45	1.34	21.01	46.36	832.38
80 INVESTMENT TRUSTS(133)	2940.13	−0.2	2947.28	2923.04	2901.37	2778.43	2.23	1.07	52.65	53.40	1012.86
89 FT-SE-A ALL-SHARE(901)	1749.74	−0.3	1754.15	1737.42	1718.30	1548.45	3.81	2.00	16.38	58.62	1441.55
FT-SE-A Fledgling	1075.46	+0.1	1074.79	1071.41	1068.01	−	2.83	1.23	35.86	25.40	1102.97
FT-SE-A Fledgling ex Inv Trusts	1073.34	+0.1	1072.66	1069.38	1065.81	−	2.98	1.28	32.74	26.43	1102.03

Fig. 6.3 FT-SE Actuaries share indices (daily)

largest UK companies in terms of market capitalisation and represents over 70 per cent of the total All-Share market capitalisation.

- **FT-SE Mid 250:** an index of the next 250 companies in market capitalisation, those directly beneath the FT-SE 100. These are companies capitalised at between £250 million and £1 billion, in total around 20 per cent of overall market capitalisation. It is calculated on two formats, one that includes and one that excludes investment trusts.

- **FT-SE-A 350:** the combination of the FT-SE 100 and the FT-SE Mid 250.

- **FT-SE-A 350 Higher and Lower Yield:** these two indices, introduced at the beginning of 1995, are calculated by a quarterly descending ranking of the 350 companies by the size of their annual dividend yield, and then their division into two equal halves as measured by total capitalisation of the 350 companies.

- **FT-SE SmallCap:** the 500 to 600 companies capitalised at between £40 million and £250 million, including the smallest 450 in the All-Share index. Like the Mid 250, this index is again calculated on two formats.

- **Industrial group:** aggregate performance measures for key industrial sectors, providing investors with a valuable yardstick for assessing the performance of a stock relative to its sector. The group comprises Mineral Extraction, General Industrials, Consumer Goods, Services and Utilities, each of which is further broken down into various sub-sectors. The sub-sectors are broken down into their constituent companies in the London share service.

- **Non-financials:** formerly known as the FT "500", this includes all companies except financial and property companies and investment trusts, and now comprises over 650 companies.

- **Financials and Investment trusts:** financial and property companies broken down into six sub-sectors plus investment trusts (see chapter 8).

- **FT-SE-A All-Share index:** the full 900-plus companies capitalised at over £40 million. Introduced on a daily basis in 1962, it is far more representative than the FT index. Its mathematical structure makes

it a reliable yardstick against which to measure portfolio performance, and hence it represents an essential tool for professional investment managers.

- **FT-SE-A Fledgling:** another index launched at the beginning of 1995, this was introduced to indicate the Stock Exchange's concern for smaller companies. It includes the over 800 companies that fail to qualify for the All-Share index (including shares quoted on the AIM), representing 1–2 per cent of total market capitalisation. It is calculated on two formats, one that includes and one that excludes investment trusts.

- **All indices:** the UK Series lists yesterday's closing value for each index as well as the percentage change on the previous day, the three previous days' closing values and the value of the index one year ago. The further performance indicators of dividend yield, net dividend cover and price/earnings ratio for each index are also provided. Sector values for these ratios can be used as benchmarks for the performance of individual stocks within a sector.

- **Ex-dividend adjustment year to date:** when a share goes ex-dividend, all else being equal, its price will drop by the amount of the dividend per share. This is the ex-dividend adjustment. The figure in the indices is the cumulative total of the aggregate of the gross ex-dividend adjustments multiplied by the relevant number of shares in issue. It allows the investor to assess the flow of income on a portfolio over the year.

- **Total return:** calculated at the close of each trading day, total return figures reflect both the price and dividend performance of stocks. The index starts the year at 1,000 and incorporates share price appreciation for the year plus ex-dividend adjustment year to date, assuming that dividends are reinvested.

Using the information

The Footsie is calculated from the price movements of the 100 largest UK companies by market capitalisation. Since it incorporates fewer companies than the All-Share index, it can be calculated more rapidly and frequently. The Footsie was the first real-time index in

the UK and was introduced mainly as a basis for dealing in equity index options and futures (see chapter 12). It rapidly became a key indicator of the stock market's mood, not least because it is quoted widely throughout the day. In many respects, the market thinks in terms of the Footsie figures with particular points being seen as psychological watersheds. For example:

> The UK equity market yesterday blasted through its all-time intra-day high point, ended the day at a record closing peak and looked set to penetrate the 3,600 level for the first time.
> (*Financial Times*, 19 October 1995)

The blue chip FT-SE 100 constituents (listed in appendix 2) are mostly multinationals and companies with strong overseas interests, while the FT-SE Mid 250 are mainly strongly UK orientated companies. As a result, the former are likely to be more influenced by overseas factors such as exchange rate movements, while the latter may be influenced more by domestic factors such as interest rate movements.

The FT All-Share accurately reflects the whole market. With over 900 constituents, it has a very broad coverage, encompassing 98 per cent of the market's aggregate capitalisation with each company weighted according to its market value so that a move in the price of a large company has more effect than that of a small one. It can be used as a measure of the market's performance over long periods. It serves as a reliable yardstick against which to assess portfolio performance. As a weighted arithmetic index it is designed to behave as an actual portfolio would behave.

The breakdown into industry groups allows investors to track the performance of particular sectors. This is of great assistance to specialist sector analysts, as well as allowing more general investors to improve their understanding of the structure of the market as a whole. Industrial classification is highly important since it is normally accepted by the stock market and institutional research departments as the basis for the analysis of companies. Correctly classifying all companies traded on the London market is the responsibility of the FT-SE Actuaries Industry Classification Committee, made up of market practitioners, investment managers and actuaries.

Institutional investors attempt to beat the index most relevant to their portfolio. Increasingly, investors want a set of indices that covers the entire equity capital structure of the UK market so that they can accurately assess the performance of large, medium and small companies within the framework of the whole market. There has also been a growing interest in the performance of medium-sized companies. The newer indices increase the visibility of many medium and small companies.

The FT-SE Actuaries 350 provides a real-time measure covering around 90 per cent of the UK equity market by value. The SmallCap and Fledgling indices are higher risk but likely to boom in a recovery. They are good for the visibility and marketability of smaller companies. Beyond the markets covered by the All-Share and Fledgling indices is OFEX, a new unregulated off-exchange dealing facility for companies not eligible for the AIM or the index. It is offered by the broker JP Jenkins Ltd.

Evaluating quarterly performance

The quarterly valuation (see Figure 6.4) surveys the market capitalisation of the FT-SE Actuaries share indices over the preceding three quarters.

- **Market capitalisation:** comparative figures for the past three quarters of the market capitalisation of the various sectors and indices that make up the All-Share index.

- **Percentage of All-Share index:** the proportion of the All-Share index that each sector and index took up at the end of each of the past three quarters.

Key indicators

A snapshot of recent price and trading activity in the equities market is provided by the graphs and key indicators published daily on the back page of the newspaper's second section (see Figure 6.5).

- **FT-SE-A All-Share index:** this index provides investors with an instant overview of movements in the UK equity market over several months. It moves more sluggishly than the FT-30 index because it has a large number of comparatively inactive constituents which lag behind the market leaders. Graphs featuring the performances of individual share prices relative to the All-Share index or the Footsie also appear frequently in the newspaper, usually linked to a news

FT - SE Actuaries Share Indices - Quarterly Valuation

	Market cap. as at 29/9/95 (£m)	% of All-Share index	Market cap. as at 30/6/95 (£m)	% of All-Share index	Market cap. as at 31/3/95 (£m)	% of All-Share index
FT-SE 100†	582,826.98	71.48	543,966.62	71.50	513,554.33	71.59
FT-SE Mid 250†	170,624.77	20.92	157,352.94	20.69	148,745.77	20.73
FT-SE Mid 250 ex. Inv. Trusts†	153,189.49	18.79	140,738.01	18.50	133,076.30	18.55
FT-SE A 350†	753,451.75	92.40	701,319.56	92.19	662,300.10	92.32
FT-SE A 350 Higher Yield†	380,352.50	46.64	377,727.05	49.65	356,554.82	49.70
FT-SE A 350 Lower Yield†	373,099.26	45.76	323,592.51	42.54	305,745.28	42.62
FT-SE SmallCap†	61,970.38	7.60	59,385.68	7.81	55,122.23	7.68
FT-SE SmallCap ex Inv. Trusts†	51,847.70	6.36	50,005.25	6.57	46,539.66	6.49
FT-SE-A ALL-SHARE	815,422.13	100.00	760,705.24	100.00	717,422.33	100.00
10 MINERAL EXTRACTION (24)	70,218.51	8.61	67,851.00	8.92	64,542.72	9.00
12 Extractive Industries (7)	12,151.23	1.49	10,890.93	1.43	10,558.88	1.47
15 Oil, Integrated (3)	53,004.12	6.50	51,642.82	6.79	48,898.42	6.82
16 Oil Exploration & Prod (14)	5,063.16	0.62	5,317.25	0.70	5,085.42	0.71
20 GEN MANUFACTURERS (279)	153,411.36	18.81	147,004.03	19.32	141,075.02	19.66
21 Building & Construction (38)	5,757.65	0.71	5,817.63	0.76	5,977.68	0.83
22 Building Matls & Merchs (31)	19,851.26	2.43	19,038.65	2.50	19,359.34	2.70
23 Chemicals (23)	18,455.86	2.26	18,112.65	2.38	15,966.75	2.23
24 Diversified Industrials (18)	35,334.42	4.33	35,173.52	4.64	35,841.26	4.99
25 Electronic & Elect Equip (36)	17,478.61	2.14	16,299.43	2.14	16,193.92	2.26
26 Engineering (72)	32,187.75	3.95	29,311.88	3.85	25,986.00	3.62
27 Engineering, Vehicles (13)	8,311.46	1.02	6,991.20	0.92	6,594.83	0.92
28 Paper, Pckg & Printing (27)	11,726.95	1.44	12,044.94	1.58	11,057.25	1.54
29 Textiles & Apparel (21)	4,307.40	0.53	4,214.13	0.55	4,097.99	0.57
30 CONSUMER GOODS (93)	156,843.63	19.23	147,948.23	19.45	136,415.77	19.01
31 Breweries (18)	15,954.05	1.96	14,566.93	1.91	13,680.16	1.91
32 Spirits, Wines & Ciders (10)	27,086.78	3.32	24,796.42	3.26	24,675.03	3.44
33 Food Producers (24)	28,755.13	3.53	28,508.70	3.75	26,921.99	3.75
34 Household Goods (10)	4,021.30	0.49	3,679.73	0.48	3,491.74	0.49
36 Health Care (17)	5,755.13	0.71	5,113.02	0.67	5,167.56	0.72
37 Pharmaceuticals (12)	58,951.16	7.22	55,212.15	7.27	48,020.18	6.68
38 Tobacco (2)	16,320.08	2.00	16,071.28	2.11	14,459.11	2.02
40 SERVICES (228)	167,812.75	20.59	149,773.25	19.69	142,034.85	19.81
41 Distributors (32)	8,003.48	0.98	7,301.42	0.96	6,688.00	0.93
42 Leisure & Hotels (29)	22,965.80	2.82	21,144.13	2.78	19,745.26	2.75
43 Media (43)	37,778.33	4.63	28,914.23	3.80	26,550.53	3.70
44 Retailers, Food (16)	25,378.96	3.11	24,402.08	3.21	22,220.21	3.10
45 Retailers, General (44)	43,040.51	5.29	38,670.29	5.09	38,460.75	5.37
48 Support Services (37)	11,718.00	1.44	10,218.06	1.34	9,394.75	1.31
49 Transport (20)	18,266.68	2.24	18,486.02	2.43	18,338.71	2.56
51 Other Services & Business (7)	660.99	0.08	637.03	0.08	636.64	0.09
60 UTILITIES (38)	102,371.32	12.55	96,500.26	12.69	91,435.15	12.74
62 Electricity (17)	29,888.70	3.67	26,669.21	3.51	25,032.71	3.49
64 Gas Distribution (2)	12,066.49	1.48	13,089.51	1.72	12,935.06	1.80
66 Telecommunications (6)	46,488.83	5.69	43,818.62	5.76	41,132.83	5.73
68 Water (13)	13,927.30	1.71	12,922.92	1.70	12,334.55	1.72
69 NON-FINANCIALS (662)	650,657.57	79.79	609,076.77	80.07	575,503.51	80.22
70 FINANCIALS (117)	135,105.28	16.57	123,787.25	16.27	115,916.53	16.16
71 Banks, Retail (9)	77,623.92	9.53	68,959.28	9.05	63,892.13	8.91
72 Banks, Maerchant (8)	3,855.79	0.47	5,849.01	0.77	5,486.05	0.77
73 Insurance (26)	16,658.26	2.04	16,101.87	2.12	15,304.05	2.13
74 Life Assurance (6)	14,009.21	1.72	11,479.20	1.51	10,535.99	1.47
77 Other Financial (22)	9,009.80	1.10	6,898.57	0.91	6,756.14	0.94
79 Property (46)	13,948.30	1.71	14,499.32	1.91	13,942.17	1.94
80 INVESTMENT TRUSTS (134)	29,659.28	3.64	27,841.22	3.66	26,002.29	3.62
89 FT-SE-A ALL-SHARE (913)	815,422.13	100.00	760,705.24	100.00	717,422.33	100.00
FT-SE-A Fledgling	14,695.99	-	13,516.69	-	12,657.30	-
FT-SE-A Fledgling ex Inv Tst	12,318.12	-	11,246.42	-	10,554.71	-

† Figures rounded due to slight pricing inconsistencies.

Fig. 6.4 FT-SE Actuaries share indices (quarterly valuation)

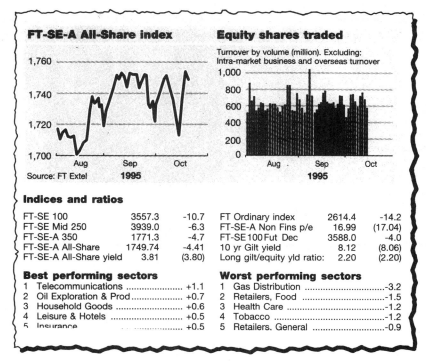

Fig. 6.5 Key indicators

item or comment in the Lex column. These "price relatives" are very valuable for comparing share performances and for assessing individual price patterns independent of overall market movements.

- **Equity shares traded:** the volume of shares traded over the same period, excluding intra-market and overseas turnover.

- **Indices, ratios and sectors:** easy reference for a number of leading market indices and ratios, plus the five best and worst performing sectors and their percentage rises and falls.

Hourly movements and industry baskets

An hourly breakdown of the previous day's trading in the UK equities market is also recorded in the share indices (see Figure 6.6).

- **Hourly movements:** the values of the key indices at hourly intervals throughout the previous day's trading, plus their highs and lows for the day. These are what are known as intra-day values.

FT - SE Actuaries Share Indices   The UK Series

■ **Hourly movements**

	Open	9.00	10.00	11.00	12.00	13.00	14.00	15.00	16.10	High/day	Low/d
FT-SE 100	3475.7	3471.9	3459.1	3468.0	3468.3	3468.0	3472.0	3476.8	3471.3	3480.9	3457.
FT-SE Mid 250	3909.0	3908.4	3912.0	3914.9	3916.9	3917.0	3917.7	3920.2	3919.7	3920.3	3906.
FT-SE-A 350	1736.7	1735.2	1730.6	1734.3	1734.6	1734.5	1736.2	1738.3	1736.1	1739.8	1730.

Time of FT-SE 100 Day's high: 2.43pm Day's low: 10.16am . FT-SE 100 1995 High: 3570.8 (13/9) Low: 2954.2 (23/1).

■ **FT-SE Actuaries 350 Industry baskets**

	Open	9.00	10.00	11.00	12.00	13.00	14.00	15.00	16.10	Close	Previous	Chan
Bldg & Cnstrcn	907.5	906.4	908.0	908.0	908.9	910.2	910.2	910.2	909.5	909.5	905.9	+3.
Pharmaceuticls	4414.4	4404.2	4400.0	4406.7	4409.1	4408.8	4415.6	4420.7	4403.3	4407.4	4387.8	+19.
Water	2131.1	2129.5	2121.6	2122.5	2123.0	2121.9	2119.3	2119.1	2115.3	2115.9	2126.1	-10.
Banks, Retail	3696.2	3707.9	3683.9	3705.1	3709.9	3720.1	3719.4	3724.4	3723.9	3726.7	3673.9	+52.

Fig. 6.6 FT-SE Actuaries share indices (daily)

- **FT-SE Actuaries 350 industry baskets:** the real-time industry sector indices for Building and Construction, Pharmaceuticals, Water and Retail Banks, a representative selection of baskets. These provide an instant view of industry performance across the market and enable investors to react quickly to industry-wide news and events.

Highs, lows and base dates

Saturday's edition of the *Financial Times* carries an expanded table of the FT-SE Actuaries All-Share index (see Figure 6.7):

- **Highs and lows:** the highs and lows for each index both for the current year and for the whole period since the FT-SE Actuaries series was started in 1962. The latter are loosely termed "all-time" highs and lows.

- **Equity section or group, base date and value:** details of the starting date and base value for each sector. Over time, as the structure of UK industry has shifted, it has been necessary to amalgamate sectors and create new ones. For example, Radio and TV, Teas and Diamonds have gone, while Health Care, Media and Electricity have been formed. When a new group is created, its initial value is set at the level of its immediate predecessor.

FT - SE Actuaries Share Indices | The UK Series

	Oct 6	Day's chge%
FT-SE 100	3526.5	−0.5
FT-SE Mid 250	3979.0	−0.3
FT-SE Mid 250 ex Inv Trusts	4003.8	−0.4
FT-SE-A 350	1763.4	−0.5
FT-SE-A 350 Higher Yield	1751.8	−0.5
FT-SE-A 350 Lower Yield	1780.0	−0.4
FT-SE SmallCap	1976.61	+0.1
FT-SE SmallCap ex Inv Trusts	1962.20	+0.1
FT-SE-A ALL-SHARE	1743.38	−0.4

	1995 High		Low		Since Compilation High		Low	
3570.8	13/9	2954.2	23/1	3570.8	13/9/95	986.9	23/7/84
3991.3	5/10	3300.9	8/3	4152.8	3/2/94	1379.4	21/1/86
4018.1	5/10	3306.4	8/3	4160.7	19/1/94	1378.3	21/1/86
1778.3	13/9	1482.4	23/1	1778.3	2/2/94	664.5	14/1/86
1761.8	13/9	1507.7	9/3	1778.3	2/2/94	100.0	14/12/94
1799.9	13/9	1454.9	23/1	1799.9	13/9/95	100.0	14/12/94
1993.11	11/9	1678.61	13/3	2094.98	4/2/94	1363.79	31/12/92
1972.36	11/9	1658.18	13/3	2060.72	4/2/94	1363.79	31/12/92
1757.58	13/9	1469.23	23/1	1764.11	2/2/94	61.92	13/12/74

Equity section or group	Base date	Base value
FT-SE 100	31/12/83	1000.00
FT-SE Mid 250 & ex I.T.s	31/12/85	1412.60
FT-SE-A 350	31/12/85	682.94
FT-SE-A 350 Higher Yield	31/12/85	682.94
FT-SE-A 350 Lower Yield	31/12/85	682.94

Equity section or group	Base date	Base value
Electricity	31/12/90	1000.00
Water	29/12/89	1000.00
Non-Financials	10/4/62	100.00
FT-SE-A All-Share	10/4/62	100.00
All Other	31/12/85	1000.00

Fig. 6.7 FT-SE Actuaries share indices (weekly)

Leaders and laggards

Saturday's newspaper also includes leaders and laggards, a table of notable performances, either good or bad, listing percentage changes in value in the current year for various indices (see Figure 6.8).

- **Index:** the percentage changes in the year in various detailed markets and subsections of the FT-SE Actuaries indices. Based on the preceding Friday's closing prices, FT and sector indices are ranked in order of percentage increase in value in the current year to date.

A further weekly table, published on Monday, collects the previous five days' values (plus this year's highs and lows, and highs and lows since compilation began) for all stock indices: the FT-SE Actuaries indices, the FT indices and the Eurotrack indices (see below). A monthly table brings together monthly averages for these indices for each of the last four months, plus the highest and lowest closing value for the main ones in the preceding month.

FT-SE-A INDICES - LEADERS & LAGGARDS

Percentage changes since December 30 1994 based on Friday October 6 1995

Pharmaceuticals ....+38.97	Insurance .... +16.03	Investment Trusts ....+9.29
Health Care ....+29.91	FT-SE 100 ....+15.04	Gen Industrials ....+9.15
Life Assurance ....+29.50	Services ....+14.94	Chemicals ....+8.94
Support Services ....+27.28	FT-SE-A 350 ....+14.71	Food Producers ....+8.12
Tobacco ....+26.66	FT-SE-A All-Share ....+14.59	FT-SE-A Fledgling ....+7.79
Banks, Retail ....+26.48	FT-SE SmallCap ex ITs ....+14.36	Electricity ....+7.54
Engineering ....+22.91	FT-SE Mid 250 ex ITs ......+14.24	Spirits, Wines & Ciders ......+7.53
Engineering, Vehicles ......+22.86	FT-SE Mid 250 ....+13.63	FT-SE-A Fledgling ex ITs ...+7.49
Consumer Goods ....+22.72	Retailers, General ....+13.36	Paper, Pckg & Printing ......+6.72
Financials ....+22.43	Non-Financials ....+13.30	Utilities ....+6.11
Banks, Merchant ....+22.42	FT-SE SmallCap ....+13.18	Textiles & Apparel ....+5.89
Retailers, Food ....+20.55	FT-SE-A 350 Higher Yld ..+12.47	Oil Exploration & Prod ....+2.69
Breweries ....+20.09	Extractive Industries ....+11.82	Property ....+2.04
Media ....+19.19	Oil, Integrated ....+10.99	Diversified Industrials ....+1.55
Electronic & Elect Equip ...+18.96	Distributors ....+10.71	Transport ....-0.49
Water ....+18.03	Mineral Extraction ....+10.50	Building Matls ....-1.34
FT-SE-A 350 Lower Yld ...+17.33	Telecommunications ....+9.57	Building & Construction ......-5.58
Leisure & Hotels ....+16.60	Household Goods ....+9.54	Gas Distribution ....-17.09

Fig. 6.8 FT-SE-A indices: leaders and laggards

Eurotrack indices

A summary of current performance in the European equities markets is provided by the European Series indices (see Figure 6.9), tracking a sample of major continental companies and providing a basis for derivative contracts.

● **FT-SE Eurotrack 100:** yesterday's hourly changes and high and low for the day, and the previous five trading days' closing values of an index monitoring 100 major companies in continental Europe. This index was launched on 26 October 1990 with a base value of 1,000. In 1991, LIFFE issued options on the index. It is based on the prices of constituent companies, London dealings only, not those of

FT-SE Actuaries Share Indices

Oct 12   THE EUROPEAN SERIES

Hourly changes	Open	11.30	12.00	12.30	13.00	14.00	15.00	Close
FT-SE Eurotrack 100	1403.02	1404.14	1404.30	1403.43	1403.59	1403.79	1404.69	1405.03
FT-SE Eurotrack 200	1511.02	1512.75	1511.49	1511.71	1512.24	1510.79	1513.47	1514.08

	Oct 11	Oct 10	Oct 9	Oct 6	Oct 5
FT-SE Eurotrack 100	1396.12	1377.54	1398.45	1401.61	1422.43
FT-SE Eurotrack 200	1508.53	1493.62	1517.79	1524.49	1541.57

Base 1000 (26/10/90); High/day: 100 - 1405.58; 200 - 1514.77 Low/day: 100 - 1402.63 200 - 1510.06 † Partial

Fig. 6.9 FT-SE Actuaries share indices: the European series

the home markets, and is intended to reflect the role of the London market as the leading international market in European shares.

- **FT-SE Eurotrack 200:** an index of 100 UK and 100 continental European stocks, with all its constituents traded in a single financial centre, London. Launched on 25 February 1991, the index combines the stocks in the UK Footsie with those in the Eurotrack 100.

By bringing together the United Kingdom and continental Europe, the Eurotrack 200 provides the investment community with an instant overview of securities trading throughout Europe. Continuous real-time prices from the Stock Exchange's SEAQ and SEAQ International allow the Eurotrack 200 to operate without interruption throughout the trading day and provide a means of measuring the performance of European financial markets. This leads to international equities, the subject of the next chapter.

"In London and New York share prices get out of line in value, but in other places they get even further out of line. You get better bargains in addition to more bargains by looking world-wide."

SIR JOHN TEMPLETON

"A random walk down Wall Street."

BURTON MALKIEL

7

INTERNATIONAL EQUITIES
The world stock markets

- **World stock markets** – share price movements on leading global markets

- **US markets** – the dominant world exchanges: the New York Stock Exchange; AMEX, NASDAQ and other US exchanges

- **International equity indices** – the standard performance measures of the world's stock markets: US equity indices; other international indices

- **The FT/S&P Actuaries World Indices** – reading the figures and using the information for these global market indicators: markets in perspective; evaluating quarterly performance

- **International equity investing** – emerging markets

The abolition of exchange control restrictions and the widespread deregulation of financial markets have made possible the globalisation of trading in equities. This has led to an upsurge in the buying and selling of shares across national boundaries. In the United Kingdom, the removal of exchange controls in 1979 led to a massive upsurge in foreign investment. During the 1980s, an increasing proportion of Japan's enormous capital surplus was for the first time being directed towards the world's equity markets. In the United States, fund managers had long taken an excessively parochial view but had made cautious moves towards greater foreign equity investment. This pace has quickened in recent years.

London remains a pivotal point in the global equity market, but it is just one market, albeit in a favourable time zone. For many years, New York has been attracting more equity business, and for a while Japan outstripped the United States in terms of market capitalisation before Tokyo's major shakeout in 1990.

WORLD STOCK MARKETS

The International Companies and Finance pages of the *Financial Times* contain the bulk of global corporate news: financial results, whether quarterly, half-yearly or annual; essential developments in bids and deals; new or revised funding arrangements; changes to shareholding structures; joint ventures; or new products or production processes. In fact they contain anything that is valuable for an accurate and timely assessment of trends and prospects for shareholders and potential investors alike.

The reports attempt to cover all companies in the FT-S&P Actuaries world indices, plus many more that are heavily traded and might have an historical relationship with the United Kingdom or with UK companies, such as those in the old Commonwealth or the Americas.

World stock price listings in the UK edition of the newspaper cover over 2,000 shares, a little over a third being US shares from the two New York exchanges (the NYSE and the American) and the national screen-based trading market (NASDAQ), and just under a quarter from Japan. The other world markets covered are Austria, Belgium and Luxembourg, Denmark, Finland, France, Germany, Italy, the Netherlands, Norway, Spain, Sweden, Switzerland, Australia, Hong Kong, Malaysia, Singapore, Canada's Toronto market and South Africa. Figure 7.1 provides examples.

● **National markets:** share prices in local currency, changes on the previous trading day, highs and lows for the year, gross dividend yields and price/earnings ratios, if available.

International editions of the newspaper expand on the coverage for these countries (notably the United States), and add listings for the Czech Republic, Greece, Poland, Portugal, Turkey, Indonesia, New Zealand, South Korea, Taiwan, Thailand and Canadian listings in Montreal. There is also a special table with the previous day's ten most active stocks in Tokyo. The prices for all national markets are as quoted on the individual exchanges and are mostly last traded prices. Highs and lows are for the year except for Toronto and Montreal which are the day's high and low.

Nowadays it is much easier to deal in foreign shares, and, because of market interactions, it is important to understand these markets. One problem for international investors is the unreliability of indicators such as price/earnings ratios for the purposes of international comparison. Different countries employ different accounting conventions, and therefore often differ in their treatment of the earnings component of such ratios.

US MARKETS

The *Financial Times* provides extensive coverage of the US stock markets, particularly in its international editions. These feature a complete listing of all shares (or common stocks as they are known in

WORLD STOCK MARKETS

/E			+/−	High	Low	Yld	P/E
6	NatBkC	11¾	....	12	8½	3.4	9.6
..	Newbdg	36⅛	+½	60¾	34	....	16.1
6	Noma A	5⅝	....	6⅛	4⅜	2.1	13.7
3	NrndaM	26¼	+⅛	30	21½	3.8	12.1
0	NorcnE	17¾	....	20⅞	15¼	3.4	11.2
1	NthTel	45½	....	56	44	1.3	20.1
	Nova	10⅝	+⅛	13¾	10¼	3.0	6.2
..	Nowsco	16	−½	17	12⅛	2.2	11.9
6	NumacE	5¾	+⅛	8⅛	5½	....	24.0
8	OshawA	22⅜	−¼	22¾	18	2.3	14.7
9	PanCnP	47½	+¼	54	37	1.7	19.9
2	Pgasus	17½	−¼	19⅜	13½	....	....
5	PtCnlR	6⅜	−⅛	7¼	6⅛	....	....
7	PlDome	32	−½	40	26	1.3	....
1	PowrCp	20⅛	+⅛	22⅞	17¼	3.5	12.8
7	PowrFn	31½	−¼	34¼	27¼	4.0	10.0
5	Prvigo	8⅝	−⅛	8¾	4⅞	....	7.8
..	Quebec	20	....	20½	17¾	6.3	11.4
3	RngOil	8	+⅛	10⅛	7⅛	1.3	....
9	ReedSt	31⅛	+⅝	35½	26	0.4	14.9
6	Ren En	30⅜	+⅝	32	23¼	....	43.4
	Repap	8¼	....	12¼	6½	....	39.3
7	Rigel	13	+⅛	16	11½	....	24.1
3	RioAlg	26¼	....	29⅝	22¾	2.3	11.1
9	RogCmB	13⅜	+⅛	18⅞	12⅜	....	7.1
1	RoyBkC	31	+¼	31¼	25⅞	4.0	9.1
8	RoyOak	5⅜	−⅛	6⅛	4	....	38.4
3	StLwrA	8⅛	....	11½	8	2.5	23.9
..	SceptR	7¾	....	10¾	7½	....	24.2
4	ScottH	8⅞	−⅛	10	6⅞	2.9	16.1
2	Seagrm	48¼	−¼	52	35½	1.7	3.4
5	SearsC	7¾	+⅛	8½	6¾	3.1	17.6
7	ShellA	41¼	−⅜	46¼	39½	3.2	8.5
6	SHL Sy	17	+⅛	17¼	7	....	....
9	Southm	14⅝	+⅛	16½	12⅜	1.4	22.5
	SparAe	14	−⅜	15¾	9¼	1.7	19.4
1	Stelco	5¾	+⅛	8½	5½	....	3.2
2	TVX Go	9¼	−⅝	11⅜	8⅛	....	44.8
3	TalisE	24⅜	−⅜	28¾	20½	0.8	33.4
0	Teck B	26⅜	−⅛	29¼	21⅞	0.8	28.4
..	Telus	16¾	+⅛	17⅛	14¾	5.5	11.4
7	Thomsn	18	+⅛	19½	16⅜	0.8	19.1
8	TorDom	23⅞	....	24⅜	19½	3.7	9.9
1	TrscnP	17⅞	−¼	18⅞	16½	5.6	10.8
5	Trnslt	14⅝	....	14¾	13	6.7	12.7
9	Trimac	12⅛	+⅛	13⅞	10	1.5	13.8
3	Trizec	10¼	....	11⅜	8⅝	....	27.6
9	UtdDom	31¼	−¼	34¼	24½	0.9	12.9
4	Westcs	20¼	−⅛	22¾	19¾	4.5	11.7
	WestnG	47¾	+⅛	49	39¼	1.5	14.2

3 4 3 4 2 5 4 9 8

EUROPE

AUSTRIA (Oct 16 / Sch)

/E			+/−	High	Low	Yld	P/E
8	AusAir	1,700	+65	2,055	1,325	2.9	....
..	BkAust	817	−3	892	702	1.2	....
5	BUAG	752	−1	756	559	....	....
2	CredPf	482	−18	637	482	2.1	....
1	EA Gen	2,660	−20	3,335	2,490	0.6	....
7	EVN	1,115	−20	1,430	1,115	2.1	....
	Lenzng	841	−17	986	762	1.2	....
8	Mayr−M	637	−7	685	550	2.2	....
2	OMV	877	−23	1,139	872	1.7	....
3	PerlZm	815	....	920	700	2.5	....
8	RadexH	314	−1	410	298	3.2	....
4	SteyrD	170	....	200	136	3.5	....
5	VA Tec	1,116	−39	1,283	973	2.2	....
0	VeitMg	215	+9	337	206	2.8	....
4	VbdBrA	582	−4	745	562	2.7	....
5	VnlAir	637	+14	662	421	1.3	....
4	VA Stl	307	+4	331	301	....	....
6	Wienbg	2,010	−55	2,718	2,010	2.1	....

BELGIUM/LUXEMBOURG (Oct 16 / Frs.)

		+/−	High	Low	Yld	P/E
Ackmns	4,875	+70	4,875	3,660	1.5	....
Almnij	7,930	+30	8,190	7,100	3.1	....
Arbed	3,365	−15	4,970	3,310	....	....
BBL	4,780	+75	5,040	3,800	4.5	....
BkInLx	17,650	+15	18,250	15,775	2.5	....
BGnLPt	26,700	−200	26,800	21,025	3.7	....
BnqNtB	38,525	−450	39,250	34,100	5.7	....
Barco	3,380	+20	3,650	2,150	1.2	....
Bekrt	21,500	....	25,075	18,500	1.9	....
CBRCim	11,825	−25	12,100	11,200	3.3	....
CMB	2,110	+20	2,630	1,950	4.8	....
Cobepa	1,006	....	1,074	954	....	....
C'cklP	157	+1	203	145	6.6	....
Colryt	7,280	−50	8,360	5,800	1.8	....
Dlhaiz	1,164	−12	1,386	1,092	2.3	....
Electb	6,510	+20	6,540	5,590	6.4	....
ElfnAC	2,850	+10	3,135	2,475	4.8	....
Fortis	3,110	....	3,295	2,555	....	....
GBL	3,765	−45	4,050	3,200	5.2	....
GIB Gp	1,186	+32	1,440	1,090	3.3	....
GenBnq	9,170	−20	9,470	7,800	5.0	....
Gvaert	1,665	+5	1,720	1,418	2.7	....
Glvbel	3,690	....	5,000	3,570	3.0	....
Immobl	2,120	−80	2,900	2,120	7.0	....
Krdbnk	7,220	....	7,350	6,010	4.0	....
Mcnver	6,710	....	7,050	5,650	4.0	....
Ptfina	8,910	−110	9,510	7,990	3.1	....
Pwrfin	3,330	+15	3,400	2,800	4.4	....
Rcticl	348	....	466	345	5.0	....
RyBelg	5,130	−70	5,600	4,000	4.2	....
SocGnB	2,145	+20	2,320	1,805	5.3	....
Sofina	13,825	+25	14,700	12,000	4.5	....
Solvac	1,800	....	1,890	1,450	5.8	....
Solvay	15,000	....	16,725	13,200	4.5	....
Trctbl	10,700	−125	11,125	8,650	4.3	....
UCB	33,000	+125	35,200	22,800	1.8	....
UnMin	1,825	−20	2,490	1,755	6.6	....

		+/−	High	Low	Yld	P/E
Dllfus	241.10	−6.90	310	228.50	2.5	....
EauxGn	426	−12	595	424.30	4.0	....
Ecco	835	−9	885	551	2.2	....
ElfAqu	334.70	−3.30	415.80	324.50	5.7	....
ElfACt	307	−3	378	282	6.4	....
ErBSay	806	+2	824	676	5.6	....
ErBCts	727	+1	810	630	6.2	....
Essilr	900	+17	915	672	1.9	....
Eurafr	1,661	+1	1,761	1,366	4.3	....
EuRSCG	472	−5	580	435	3.8	....
EurDis	16.05	−.35	19.90	9.80	4.2	....
Finxtl	64.10	−.90	97.50	61	7.8	....
FoncLy	615	−10	814	545	3.9	....
FrmBel	4,450	+10	4,852	3,980	1.3	....
GTMEnt	322	−2	465	310	3.7	....
GalLaf	1,522	−88	2,349	1,480	1.1	....
Gaumnt	306.30	+5.30	308	237.50	0.7	....
G'phys	160.60	+.60	400	157	7.5	....
Havas	333.10	−8.20	445.90	331	3.8	....
Imetal	574	−1	630	438.10	3.3	....
ImmFr	229.10	−.90	414	195.10	9.8	....
Immbnq	695	....	865	675	8.6	....
Intbai	303	....	372	296.50	11.9	....
Intrtc	500	−7	629	489	7.0	....
LVMH	934	−9	971	777	2.0	....
Lfarge	321.10	−4.40	395.80	298.50	4.7	....
Lgardr	88	−1	127.50	82.60	4.8	....
LOreal	1,242	−31	1,345	1,041	1.5	....
Legrnd	811	−21	844	621	5.4	....
Legris	155.10	+.10	420	150.50	....	....
LyEaux	451.50	−13.50	539	408.50	3.8	....
MchlnB	208.40	−3.90	232.90	188.70	1.6	....
Moulnx	100	−1	129	97.30	6.0	....
NavMxt	718	+20	1,075	695	8.4	....
NrdEst	110	−3	148	108.10	7.5	....
Pariba	259.30	−1.40	356.70	245.50	6.9	....
ParisR	348.60	−1.40	411	311	8.6	....
Pchnln	114	+.30	163.50	108.30	4.5	....
PrnRic	291.80	−3:10	355.50	271.50	2.2	....
Peug't	666	+2	782	621	1.4	....
PinPr	1,073	....	1,165	925	3.1	....
Prom'd	1,230	−21	1,265	885	1.3	....
Radtch	248.80	−.70	592	243	6.0	....
RemyC	137	−1	198	126	5.0	....
Rnault	150.50	−2	184.60	133.20	3.5	....
RhonPA	102.10	+.40	137.50	94	4.1	....
RUclaf	778	−17	847	608	2.8	....
SILIC	668	−25	778	627	8.4	....
SGSThm	228.10	−10.90	288	119	....	....
Sagem	2,705	−20	2,900	2,412	1.2	....
StGobn	580	+2	684	563	4.0	....
StLoui	1,375	−44	1,600	1,280	4.1	....
Sanofi	309.50	−.10	312	213	2.9	....
Schndr	192.70	−1.30	275	131	....	....
Seb SA	600	−5	635	442	2.3	....
Sefimg	310	−3	381.10	266	6.9	....
Seita	168.90	+1.90	191	123.10	4.6	....
Simco	393	−4	480	372.10	7.9	....
Skis R	1,299	−1	1,658	970	2.5	....
SocGen	516	−8	608	466	4.7	....
SommrA	1,426	+1	1,978	1,320	4.0	....
SuezCi	182.20	−5.20	278	180.70	6.8	....
Synthl	327	−.80	328.80	212	1.7	....
Taittn	2,010	+10	2,745	1,990	1.6	....
Tchnip	313	−4.50	333.50	240.50	....	....
ThmCSF	99.50	−2.40	164.90	96	3.0	....
TotalB	294.10	−7.90	330.60	254.50	4.1	....
UAP	111.30	−3.50	151	108.20	4.0	....
UFBLoc	373.90	+.10	442	335	4.0	....
Unibai	446.10	−3.90	540	440	5.8	....
UnlmFr	424	+4	505	388	7.8	....
Usinor	79.50	−1.15	91.80	78.70	....	....
Valeo	234.10	+.10	295	209.20	1.4	....
Vallrc	210	+2	280	193	4.5	....
Worms	212.50	+4.50	272	197.10	5.6	....

GERMANY (Oct 16 / Dm.)

		+/−	High	Low	Yld	P/E
AEG	140	+1	152.50	121	1.2	....
AGIndV	34.90	+.20	51.50	34.70	34.4	....
AaMnRg	950	+10	1,120	870	1.5	....
Allnz	2,596	+3	2,761	2,206	0.6	....
Altana	820	−4	898	613	1.6	....
Asko	790	−62	940	535	1.3	....
AskoPf	750	−39	800	515	1.5	....
BASF	316	−2.30	338.50	274.50	3.2	....
Bdnwrk	503	+1	530	496	1.7	....
Bnkges	416	+2	416	314	2.6	....
Bayer	372.20	+.20	389.80	330.60	3.5	....
BayerH	34.30	−.43	41	34.12	4.2	....
BMWBr	763	−5	838	665	1.6	....
BayerV	40.35	−.20	44	38.25	....	....
B'sdor	1,030	....	1,200	955	1.6	....
BerlKr	394	−2	400	268.50	1.8	....
BHF Bk	37.90	−.55	40.25	35.25	....	....
BilfBg	591	−6	798	588	2.3	....
ColPrf	860	+7	948	633	1.5	....
ColKnz	1,155	−15	1,282	970	1.0	....
Cmmzbk	325.70	+.20	352	312	3.7	....
Contnt	21	−.28	23.40	18.60	19.0	....
DLW	340	−3	415	325	0.6	....
Daimlr	697.50	+2.70	762	597.50	1.6	....
Dgussa	456	−2	486.80	382	2.2	....
Dt Bab	143.70	−.50	205	136.50	3.5	....
DschBk	67.21	+.11	73.25	63.75	2.5	....
DidWrk	121	−2	142	105	3.3	....
Dougls	56.10	−.30	60.30	41.50	25.0	....
Drgwk	252	....	295	235	2.6	....
DrsdBk	38.70	+.20	41.85	37.25	3.5	....
GEHE	703.50	+17	705	483	1.4	....
Grrshm	266	−3	295	220	1.9	....
Gldsch	600	−20	822.20	600	2.3	....
HambEl	382	+.90	382	220	1.7	....
HeidZm	900	−27	1,124	909	1.6	....
HnkelP	536	+1	588	506	2.1	....
Hrlitz	265	−4	309.50	248	3.8	....
Hochtf	652	−16	934	652	2.1	....
H'chst	353.50	−3.20	375.80	276.50	2.8	....
Hlzmnn	590	−9	850	581	2.3	....
[illegible]	216	....	221	207.50	4.2	....

Sirti
SniaBP
TIM
Telecm
ToroAs
TosiFr
Unicem
NETHEI
ABNAm
AEGON
Ahold
AKZO N
BolsDR
BoskDF
CSM
DSM
DschPe
EVC
Elsevr
FkkDpI
FAmvD
Gamm
GBrDp
Hagm
Heinkı
HollBe
HgvDı
HunD
IHCCa
INGDı
IntMu
KLM
KNP E
KPN
KPkD
KNdly
NutrD
OceV
Philip
PolG
Robec
Rodm
Rolinc
Roren
RDutc
Storkl
TenCt
UnilDı
VNU
VOmr
VndxD
WKIDı
NORW
Aker /
Brgsn.
ChrBn
DNB A
Dynolr
Elkem.
HafNy
Kvaen
Leif H
NskHy
NSkog
OrklaA
RiebrB
RiebrA
Saga A
SagaBf
Schbst
StrliB
Unitor
Vard A
SPAIN
AGFUnI
Alba
Argntr
BBV
BCH
BExter
BPoplr
BSantd
Bnesto
CEPSA
CarbMt
Cubrts
Drgdos
EbroAg
ElVies
EndsBr
Fecsa
GrDurF
HidCan
Iberdr
Koipe
Mapfre
Mtrova
PortV
Pryca
Repsol
SNIACE
Sarrio
Sev El
TabacA
Telefn
Un Fen
Uralit
Vallhm
Viscfn

Fig. 7.1 World stock markets

the United States), including prices, volumes traded, yields and price/earnings ratios quoted on the New York Stock Exchange, together with extensive coverage of the American Stock Exchange (AMEX) and the market for over the counter stocks, the National Association of Securities Dealers Automated Quotation service (NASDAQ). The UK edition also lists details on a significant number of leading US stocks, and all editions carry the main composite indices, ratios and trading activity on the US markets.

With many major stocks traded in both London and New York, and increasing interaction between the two markets, the performance of equity prices on Wall Street can have a significant impact on prices in London, and *vice versa*. This internationalisation of major equity markets was graphically illustrated during the October 1987 crash, the impact of which spread rapidly from Wall Street to the London Stock Exchange.

The New York Stock Exchange

The New York Stock Exchange (NYSE) is the main US exchange (see Figure 7.2). It lists the largest US corporations and is known colloquially as the Big Board.

- **NYSE stocks:** each stock listing begins with information on the price highs and lows for the year to date, and the abbreviated name by which the stock is known. For example, UAL is United Airlines.

- **Dividend, yield, p/e and sales:** the last declared dividend worked out at an annual rate in dollars (dividends are usually paid quarterly); the current dividend yield, a percentage calculated as the dividend divided by the current price multiplied by 100; the price/earnings ratio, calculated as the current price divided by the current annual earnings per share; and 'Sales 100s', the volume of round lots (100 shares each) of the stock traded on the previous day.

- **Prices:** the price high and low for the day, the closing quote and the change on the previous day's closing price.

NYSE COMPOSITE PRICES

High	Low	Close Quote	Ch'ge Prev. Close
56 1/4	55 1/2	55 7/8	-3/8
u26 1/4	25 3/4	25 3/4	-1/8
17	16 1/2	16 5/8	-3/8
6 1/2	6 3/8	6 1/2	+1/8
44 3/8	44 1/8	44 1/4	-1/8
55 1/8	54 1/8	54 5/8	+5/8
62 3/8	61 3/4	61 7/8	-1/8
25 1/4	24 3/8	24 7/8	
14 7/8	13 3/4	14 7/8	+1 1/4
16 5/8	16 1/2	16 1/2	
u54 5/8	53 5/8	54 3/8	+1/8
38 3/8	38 1/8	38 1/4	-1/8
14 5/8	14 1/2	14 1/2	-1/8
10 5/8	10 3/8	10 1/2	-1/8
18 1/8	18	18 1/8	+1/8
15 3/4	15 3/4	15 3/4	
u49 3/4	48 1/4	48 1/4	-5/8
37 1/8	36 1/2	36 5/8	-1/8
17 1/2	17	17 1/4	
27 5/8	26 1/4	27 5/8	+1
36 7/8	35 3/4	36 7/8	+7/8
17 5/8	17 3/8	17 1/2	
12 1/4	12 1/8	12 1/4	+1/8
21 1/2	20 3/4	20 3/4	-5/8
25 1/4	25	25	-1/4
31 3/4	31 3/4	31 3/4	
39 3/8	38	39 1/8	+1 3/8
28 1/2	28 1/8	28 1/4	+1/8
5 5/8	5 3/8	5 3/8	-1/4
47 1/8	46 1/2	46 1/2	-3/4
14 3/8	14	14 1/4	+1/4
34 1/2	34	34 3/8	
13 1/4	13	13 1/4	+3/8
70 3/8	70 1/8	70 3/8	+1/8
37 5/8	37 3/8	37 1/2	-1/8
11 1/2	11	11 3/8	+1/4
u25 1/4	25	25	+1/4
23 3/8	23 1/4	23 1/4	-1/8
6 1/2	6 1/2	6 1/2	
24 1/4	23 3/4	24 1/4	-1/4
36 1/2	35 3/8	35 5/8	-5/8
9	d9	9	-1/4
4 1/8	4	4	
18	17 3/4	17 7/8	+1/8
u8 3/4	8 3/8	8 3/8	
9/32	d1/8	0.15	
16 1/4	15 7/8	16 1/4	+1/8
51 1/4	50 3/4	51	+3/8
50 1/2	50	50 1/8	+1/8
23 3/8	22	23	+7/8
20 1/4	19 7/8	19 7/8	-1/8
u43 1/8	42 5/8	42 7/8	+1/4
10 7/8	10 3/4	10 3/4	+1/8
u43 5/8	42 1/2	42 3/4	-7/8
29 1/4	29	29 1/4	+1/8
25 1/4	24 3/4	24 3/4	-1/4
47 3/8	46 7/8	47 3/8	-1/4
14 7/8	14 5/8	14 3/4	
41 5/8	40 3/4	41 1/8	+5/8
35 1/4	35 1/4	35 1/4	
20 3/4	20 1/2	20 5/8	-1/8
16 3/4	16 3/8	16 1/2	-1/8
18 7/8	18 5/8	18 7/8	+1/4
25 7/8	25 5/8	25 3/4	-1/8
23 3/8	23 1/8	23 1/8	-3/8
u34 1/4	34 1/8	34 1/8	+1/8
36 1/8	35 7/8	36 1/8	
22 5/8	21 3/4	22 3/8	+3/4
15 3/4	15 3/8	15 5/8	+1/4
12 5/8	12 1/4	12 3/8	-1/4
33 5/8	33 1/4	33 3/8	-1/8
8 1/2	8 1/4	8 3/8	-1/8
4	3 7/8	3 7/8	
14 1/4	13 7/8	13 7/8	-3/8
42 1/8	41 3/4	41 3/4	-3/8
38 1/2	37 1/2	38 3/8	+1/4
16 3/8	16 1/4	16 3/8	
1 5/8	1 1/2	1 1/2	-1/8
10 3/4	10 3/4	10 3/4	
37 3/8	36 3/4	36 7/8	-1/4
16 5/8	16 1/2	16 1/2	-1/8
6 1/2	6 3/8	6 3/8	
15 1/2	15 3/8	15 1/2	+1/8
33 1/4	32 7/8	32 7/8	
30 1/2	30 1/4	30 1/4	-1/8
49 1/4	48	48 1/2	
56 1/4	55 7/8	56	-1/4
22 7/8	22 7/8	22 7/8	
42 1/4	41 3/4	42	+1/8
u10 1/8	9 7/8	10	+1/4
8 3/4	8 1/2	8 3/4	+3/8
18 7/8	18 1/2	18 3/4	+3/8

1995 High	1995 Low	Stock	Div	Yld. %	P/E	Sls 100s	High	Low	Close Quote	Ch'ge Prev. Close
28 5/8	19 1/4	Taiwan Fd	0.02	0.1		201	21 1/2	21 1/8	21 1/8	-1/2
10 7/8	7 3/8	Talleyind x	0.42	5.2	33	64	8 3/8	8 1/8	8 1/4	-1/8
17 1/8	12 1/2	Talley Pf x	1.00	6.3		2	15 3/4	15 3/4	15 3/4	
48 1/8	37 7/8	Tmbrds	1.76	3.8	19	324	46 1/8	45 7/8	46	
19 3/4	10	Tandem			13	6135	12 1/4	11 3/4	12	+1/8
64 3/8	43 1/2	Tandy	0.72	1.6	14	6096	45 7/8	43 5/8	45 7/8	+1 1/4
10 1/8	9	Taurus Mun	0.64	6.3		186	u10 1/4	9 3/4	10 1/4	+1/2
3	1 3/4	TCCInd			14	6	2 5/8	2 5/8	2 5/8	
24 1/2	20	Teco Energ x	1.06	4.4	16	298	24	23 3/4	23 7/8	-1/8
61 7/8	31 3/8	Tktrnx	0.60	1.0	20	1410	58 3/4	58 3/8	58 3/4	+1/4
29 1/4	24 1/4	TeleDa	0.93	3.6	2	932	25 7/8	25 5/8	25 7/8	
27 5/8	19 3/4	Teldyn x	0.40	1.6	9	462	24 7/8	24 5/8	24 3/4	+1/4
44	33 1/4	TeleEspSA	1.19	3.1	14	765	38 1/2	37 3/4	38 3/8	+5/8
41 1/2	23	Telmex	0.87	3.2	8	16205	27 3/8	26 5/8	26 7/8	-1/4
55 3/4	41 1/2	Tmplnl	1.20	2.6	9	2899	45 3/4	45 1/4	45 3/4	+5/8
22 1/8	16 5/8	TempltEmMk	0.10	0.6		321	17 1/4	17 1/8	17 1/4	+1/8
7 1/8	6 1/4	TempltGlob x	0.60	8.6		130	u7 1/8	7	7	-1/8
7 1/4	6 3/8	TempltGIFd	0.60	8.6		917	7 1/8	7	7	-1/8
50 1/4	41 7/8	Tnneco	1.60	3.6	11	2219	44 7/8	44 1/4	44 1/2	-1/4
35 1/4	25 1/4	Teppco Pts x	2.60	7.6	11	47	34 3/8	34 1/8	34 3/8	
43	16	Teradyne			19	7272	35	32 7/8	33 7/8	+1/2
7 1/8	3 1/8	Terex	0.06	1.1	2	189	5 1/4	4 7/8	5 1/4	
14 7/8	9 3/4	Terra Inds	0.12	0.9	6	1692	13 3/8	13	13 1/4	+1/8
12	7 1/4	Tesoro			3	148	8 1/8	7 3/4	8	-1/8
69 5/8	59 3/4	Texaco x	3.20	4.7	14	3133	67 3/4	67 1/4	67 5/8	+3/8
54	30 1/8	Texas Ind x	0.40	0.8	11	96	53	52 1/2	52 5/8	-1/2
83 1/2	34 1/2	Txinst	0.68	1.1	12	27149	65 3/8	62	62 1/2	-3
28 3/4	17	Texas Pac	0.40	1.7	19	7	23 7/8	23 3/4	23 7/8	+1/4
37 1/2	30 1/8	TxUtil	3.08	8.3	45	7584	37 3/8	36 7/8	37 1/4	
3 3/8	2 3/8	Texfi Inds	1.10	44.0	41	5	2 1/2	2 1/2	2 1/2	
70 1/8	48 5/8	Textrn	1.56	2.2	13	1414	69 7/8	69 3/8	69 3/8	-1/2
5 5/8	3 5/8	Thackeray			64	2	4 1/2	4 1/2	4 1/2	
19	13 1/8	Thai Cap	1.90	12.9		41	14 7/8	14 3/4	14 3/4	
28 1/2	19 1/4	Thai Fund	0.07	0.3		111	23 3/8	23 1/8	23 3/8	+1/8
47 1/4	29.21	ThermoElec	0.12	0.3	30	1643	u47 1/2	46 1/2	46 3/4	-1/2
37 1/8	25 3/8	Thiokl	0.68	2.0	12	190	34 1/4	33 7/8	34	-1/8
70 7/8	62	ThBett	2.24	3.3	141	247	67 3/4	67 1/2	67 3/4	+3/8
23	13 5/8	Thomas Ind	0.40	1.8	19	517	u23	22 3/4	22 3/4	-1/4
29 1/2	16 1/2	Tidwtr x	0.50	1.8	27	5998	28 1/8	27 3/4	28	+3/8
46 1/2	29	Tiffany	0.28	0.6	23	773	46 3/8	45 1/2	46 3/8	+1/8
45 1/2	33 5/8	TmWarn	0.36	1.0	82	7084	37	36 1/2	36 1/2	-1/8
32 5/8	17 1/4	TmMirA	0.24	0.9	14	2176	28 1/2	28 1/8	28 1/8	-1/4
48	32 1/2	Tmkn♣	1.08	2.7	11	361	40	39 1/4	39 3/8	-7/8
10 3/8	5 1/2	TitanCrp			35	108	7 7/8	7 3/4	7 3/4	-1/8
13 1/4	10 7/8	Titan Pf x	1.00	8.0		9	12 3/4	12 1/2	12 1/2	
7 1/8	5	Todd Shp			15	145	6 1/8	6 1/8	6 1/8	
9 3/8	6 1/2	Tokheim Co	0.56	7.7	45	131	7 1/4	6 7/8	7 1/4	+1/4
19	10	Toll Bros			12	387	18	17 7/8	18	-1/8
41	29	Tootsie Rl	0.25	0.7	20	45	37	36 3/8	36 1/2	-1/2
44 3/4	34 1/4	Tchmrk	1.16	2.8	11	440	41 3/4	41 1/4	41 3/4	-1/4
32 1/4	25 5/8	Toro Corp	0.48	1.7	10	162	29	28 3/4	28 3/4	-1/4
36 1/2	27 1/2	Tosco	0.64	1.8	21	423	35 7/8	35 5/8	35 7/8	+1/4
24 1/8	13 3/8	TotalSyst	0.09	0.4	58	49	22 1/2	22 1/4	22 3/8	
30 7/8	21 5/8	TysRUs			13	20949	24 1/8	23 1/8	24 1/8	+1 1/8
26	21	Transaminc x	1.92	7.6	11	48	25 5/8	25 3/8	25 3/8	
71 1/2	49 1/2	TrAm♣	2.00	2.9	12	519	69 7/8	69 1/2	69 3/4	
70 3/8	52 1/4	Transatlan	0.40	0.6	12	131	70	69 5/8	70	+1/2
16 1/2	14 5/8	Transcnt R			5	9	15 5/8	15 1/8	15 1/8	-1/4
17 3/4	9 5/8	Transpro				357	9 7/8	d9 5/8	9 3/4	-1/8
15 1/8	10	Transtech	0.26	2.0	9	10	13 1/4	13 1/8	13 1/8	+1/8
55	32 3/8	Travlr x	0.80	1.5	11	6492	54 3/4	53 3/8	54 5/8	+1 1/8
32	17 3/8	Tredegar	0.24	0.8	12	46	29 5/8	29 1/4	29 5/8	-1/8
35	30 7/8	TriCont2.5	2.50	7.2		11	34 5/8	34 1/2	34 5/8	
16 3/4	9 1/2	Triarc			40	341	10 1/4	9 3/4	10	
68 7/8	50 3/4	Trbune	1.12	1.8	16	665	63 1/2	62 7/8	63 3/8	+1/4
24	19 7/8	TriCon	0.72	3.1		592	23 1/2	23 1/4	23 1/2	+1/8
40 3/8	28 3/4	Trinity	0.68	2.3	11	562	29 7/8	29 7/8	29 7/8	
38 3/4	23 1/2	Trnova	0.72	2.5	9	480	29	28 3/8	28 5/8	+1/4
55 1/2	30 3/4	Triton	0.10	0.2	60	936	50 1/8	49 1/4	49 3/8	-1/8
21 3/4	15 3/4	TrueN	0.60	3.1	23	236	19 1/2	19 1/4	19 1/4	-3/8
3 3/4	2 7/8	Tucson El			12	758	3 1/8	3	3	
6 1/2	4 1/8	Tultex Crp	0.20	4.3	14	28	4 3/4	4 5/8	4 5/8	-1/8
7 5/8	5 1/8	Turkish In x	0.12	2.1		52	5 3/4	5 5/8	5 5/8	-1/4
17 3/4	10 3/8	Twth Cent	0.64	3.9	5	76	16 7/8	16 1/2	16 1/2	-3/8
25 1/4	18 3/8	Twin Disc	0.70	3.0	11	6	23 3/8	23 3/8	23 3/8	-1/8
63 1/4	46 1/2	Tyco L	0.40	0.6	20	935	62	61 1/2	61 7/8	-1/8
7 1/2	4 1/4	Tyco T	0.10	1.8	7	469	5 1/2	5 3/8	5 1/2	
3 7/8	2 5/8	Tyler			14	11	3 1/4	3 1/4	3 1/4	
		- U -								
37 1/4	24 1/8	UJB Fin	1.16	3.6	11	588	32 5/8	32 1/4	32 5/8	+3/8
6 7/8	5 1/8	URS			9	66	6 5/8	6 1/2	6 1/2	-1/8
51	43 5/8	USF&G 4.1	4.10	8.1		18	50 3/4	50 1/4	50 3/4	+1/4
29 7/8	19 1/4	USG			31	475	29 1/2	29 1/8	29 1/2	+3/8
32 5/8	26 5/8	UST	1.30	4.2	14	2109	31	30 3/4	30 7/8	-1/4
185	87 5/8	UAL			7	902	u187	182 1/2	186 3/4	+2 3/8
22 1/8	18 7/8	UGI Corp	1.40	6.5	49	717	21 5/8	21 3/8	21 3/8	-1/8
6 3/4	4 5/8	UNC Inc			7	1213	5 7/8	5 5/8	5 3/4	-1/8
33 3/4	23 1/4	Unicom	1.60	4.9	10	2588	33 1/2	32 7/8	32 7/8	-5/8
29 1/8	21 7/8	Unifi Inc x	0.52	2.2	15	450	23 1/4	22 5/8	23 1/8	+1/2
14 7/8	11	Unifirst	0.10	0.7	14	290	14 3/4	14 5/8	14 3/4	-1/8
82 5/8	71	Unilvr x	1.81	2.4	14	7	77	76 1/2	76 1/2	-1/4
137 1/4	114 1/4	UnilNV	3.15	2.4	15	1138	130 3/8	129 3/4	130	-3/8
61 1/4	46 5/8	UnCamp	1.80	3.7	7	2176	49	48 1/2	48 5/8	-1/8
42 5/8	25 1/2	UnCarb	0.75	2.0	6	4470	38	37 1/8	37 1/8	-1

1995 High	1995 Low	Stock	Div	Yld. %
		- V		
57 1/8	46 3/4	VF Cp	1.36	2.8
25 5/8	16 1/8	VleroE x	0.52	2.2
8 5/8	6 5/8	Valhi Inc	0.12	1.8
40 3/4	21 1/4	ValueHlth		
7	5 1/2	VanKamp HI	0.70	10.6
9 1/8	7 3/8	VanKampMer	0.96	11.0
11 3/8	9 3/4	VanKampMeM	0.78	7.4
11 7/8	6	Varco Intl		
57 3/8	34 1/2	Varian	0.28	0.6
50 3/4	33 5/8	Varity		
38	27	Vencor		
14	11 3/4	Vestaur	1.08	7.9
72 3/4	56 1/2	VirE&P5.00	5.00	6.9
44 3/8	23	Vishay Int		
35 7/8	26 5/8	Vivra Inc		
45	27 1/4	Vodafone	0.56	1.3
12 1/2	6 1/8	Volunteer		
26 3/4	17 5/8	Von Cos		
39	32 5/8	Vrnado x	2.24	6.5
60 3/8	48 1/8	VulcnM	1.46	2.6
		- W		
24 1/4	16 3/8	WMS Ind		
31 5/8	27 1/4	WPL Holdin x	1.94	6.3
20 3/8	13 1/2	Waban Inc		
48 1/4	32	Wchva x	1.44	3.2
19	10 1/2	Wackenhut	0.30	1.8
5	3 1/4	Wainoco		
29 1/4	21 3/4	Walgrn	0.39	1.3
60	27 1/2	WallaceCS	0.86	1.5
27 1/2	20 1/2	WalMrt	0.20	0.9
3	13/16	Warner Ins	0.04	4.0
98	73 3/8	WnrLam x	2.60	3.0
19	13	WshEnergy	1.00	5.3
21	16 1/4	WashGL	1.12	5.6
25 3/8	17 3/4	WashNat	1.08	4.6
315	237 1/2	WashPB	4.40	1.5
57	29 3/4	WatkJn	0.48	1.0
1 5/8	13/16	Waxman Ind	0.08	8.5
27 3/4	16 1/2	WthrfdEnt		
25	16 5/8	Webb (Del) x	0.20	0.9
38 1/8	34 1/4	Weingarten	2.40	7.1
9 3/8	4 3/8	Weirton St	0.64	14.2
29	24	WeisMk	0.84	3.0
30	22 1/4	Wellman	0.28	1.1
230 1/4	141	WellsF x	4.60	2.2
22 3/4	14 3/8	Wendys	0.24	1.2
30 5/8	24 1/4	West Co	0.52	2.0
16 3/8	13 7/8	Westcst E	0.92	6.3
52 1/8	35 5/8	WAtlas		
22 1/8	13 1/8	WDigital		
24 1/4	15	WestnGas	0.20	1.3
27 3/4	19	Westn Mng	0.60	2.31
34	28 5/8	Wstn Res	2.02	6.0
16 3/8	12 1/4	WstgEl x	0.20	1.41
6 3/4	2 1/2	WstmrCoal	0.32	9.1
24 1/2	14 7/8	Wstn Waste		
20 3/4	16 3/8	Westpac	0.73	3.6
31 3/4	24	Wstvco	0.88	3.2
50 3/8	36 7/8	Wyrhsr x	1.60	3.6
17 1/2	12 1/2	Wheelabrtr	0.11	0.7
60 7/8	49 1/4	Whirlpl	1.36	2.6
40 1/2	20 1/8	Whitehall		
22 1/2	15 5/8	Whitmn	0.38	1.8
24 1/2	17 3/8	Whittaker		
30 7/8	26 5/8	Wicor Inc	1.64	5.4
40 5/8	24 1/2	Willms	1.08	2.8
7	5 3/4	Wilshire	0.07	1.1
10 1/8	5 7/8	Windmere	0.20	2.9
66 3/8	51 1/8	WinnDx	1.80	2.7
10 3/4	7 3/8	Winnebago x	0.40	5.1
30 1/4	25 3/4	WiscEn x	1.47	5.1
15	10 7/8	WiserO	0.40	3.6
35 5/8	24 1/4	Witco Corp	1.12	3.9
32 1/2	25 3/4	WMX T	0.60	2.1
32 1/2	15 1/2	Wolverine	0.14	0.5
19 3/8	12 3/4	Woolwth	0.60	4.2
16 1/2	13 1/4	World Wide	0.10	0.6
13 5/8	7 1/4	Worldcorp		
31 7/8	26 3/4	WPS Rs	1.86	5.9
51 1/4	42 7/8	Wrigley	0.68	1.4
46 1/2	19 3/8	Wyle Labor	0.28	0.6
28 1/4	19 1/2	Wynns Int	0.52	1.9

Fig. 7.2 NYSE composite prices

AMEX, NASDAQ and other US exchanges

The second stock exchange in New York, and the second largest traditional market is the AMEX. Elsewhere in the country, there are five more of these traditional exchanges: the Pacific Stock Exchange (with trading floors in both Los Angeles and San Francisco), the Midwest Stock Exchange in Chicago, the Boston Stock Exchange, the Philadelphia Stock Exchange and the Cincinnati Stock Exchange. Each of these smaller exchanges has some exclusive stocks, usually small or locally owned companies, but they also trade stocks that are listed on the NYSE or the AMEX, "dual listed" stocks; no stocks trade on both the NYSE and the AMEX.

The smaller regional exchanges offer some distinct features. For example, as it is three hours behind New York, the Pacific market offers continued trading in dual listed NYSE shares after the NYSE has closed. The Midwest market makes no extra charge for odd-lot transactions, deals of less than a round lot of 100 shares, and odd-lot orders on the NYSE for dual listed stocks are often transferred there. The Philadelphia market carries a number of options, including an option on the sterling/dollar exchange rate, prices for which are carried on the FT Currencies and Money page (see chapter 11).

Like the London market, the Cincinnati has no trading floor with all transactions conducted by computer and telephone. A more prominent electronic exchange is the NASDAQ. Run by the National Association of Securities Dealers, this automated quotations system is the world's second largest stock market (in terms of the dollar value of trading) after its arch-rival, the NYSE. It was established in 1971 to provide a high-tech method of setting stock prices and trading securities "over the counter". Through a network of computer screens, more than 500 marketmakers post the prices at which they are prepared to buy and sell shares. The best bid and offer prices are displayed on dealers' screens and deals are done over the telephone.

This dealer driven mechanism of making prices is similar to that adopted by the London Stock Exchange after the Big Bang deregulation of 1986. It differs from the order-driven process used by the NYSE where supply and demand for shares meet through a single "specialist" or marketmaker. The system also has less onerous listing

requirements than the NYSE, enabling young or small companies in fast-growing industries such as computers and biotechnology to obtain a quotation and access to the capital markets. Microsoft, Apple Computers and Intel all started here.

The *Financial Times* international edition listings for the NASDAQ National Market (the most actively traded NASDAQ stocks) are a little less detailed than for the NYSE, providing everything but the year's highs and lows. Similar information is given for a selection of stocks traded on the AMEX.

INTERNATIONAL EQUITY INDICES

The international equity indices are a useful tool in the world of international investment, acting as valuable barometers of local market performance for investors faced with limited background knowledge of foreign stocks. In such circumstances the active management of an international portfolio may be too costly and risky an exercise, and many fund managers may aim merely to match the performance of equity indices. The more passive management of indexed funds relies largely on the computerised tracking of price movements, and international equity indices have become the key benchmarks for performance measurement.

US equity indices

The United States provides the largest range of stock price indices (see Figure 7.3):

- **Dow Jones:** Industrials or the Dow Jones Industrial Average (DJIA), the main US index, takes the stock prices of thirty blue chip companies and measures their movements. It is calculated by adding the New York closing prices and adjusting them by a "current average divisor", an adjustable figure formulated to preserve the continuity of the Dow over time amid changes in its component parts. Specialist indices are also provided for three other groups of stocks: Home Bonds, Transport (twenty airlines, railroads and

US INDICES

Dow Jones	Oct 11	Oct 10	Oct 9	1995 **High**	1995 Low	Since compilation **High**	Since compilation Low
Industrials	4735.25	4720.80	4726.22	**4801.80** (14/9)	3832.08 (30/1)	**4801.80** (14/9/95)	41.22 (2/7/32)
Home Bonds	(u)	103.48	103.41	**103.75** (13/7)	93.63 (3/1)	**109.77** (18/10/93)	54.99 (1/10/81)
Transport	1925.80	1892.31	1898.27	**2000.39** (18/9)	1473.19 (3/1)	**2000.39** (18/9/95)	12.32 (8/7/32)
Utilities	217.04	217.44	215.59	**217.44** (10/10)	183.03 (3/1)	**256.46** (31/8/93)	10.50 (8/4/32)

DJ Ind. Day's high 4773.91 (4745.74) Low 4686.48 (4638.43) (Theoretical♠)
Day's high 4738.86 (4726.58) Low 4711.41 (4660.47) (Actual♠)

Standard and Poors							
Composite ‡	579.46	577.52	578.37	**586.77** (20/9)	459.11 (3/1)	**586.77** (20/9/95)	4.40 (1/6/32)
Industrials♥	675.98	674.59	676.27	**691.27** (20/9)	546.28 (3/1)	**691.27** (20/9/95)	3.62 (21/6/92)
Financial	60.34	59.77	59.93	**60.34** (11/10)	41.64 (3/1)	**60.34** (11/10/95)	8.64 (1/10/74)
NYSE Comp.	310.51	309.41	310.35	**314.33** (20/9)	250.73 (3/1)	**314.33** (20/9/95)	4.46 (25/4/42)
Amex Mkt Val	527.54	525.22	527.48	**553.58** (12/9)	433.12 (6/1)	**553.58** (12/9/95)	29.31 (9/12/72)
NASDAQ Cmp	1001.57	983.47	984.74	**1067.40** (13/9)	743.58 (3/1)	**1067.40** (13/9/95)	54.87 (31/10/72)

■ RATIOS

	Oct 6	Sep 29	Sep 22	Year ago
Dow Jones Ind. Div. Yield	2.43	2.42	2.42	2.79
	Oct 4	Sep 27	Sep 20	Year ago
S & P Ind. Div. yield	2.08	2.07	2.05	2.43
S & P Ind. P/E ratio	17.87	17.94	18.14	20.33

■ NEW YORK ACTIVE STOCKS

Wednesday	Stocks traded	Close price	Change on day
Union Pac	8,937,900	22	+1
Motorola	7,743,600	64¼	+¼
Micron Tech	7,125,900	67¾	+⅝
Allmerica Fin	6,137,300	24¼	+3¼
Abbott Labs	6,122,100	39¼	-¾
Wal-Mart	5,907,700	22⅞	-1
EMC	5,838,200	14⅛	+⅜
Ford Motor	4,061,400	30⅛	+¾
Freeport Mcn	3,986,200	6¼	+⅝
Seagate Tech	3,611,300	40⅝	+1⅞

■ TRADING ACTIVITY

● Volume (million)

	Oct 11	Oct 10	Oct 9
New York SE	343.060	416.328	278.386
Amex	15.566	18.479	13.267
NASDAQ	(u)	557.685	417.697
NYSE			
Issues Traded	3,036	3,037	2,995
Rises	1,433	846	616
Falls	803	1,443	1,631
Unchanged	800	748	748
New Highs	113	67	69
New Lows	38	72	60

	Open	Sett price	Change	High	Low	Est. vol.	Open int.
■ S&P 500							
Dec	581.25	583.35	+2.10	585.75	580.90	94,512	192,185
Mar	587.50	588.00	+2.10	588.45	586.05	1,031	8,141
■ Nikkei 225 (Oct 9)							
Dec	18180.0	17920.0	-390.0	18190.0	17900.0	22,110	153,962
Mar	18160.0	18120.0	-200.0	18160.0	18120.0	2	4,363

Open interest figures for previous day.

Excluding bonds. ‡ Industrial, plus Utilities, Financial and Transportation.
and lows are the averages of the highest and lowest prices reached during the day by each
ws (supplied by Telekurs) represent the highest and lowest values that the index has reached
previous day's). ♥ Subject to official recalculation.

Fig. 7.3 US indices

trucking companies) and Utilities (fifteen gas and power companies). For all four indices, the information provided comprises: the closing figures for the day alongside the closing for the previous three trading days; the highest and lowest trading level for the year with dates; and the highest and lowest trading level since compilation began, also with dates.

- **Standard & Poor's (S&P):** the Composite index consists of 500 companies listed on the New York Stock Exchange; the other two indices cover the Composite's Industrials (400 companies) and Financial stock (forty companies) sub-groups. The remaining companies are twenty transport companies and forty utilities. While not as comprehensive as the NYSE Composite nor as famous as the DJIA, the S&P 500 is generally regarded as a more comprehensive guide to the US market, accounting for nearly 80 per cent of the total NYSE capitalisation. Like the FT-SE Actuaries series, individual companies are weighted according to their market capitalisation, allowing for the fact that some stocks exhibit a greater influence over the market than others.

- **NYSE Composite index:** the most broadly based of the US indices, covering all common stocks on the exchange.

- **AMEX Market Value index:** an index of over 800 companies listed on the American Stock Exchange.

- **NASDAQ:** an index of the electronic stock market. This index is often used as an indicator of the market for stocks in technology and the industries of the future.

- **Ratios:** Dividend yields and price/earnings ratios: yields for the Dow and S&P are calculated on the basis of the last declared dividend worked out at an annual rate. The S&P industrials' p/e ratio is measured by dividing the last four quarterly earnings figures into the latest share price.

- **New York Active Stocks:** figures on the previous day's ten most actively traded stocks, including the number of shares traded and the stocks' closing prices and changes on the previous day.

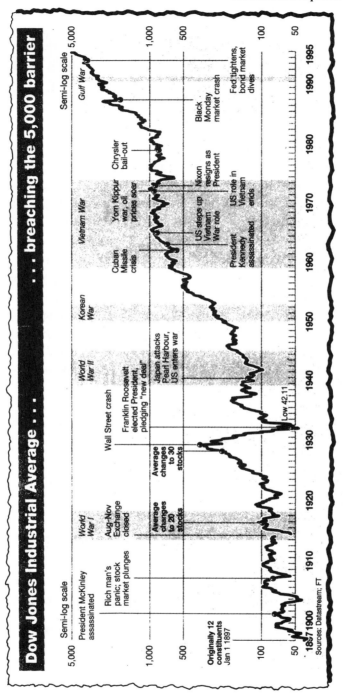

Fig. 7.4 Dow Jones Industrial Average

● **Trading Activity:** the volume of stocks traded on the NYSE, the AMEX and the NASDAQ on the last three trading days, together with information on the number of issues traded, aggregate rises and falls, and new highs and lows on the NYSE. These are broad indicators of the recent pattern of the market's movements and the level of activity.

The Dow often reaches new "highs" but since it is not adjusted for inflation it can only reliably indicate direction of movement. The Dow – not an index but an "average" – is the most widely followed indicator in the United States, providing a guide to the daily mood of the industrial stock markets in the same way that the FT-30 share index does for the United Kingdom. Its breaching of the 5,000 mark in 1995 was an occasion for reflection on its movements over the twentieth century, as shown in Figure 7.4. The semi-log scale used allows perspective on the relative importance of major movements at different times: a move of 50 points when the average is below 100 is far more significant than one when the average is over 1,000.

Typical FT coverage of what is happening on Wall Street (the collective noun for American financial markets, analogous to "the City" for London's markets) looks like this:

> Blue chip issues posted gains yesterday, but otherwise US stock prices were mostly flat to lower in light trading. At the close, the Dow Jones Industrial Average was up. The more broadly based Standard & Poor's 500 ended 0.24 off, the American SE composite eased 0.15, and the NASDAQ composite was 2.59 weaker. Trading volume on the New York SE totalled a moderate 236.2m shares.
> (*Financial Times*, 7 July 1994)

"Off", "weaker" and "eased" (the opposite of "firmed") all mean that prices went down.

Other international indices

Figure 7.5 shows indices for other international markets.

● **Indices:** for most markets, a single national index is recorded daily with the base date indicated. The base figure for almost all indices is 100 and the few exceptions are listed at the bottom of the page.

INDICES

	Oct 12	Oct 11	Oct 10	1995 High	1995 Low
Argentina					
General (29/12/77)	13999.21	14149.65	14049.81	16531.10 2/1	9831.09 9/3
Australia					
All Ordinaries(1/1/80)	2078.4	2068.6	2062.2	2166.00 18/9	1823.30 8/2
All Mining(1/1/80)	932.2	933.1	930.0	1029.50 7/8	795.30 8/2
Austria					
Credit Aktien(30/12/84)	343.36	351.92	355.36	395.42 2/1	343.36 12/10
Traded Index(2/1/91)	936.11	962.83	973.41	1056.31 2/1	934.83 30/3
Belgium					
BEL20 (1/1/91)	1407.71	1414.98	1414.97	1491.39 2/8	1271.53 9/3
Brazil					
Bovespa (29/12/83)	(c)	45007.0	44095.0	49612.00 19/9	4531.60 8/9
Canada					
Metals Mins♦(1975)	4624.70	4590.76	4599.15	5252.77 21/8	3808.63 1/3
Composite♦ (1975)	4476.70	4474.60	4472.30	4710.30 12/7	3691.41 30/1
Portfolio§§ (4/1/83)	2183.58	2189.35	2191.27	2307.81 12/7	1963.36 30/1
Chile					
IGPA Gen♥(31/12/80)	(c)	5896.0	5873.6	6363.10 11/7	4576.90 9/3
Denmark					
CopenhagenSE(3/1/83)	(u)	(u)	359.47	375.44 25/8	330.01 29/3
Finland					
HEX General(28/12/90)	2088.85	2057.49	1978.53	2332.22 14/9	1555.30 29/3
France					
SBF 250 (31/12/90)	1205.33	1199.27	1192.91	1322.30 12/5	1154.41 13/3
CAC 40(31/12/87)	1803.75	1794.43	1777.96	2017.27 12/5	1721.80 13/3
Germany					
FAZ Aktien(31/12/58)	791.61	785.73	792.41	846.76 19/9	708.87 30/3
Commerzbank(1/12/53)	2282.7	2263.3	2282.8	2427.60 19/9	2018.70 30/3
DAX (30/12/87)‡	2158.12	2145.30	2138.77	2317.01 15/9	1910.96 28/3
Greece					
Athens SE(31/12/80)	914.14	925.43	924.42	992.59 4/8	787.15 16/3
Hong Kong					
Hang Seng(31/7/64)	9685.14	9635.06	9730.92	9939.95 4/10	6967.93 23/1
India					
BSE Sens.♥(1979)	3561.40	3572.22	3557.80	3832.09 2/1	3015.07 2/5
Indonesia					
Jakarta Comp.(10/8/82)	494.52	496.28	495.99	519.18 11/8	414.21 19/4
Ireland					
ISEQ Overall(4/1/88)	2139.42	2123.33	2110.66	2170.73 15/9	1813.59 23/1
Italy					
Banca Comm Ital (1972)	600.29	594.41	594.73	680.54 10/2	587.99 23/3
MIB General (2/1/95)	948.0	939.0	939.0	1076.00 10/2	929.00 23/3
Japan					
Nikkei 225 (16/5/49)	17971.40	17891.19	(c)	19684.04 4/1	14485.41 3/7
Nikkei 300 (1/10/82)	267.10	267.24	(c)	286.16 4/1	222.26 13/6

	Oct 12	Oct 11	Oct 10	1995 High	1995 Low
Japan					
Topix (4/1/68)	1426.12	1427.04	(c)	1553.40 4/1	1193.16 13/6
2nd Section (4/1/68)	1862.18	1868.61	(c)	2130.68 4/1	1441.90 13/6
Malaysia					
KLSE Comp.(4/4/86)	.961.94	958.80	970.75	1085.04 5/6	840.87 24/1
Mexico					
IPC (Nov 1978)	(u)	2353.68	2237.78	2622.21 8/9	1447.52 27/2
Netherland					
CBS TtlRtnGen(End 83)	499.1	498.7	496.5	511.80 19/9	422.90 23/3
CBS All Shr (End 83)	302.5	302.3	300.9	311.10 15/9	265.20 23/3
New Zealand					
Cap. 40 (1/7/86)	2113.52	2091.33	2081.61	2155.79 18/5	1901.43 5/1
Norway					
Oslo SE(Indx)(2/1/83)	1245.23	1230.45	1224.31	1291.58 19/9	1036.00 10/3
Philippines					
Manila Comp (2/1/85)	2599.80	2588.82	2600.0	2958.12 10/7	2248.39 27/3
Portugal					
BTA (1977)	2603.7	2605.6	2611.1	2911.60 9/1	2580.70 25/9
Singapore					
SES All-S'pore(2/4/75)	517.26	517.60	518.01	535.06 5/1	472.90 23/1
South Africa					
JSE Gold (28/9/78)	1455.8♥	1459.7	1473.2	2023.00 2/1	1317.20 19/5
JSE Indl. (28/9/78)	7302.7♥	7257.1	7221.2	7302.7 12/10	6222.00 31/1
South Korea					
KoreaCmpEx(4/1/80)**	1016.66	1011.00	1004.16†	1027.37 2/1	847.09 27/5
Spain					
Madrid SE (30/12/85)	(c)	297.38	295.36	318.98 13/9	203.30 26/6
Sweden					
AffarsvardnGen (1/2/37)	1800.6	1774.3	1753.1	1872.10 19/9	1439.80 29/3
Switzerland					
Swiss Bk Ind (31/12/58)	1424.77	1419.71	1404.58	1424.77 12/10	1174.63 13/3
SBC General (1/4/87)	1064.45	1060.96	1054.19	1084.45 12/10	870.58 13/3
Taiwan					
WeightedPr.(30/6/66)**	5108.93	5165.36	(c)	7051.49 5/1	4503.37 14/8
Thailand					
Bangkok SET (30/4/75)	1323.26	1323.00	1317.26	1472.04 10/7	1135.69 16/3
Turkey					
Istanbul Cmp.(Jan 1986)	43101.7	45395.1	44428.9	54653.90 21/4	24644.31 23/1
WORLD					
MS Capital Int (1/1/70)§	695.2*	691.1	693.7	703.80 29/9	596.21 23/1
CROSS-BORDER					
Eurotrack 100(26/10/90)	1405.03	1396.12	1377.54	1480.69 15/9	1222.41 13/3
Euro Top-100 (26/6/90)	1270.37	1267.66	1257.88	1316.68 15/9	1117.34 9/3
JCapelDrgns (31/12/88)	(u)	330.78	332.97	349.47 14/7	262.07 23/1
Barings Emerg.(7/1/92)	146.33	145.56	145.98	158.07 2/1	117.15 10/3

Fig. 7.5 International indices

All these indices are benchmarks commonly used by local investors. They are designed to provide an accurate reflection of the daily movement of individual markets. More than one national index is published in the case where a single index does not give the full picture or where two or more are commonly used. For example, one national index may comprise the market's major companies while a second may reflect a wider market. In Australia, the Metals and Minerals index is given alongside the All-Share Ordinary Index because of the heavy weighting of resource stocks in the Australian market.

In Canada, there are two indices for Toronto, the most widely used of which is the Toronto Composite (a broadly based index similar to the S&P 500), and a much smaller one for the market in Montreal.

For France there are two indices: the broadly based SBF 250 and the CAC 40, a real-time index of the largest stocks. In Germany,

three indices are commonly used: the Frankfurter Allgemeine Zeitung, the Commerzbank, and the DAX real-time index introduced at the end of 1987.

The Nikkei is the most widely quoted measure of stock price movements on the Tokyo Stock Exchange, the world's second biggest in terms of market capitalisation. Not strictly an index but an average of 225 shares, it is not weighted according to market capitalisation, so smaller firms can move the index as much as bigger ones. The index is run by the *Nihon Keizai Shimbun*, Japan's main financial daily newspaper. Nikkei is an abbreviation of the newspaper's name. The Nikkei is a benchmark similar to the Dow or the FT-30 but is more widely followed than the comprehensive Tokyo Stock Exchange index (Topix). The latter provides a more accurate guide to the state of the overall market.

In South Africa, the heavy preponderance of gold shares makes publication of the Gold Index indispensable. Since the index moves very closely in line with the gold price, the Johannesburg Stock Exchange (JSE) Industrial index is used to monitor the rest of the market.

Local indices carry great credibility in their local markets, but do not provide the whole picture for the global investor. For example, they may include equities not freely available to international fund managers or some national issues may be illiquid from the viewpoint of committing funds globally.

Monday's newspaper carries substantial analysis of world stock markets, including a regular column "Global Investor" on its Markets: This Week pages, and a separate Equity Markets: This Week page. The latter examines prospects for the week ahead in New York and London as well as a range of other markets, including Frankfurt, Milan, Tokyo, Amsterdam, Helsinki, Zurich, Madrid and Johannesburg. Half-yearly, the newspaper presents ending index values for each of the three previous six-month periods on the key index in fifteen countries.

A table in Saturday's newspaper lists the key world market indices, their latest values, and their percentage changes on a week previously and on the beginning of the year (see Figure 7.6):

■ Market week		Friday's value	% change: since 1 week	30/12/94
UK	FT-SE-A All-Share	1772.82	0.2	16.5
UK	FT-SE 100	3624.00	0.4	18.2
UK	FT-SE Mid 250	3942.80	−0.5	12.6
UK	FT-SE SmallCap	1949.48	0.0	11.6
UK	FT-SE-A Fledgling	1094.82	0.1	9.5
UK	Hoare Govett Sml Cos	1739.26	0.1	10.7
UK	Gilts: FT-A All Stocks	143.89	0.7	5.6
Global	FT/S&P-A World ($)	195.52	0.6	13.0
Global	FT/S&P-A World(local)	163.38	0.4	11.3
Global	Barings Em Mkts($)	139.05	3.2	−12.0
US	Dow Jones Indl	5048.84	1.2	31.7
Japan	Nikkei 225	18215.23	0.4	−7.6
Europe	FT-SE Eurotrack 100	1450.97	1.3	8.8
Germany	Dax	2198.16	−0.1	4.3
France	CAC40	1890.95	0.0	0.5
Italy	Comit 30	134.70	−1.4	−8.7
HK	Hang Seng	9488.75	2.2	15.8

† Thursday's closing index shown. ♥ Latest available for this edition.   Sources: Hoare Govett, Telekurs, Reuters

Fig. 7.6 Market week

THE FT/S&P ACTUARIES WORLD INDICES

The FT/S&P Actuaries world indices table covers global equity markets, expressing the various market indices in terms of both local and key international currencies (see Figure 7.7). Owned by FT-SE International, Goldman, Sachs and Standard & Poor's, calculated in conjunction with the Institute and Faculty of Actuaries, launched in March 1987, and based on over 2,200 equity securities from 26 countries, these indices represent at least 70 per cent of the total market capitalisation of the world's main stock exchanges.

Reading the figures

- **Regional indices:** the complete world series has eleven regional indices. Figures are shown for these and the main country indices.

FT/S&P ACTUARIES WORLD INDICES

The FT/S&P Actuaries World Indices are owned by The Financial Times Ltd., Goldman, Sachs & Co. and Standard & Poor's. The Indices are compiled by The Financial Times and Goldman Sachs in conjunction with the Institute of Actuaries and the Faculty of Actuaries. NatWest Securities Ltd. was a co-founder of the Indices.

NATIONAL AND REGIONAL MARKETS Figures in parentheses show number of lines of stock	FRIDAY SEPTEMBER 29 1995							THURSDAY SEPTEMBER 28 1995						DOLLAR INDEX		
	US Dollar Index	%chg since 30/12/94	Pound Sterling Index	Yen Index	DM Index	Local Currency Index	Local chg from 30/12/94	Gross Div. Yield	US Dollar Index	Pound Sterling Index	Yen Index	DM Index	Local Currency Index	52 week High	52 week Low	Year ago (approx)
Australia (82)	185.82	8.3	174.06	115.88	137.48	163.75	11.3	3.97	184.04	172.47	115.79	135.98	162.56	191.01	157.95	171.16
Austria (26)	180.67	-1.1	169.23	112.66	133.66	133.57	-9.2	1.34	180.06	168.74	113.28	133.04	132.95	199.28	167.48	184.83
Belgium (35)	195.61	16.1	183.23	121.98	144.71	141.01	6.7	3.71	194.98	182.73	122.67	144.06	140.45	201.12	161.66	165.22
Brazil (28)	152.53	-6.5	142.87	95.11	112.84	267.59	5.2	1.58	149.75	140.34	94.21	110.64	263.05	—	—	—
Canada (101)	144.53	11.7	135.38	90.13	106.93	140.98	7.3	2.63	144.04	134.99	90.62	106.43	140.93	150.83	121.81	138.52
Denmark (33)	282.30	12.1	264.43	176.04	208.84	212.04	1.7	1.53	280.25	262.63	176.32	207.07	210.60	295.99	236.61	250.42
Finland (25)	265.87	43.0	249.03	165.79	196.69	237.71	28.5	1.35	258.16	241.93	162.42	190.74	231.21	276.11	171.13	178.37
France (100)	172.85	5.7	161.91	107.79	127.88	133.14	-2.8	3.29	171.20	160.44	107.71	126.49	131.85	191.17	157.79	165.51
Germany (59)	159.47	11.3	149.38	99.41	117.97	117.97	2.2	2.02	158.65	148.68	99.82	117.22	117.22	167.74	134.99	140.26
Hong Kong (55)	375.42	15.1	351.65	234.10	277.74	372.64	15.0	3.85	373.94	350.43	235.26	276.29	371.23	399.17	277.40	399.17
Ireland (16)	249.46	21.0	233.67	155.56	184.55	217.19	15.4	3.49	247.65	232.08	155.81	182.98	215.72	249.46	195.34	206.63
Italy (59)	76.25	-1.3	71.42	47.55	56.41	91.76	0.6	1.66	75.69	70.93	47.62	55.93	90.99	85.60	65.45	85.60
Japan (483)	147.76	-5.8	138.41	92.14	109.32	92.14	-6.9	0.83	146.04	136.86	91.88	107.90	91.88	164.82	136.95	160.28
Malaysia (107)	495.59	3.5	464.59	309.29	366.94	479.56	1.7	1.72	492.69	461.72	309.97	364.04	476.46	567.20	398.16	562.07
Mexico (18)	1092.12	-22.9	1022.98	681.02	807.94	7600.21	-0.3	1.83	1073.54	1006.05	675.41	793.19	7594.15	2302.16	647.81	2302.16
Netherland (19)	259.42	19.6	243.00	161.77	191.92	188.60	9.8	3.46	257.34	241.16	161.90	190.14	186.88	263.99	205.92	210.73
New Zealand (14)	78.83	11.9	73.84	49.16	58.32	63.57	8.8	4.51	77.75	72.87	48.92	57.45	63.06	85.49	69.56	72.77
Norway (33)	236.88	11.1	221.88	147.71	175.24	201.14	2.8	2.10	235.58	220.77	148.21	174.06	200.28	243.79	192.92	196.84
Singapore (44)	371.40	-0.4	347.89	231.60	274.77	243.21	-3.0	1.70	368.12	344.99	231.60	272.00	241.65	414.26	313.94	380.97
South Africa (45)	351.67	4.5	329.41	219.30	260.17	280.66	-6.4	4.15	351.18	329.11	220.94	259.48	279.96	363.22	281.06	312.87
Spain (38)	151.01	14.4	141.45	94.17	111.72	140.93	7.1	3.96	149.87	140.45	94.29	110.74	139.63	160.51	124.10	140.07
Sweden (48)	320.43	38.6	300.15	199.82	237.06	328.60	29.2	1.82	312.11	292.49	196.36	230.61	323.15	320.43	219.88	222.28
Switzerland (43)	215.21	30.3	201.58	134.20	159.21	153.30	14.4	1.74	214.08	200.62	134.69	158.18	152.30	216.36	158.38	163.83
Thailand (46)	163.05	3.1	152.73	101.67	120.62	158.71	3.0	2.57	163.07	152.82	102.59	120.49	158.82	—	—	—
United Kingdom (200)	224.72	15.3	210.49	140.13	166.25	210.49	14.0	4.11	222.76	208.76	140.15	164.59	208.76	227.07	187.07	192.79
USA (504)	239.12	27.4	223.98	149.11	176.90	239.12	27.4	2.46	239.64	224.58	150.77	177.06	239.64	239.87	182.33	188.77
Americas (651)	218.62	25.5	204.78	136.33	161.74	183.38	25.7	2.45	218.97	205.21	137.76	161.79	183.72	199.02	163.04	168.76
Europe (734)	195.12	15.5	182.77	121.67	144.35	164.17	9.0	3.08	193.42	181.26	121.69	142.91	162.76	199.02	163.04	216.80
Nordic (139)	295.02	31.4	276.34	183.97	218.26	255.34	21.3	1.72	288.69	270.54	181.63	213.30	251.35	295.35	213.93	170.19
Pacific Basin (831)	158.25	-3.7	148.23	98.68	117.08	102.71	-4.8	1.25	156.54	146.70	98.48	115.66	102.37	173.52	145.93	169.46
Euro-Pacific (1565)	173.51	4.4	162.53	108.20	128.36	125.94	0.8	2.11	171.81	161.01	108.09	126.94	125.21	178.33	154.73	185.64
North America (605)	233.27	26.7	218.50	145.46	172.57	232.55	26.5	2.46	233.73	219.04	147.05	172.70	233.03	233.93	178.86	152.01
Europe Ex. UK (534)	174.93	15.6	163.85	109.08	129.41	138.59	6.3	2.51	173.41	162.50	109.10	128.12	137.37	179.46	146.45	265.91
Pacific Ex. Japan (348)	258.26	8.4	241.91	161.05	191.06	126.10	8.5	3.22	256.49	240.37	161.37	189.51	224.83	266.72	211.19	171.47
World Ex. US (1757)	174.50	4.3	163.45	108.81	129.51	129.51	0.8	2.15	172.82	161.96	108.73	127.69	128.78	178.73	155.42	174.56
World Ex. UK (2061)	191.32	11.9	179.21	119.30	141.54	156.35	9.4	2.07	190.44	178.47	119.81	140.71	156.04	191.32	163.46	186.69
World Ex. Japan (1778)	220.40	20.0	206.44	137.43	163.05	205.20	17.4	2.76	219.78	205.97	138.28	162.39	204.69	220.98	178.95	176.18
The World Index (2261)	194.25	12.2	181.95	121.13	143.70	161.11	9.8	2.27	193.27	181.12	121.59	142.80	160.70	194.25	165.92	176.18

Fig. 7.7 FT/S&P Actuaries world indices

Seven broad economic groups are made up from more than thirty composite industry indices, derived from over 100 sub-industry categories. For example, the consumer goods/services sector has twelve industry groups and as many as thirty-six subsectors ranging from automobiles to tobacco manufacturers, from health care to the broadcast media.

- **Currencies:** the series is calculated nightly at the US close in five currencies (the dollar, pound sterling, yen and D-Mark plus the local currency) with the percentage change on the beginning of the year shown in terms of the dollar and the local currency. The figures for the five currency indices are shown for the previous trading day plus the highs and lows for the last fifty-two weeks and the value for the dollar index a year ago.

Using the information

The standard equity indices of Figure 7.5 act as barometers of local market performance for investors faced with limited background knowledge of foreign stocks. Designed to give an accurate reflection of the daily movement of individual markets, they carry great credibility in their local markets. But they may not provide the whole picture for the global investor, particularly if they include equities not freely available to overseas investors or in closely held local companies. That is the advantage of the FT/S&P Actuaries series, a set of high quality indices of the international equity market for use as a benchmark by the global investment community.

Markets, companies and securities are only included under the following criteria: the local exchange must permit direct equity investment by non-nationals; accurate and timely data must be available; no significant exchange controls should exist which would prevent the timely repatriation of capital or dividends; significant international investor interest in the local equity market must have been demonstrated; and adequate liquidity must exist. Also excluded are companies where 75 per cent or more of the issued capital is controlled by dominant shareholders, or where less than 25 per cent of the shares are available to investors through the local market. Each subset aims to capture at least 70 per cent of the total market value of

all shares listed on the domestic exchange or 85 per cent of the eligible universe of stocks. In some countries, this is not possible because of restrictions on foreign shareholdings.

The indices aim to cover a significant proportion of the stocks listed in each market rather than concentrating merely on the largest companies, and encompass around 15 per cent of an estimated universe of more than 15,000 listed companies. Companies and markets are only included where a timely and reliable source of daily price movements is available, but the number of US companies (by far the most broadly based of the world's equity markets) is limited to just over 500 under the rules of the indices. To ensure that they reflect a reasonable marketability of shares, companies with a market capitalisation of less than $100 million are generally excluded. This cut-off level is lowered, however, in the case of countries whose average market capitalisation is less than $100 million.

The index is designed to represent global equity markets and to reflect the increases in cross border equity investment, particularly from the United States and Japan. It is intended mainly for such end-users as pension fund managers, consultants and money managers. Its primary function is global equity performance measurement, hence it is essential that shares that make up the index can be purchased and sold. But it is also being used for the creation of derivative products, such as stock index funds. An increasing number of companies are running funds designed to track the world indices or one or more of their sub-series.

Markets in perspective

Derived from the FT/S&P Actuaries world indices, a further chart published in the *Financial Times* on Tuesday (see Figure 7.8) records movements in leading international market indices in terms of local currencies, dollars and sterling.

- **National markets:** percentage changes in market indices in a number of leading markets from a week ago, a month ago, a year ago and from the start of the year. Figures are given in local currencies, and in dollars and sterling for changes from the start of the year.

MARKETS IN PERSPECTIVE

	% change in local currency †				% change sterling †	% change in US $ †
	1 Week	4 Weeks	1 Year	Start of 1995	Start of 1995	Start of 1995
Austria	+0.01	-3.82	-7.72	-9.25	-2.43	-1.40
Belgium	-0.84	-0.87	+10.34	+5.76	+13.36	+14.55
Denmark	-0.49	-3.90	+5.37	+1.24	+9.84	+10.99
Finland	-4.36	-7.85	+26.15	+22.91	+33.70	+35.09
France	+1.16	-1.99	+0.13	-1.62	+3.61	+4.69
Germany	-0.54	-4.42	+8.25	+1.60	+9.22	+10.36
Ireland	-0.72	+0.62	+19.48	+14.60	+18.28	+19.51
Italy	-1.83	-5.35	-3.19	-1.25	-1.96	-0.94
Netherlands	-0.13	-0.17	+15.91	+9.66	+17.65	+18.88
Norway	-1.40	-2.88	+10.49	+1.34	+7.57	+8.69
Spain	-2.93	-6.05	+3.67	+3.96	+9.44	+10.58
Sweden	-2.33	-0.76	+33.79	+26.18	+32.07	+33.45
Switzerland	+0.90	+1.62	+21.64	+15.42	+30.15	+31.51
UK	+0.55	-0.81	+17.58	+14.63	+14.63	+15.82
EUROPE	**-0.06**	**-1.75**	**+12.55**	**+8.93**	**+13.63**	**+14.81**
Australia	-1.60	-2.04	+7.72	+9.49	+6.34	+7.46
Hong Kong	+2.34	+4.47	+0.83	+17.72	+16.57	+17.78
Japan	+2.18	+2.50	-5.86	-4.88	-6.77	-5.80
Malaysia	-1.69	-0.71	-15.76	+0.00	-0.37	+0.67
New Zealand	-1.42	-1.46	+1.34	+7.24	+9.79	+10.94
Singapore	+2.01	+3.14	-5.38	-1.02	-0.02	+1.03
Canada	-0.91	-2.47	+5.41	+6.29	+10.78	+11.94
USA	-0.23	+2.00	+29.13	+27.06	+25.75	+27.06
Mexico	+1.09	-7.18	-6.15	+0.75	-24.85	-24.07
South Africa	+1.82	+2.42	+17.01	-4.71	+4.97	+6.06
WORLD INDEX	**+0.45**	**+0.94**	**+10.81**	**+10.30**	**+10.84**	**+12.00**

† Based on October 6th 1995. © Copyright 1995 Financial Times Limited, Goldman, Sachs & Co., Standard & Poor's. All rights rese

Fig. 7.8 Markets in perspective

Evaluating quarterly performance

The FT/S&P Actuaries world indices quarterly valuation (see Figure 7.9) carries quarterly assessments of market capitalisation and relative market size for the major national and regional markets.

- **Market capitalisation:** calculated for each market by multiplying the total number of shares in issue by the market price per share.

- **Percentage of world index:** the relative size of each market to the whole. This indicates the dominance of the US and Japanese markets with the United Kingdom also standing out.

FT/S&P ACTUARIES WORLD INDICES QUARTERLY VALUATION

The market capitalisation of the national and regional markets of the FT/S&P Actuaries World Indices as at SEPTEMBER 29, 1995 expressed below in millions of US dollars and as a percentage of the World Index. Similar figures are provided for the preced quarter. The percentage change for each US dollar Index value since the end of the calendar year is also provided.

NATIONAL AND REGIONAL MARKETS (number of lines of stock)	Market cap. as at 29/09/95 (US$m)	% of World Index	Market cap. as at 30/06/95 (US$m)	% of World Index	% chge in $ in since 31/12/9
Australia (82)	172562.9	1.60	151306.2	1.48	8.27
Austria (26)	16795.0	0.16	18304.0	0.18	-1.14
Belgium (35)	75247.7	0.70	74710.3	0.73	16.14
Brazil (28)	46365.2	0.43	39748.9	0.39	-6.52
Canada (101)	164707.2	1.53	164661.0	1.61	11.70
Denmark (33)	38435.6	0.36	37587.8	0.37	12.11
Finland (25)	42058.5	0.39	37506.6	0.37	42.97
France (100)	356932.7	3.32	366020.0	3.58	5.69
Germany (59)	389028.9	3.62	382246.8	3.74	11.28
Hong Kong (55)	190213.0	1.77	181734.9	1.78	15.11
Ireland (16)	18543.2	0.17	17543.3	0.17	20.96
Italy (59)	138679.6	1.29	133113.9	1.30	1.26
Japan (483)	2712496.3	25.22	2611495.6	25.54	-5.85
Malaysia (107)	117167.1	1.09	112200.1	1.10	3.47
Mexico (18)	40794.8	0.38	38411.3	0.38	-22.88
Netherland (19)	219881.2	2.04	209808.0	2.05	19.61
New Zealand (14)	21842.3	0.20	21609.1	0.21	11.89
Norway (33)	24879.2	0.23	24482.3	0.24	11.12
Singapore (44)	58474.6	0.54	60340.0	0.59	-0.44
South Africa (45)	127341.8	1.18	133571.3	1.31	4.45
Spain (38)	105916.3	0.98	102949.2	1.01	14.44
Sweden (48)	138801.6	1.29	115437.5	1.13	38.65
Switzerland (43)	298183.7	2.77	280778.9	2.75	30.28
Thailand (46)	21767.9	0.20	22672.8	0.22	3.09
United Kingdom (200)	1033641.3	9.61	986544.3	9.65	15.34
USA (504)	4184216.8	38.90	3901748.4	38.15	27.35
Americas (651)	4436083.9	41.25	4144569.5	40.53	25.56
Europe (734)	2897024.5	26.94	2787032.7	27.25	15.48
Nordic (139)	244174.9	2.27	215014.2	2.10	31.42
Pacific Basin (831)	3294524.1	30.63	3161358.8	30.91	-3.68
Euro-Pacific (1565)	6191548.7	57.57	5948391.5	58.17	4.44
North America (605)	4348924.0	40.44	4066409.4	39.76	26.68
Europe Ex. UK (534)	1863383.2	17.33	1800488.5	17.61	15.58
Pacific Ex. Japan (348)	582027.8	5.41	549863.2	5.38	8.41
World Ex. US (1757)	6570757.6	61.10	6324783.9	61.85	4.30
World Ex. UK (2061)	9721333.1	90.39	9239988.1	90.35	11.9
World Ex. Japan (1778)	8042478.1	74.78	7615036.7	74.46	20.0
The World Index (2261)	10754974.4	100.00	10226532.3	100.00	12.2

Fig. 7.9 FT/S&P Actuaries world indices (quarterly valuation)

INTERNATIONAL EQUITY INVESTING

Direct investing in international equities is an increasingly attractive proposition. The widespread deregulation of financial markets has made dealing shares across national boundaries much easier. Nowadays, it is quite possible to get a stake in industries that do not exist

at home and in economies with more favourable growth prospects or at different stages of the business cycle. International investments are also likely to afford superior returns to those available in a single market, especially if they encompass some of the emerging markets of the newly industrialising world. There are greater risks associated with such returns, but the range of choice in the global equity market offers strong potential for diversification.

At the level of the individual company, there are frequently problems in comparing the relative merits of companies across markets. It is important to remember that financial reporting and accounting standards vary, and that indicators such as price/earnings ratios are often unreliable for international comparisons. Countries employ a variety of accounting conventions in their treatment of corporate profits. There are also differences in dealing and settlement arrangements, in rules on the size of investments, and in provisions for the custody and transfer of share certificates.

There is also the danger of adverse currency fluctuations: foreign exchange risk is likely to be the biggest threat to overseas transactions. Linkages between world equity markets can also affect the performance of an international portfolio. For example, with many major stocks traded in both London and New York, the two markets have become highly interdependent. Others might have a lower degree of correlation, if they respond in different ways to prevailing global economic conditions.

Another attractive area for the international equity investor is that of new issues. Buying shares the first time they are offered to the public, whether in privatisations of state-owned corporations or previously private companies coming to market, can be very profitable, perhaps especially for investors with relatively short investment horizons. In Europe, the new issue boom has partly arisen from the UK government's programme of privatisation, encouraging investors and issuers to enter the market, and other countries to launch their own selling agendas. Worldwide, it has been influenced by the weight of demand from investing institutions and the stress they place on quality control in new issues.

The success of the UK privatisation program has inspired numerous other governments to turn their public sector companies into publicly quoted ones. For the global investor, there may be opportunities in the Far East, Latin America, and the formerly planned

economies as well as in continental Europe. Many of the companies on the block are large, stable businesses with leading positions in their market sectors. After privatisation, they will become answerable to shareholders, presumably focusing far more on profitability, growth and cash flow. This could lead to some major gains in their value over the longer term in addition to first day appreciation. Potentially dramatic increases in profitability also offer the prospect of fast growth in dividends.

Important considerations with global issues include international differences in accounting practices and settlement arrangements; the identity and reputation of the sponsor; the language in which the prospectus is written; whether some issues are not available to non-residents; and the procedures for scaling down an application in the event of oversubscription.

Emerging markets

Both for multinational businesses and for private and institutional investors, the markets of the developing world are becoming more and more appealing. This is partly a response to such political developments as the collapse of communism and the increasingly global embrace of liberal democratic values, which may have reduced the sovereign or country risk of overseas investments. But naturally enough, economic forces also play a critical role: relatively lower labour costs are an attraction to multinationals to shift production to the developing world, as are the vast markets those workers represent for global brands like Coca Cola, Marlboro and McDonald's.

Emerging markets currently account for 13 per cent of world market capitalisation, but predictions suggest that by 2010 these markets will be 45 per cent of total capitalisation as more firms become listed and as faster growth in output and profits than in developed economies boost share prices. By 2010, China, India, Brazil and Russia could rival America, Japan and the United Kingdom as the world's biggest stock markets.

The terms emerging market and emerging economy tend to be used interchangeably, and the definition is somewhat hazy. Some so-called emerging economies, for example, have larger market capi-

talisations than developed ones: the markets of Hong Kong, Malaysia, Singapore and Taiwan all have higher capitalisation per head than Germany.

In emerging markets, currency risks are likely to be compounded by political risks, the greater sensitivity of investors to the signs of impending devaluation or depreciation, and the impact of fundamental economic events elsewhere in the world. The "flight to quality" following the Mexican devaluation of early 1995 showed all of these in action: the arrival of a new government with untested macroeconomic policies, the dangers of current account deficits and limited reserves, and the increases in US interest rates making dollars relatively more appealing than pesos (see chapters 10 and 15).

Each Monday and Thursday, the *Financial Times* carries data on the emerging stock markets of Latin America, east and south Asia, Europe and the Middle East, which are attracting increasing investor attention. Thursday's tables are prepared by the International Finance Corporation, a subsidiary of the World Bank, as a complement to the much more comprehensive daily coverage of the FT/S&P Actuaries world series (see Figure 7.10 overleaf).

- **Market and number of stocks:** countries' stock exchanges and the number of stocks listed on it that are included in the index.

- **Dollar terms:** the latest value of the local market index, the percentage change over the previous week, and from the end of the previous year.

- **Local currency terms:** the same figures in the local currency.

Monday's newspaper has an entire Emerging Markets page with a column on "The Emerging Investor", a news round-up, a table of the ten best performing emerging market stocks by percentage price rise of the previous week, and a further table of emerging market indices prepared by Baring Securities (see Figure 7.11 on p 153).

- **Market, number of stocks and latest value:** markets in five Latin American countries, three European (plus South Africa) and seven Asian plus composites for Latin America, Europe, Asia and the

EMERGING MARKETS: IFC WEEKLY INVESTABLE PRICE INDICES

Market	No. of stocks	Dollar terms October 6 1995	% Change over week	% Change on Dec '94	Local currency terms October 6 1995	% Change over week	% Chang on Dec '‹
Latin America	(252)	489.66	-1.4	-15.6			
Argentina	(30)	699.49	+2.6	-4.7	429,003.34	+2.6	-4
Brazil	(72)	334.03	-2.5	-13.1	1,197.88	-1.9	-1
Chile	(36)	745.32	-0.8	-5.0	1,197.94	-0.3	-8
Colombia[1]	(16)	605.20	-5.0	-25.4	1,049.38	-3.6	-12
Mexico	(67)	470.02	-1.8	-22.7	1,324.36	+0.8	+2
Peru[2]	(19)	195.52	-0.5	+9.6	269.41	-0.2	+13
Venezuela[3]	(12)	458.40	+13.5	-7.4	1,789.19	+13.5	-
Asia	(657)	239.92	-0.1	-3.8			
China[4]	(20)	67.58	+1.0	-10.9	71.01	+1.0	-1
South Korea[5]	(159)	143.83	+1.5	+5.2	145.30	+1.6	+
Philippines	(25)	265.68	+2.2	-10.9	332.28	+1.6	-
Taiwan, China[6]	(93)	115.45	+4.1	-29.8	116.59	+3.5	-2
India[7]	(101)	96.62	+3.8	-21.8	116.36	+3.8	-1
Indonesia[8]	(42)	108.49	+1.2	+8.8	133.62	+1.3	+1
Malaysia	(114)	269.64	-2.8	+0.3	252.41	-1.8	-
Pakistan[9]	(36)	290.56	-0.8	-20.6	416.81	-0.5	-1
Sri Lanka[10]	(19)	107.66	+1.2	-37.4	121.78	+1.0	-3
Thailand	(68)	391.72	+3.0	+2.1	390.60	+3.2	+
Euro/Mid East	(210)	137.00	+1.4	+15.6			
Greece	(40)	244.97	-4.8	+8.6	389.30	-3.6	+
Hungary[11]	(5)	125.17	-1.5	-17.5	198.02	-0.4	-
Jordan	(8)	186.63	+0.6	+24.4	280.23	+0.9	+2
Poland[12]	(16)	465.19	-4.2	-0.9	715.86	-3.8	-
Portugal	(28)	120.45	+1.9	-0.5	124.30	+2.3	-
South Africa[13]	(64)	238.75	+1.2	+6.2	180.50	+1.5	-
Turkey[14]	(44)	137.62	+6.6	+13.0	3,237.68	+8.5	+4
Zimbabwe[15]	(5)	260.38	-1.4	+6.4	339.53	-1.1	+1
Composite	(1119)	279.39	-0.1	-9.1			

Indices are calculated at end-week, and weekly changes are percentage movement from the previous Friday. Base date: Dec 1988=100 except those r which are: (1)Feb 1 1991; (2)Dec 31 1992; (3)Jan 5 1990; (4)Dec 31 1992; (5)Jan 3 1992; (6)Jan 4 1991; (7)Nov 6 1992; (8)Sep 28 1990; (9)Mar 1 1991 Dec 31 1992; (11)Dec 31 1992; (12)Dec 31 1992; (13)Dec 31 1992; (14)Aug 4 1989; (15)June 2 1993.

Fig. 7.10 Emerging markets (IFC indices)

world; the number of individual stocks in each index; and the index value at the end of the previous week.

- **Week on week, month on month and year to date:** movement of the index over each of these three periods, both in actual index number terms and as a percentage of the total index value.

Baring Securities emerging markets indices							
dex	22/9/95	Week on week movement		Month on month movement		Year to date movement	
		Actual	Percent	Actual	Percent	Actual	Percent
World (352) 146.98		-3.11	-2.07	-0.57	-0.39	-11.05	-6.99
Latin America							
Argentina (23)	78.75	-1.51	-1.88	-0.22	-0.28	-7.36	-8.55
Brazil (22)	197.76	-5.96	-2.93	-1.95	-0.98	-11.61	-5.55
Chile (13)	186.79	-5.06	-2.64	-3.575	-1.87	-24.78	-11.71
Mexico (24)	75.59	-4.33	-5.42	-2.48	-3.18	-22.04	-22.58
Peru (15)	1,007.37	-55.60	-5.23	-39.44	-3.77	+158.70	+18.70
Latin America (97) 122.97		-4.57	-3.58	-2.23	-1.78	-15.80	-11.39
Europe							
Greece (18)	106.93	-1.00	-0.93	+2.72	+2.61	+19.94	+22.92
Portugal (22)	115.68	+0.23	+0.20	+2.77	+2.46	-0.60	-0.51
Turkey (21)	98.61	-3.59	-3.51	-11.37	-10.34	+22.50	+29.56
South Africa (34)	138.00	+0.06	+0.04	+3.08	+2.28	+10.06	+7.86
Europe (95) 114.29		-0.33	-0.29	+1.53	+1.35	+16.60	+16.99
Asia							
Indonesia (28)	141.40	-1.74	-1.22	-6.18	-4.19	+7.71	+5.77
Korea (24)	150.81	-1.12	-0.74	+14.82	+10.90	+10.92	+7.81
Malaysia (21)	227.41	-5.18	-2.23	-2.95	-1.28	+16.56	+7.85
Pakistan (16)	87.47	-3.52	-3.86	-5.73	-6.15	-18.73	-17.64
Philippines (14)	262.97	-7.34	-2.71	-13.17	-4.77	-19.15	-6.79
Thailand (25)	251.20	-2.59	-1.02	-6.46	-2.51	-0.44	-0.18
Taiwan (32)	130.69	+1.82	+1.42	+5.16	+4.11	-53.46	-29.03
Asia (160) 206.71		-2.62	-1.25	+0.60	+0.29	-3.90	-1.85

indices in $ terms, January 7th 1992=100. Source: Baring Securities

Fig. 7.11 Emerging markets (Baring Securities indices)

" The management of stock exchange investments of any kind is a low pursuit from which it is a good thing for most members of our society to be free."

JOHN MAYNARD KEYNES

" Put not your trust in money, but put your money in trust."

OLIVER WENDELL HOLMES

8

TRUSTS AND FUNDS
The managed money markets

- **The managed funds service** – reading the figures and using the information on authorised unit trusts; other UK unit trusts

- **Investment trusts**

- **Insurances;** management services

- **Offshore and overseas** – opportunities for non-UK investors: SIB recognised funds; regulated funds; offshore insurances; and other offshore funds

- **US mutual funds**

Managed funds are collective investment vehicles that are run by investment companies to provide professional management of investors' money. These funds in turn may be linked to other financial products. Managed funds are an easy way to get into share-buying for small, private investors.

THE MANAGED FUNDS SERVICE

The *Financial Times* managed funds service provides investors with information relating to a substantial number of managed funds. The information is provided by the individual management groups to a specific formula laid down for UK authorised bodies by the regulatory organisations. The address and telephone number of the group are normally given under its name, except in the case of those offshore funds that have not been authorised by the Securities and Investments Board (SIB) or the Department of Trade and Industry (DTI) to be promoted for general sale in the United Kingdom. This does not mean that they are in some way suspect; it merely signifies that the country in which they are based has not applied for designated territory status. This status is only given if the country's regulatory system is deemed to be at least equal to that ruling in the United Kingdom.

Authorised unit trusts

Unit trusts offer professional management of funds pooled together and divided into units whose value is based on the market valuation of the securities acquired by the fund. Hence the value of the units varies in accordance with the movement of the market prices of the securities owned by the fund. Authorised unit trusts are unit trusts that have been approved as being suitable for general promotion and sale in the United Kingdom.

The attraction of unit trusts is that they enable small investors to achieve the advantages available to large investors of cheaper dealing costs and a spread of investments to reduce risk. They can also be tailored to meet the particular needs of investors looking for capital growth or income, or to go into specific sectors and overseas markets. They are therefore also widely used by stockbrokers and fund management groups. Since capital gains tax on sales and purchases made within the fund does not have to be paid, unit trusts have the additional advantage of favourable tax treatment.

A unit trust is divided into equal portions called units. Their prices are calculated daily to reflect the actual market value of the assets of the trust. Under the deed creating the trust, unit trust management groups have an obligation to keep investors properly informed about movements in the value of these units. Instead of having to circulate information to each unit holder individually, it is accepted by the authorities that this obligation can be discharged by regular publication of the unit prices in certain national newspapers, in particular the *Financial Times* (see Figure 8.1).

Reading the figures

- **Name of the investment group, its pricing system and trust name:** each investment group is listed together with its component trusts, and the basis of its pricing system. The price regime for each group is measured at a certain cut-off point, the figure in brackets representing a time, and calculated on a forward (F) or historical (H) basis. The trust name will indicate what kind of assets the trust invests in.

- **Initial charge:** the second column indicates the percentage charge imposed on buyers of the fund by the manager to cover the "front load" costs of administration and marketing plus commission paid to intermediaries. The initial charge is included in the buying price of units. If the initial charge is 5 per cent, out of every £100 invested, £5 is retained by the management group to cover its costs, leaving the remaining £95 to be actually invested in the fund.

- **Notes:** the third column notes any special features of the trust. For example, the letter E denotes that there may be exit charges when

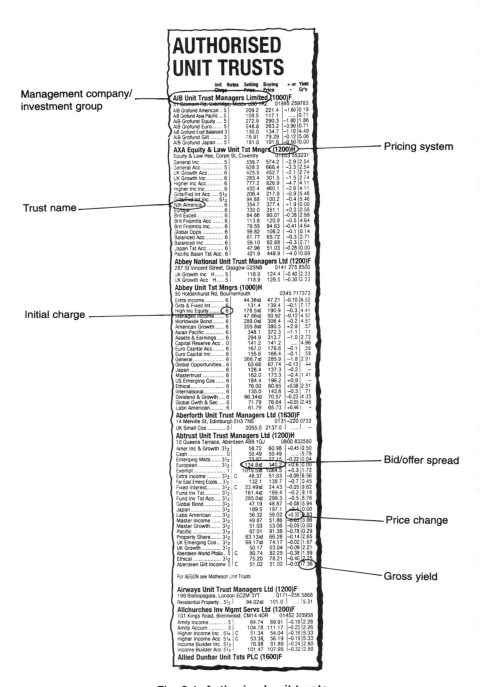

Management company/investment group

Pricing system

Trust name

Initial charge

Bid/offer spread

Price change

Gross yield

Fig. 8.1 Authorised unit trusts

units are sold, and the letter C indicates that there will be a periodic management charge, typically 1–1.5 per cent annually.

- **Selling price/buying price:** the fourth and fifth columns show the gap between the selling or bid price, at which units can be sold, and the buying or offer price, at which they can be bought. These are calculated by the group assessing the value of the underlying securities held at the most recent lowest market dealing price (plus other assets like uninvested income and undistributed income), adding the various costs involved such as dealing charges, and dividing the total by the number of units issued.

- **Price change:** the sixth column compares the mid-point between the selling and buying prices with the previous quotation. It may be unchanged, or show an upward or downward trend, according to changes in the value of the underlying securities or an alteration in the bid/offer spread. Since Saturday's newspaper carries the price change for the last day's trading of the week, the Monday paper replaces this column with the trust's Cityline number. Real-time unit trust prices can be obtained by dialling 0891 430010 plus the relevant five digit code.

- **Gross yield:** the last column indicates gross income paid by the unit trust as a percentage of the offer price. The quoted yield reflects income earned by the fund during the previous twelve months, and therefore only relates to past performance. The figure is gross since it does not reflect the unit holder's tax liability, but as most unit trusts charge their management expenses against income, the gross yield is net of expenses. However, a rule change has allowed trusts to charge some or all of their management expenses to capital, thus inflating the yield. The managed funds service identifies those trusts which charge to capital.

Using the information

The information provided means that investors can calculate how much their unit trust holdings are worth, and how they are performing on a day-to-day basis. Details of charges made by individual fund groups are also provided.

The spread is used by unit trust groups to collect the initial charge imposed to cover the expense of setting up and promoting the fund as well as recouping other costs. Under the formula laid down by the SIB, the spread for unit trusts can only be moved up and down within a limited scale. If there is a surplus of sellers, the spread tends to be based at the bottom end of the scale. Conversely, if there is an excess of buyers, the spread is raised to the upper end of the scale, enhancing the value of the fund. The spread also reflects the fact that there are spreads in the prices of the shares in which trusts invest: like all investors, they buy at offer prices and sell at bid prices.

It is important to be aware of a unit trust's pricing policy, whether "historic", based on the price set at the most recent valuation of its portfolio of assets, or "forward", based on the price to be set at the next valuation. In the latter case, investors can be never be sure of the price of a purchase or sale in advance of it being carried out.

Unit trusts are open-ended in that within reason there is no limit to the number of units a given trust can issue. An investor who wants to sell his or her units back to the trust will cause the trust either to find other willing owners or to sell some of its assets to pay for the buyback.

The income received by unit trusts on their investments must be paid out to unit holders, but there is often a distinction between income and accumulation units. With the former, the investor receives the appropriate share of dividends earned by the trust as cash; with the latter, income is added to the value of each unit, that is, the income is reinvested (net of tax). There are often separate listings for the prices of income and accumulation units, the latter being higher because of the reinvested income.

Unit trusts with low, or even nil, yields are those concentrating on capital growth rather than providing income. If there is a yield, UK investors have to deduct their top rate of income tax from this yield to calculate the true (net) return they will receive. Hence a gross yield of 10 per cent is currently only equivalent to 6 per cent for the top-rate taxpayer.

Unit trusts were originally conceived to offer a spread of investments across the market, but they are now often much more focused, specialising by asset type (mainly equities but also bonds

and currencies) and by the countries and regions in which they are invested, by the size of companies and the kind of industries, and by whether they are primarily pursuing income, capital apprecia-tion or a combination of the two. The relationship between risk and return in the chosen market is important to selection, as are the investor's own investment goals: income, capital growth or total return. Unit trusts should generally be seen as a long-term invest-ment: they need time to recoup the dealing charges.

The performance of unit trusts is assessed in more detail in Satur-day's *Financial Times*. A half page presents information on the over-all winners and losers (the top and bottom five funds in terms of returns over one, three, five and ten years), and the top five and sector average performances for these four periods for over twenty different fund types ranging from those investing in UK smaller com-panies' equities to those trading international bonds. Figure 8.2 shows a couple of examples as well as a table for various indices.

■ Indices	1 year (£)	3	5	10	Volatility	Yld %
Average Unit Trust	1037	1529	1924	3131	4.1	2.7
Average Investment Trust	1060	1820	2094	3880	5.9	4.8
Bank	1039	1118	1258	1816	0.0	5.3
Building Society	1035	1111	1283	1953	0.0	4.7
Stockmarket: FT All-Share	1187	1618	2070	3785	3.5	3.8
Inflation	1039	1080	1165	1578	0.4	-

■ UK General	1 year (£)	3	5	10	Volatility	Yld %
Newton Foundation	1104	1756	-	-	3.9	2.4
M&G Second General	1047	1736	1952	3370	3.9	3.6
M&G Midland & General	980	1727	1773	3763	4.4	3.1
GAM UK Diversified Inc	1029	1713	1970	-	4.4	3.3
Cazenove UK Income & Growth	1113	1645	1939	-	2.8	3.1
SECTOR AVERAGE	1087	1478	1783	3104	3.6	2.8

■ UK Growth						
Fidelity Recovery	1013	2169	2090	-	4.3	-
Fidelity Special Situations	1118	1992	2006	4849	4.1	-
Guinness Flight Recovery	971	1988	1669	3356	5.2	2.1
Exeter Capital Growth	999	1970	1890	-	5.4	-
Provident Mutual Equity Growth	1214	1965	2079	-	4.0	1.3
SECTOR AVERAGE	1095	1545	1822	3047	3.7	2.1

Fig. 8.2 Unit trusts

The tables show the result of investing £1,000 in a trust over the four different time periods. It is important to remember that these are merely a historical record and cannot be a guide to future performance. The volatility figure shows the absolute variability of the trust's performance, measured by standard deviation of monthly price movements over three years. As a rule of thumb, the more volatile a fund's progress (the higher the figure), the higher the return investors demand from it to compensate for the additional risk, and the more wary potential new investors should be. The yield is the annual income paid gross to unit holders as a percentage of the units' value. For some funds, there is no yield shown since income is reinvested rather than distributed to unit holders.

The indices show performance, volatility and yield figures for an average unit trust, an average investment trust, representative bank and building society accounts, the FT All-Share index and inflation.

Saturday's newspaper also generally includes a table of new unit trust launches with details of their target yields, charges, minimum investment levels, availabilities to participate in tax-free savings schemes and any special offer discounts. Unit trusts are generally offered at a fixed price for a limited period.

Other UK unit trusts

These are trusts that are not authorised by the SIB and which are therefore not open to investment by members of the general public. They are available only to specific buyers such as pension funds, charities and local authorities.

INVESTMENT TRUSTS

Investment trusts are companies that exist to invest in the equity of other companies, and their business consists entirely of buying, selling and holding shares. Like unit trusts, they provide an accessible vehicle for small investors to achieve a wide spread of investments. Investment trusts differ from unit trusts, however, in the sense that they issue equity themselves, and hence their shareholders hold a direct stake in the profits of the trust rather than merely the profits of a unit of shareholdings. They are also closed-ended; there is a finite

number of shares in issue. Their performance is listed in the FT London share service (see Figure 8.3).

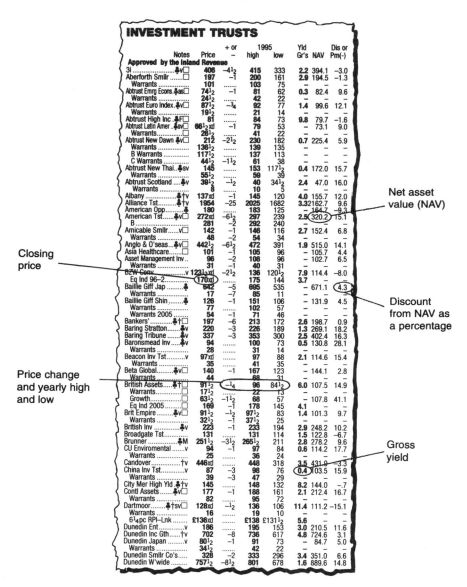

Fig. 8.3 London share service: Investment trusts

- **Prices and yields:** latest prices, price changes, highs and lows for the year and gross yield as in the standard share coverage.

● **Net asset value (NAV), discount and premium:** the NAV figure is the market value per share of the various securities in which the trust has invested, and therefore what, in theory, the trust might be worth if it were liquidated immediately. The discount (rarely is it a premium) is where the share price typically stands in relation to the NAV per share. The amount of the discount is calculated as a percentage of the NAV per share. These figures are of key importance to investors in making their buying and selling decisions.

The figures are supplied by a leading broker and are the result of a daily simulation of changes in portfolio values. Calculations of the discount are generally reliable but, in some cases, such as recent new issues with substantial uninvested cash or funds which have radically restructured their portfolios, the estimates may need to be treated with caution.

Investment trust shares traditionally sell at a discount to their underlying asset value. In the 1974 bear market, discounts were as wide as 45 per cent and although they have mainly narrowed to well under 10 per cent, they add an additional uncertainty to investment trust share price prospects. In general, the more significant the discount from net asset values per share to share prices, the more tempting an investment trust will be as a takeover target.

Compared to unit trusts, the commission charged on investment trusts is usually cheaper and the bid/offer spread narrower. But it is not possible to make minute comparisons of unit and investment trusts: the unit trust figures take account of the spread between buying and selling prices while the investment trust figures take mid-prices in both cases. Comparisons thus flatter investment trusts. In addition, the narrowing of investment trust discounts makes them look better than unit trusts on longer term comparisons.

Below the unit trust analysis in Saturday's *Financial Times* is a half page of figures for investment trusts. As with unit trusts, this includes the overall winners and losers (the top and bottom five funds in terms of returns over one, three, five and ten years), and the top five and sector average performances for these four periods for twenty different fund types. These fall into six broad categories: general trusts with an international portfolio of shares; trusts investing in specific geographical areas; trusts investing in specific market sectors;

trusts aiming to generate high income; trusts aiming for capital growth; and trusts with a split capital structure.

Ten per cent of funds under investment trust management are in split capital trusts. These are companies with more than one class of share capital. The traditional variety is relatively simple: income shares get all the income, and capital shares get any capital growth over the life of the trust. Nowadays splits are highly complex with several different types of security with differing rights and risks, and aiming to satisfy different investment needs. For example, at one extreme, zero dividend and preference shares offer a low risk investment with a predetermined return; at the other, capital shares offer the potential for a high capital return at winding up but also the possibility that the shares will be valueless at the end of the trust's life.

Some but not all unit and investment trusts can be put into a general personal equity plan (PEP), which shields investors against both income and capital gains tax. PEPs are personal investment vehicles launched in the United Kingdom in 1987. The PEP rules are that an investor can put £6,000 into a general PEP, and a further £3,000 into a single company PEP. To qualify for the full £6,000 general PEP allowance, a minimum of a plan's assets must be held in European Union shares, trusts or qualifying corporate bonds. A PEP must be run by a professional fund manager.

Saturday's newspaper typically lists new investment trust launches with details of their target sizes and yields, charges, issue prices, minimum NAVs, relationships with tax-free savings schemes and PEPs, and offer periods. Since investment trusts typically trade at a discount to their NAV, investments in new issues may initially fall in value.

INSURANCES

These are funds that are managed by insurance companies and are linked to other savings products such as investment bonds, regular premium policies or pension contracts. The FT listings follow the same pattern as for unit trusts except there is rarely a yield figure since income is automatically reinvested (see Figure 8.4).

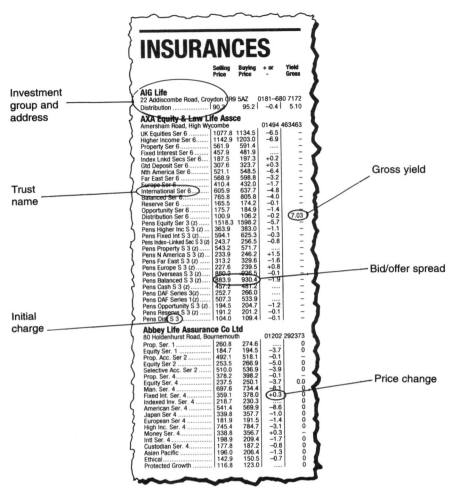

Fig. 8.4 Insurances

Management services

These are unit-linked insurance funds which are managed mainly by intermediaries. They are often known as "broker bonds". Many of them are underwritten by insurance companies.

OFFSHORE AND OVERSEAS

These are funds that operate like unit trusts but are based in foreign countries, often with a more liberal tax regime than the

United Kingdom, but still effectively operating under the advice or management of groups offering authorised unit trusts in the United Kingdom (see Figure 8.5). They are often located in the Channel Islands, Bermuda and the Cayman Islands. For the UK-based investor, there is no tax advantage in investing in these funds, but there may well be for the expatriate or other overseas investor. Readers seeking further information are referred to Leo Gough's *The Investor's Guide to Offshore Investment: International Tactics for the Active Investor* (*Financial Times* Pitman Publishing, 1995).

SIB recognised funds

These are offshore funds that are based in designated territory-status countries and the European Union and for which authorisation for promotion in the United Kingdom has been secured from the SIB. These funds can be sold freely without any restrictions and their full names, addresses and telephone numbers are therefore included in the listing.

Regulated funds

These funds are based in designated territory-status countries which comply with local regulations but have not applied for official SIB recognition for sale in the United Kingdom. They cannot be promoted in the United Kingdom and therefore only the names are listed.

Offshore insurances

These are funds that are run by insurance companies which are based in countries with designated territory status for insurance products. The funds listed are linked to products which the companies are authorised to promote in the United Kingdom. Such authorisation must be sought from the SIB.

Other offshore funds

These are funds based in countries throughout the world but predominantly in tax havens. They cannot be advertised in the United Kingdom and again only the names are listed.

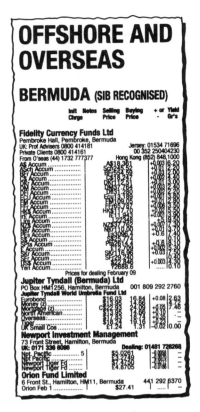

Fig. 8.5 Offshore and overseas

US MUTUAL FUNDS

The US equivalent of the UK managed money market is the mutual fund industry. As with unit trusts and investment trusts, the money invested in a mutual fund is pooled to buy a range of stocks, bonds and/or other assets. This offers the benefits to the small investor of diversification, flexible investing, professional management, automatic reinvestment or payment of income and liquidity. Investors who buy stocks directly face much higher trading costs because they cannot match the pooled funds' ability, for example, to negotiate lower commissions from stockbrokers.

The *Financial Times* does not carry information on US mutual funds but they are well covered in the *Wall Street Journal*. The US newspaper covers both open-end funds for which the fund will sell as many shares as investors want (the equivalent of unit trusts) and closed-end funds for which there are only a limited number of shares (the equivalent of investment trusts). There is also a distinction between load funds, which charge a commission when bought and sold, and no-load funds, which only charge a management fee. The typical fund charges 0.75 per cent of an investor's assets.

The US mutual fund market has grown dramatically in the last fifteen years. The most popular funds are simply cash substitutes known as money market funds (the UK equivalent are discussed in chapter 1), which invest in very short-term interest-bearing securities. Next are bond funds, which own securities with average maturities exceeding ninety days. Lastly, there are equity funds, which invest across a range of different US and international stocks and shares.

"I used to think that if there was reincarnation, I wanted to come back as the president or the pope. But now I want to be the bond market: you can intimidate everybody."

JAMES CARVILLE,
ADVISER TO BILL CLINTON

"Every intelligent investor should know something about bonds just to fill in a vital part of the background."

LOUIS ENGEL, *HOW TO BUY STOCKS*

9

BONDS AND EUROBONDS
The international capital markets

- **Government bonds** – the UK gilt market: UK gilts prices; fixed interest indices; benchmark government bonds

- **Corporate bonds** – fixed income securities from non-sovereign debtors: Eurobonds; new international bond issues; reading the figures and using the information in the FT/ISMA international bond service

Bonds are debt instruments, securities sold by governments, companies and banks in order to raise capital. They normally carry a fixed rate of interest, known as the coupon, have a fixed redemption value, the par value, and are repaid after a fixed period, the maturity. Some carry little or no interest (deep discount and zero coupon bonds), rewarding the buyer instead with a substantial discount from their redemption value and, hence, the prospect of a sizeable capital gain.

As seen in chapter 1, the prices of bonds fluctuate in relation to the interest rate. The secondary market for bonds provides the liquidity necessary for a thriving primary market. This now exists not only for government bonds, but also on an international scale for all kinds of debt instruments.

National boundaries are no longer an obstruction to lenders and borrowers meeting in a market to buy and sell securities. It is possible for borrowers in one country to issue securities denominated in the currency of another, and for these to be sold to investors in a third country. Often, such transactions will be organised by financial institutions located in yet another country, usually one of the three primary centres of these international capital markets – London, New York and Tokyo. These are the Euromarkets.

The International Capital Markets pages of the *Financial Times* attempt to keep track of developments in the Euromarkets and other areas which involve the raising of capital across borders. These include the growing markets in derivative products (such as futures, options, and interest rate and currency swaps) and in crossborder new equity issues. The newspaper also tracks developments in important government bond markets such as the US Treasury bond market and, of course, the market in UK government bonds, known as gilt-edged stock or gilts.

From Tuesday to Friday, daily reports cover the market in international bonds, including Eurobonds and government bonds. On Monday, the World Bond Markets page examines the prospects for the week ahead, particularly focusing on the markets in New York,

London, Frankfurt and Tokyo. These markets, like the international equity markets, are not compartmentalised. In the interdependent world of international finance, developments in one market will often influence many others. For example, a sharp rally in gilts is likely to prompt a similar rally in Eurosterling bonds, which may in turn encourage borrowers to launch new issues.

GOVERNMENT BONDS

As discussed in chapter 4, the government of a country finances many of its activities through borrowing from lenders by issuing bonds. In the United Kingdom, government bonds are known as gilt-edged securities and they trade in a secondary market run by leading marketmakers.

UK gilts prices

Detailed price information on the UK government bond market is published daily under the heading UK Gilts Prices. These are classified under four headings based on their time to redemption: "shorts" with lives up to five years, "medium-dated" with lives from five to fifteen years, "longs" with lives of over fifteen years, and undated, irredeemable stocks like Consols and War Loan. The classifications reflect the current life of the stock rather than the life when it was issued, and so stocks get reclassified as their date of maturity draws closer. There is also a fifth category, index-linked gilts, the yields of which are tied to the rate of inflation.

The gilt market is moved by economic and financial news, notably the movements of interest rates and inflation. The key to understanding it is that as interest rates go up, bond prices go down, making the coupon an effective rate of interest. Since high rates may be used to support a weak currency, a weakness in the currency may signal future increases in the interest rate, and a damaging effect on gilt prices. Similarly, prospects of inflation may lead to rate increases and bond price falls. Inflation also erodes the value of bonds since their prices and yields, unless index-linked, do not keep pace with rising prices generally. Hence, it is important for investors in bonds to look for changes in expectations about the future rates of interest and

inflation. Other price determinants include the degree of risk (credit risk in the case of companies), the opportunity cost of other potential investments, and the time value of the bonds.

The market for gilts is run by primary dealers, the gilt-edged marketmakers (GEMMs) who have an obligation to maintain a market and a right to deal directly with the Bank of England in, for example, bidding for tap stock (see below). Information on gilt prices is carried on SEAQ and transactions are for immediate or cash settlement. Institutional investors generally deal directly with the primary dealers. Figure 9.1 shows FT listings of UK gilts prices.

- **Stock name and coupon:** the name given to a gilt is not important except as a means of differentiating it from others. The coupon, however, indicates how much nominal yield the owner is entitled to receive annually. Most gilts are issued in units of £100 (their par value), and so the percentage is equivalent to the number of pounds the owner receives. The coupon is a good indication of the interest rates the government was obliged to pay at the time of issue, and of the broad movements in the rate over the years.

- **Redemption date:** the year of redemption by the government, the specific date on which repayment of the loan will take place. If there are two dates, there is no specific date for repayment, but the stock will not be redeemed before the first one, and must be by the second one.

- **Interest yield:** this yield (also known as the income, earnings or flat yield) depends on the current price of the stock. It is calculated by dividing the coupon by the current price. This explains mathematically why bond prices always fall when interest rates rise and vice versa: since the coupon is, by definition, fixed, the price and yield are in an inverse relationship. To maintain a competitive yield when interest rates rise, the price has to fall. Gross redemption yield is the interest rate plus the capital gains or losses.

- **Redemption yield:** this figure indicates the total return to be secured by holding on to a stock until it is finally redeemed by the government. It thus includes the capital gains or losses made at redemption as well as the income from the coupon. If the current

UK GILTS PRICES

Shorts" (Lives up to Five Years) Notes	Yield Int	Yield Red	Price £	+ or –	1995 High	1995 Low
Treas $12\frac{3}{4}$pc 1995‡‡	12.68	6.27	$100\frac{9}{16}$xd	$-\frac{1}{32}$	$104\frac{7}{8}$	$100\frac{9}{16}$
14pc 1996	13.73	6.49	102	$-\frac{3}{32}$	$106\frac{7}{8}$	102
$15\frac{1}{4}$pc 1996‡‡	14.55	6.58	$104\frac{25}{32}$xd	$-\frac{1}{8}$	$109\frac{5}{8}$	$104\frac{25}{32}$
Exch $13\frac{1}{4}$pc 1996‡‡	12.76	6.64	$103\frac{7}{8}$xd	$-\frac{1}{16}$	$107\frac{1}{4}$	$103\frac{7}{8}$
Conversion 10pc 1996	9.65	6.55	$103\frac{5}{8}$xd	....	$104\frac{15}{32}$	$103\frac{3}{32}$
Treas $13\frac{1}{4}$pc 1997‡‡	12.28	6.61	$107\frac{15}{16}$	$-\frac{1}{16}$	$109\frac{23}{32}$	$107\frac{13}{32}$
Exch $10\frac{1}{2}$pc 1997	10.02	6.67	$104\frac{25}{32}$	$-\frac{3}{32}$	$105\frac{25}{32}$	$104\frac{1}{32}$
Treas Cnv 7pc 1997‡‡	6.98	6.81	$100\frac{7}{32}$	$-\frac{1}{16}$	$100\frac{13}{16}$	$97\frac{1}{8}$
Treas $8\frac{3}{4}$pc 1997‡‡	8.47	6.85	$103\frac{1}{4}$	$-\frac{1}{16}$	$103\frac{15}{16}$	$100\frac{1}{32}$
Exch 15pc 1997	13.03	6.90	$115\frac{5}{32}$xd	$-\frac{1}{16}$	$117\frac{3}{16}$	$114\frac{15}{16}$
$9\frac{3}{4}$pc 1998	9.24	7.04	$105\frac{17}{32}$	$-\frac{1}{8}$	$107\frac{5}{16}$	$102\frac{3}{4}$
Treas $7\frac{1}{4}$pc 1998‡‡	7.23	7.11	$100\frac{5}{16}$	$-\frac{1}{16}$	$101\frac{3}{32}$	$96\frac{5}{16}$
Treas $6\frac{3}{4}$pc 1995–98‡‡	6.82	7.21	$98\frac{15}{16}$xd	$-\frac{1}{8}$	$99\frac{27}{32}$	$94\frac{13}{16}$
Treas $15\frac{1}{2}$pc '98‡‡	12.74	7.26	$121\frac{5}{8}$	$-\frac{5}{32}$	$124\frac{1}{8}$	$120\frac{3}{8}$

Over Fifteen Years						
Treas 6 1/4pc 2010	7.60	8.33	$82\frac{1}{4}$	$-\frac{5}{32}$	$86\frac{15}{32}$	$79\frac{9}{32}$
Conv 9pc Ln 2011 ‡‡	8.50	8.32	$105\frac{7}{8}$	$-\frac{1}{4}$	$111\frac{1}{16}$	$101\frac{27}{32}$
Treas 9pc 2012‡‡	8.49	8.32	$106\frac{1}{32}$	$-\frac{3}{32}$	$111\frac{13}{32}$	$102\frac{1}{32}$
Treas $5\frac{1}{2}$pc 2008–12‡‡	7.11	7.99	$77\frac{3}{8}$	$-\frac{3}{32}$	$80\frac{5}{8}$	$72\frac{3}{4}$
Treas 8pc 2013‡‡	8.25	8.33	$96\frac{15}{16}$	$-\frac{1}{4}$	$102\frac{1}{4}$	$93\frac{15}{32}$
$7\frac{3}{4}$pc 2012–15‡‡	8.21	8.35	$94\frac{3}{8}$	$-\frac{1}{4}$	$99\frac{13}{16}$	$91\frac{21}{32}$
8pc 2015	8.25	8.31	$96\frac{15}{16}$	$-\frac{1}{4}$	$102\frac{27}{32}$	$93\frac{21}{32}$
Treas $8\frac{3}{4}$pc 2017‡‡	8.42	8.36	$103\frac{7}{8}$	$-\frac{5}{16}$	$110\frac{15}{32}$	$100\frac{21}{32}$
Exch 12pc 2013–17	9.01	8.40	$133\frac{1}{8}$	$-\frac{9}{32}$	$139\frac{27}{32}$	$127\frac{9}{16}$
Undated						
Consols 4pc	8.56	–	$46\frac{23}{32}$	$-\frac{7}{32}$	$49\frac{15}{16}$	$45\frac{1}{8}$
War Loan $3\frac{1}{2}$pc‡‡	8.36	–	$41\frac{7}{8}$	$-\frac{1}{8}$	$45\frac{3}{16}$	$40\frac{15}{32}$
Conv $3\frac{1}{2}$pc '61 Aft.	5.89	–	$59\frac{3}{8}$	$+\frac{1}{8}$	$61\frac{3}{16}$	$57\frac{15}{32}$
Treas 3pc '66 Aft	8.48	–	$35\frac{3}{8}$	$+\frac{5}{16}$	$37\frac{5}{16}$	$34\frac{1}{4}$
Consols $2\frac{1}{2}$pc	8.37	–	$29\frac{7}{8}$	$-\frac{1}{8}$	$31\frac{7}{8}$	$28\frac{23}{32}$
Treas. $2\frac{1}{2}$pc	8.47	–	$29\frac{1}{2}$	$-\frac{5}{16}$	$31\frac{5}{8}$	$28\frac{3}{8}$

n basis. xd Ex dividend. Closing mid-prices are shown in pounds per

Index–Linked Notes (b)	Yield (1)	Yield (2)	Price £	+ or –	1995 High	1995 Low
2pc '96 (67.9)	0.72	3.33	$212\frac{19}{32}$	$-\frac{3}{32}$	$213\frac{3}{16}$	$201\frac{1}{16}$
$4\frac{5}{8}$pc '98‡‡ (135.6)	2.21	3.27	$111\frac{3}{16}$xd	$-\frac{1}{8}$	$112\frac{3}{32}$	$106\frac{5}{16}$
$2\frac{1}{2}$pc '01 (78.3)	3.21	3.67	$174\frac{15}{16}$	$-\frac{3}{16}$	$177\frac{27}{32}$	$165\frac{25}{32}$
$2\frac{1}{2}$pc '03 (78.8)	3.34	3.69	$170\frac{7}{8}$	$-\frac{5}{16}$	$173\frac{7}{8}$	$161\frac{13}{16}$
$4\frac{3}{8}$pc '04‡‡ (135.6)	3.38	3.71	$113\frac{1}{8}$xd	$-\frac{5}{16}$	$115\frac{13}{16}$	$108\frac{3}{32}$
2pc '06 (69.5)	3.41	3.67	$179\frac{1}{8}$	$-\frac{7}{16}$	$183\frac{1}{16}$	$168\frac{7}{32}$
$2\frac{1}{2}$pc '09 (78.8)	3.51	3.73	$161\frac{5}{16}$	$-\frac{7}{16}$	$165\frac{21}{32}$	$152\frac{3}{32}$
$2\frac{1}{2}$pc '11 (74.6)	3.54	3.73	167	$-\frac{1}{2}$	$171\frac{5}{8}$	$157\frac{3}{16}$
$2\frac{1}{2}$pc '13 (89.2)	3.58	3.76	$137\frac{3}{16}$	$-\frac{11}{32}$	$141\frac{9}{16}$	$129\frac{9}{32}$
$2\frac{1}{2}$pc '16 (81.6)	3.61	3.78	146	$-\frac{3}{8}$	$150\frac{19}{32}$	$137\frac{5}{8}$
$2\frac{1}{2}$pc '20 (83.0)	3.65	3.79	$139\frac{15}{16}$xd	$-\frac{19}{32}$	$144\frac{21}{32}$	$131\frac{27}{32}$
$2\frac{1}{2}$pc '24‡‡ (97.7)	3.65	3.78	$116\frac{1}{8}$	$-\frac{9}{16}$	$120\frac{21}{32}$	$109\frac{1}{4}$
$4\frac{1}{8}$pc '30‡‡ (135.1)	3.66	3.79	115	$-\frac{19}{32}$	$119\frac{13}{16}$	$108\frac{9}{32}$

Prospective real redemption rate on projected inflation of (1) 10% and (2) 5%. (b) Figures in parentheses show RPI base for indexing (ie 8 months prior to issue) and have been adjusted to reflect rebasing of RPI to 100 in February 1987. Conversion factor 3.945. RPI for January 1995: 146.0 and for August 1995: 149.9.

Other Fixed Interest

Notes	Yield Int	Yield Red	Price £	+ or –	1995 High	1995 Low
Asian Dev $10\frac{1}{4}$pc 2009	9.01	8.51	$113\frac{25}{32}$	....	$116\frac{9}{16}$	$108\frac{11}{16}$
B'ham $11\frac{1}{2}$pc 2012	9.50	9.05	121	....	$122\frac{1}{2}$	$116\frac{1}{2}$
Ireland Cap $8\frac{1}{2}$pc '10	8.19	–	$103\frac{3}{4}$	....	106	$96\frac{3}{4}$
9pc Cap 1996	8.65	–	104	....	$104\frac{3}{4}$	100
13pc '97–2	11.76	–	$110\frac{1}{2}$	....	$111\frac{7}{8}$	107
Hydro Quebec 15pc 2011	10.33	9.41	$145\frac{7}{32}$	....	$154\frac{15}{32}$	$138\frac{31}{32}$
Leeds $13\frac{1}{2}$pc 2006	10.34	–	$130\frac{1}{2}$	....	$133\frac{1}{2}$	$126\frac{1}{2}$
Liverpool $3\frac{1}{2}$pc Irred.	10.61	–	33	....	40	33
LCC 3pc '20 Aft.	10.81	–	$27\frac{3}{4}$	....	$34\frac{1}{2}$	$27\frac{3}{4}$
Manchester $11\frac{1}{2}$pc 2007	9.70	8.95	$118\frac{1}{2}$	....	$119\frac{1}{2}$	$113\frac{1}{2}$
Met. Wtr. 3pc 'B'	4.26	8.39	$70\frac{1}{2}$	....	72	$69\frac{1}{4}$
N'wide Anglia $3\frac{7}{8}$pc 2021	–	4.51	$137\frac{1}{4}$	....	$143\frac{1}{2}$	$130\frac{1}{2}$
$4\frac{1}{4}$pc IL 2024	–	4.47	$131\frac{3}{4}$	....	$138\frac{1}{2}$	$123\frac{7}{8}$
Utd Mex States $16\frac{1}{2}$pc 2008	13.41	–	123	....	139	$113\frac{1}{2}$

£100 nominal of stock.

Stock name and coupon
Redemption date
Interest yield
Redemption yield
Closing price
Price change
Price high and low for the year

Fig. 9.1 UK gilts prices

price is below £100, the redemption yield will be bigger than the interest yield since, assuming the bond is held to redemption, there will also be a capital gain.

- **Price, price change and the year's high and low points:** the price is the middle price between the buying and selling price quoted by marketmakers in pounds and fractions of pounds (usually in thirty-seconds) for a nominal £100 of stock. Each gilt has this par value, and moves of a point mean that it has risen or fallen by £1 in price. Like a share, gilts can be "ex-dividend" (xd) which means a buyer is not entitled to receive the latest coupon.

- **Tap stock:** a large black dot signals a tap stock. This is a gilt issue of which the Bank of England, performing its role as the government's broker, still holds a part, which it is ready to supply to the market. When the Bank announces a new stock, part of the issue is often left unsold to release to the market in the future. This minimises any effect of depressing gilt prices overall that a new issue might have.

- **Index-linked gilts:** with these bonds, the interest and redemption value are adjusted to account for movement in the retail prices index with a time lag of eight months. In this way, they maintain their real value, and hedge their owners against inflation. The price of the hedge is the lower nominal coupon rate compared to that earned by non-index-linked gilts. The yield columns of the table give two possible redemption yields, one based on the assumption of 10 per cent inflation, the other on the assumption of 5 per cent inflation. The table also indicates the base date for the indexation calculation.

Monday's newspaper has a variation on the listing for UK gilts, indicating the percentage price change on the previous week, the total amount of the stock in issue in millions of pounds (a fixed sum since the stock is guaranteed by the government to be redeemed at that amount, the bond equivalent of market capitalisation), the dates on which the interest is paid (twice yearly), the last ex-dividend payment of interest and the Cityline telephone number for real-time updates on the gilt price.

The market price of a gilt reflects its redemption value, coupon and other rates. It is not directly determined by its redemption value until the redemption date gets closer. As a gilt approaches redemption, its price will get closer and closer to £100, the amount for which it will be redeemed.

Long-dated gilt prices move most in response to expectations of rate changes. Since their maturity value is fixed, they are a good indicator of expected trends in the rate of interest and the rate of inflation. As explained in chapter 1, investors expect higher rates of return for longer term investments. If short-term rates become higher than long-term rates, investors will move out of long-term assets. Thus, short- and long-term rates tend to move together. The yield curve is a means of comparing rates on bonds of different maturities, as well as giving an indication of the tightness of monetary conditions. Longer term yields are usually higher because of the greater degree of risk (time and inflation risk). When short-term rates are higher, there is a negative yield curve.

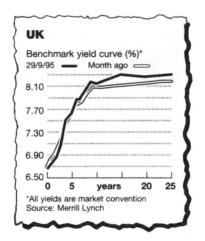

Fig. 9.2 UK benchmark yield curve

Monday's newspaper includes a picture of the current yield curve for benchmark UK government bonds (see Figure 9.2) as well as of the yield curve for national government bonds in New York, Frankfurt and Tokyo. These indicate the yields on typical bonds for each possible time to maturity. In this example, yields on longer term

bonds are higher up to a point but then flatten out, suggesting that monetary conditions might tighten through increased short-term rates or that they are at least expected to tighten.

Interest and redemption yields quoted only apply to a new buyer. The yields for investors already in possession will depend on the price they paid. But, in both cases, the yields can be calculated exactly, in contrast with equities where both the dividend and capital gain or loss are uncertain. This reflects the greater degree of risk associated with investment in equities.

$$\text{Interest yield} = \frac{\text{coupon} \times 100}{\text{gilt price}}$$

The difference between interest yield and redemption yield is important to the investor because of the tax implications. Income from gilts is taxed but capital gains are not. Hence, the net return is determined by the composition of the total return.

The investor will also want to compare bond and equity yields. The yield gap (long-term bond yields minus the dividend yield on shares) is a good indicator of the relative rates, though generally, due to fears of inflation and the opportunities for capital gains on shares, there is a reverse yield gap. An alternative indicator (carried in Saturday's Money Watch table, Figure 1.3 in chapter 1) is the yield ratio, the long gilt yield divided by the equity dividend yield. This ratio usually exceeds 2.

Index-linked bonds pay investors a known rate of interest independent of the inflation rate: both the coupon and the redemption payment are revalued in line with inflation. Along with Australia, Canada and Sweden, the UK is one of the few countries to issue such bonds, which now account for about 17 per cent of the government's outstanding stock of debt.

Index-linked stocks are valuable when inflation is feared; they are not so good when the real rates of return on gilts are high, that is, when nominal yields are above the rate of inflation. The difference between the long bond yield and the real yield on index-linked stocks is an indicator of expected inflation.

Private investors are becoming increasingly interested in bonds and gilts as investments. Banks recognise this and are promoting actively to

this group; Saturday's newspaper now regularly features advertisements and brochures for bond issues clearly directed at the private investor. It also includes a table examining gilt issues in terms of the best value for investors in different tax brackets (see Figure 9.3). The table takes three different levels of tax status and lists the best yielding gilts in each of five categories, providing the stock names and their current prices, yields and volatility. The basic principle behind the table is that since interest on gilts is taxed but capital gains are not, the higher the proportion of total return that is capital gains the better for higher rate taxpayers.

■ Gilt issues - best value v tax status

These redemption yields are applicable to private investors holding £200,000 or less in gilt-edged stock and relevant bonds. Your capital gain on a gilt – a UK government bond – is tax free. However, you pay tax on the interest. Therefore, gilts which deliver a higher proportion of their total return as capital gain are more tax efficient, and – other things being equal – more attractive to higher rate taxpayers.

NON-TAXPAYERS		Stock	Price	Yield %	Volatility %
CONVENTIONAL	<5yr	Treasury 13%, 2000	123 1/2	6.94%	3.46%
	5-10yr	Conversion 9.5%, 2005	112 11/16	7.58%	6.29%
	10-15yr	Treasury 6.25%, 2010	86 7/16	7.80%	9.14%
	>15yr	Treasury 8.75%, 2017	109 23/32	7.81%	9.95%
INDEX-LINKED		Indx-Linkd 2.5%, 2020	145	6.84%* 3.64%§	16.87%
		Indx-Linkd 4.125%, 2030	119 11/16	6.83%* 3.63%§	18.48%

25% TAXPAYERS		Stock	Price	Yield %	Volatility %
CONVENTIONAL	<5yr	Treasury 6%, 1999	97 19/32	5.28%	3.19%
	5-10yr	Treasury 6.75%, 2004	94 31/32	5.86%	6.55%
	10-15yr	Treasury 6.25%, 2010	86 7/16	6.15%	9.14%
	>15yr	Treasury 8%, 2013	102	5.90%	9.36%
INDEX-LINKED		Indx-Linkd 2.5%, 2003	173 7/8	6.12%* 2.93%§	6.54%
		Indx-Linkd 2%, 2006	182 11/16	6.22%* 3.03%§	9.07%

40% TAXPAYERS		Stock	Price	Yield %	Volatility %
CONVENTIONAL	<5yr	Treasury 6%, 1999	97 19/32	4.31%	3.19%
	5-10yr	Treasury 6.75% 2004	94 31/32	4.75%	6.55%
	10-15yr	Treasury 6.25%, 2010	86 7/16	5.05%	9.14%
	>15yr	Treasury 8%, 2013	102	4.63%	9.36%
INDEX-LINKED		Indx-Linkd 2.5%, 2003	173 7/8	5.72%* 2.54%§	6.54%
		Indx-Linkd 2%, 2006	182 11/16	5.89%* 2.70%§	9.07%

Yield is redemption yield and takes account of any change in the capital value over period to maturity. Volatility is a measure of the sensitivity of the stock price to changes in yield. *Money yield (current inflation assumed). § Real yield.   Source: BZW.

Fig. 9.3 Gilt issues: best value v tax status

By the end of 1996, the UK government will be issuing a new type of gilt-edged security called a strip. These are created when a conven-

tional bond is broken down into its constituent parts, which can then be held or traded separately. A normal ten year bond, for example, pays a coupon twice a year for ten years and a final large principal repayment at the end of the ten years. Under the new arrangements, an investor who owns a conventional gilt would be able to approach the Bank of England to have the bond stripped to make twenty-one separate instruments: twenty strips based on the coupons, which would mature after six months, a year, eighteen months, two years and so on; and one strip based on the principal which would mature after ten years.

The strips would pay no interest but since they would be zero coupon instruments, they would be sold at a discount, offering the investor a capital gain when they mature at their face value. The idea is that because these offer investing institutions exactly the kind of maturity profile that they want, they might be willing to pay more for them. Other countries' experience is that strips tend to trade at a small premium to conventional bonds.

A typical report on the UK market for gilts looks like this:

> Gilt markets will have their regular mid-month menu of UK economic data to feast on this week. April saw an unexpected fall in average earnings growth. Expectations are for the annual rate to be unchanged in May but any acceleration would re-awaken inflationary fears, as would any further signs of a knock-on effect of higher commodity prices on the producer prices or retail prices data. One eye will have to be kept on the international situation, in case dollar weakness prompts either concerted G7 action, or unilateral US Fed action, on interest rates. Also keenly watched will be the announcement of the next gilt auction on Friday.
>
> (*Financial Times*, 11 July 1994)

This demonstrates the major influences on the gilt market. For example, the threat of higher inflation (driven by the prospect of higher earnings and higher commodity prices feeding through to producer and retail prices) implies returns, in terms of both interest and capital appreciation, that are eroded in value. The threat of higher inflation also suggests the possibility of higher interest rates which, though promising for income, implies the prospect of falling bond prices. The government's regular gilt auction gives an indication of its intentions towards the interest rate, further clues as to prospects for bond prices.

Friendly

CLUB

Shareholder

Name
Dr V CHONG

This is not a credit card and is not valid for payment of accounts. This card entitles the holder to enjoy all Friendly Club benefits as announced from time to time by Friendly Hotels PLC.

Signature

Exchange rates also play an important role in the bond market, as the above extract indicates. The weakness of the dollar suggests that the US authorities may be obliged to raise local interest rates, leading to falling US bond prices. Given the extensive interconnections of global bond markets, the movements of interest rates and bond prices in the United States are likely to affect UK rates and prices in the same direction. For example, lower bond prices and higher yields in the United States than in the United Kingdom might tempt international bond investors to move out of UK gilts and into US bonds, pushing down the prices of the former.

In fact, the two economies (and indeed the rest of the world) are linked even more fundamentally in the patterns of their economic growth and business cycles. For example, indications of resurgent economic growth suggest that there will be the future threat of inflationary pressures from a boom. Furthermore, since the rate of interest typically goes up in a time of economic buoyancy, bond prices tend to fall on the upswing of the business cycle.

Fixed interest indices

As well as individual bond prices, the *Financial Times* provides indices for a broad range of fixed interest instruments (see Figure 9.4):

FT FIXED INTEREST INDICES

	Oct 10	Oct 9	Oct 6	Oct 5	Oct 4	Yr ago	High*	Low*
Govt. Secs. (UK)	92.78	92.94	93.11	93.34	93.44	90.88	95.51	90.22
Fixed interest	111.04	111.44	111.55	111.78	111.74	107.60	114.66	108.77

GILT EDGED ACTIVITY INDICES

	Oct 9	Oct 6	Oct 5	Oct 4	Oct 3
Gilt Edged bargains	73.5	84.6	72.0	77.2	89.9
5-day average	79.5	79.7	79.7	83.0	90.1

* for 1995. Government Securities high since compilation: 127.40 (9/1/35), low 49.18 (3/1/75).
Fixed Interest high since compilation: 133.87 (21/1/94) low 50.53 (3/1/75) .
Basis 100: Government Securities 15/10/ 26 and Fixed Interest 1928. SE activity indices rebased 1974.

Fig. 9.4 FT fixed interest indices

- **Government securities (UK):** the movements of a representative cross-section of gilt-edged stocks, the Government Securities Index, over the past five trading days, the value of the index a year ago and its high and low points for the year to date. This index began from a base of 100 in 1926, and the notes to the table detail its high and low since compilation.

- **Fixed interest:** the movements of a broader range of fixed interest stocks, including those issued by the UK government, local government, public boards and by UK industrial companies. As with the gilts index, this charts the index values over the past five trading days, one year ago and at its zenith and nadir both for the year and since compilation.

- **Gilt-edged activity indices:** gilt-edged bargains and five-day average are a measure of the level of gilt-edged activity, the number of transactions on the five previous days and a rolling five-day average. They are an indicator of the liquidity of the market.

The FT-Actuaries fixed interest indices (see Figure 9.5) are designed to perform roughly the same service for professional investors in gilt-edged stocks as the corresponding FT-SE Actuaries equity indices have provided for investors in ordinary shares. They are produced at the close of business each day that the Stock Exchange is open and published in the following day's newspaper, normally Tuesday to Saturday. The indices cover UK gilts and index-linked government securities, with the number of stocks in each sector on each day shown after the name of that sector. The information displayed falls into two sections: price indices and yield indices.

- **Price indices:** there are eight indices, five covering the market for all conventional UK government stocks (shorts, medium-dated, longs, irredeemable, and all stocks) and three for index-linked securities (one each for under and over five years to redemption plus all stocks).

- **Yield indices:** there are fourteen indices of "average gross redemption yields", three each based on maturity for each of the three categories of coupon (low, medium and high), one for irredeemables and four for index-linked securities, based on different maturities and inflation assumptions. The number of yield indices is a compromise between the need for an easily comprehensible snapshot of the market, and the need to represent some of its complexities.

FT-ACTUARIES FIXED INTEREST INDICES

Price Indices UK Gilts	Tue Oct 10	Day's change %	Mon Oct 9	Accrued interest	xd adj. ytd		Low coupon yield Oct 10	Oct 9	Yr. ago	Medium coupon yield Oct 10	Oct 9	Yr. ago	High coupon yield Oct 10	Oct 9	Yr. ago
1 Up to 5 years (23)	121.19	-0.07	121.27	1.57	8.88	5 yrs	7.66	7.63	8.59	7.67	7.63	8.66	7.76	7.73	8.80
2 5-15 years (21)	144.22	-0.12	144.40	1.93	9.78	15 yrs	8.27	8.25	8.57	8.31	8.28	8.71	8.39	8.36	8.95
3 Over 15 years (9)	159.30	-0.20	159.62	2.71	9.84	20 yrs	8.31	8.29	8.54	8.35	8.33	8.71	8.42	8.39	8.83
4 Irredeemables (6)	181.85	-0.33	182.46	3.83	8.83	Irred.†	8.41	8.37	8.64						
5 All stocks (59)	140.09	-0.12	140.26	1.96	9.54										

Index-linked

	Tue Oct 10	Day's change %	Mon Oct 9	Accrued interest	xd adj. ytd		Inflation 5% Oct 10	Oct 9	Yr. ago	Inflation 10% Oct 10	Oct 9	Yr. ago
6 Up to 5 years (1)	192.19	-0.10	192.39	-0.38	8.37	Up to 5 yrs	3.27	3.22	4.01	2.22	2.16	2.93
7 Over 5 years (11)	183.32	-0.28	183.84	0.99	4.00	Over 5 yrs	3.76	3.73	3.89	3.57	3.54	3.70
8 All stocks (12)	183.39	-0.28	183.91	0.95	4.10							

Average gross redemption yields are shown above. Coupon Bands: Low: 0%-7¾%; Medium: 8%-10¾%; High: 11% and over. † Flat yield. ytd Year to date.

Fig. 9.5 FT-Actuaries fixed interest indices

The tables provide the following information:

- **Value:** the first three columns of the price indices list current value, the percentage change on the previous trading day's value and the previous day's value.

- **Accrued interest:** interest on gilt-edged stocks is paid in twice-yearly instalments. Accrued interest simply records the amount of interest included in each day's price index that has accumulated on the stock since the last dividend payment.

- **Ex-dividend adjustment to date:** the amount of income that a holder of a portfolio of stocks proportionate to the index would have received in the year to date, credited on the ex-dividend date for each stock.

- **Redemption yields:** the three columns for each yield index give the two previous days' value and an approximation of the value a year ago. The whole table, subdividing coupon categories into short, medium and long terms to redemption, provides a representative picture of yields across the market. It indicates the shape of the market's time-related yield curve.

- **Highs and lows:** Saturday's newspaper adds information on the highs and lows for the year, with dates, for the fourteen yield indices.

The price indices and the ex-dividend adjustment can be used to work out an appropriate market rate of return, using whatever tax rate is appropriate on income. The indices can provide a basis for performance measurement.

The FT yield indices can be used to monitor the difference in yield between gilt-edged stocks and equities (the yield gap), as a guide to market rates in making valuations and in setting the terms for new issues. Stocks are divided into low, medium and high coupons because investors' tax liabilities lead to very different yields being established in the market.

Benchmark government bonds

Coverage of government bond markets outside the United Kingdom picks out items of importance or interest from internationally trade-able government bond markets throughout the world and, where relevant, related futures and options activity. Figure 9.6 shows the daily FT table of benchmark bonds in key markets.

WORLD BOND PRICES

BENCHMARK GOVERNMENT BONDS

		Coupon	Red Date	Price	Day's change	Yield	Week ago	Month ago
Australia		7.500	07/05	93.1200	−0.320	8.55	8.58	9.00
Austria		6.875	06/05	99.2000	+0.030	6.98	6.90	7.01
Belgium		6.500	03/05	95.5900	−	7.15	7.03	7.21
Canada *		8.750	12/05	107.5600	−0.300	7.66	7.78	8.05
Denmark		7.000	12/04	93.8400	+0.160	7.97	7.85	8.02
France	BTAN	7.750	04/00	103.3750	−0.130	6.87	6.71	6.60
	OAT	7.750	10/05	101.1400	+0.229	7.58	7.44	7.37
Germany Bund		6.875	05/05	101.9800	−0.030	6.58	6.56	6.71
Ireland		6.250	10/04	87.5000	−0.050	8.27	8.17	8.33
Italy		10.500	04/05	93.6500	+0.280	11.62†	11.55	11.47
Japan	No 129	6.400	03/00	120.0210	+0.063	1.56	1.53	2.09
	No 174	4.600	09/04	113.6250	−	2.71	2.60	3.12
Netherlands		7.000	06/05	102.3000	−0.060	6.66	6.62	6.73
Portugal		11.875	02/05	103.0800	−0.050	11.30	11.20	11.28
Spain		10.000	02/05	94.1900	−0.050	10.98	10.83	11.07
Sweden		6.000	02/05	79.0790	+0.330	9.47	9.31	10.24
UK Gilts		8.000	12/00	101−23	−2/32	7.58	7.44	7.63
		8.500	12/05	102−13	−3/32	8.14	8.00	8.05
		9.000	10/08	105−29	−5/32	8.25	8.13	8.16
US Treasury *		6.500	08/05	102−30	−5/32	6.10	6.20	6.24
		6.875	08/25	105−21	−9/32	6.45	6.51	6.59
ECU (French Govt)		7.500	04/05	97.6800	+0.380	7.84	7.73	7.68

London closing, *New York closing   Yields: Local market standard.
† Gross (including withholding tax at 12.5 per cent payable by nonresidents)
Prices: US, UK in 32nds, others in decimal   Source: MMS International

Fig. 9.6 Benchmark government bonds

- **National markets:** a summary of daily movements in important benchmark bonds in a number of major markets.

- **Benchmarks:** bonds are described by coupon and redemption date, the price and change on the previous day, the yield according to the local market standard (as standards vary, yields are not necessarily comparable) and the yields prevailing one week and one month earlier.

The yield differential is the gap between bond yields in different countries. It is an indication of the relative attractiveness of different currencies.

CORPORATE BONDS

Bonds issued by institutions other than governments make up a substantial part of the world's largest bond markets. Because the bulk of bonds issued by non-sovereign debtors are issued by corporations, these fixed income securities are called corporate bonds. The corporate bond markets fall into four broad categories: the relatively small markets denominated in lira, French francs and pesetas; the predominantly Eurobond markets denominated in pounds, Canadian dollars and ecus; the bank-dominated markets in yen and D-Marks; and the highly fragmented markets denominated in dollars and Swiss francs where there are high numbers of issuing institutions.

The yields on corporate bonds are generally higher and the prices lower, reflecting the more variable creditworthiness of their issuers and a greater risk of default. These bonds are often classified by rating agencies such as Standard & Poor's and Moody's, which rate bonds according to the risk they carry (ranging from high-quality *AAA* to below-grade *D*).

Low-grade corporate bonds rated as being below investment quality may be issued offering very high yields. Known colloquially as junk bonds, these essentially unsecured, high-yield debt securities peaked in popularity in the late 1980s, and financed a significant portion of the merger and acquisition boom in the United States. When new corporate bonds are issued, their yields are generally set with reference to benchmark government bonds, offering a spread over the gilt yield in order to make up for the greater risk of default that they bear. Companies unlike governments can always go under, they have a finite lifespan and the market for their bonds is less liquid than the gilt market.

The domestic US corporate bond market is particularly well developed, but the domestic market is also growing in the United King-

dom, partly in response to tax free status for investors who buy them through PEPs. Saturday's *Financial Times* Weekend Money section periodically carries a table of details on corporate bond PEPs. For the most part, however, FT bond coverage focuses on the market for international bonds.

The International Capital Markets pages in Tuesday to Friday's newspaper carry reports on new international bond issues together with tables of the previous day's prices and issues. These markets have emerged with the growth of what have come to be known as Eurocurrencies. A Eurocurrency is a currency deposited outside its country of origin. For example, a UK exporter might receive dollars but not convert them into pounds. Since the United States, in running persistent trade deficits, exports dollars, banks accumulate these deposits which are then put to work. This stateless money is free of local regulations and London is its centre. Eurocurrencies are borrowed by loans or the issue of various kinds of debt instrument that "securitise" the money: Euronotes, Eurocommercial paper and Eurobonds.

Eurobonds are the most common. They tap the large stateless pool of cash and are traded in a secondary market of screens and telephones. These are volatile and unregulated markets and they can become illiquid since there is no obligation for anyone to take part.

In many aspects trading activity in these markets is similar to trading in domestic stock markets, particularly in the case of sterling bond issues, industrial debentures and corporate bonds.

New international bond issues

Monday's newspaper rounds up the issues of the previous week with a table of new international bond issues, broken down according to the issuing currency. On Tuesday to Friday, the previous day's issues are listed (see Figure 9.7).

- **All new issues launched the previous day:** the table gives details of the borrower, currency, amount, coupon, price, maturity, the fees payable to the underwriters, the yield spread over a comparable government bond, and the issue's arranger. The table also carries details of bonds on which terms have been altered or finalised sub-

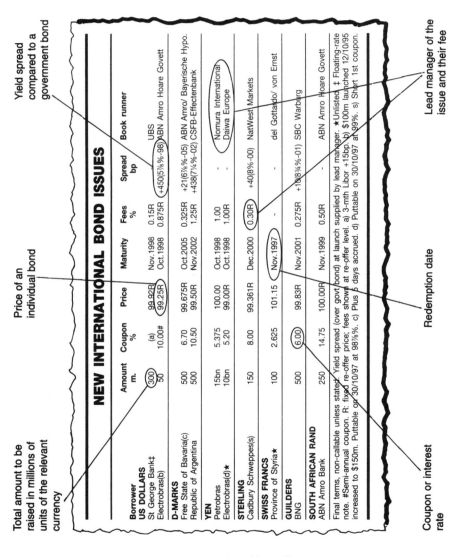

Fig. 9.7 New international bond issues

The figure shows a table titled "NEW INTERNATIONAL BOND ISSUES" with annotations:

- Total amount to be raised in millions of units of the relevant currency
- Price of an individual bond
- Yield spread compared to a government bond
- Lead manager of the issue and their fee
- Redemption date
- Coupon or interest rate

Borrower	Amount m.	Coupon %	Price	Maturity	Fees %	Spread bp	Book runner
US DOLLARS							
St George Bank‡	300	(a)	99.92R	Nov.1998	0.15R	-	UBS
Electrobras(b)	50	10.00#	99.25R	Oct.1998	0.875R	+450(5⅞%-98)	ABN Amro Hoare Govett
D-MARKS							
Free State of Bavaria(c)	500	6.70	99.675R	Oct.2005	0.325R	+21(6⅞%-05)	ABN Amro/ Bayerische Hypo.
Republic of Argentina	500	10.50	99.50R	Nov.2002	1.25R	+438(7¼%-02)	CSFB-Effectenbank
YEN							
Petrobras	15bn	5.375	100.00	Oct.1998	1.00	-	Nomura International
Electrobras(d)★	10bn	5.20	99.00R	Oct.1998	1.00R	-	Daiwa Europe
STERLING							
Cadbury Schweppes(s)	150	8.00	99.361R	Dec.2000	0.30R	+40(8%-00)	NatWest Markets
SWISS FRANCS							
Province of Styria★	100	2.625	101.15	Nov.1997	-	-	del Gottardo/ von Ernst
GUILDERS							
BNG	500	6.00	99.83R	Nov.2001	0.275R	+10(8¾%-01)	SBC Warburg
SOUTH AFRICAN RAND							
ABN Amro Bank	250	14.75	100.00R	Nov.1999	0.50R	-	ABN Amro Hoare Govett

Final terms, non-callable unless stated. Yield spread (over govt/bond) at launch supplied by lead manager. ★Unlisted. ‡ Floating-rate note. #Semi-annual coupon. R: fixed re-offer price; fees shown at re-offer level. a) 3-mth Libor +15bp. b) $100m launched 12/10/95 increased to $150m. Puttable on 30/10/97 at 98⅞%. c) Plus 5 days accrued. d) Puttable on 30/10/97 at 99%. s) Short 1st coupon.

sequent to launch.

- **Book runner:** the issuer gives a mandate to one or more lead banks to manage the issue. The fee is paid in the form of a discount on the issue price.

FT/ISMA international bond service

From Tuesday to Friday, the newspaper carries information on the secondary market prices of recently issued and actively traded bonds in the Eurobond market. Provided by the International Securities Market Association (ISMA) at close of business on the previous trading day, it covers Eurobonds picked from the sectors that best represent current market conditions, aiming to include certain "benchmark" issues. The table also tries to maintain a selection of securities involving a broad spread of borrowers and currency groups (see Figure 9.8).

Reading the figures

- **Straights:** fixed interest bonds, differentiated according to currency of denomination: US dollars, D-Marks, Swiss francs, yen, and other currencies, including sterling, Australian and Canadian dollars and ecus. Straights are traditional fixed interest bonds with a redemption date and no conversion rights. For straights, the table shows the amount of the bond issue (in millions of currency units), the prices bid and offered (the spread), the changes on the day and week and the yield to redemption of the bid price.

- **Floating rate notes (FRNs):** these pay interest which is adjusted regularly in line with short-term international money rates. They are denominated in dollars unless otherwise indicated, and the coupon shown is minimum. There are also FRNs that convert into fixed rate notes at the option of the investor (debt convertible), become fixed rate at a certain level (droplock) and that have caps and floors. The rates of interest on FRNs (the fourth column "current coupon") are usually set by reference to the London Inter-Bank Offered Rate (LIBOR), which acts as the benchmark against which rates vary (often so many basis points above the LIBOR).

FT/ISMA INTERNATIONAL BOND SERVICE

Listed are the latest international bonds for which there is an adequate secondary market. **Closing prices on October 16**

U.S. DOLLAR STRAIGHTS

	Issued	Bid	Offer	Chg.	Yield
Abbey Natl Treasury 5 97	1000	98 7/8	99	+1/8	5.91
Abbey Natl Treasury 6 1/2 03	1000	100	100 1/4		6.49
ABN Ambro Bank 7 1/4 05	1000	104 3/8	104 5/8	+1/4	6.74
African Dev Bk 7 3/8 23	500	103	103 1/2	+3/8	7.12
Alberta Province 7 5/8 98	1000	104 1/2	104 3/4		5.97
Austria 8 1/2 00	400	108 5/8	109		6.13
Baden-Wuertt L-Fin 8 1/8 00	1000	107 1/8	107 3/8		6.17
Bank Ned Gemeenten 7 99	1000	103 1/4	103 1/2		6.02
Bayer Vereinsbk 8 1/8 00	500	107 1/8	107 1/4		6.17
Belgium 5 1/2 03	1000	94 1/4	94 1/2	+1/8	6.44
BFCE 7 3/4 97	150	102 1/4	102 5/8		5.97
British Columbia 7 3/4 02	500	107 1/2	107 3/4	+1/8	6.33
British Gas 0 21	1500	15	15 1/4	+1/8	7.55
Canada 6 1/2 97	2000	101	101 1/8		5.85
Cheung Kong Fin 5 1/2 98	500	95 1/2	96 1/4		7.24
China 6 1/2 04	1000	96 1/2	97 1/8	+1/4	7.19
Credit Foncier 9 1/2 99	300	109 7/8	110 1/4		6.13
Denmark 5 3/4 98	1000	99 7/8	100 1/8		5.79
East Japan Railway 6 5/8 04	600	100 7/8	101 1/4		6.48
ECSC 8 1/4 96	193	102 3/8	102 3/4		5.98
EIB 6 04	500	97 7/8	98 1/8	+1/8	6.33
EIB 9 1/4 97	1000	106 3/4	107		5.71
Elec de France 9 98	200	106 3/8	106 7/8		6.05
Ex-Im Bank Japan 8 02	500	109	109 3/8	+1/8	6.28
Export Dev Corp 9 1/2 98	150	108 3/8	108 3/4		6.07
Fed Home Loan 7 1/8 99	1500	103 7/8	104 1/8		6.05
Federal Natl Mort 7.40 04	1500	107 1/2	107 3/4	+1/8	6.37
Finland 6 3/4 97	3000	101 3/4	102		5.94
Ford Motor Credit 6 1/4 98	1500	100 3/8	100 5/8		6.16
Ind Bk Japan Fin 7 7/8 97	200	102 1/8	102 3/8	+1/8	6.30
INTER-AMER DEV 7 1/2 05	500	107 5/8	107 7/8	+1/8	6.39
Intl Finance 5 1/4 99	500	98 1/4	98 1/2	+1/8	5.85
Italy 6 03	2000	96 5/8	97	+1/8	6.66
Italy 6 7/8 23	3500	93 1/2	94	+3/8	7.57
Japan Dev Bk 8 3/8 01	500	109 1/2	109 3/4	+1/8	6.21
Korea Elec Power 6 3/8 03	1350	98 3/8	98 7/8	+1/8	6.75
LTCB Fin 8 97	200	101 7/8	102 1/8	+1/8	6.35
Matsushita Elec 7 1/4 02	1000	105 1/8	105 3/8	+1/8	6.41
Norway 7 1/4 97	1000	101 7/8	102 1/8		5.87
Ontario 7 3/8 03	3000	105 1/2	105 3/4	+1/8	6.52
Oster Kontrollbank 8 1/2 01	200	110 1/8	110 1/2		6.22
Portugal 5 3/4 03	1000	96 1/4	96 1/2	+1/8	6.46
Quebec Hydro 9 3/4 98	150	108 7/8	109 1/4		6.35
Quebec Prov 9 98	200	105 7/8	106 1/4		6.33
SAS 10 99	200	110 1/8	110 3/4	+1/8	6.53
SNCF 9 1/2 98	150	108 5/8	108 7/8	+1/8	6.00
Spain 6 1/2 99	1500	101 5/8	101 7/8	+1/8	6.02
Sweden 6 1/2 03	2000	101 1/4	101 1/2	+1/8	6.38
Tennessee Valley 6 3/8 05	2000	100 3/4	100 7/8	+1/4	6.37
Tokyo Elec Power 6 1/8 03	1000	98	98 3/8		6.45
Tokyo Metropolis 8 1/4 96	200	102 1/4	102 1/2		5.98
Toyota Motor 5 5/8 98	1500	99 1/2	99 3/4		5.83
United Kingdom 7 1/4 02	3000	106	106 1/8	+1/8	6.18
World Bank 6 3/8 05	1500	101 1/8	101 3/8	+1/8	6.31
World Bank 8 3/8 99	1500	108 5/8	108 3/4	+1/8	5.99
World Bank 8 3/4 97	1500	104 1/4	104 1/2		5.57

DEUTSCHE MARK STRAIGHTS

	Issued	Bid	Offer	Chg.	Yield
Austria 6 1/2 24	2000	88 3/4	89	+3/8	7.46
Baden-Wuertt L-Finance 6 99	2000	102 5/8	102 3/4	+1/8	5.16
Credit Foncier 7 1/4 03	2000	102	102 3/8	+1/4	6.88
Denmark 6 1/8 98	2000	103 1/8	103 1/4	+1/8	4.75
Depfa Finance 6 3/8 03	1500	97 5/8	97 3/4	+1/8	6.77
Deutche Bk Fin 7 1/2 03	2000	104 1/4	104 1/2	+1/8	6.74
EEC 6 1/2 00	2900	103 1/4	103 3/8		5.63
EIB 6 1/4 00	1500	102 3/8	102 3/4	+1/4	5.62
Finland 7 1/2 00	3000	106 1/2	106 5/8	+1/8	5.73
Italy 7 1/4 98	5000	105	105 1/8		4.90
LKB Baden-Wuertt 6 1/2 08	2250	95	95 1/4		7.10
Norway 6 1/8 98	1500	103 3/8	103 1/2	+1/8	4.68
Ontario 6 1/4 04	1500	96 1/8	96 3/8	+1/8	6.88
Spain 7 1/4 03	4000	103 3/4	103 3/4	+1/4	6.58
Sweden 8 97	2500	106 3/8	106 1/2		4.67
United Kingdom 7 1/8 97	5500	104 7/8	105		4.56
Volkswagen Intl Fin 7 03	1000	101 3/8	101 5/8	+3/8	6.75
World Bank 0 15	2000	26	26 3/8	+1/8	6.90
World Bank 5 7/8 03	3000	96	96	+1/8	6.53

SWISS FRANC STRAIGHTS

	Issued	Bid	Offer	Chg.	Yield
Austria 4 1/2 00	1000	104 1/4	104 3/8		3.42
Council Europe 4 3/4 98	250	103 1/2	103 3/4		3.16
Denmark 4 1/4 99	1000	103 1/2	103 5/8		3.29
EIB 3 3/4 99	1000	102 5/8	102 3/4	+1/8	2.90
EIB 6 3/4 04	300	113 1/4	113 3/4		4.89
Finland 7 1/4 99	300	112 3/4	113 1/4		3.74
Hyundai Motor Fin 8 1/2 97	100	108	109		4.04
Iceland 7 5/8 00	100	115	115 1/2		4.10
Kobe 6 3/8 01	240	111 1/2	112		4.10
Ontario 6 1/4 03	400	109 3/4	110 1/2	+1/4	4.64
Quebec Hydro 5 08	100	98	99	+1	5.22
SNCF 7 04	450	117 1/4		+1/4	4.61
Sweden 4 3/4 03	500	102 3/4	103		4.33
World Bank 0 21	700	26 7/8	27	+1/8	5.16
World Bank 7 01	600	114 1/4	114 1/2		4.00

YEN STRAIGHTS

	Issued	Bid	Offer	Chg.	Yield
Belgium 5 99	75000	113 1/2	113 3/4	+1/4	1.62
CREDIT FONCIER 4 3/4 02	75000	112	112 1/4	+1/4	2.79
EIB 6 5/8 00	100000	120 1/2	120 3/4	+1/4	1.75
Ex-Im Bank Japan 4 3/8 03	105000	111 3/8	111 5/8	+3/8	2.76
Inter Amer Dev 7 1/4 00	30000	123 1/2	123 3/4	+1/4	1.85
Italy 3 1/2 01	300000	105 1/4	105 3/8	+3/8	2.52
Japan Dev Bk 5 99	100000	113 5/8	113 3/4	+1/4	1.43
Japan Dev Bk 6 1/2 01	120000	123 1/4	123 3/8	+3/8	2.26
Norway 5 3/8 97	150000	106 1/2	106 5/8		0.45
SNCF 6 3/4 00	30000	121	121 1/4	+1/4	1.72
Spain 5 3/4 02	125000	119 1/8	119 3/8	+3/8	2.49
Sweden 4 5/8 98	150000	108 1/2	108 5/8	+1/8	0.87
World Bank 5 1/4 02	250000	117 3/8	117 1/2	+3/8	2.33

OTHER STRAIGHTS

	Issued	Bid	Offer	Chg.	Yield
Finland 8 04 LFr	5000	104 3/8	105 1/8		7.31
Genfinance Lux 9 1/8 99 LFr	1000	107 7/8	108 7/8		6.51
IKB Deut Industbk 8 1/2 03 LFr	3000	105 1/2	106 1/2		7.48
ABN Amro 6 5/8 00 Fl	1000	103 1/8	103 1/2		5.80
Bank Ned Gemeenten 7 03 Fl	1500	102 3/4	103 1/8		6.51
Bell Canada 10 5/8 99 C$	150	109 3/8	109 7/8		7.63
British Columbia 7 3/4 03 C$	1250	100 1/4	100 5/8		7.85
Canada Mtg & Hsg 8 1/4 99 C$	1000	103 3/8	103 5/8		7.33
EIB 10 1/8 98 C$	130	106 1/2	107 1/4	−1/8	7.05
Elec de France 9 3/4 99 C$	275	107 3/4	108 1/8		7.38
KfW Int Fin 10 01 C$	400	109 3/4	110 1/8		7.70
Nippon Tel Tel 10 1/4 99 C$	200	109 1/4	109 3/4	−1/8	7.49
Ontario 8 03 C$	1500	101 1/4	101 5/8	−1/8	7.93
Ontario Hydro 10 7/8 99 C$	500	110 1/8	110 1/2		7.41
Oster Kontrollbank 10 1/4 99 C$	150	109	109 1/2		7.41
Quebec Hydro 7 04 C$	1000	93	93 1/4		8.31
Quebec Prov 10 1/2 98 C$	200	108 1/8	108 1/2		7.47
Council Europe 9 01 Ecu	1100	107 1/8	107 3/8	+1/8	7.49
Credit Foncier 8 3/8 04 Ecu	1000	100 7/8	101 1/4		8.21
Denmark 8 1/2 02 Ecu	1000	104 3/4	105		7.54
EC 6 00 Ecu	1000	95 5/8	95 7/8		7.06
EIB 10 97 Ecu	1125	105 1/4	105 1/2		5.73
Ferro del Stat 10 1/8 98 Ecu	500	107 1/8	107 1/2	+1/8	6.56
Italy 10 3/4 00 Ecu	1000	112 3/8	112 3/4		7.40
United Kingdom 9 1/8 01 Ecu	2750	107 7/8	108		7.28
AIDC 10 99 A$	100	105 7/8	106 3/8	+1/4	8.07
Comm Bk Australia 13 3/4 99 A$	100	118 3/8	118 3/4	+3/8	8.10
EIB 7 3/4 99 A$	350	101 3/8	101 3/4	+3/8	7.45
NSW Treasury Zero 0 20 A$	1000	12	13 1/8	+1/2	8.81
R & I Bank 7 3/4 03 A$	125	95 1/8	95 1/2	+3/4	8.63
State Bk NSW 9 02 A$	300	102 7/8	103 1/4	+5/8	8.43
Sth Aust Govt Fin 9 02 A$	150	102 3/8	102 3/4	+5/8	8.53
Unilever Australia 12 98 A$	150	108 3/4	109 1/4	+1/4	7.92
Western Aust Treas 7 5/8 98 A$	100	99 5/8	100	+1/4	7.76
Abbey Natl Treasury 8 03 £	1000	97 1/4	97 1/2		8.
Alliance Leics 11 3/8 97 £	100	105 3/4	106		7.
British Land 8 7/8 23 £	150	90 1/2	90 7/8	−1/2	10.
Denmark 6 3/4 98 £	800	98	98 1/8		7.
EIB 8 03 £	1000	98 1/4	98 3/8		8.
Halifax 10 3/8 97 £	100	103 7/8	104 1/4	−1/8	7.
Hanson 10 3/8 97 £	500	105 1/8	105 3/8		7.
HSBC Holdings 11.69 02 £	153	113 5/8	114 1/8	−1/4	8.
Italy 10 1/2 14 £	400	108 1/4	108 1/2	−1/8	9.
Japan Dev Bk 7 00 £	200	96 1/2	96 7/8		7.
Land Secs 9 1/2 07 £	200	102 3/8	102 3/4	−1/2	9.
Ontario 11 1/8 01 £	100	111 3/4	112 1/8		8.
Powergen 8 7/8 03 £	250	101 1/8	101 1/2	−1/8	8.
Severn Trent 11 1/2 99 £	150	110 3/4	111 1/8		8.
Tokyo Elec Power 11 01 £	150	112	112 3/8		8.
TCNZ Fin 9 1/4 02 NZ$	75				
World Bank 12 1/2 97 NZ$	250				
Credit Local 6 01 FFr	7000	94 1/4	94 3/8	−1/8	7.
Elec de France 8 3/4 22 FFr	3000	103 7/8	104 1/4	−1/4	8.
SNCF 9 1/4 97 FFr	4000	103 3/4	104	−1/8	6.

FLOATING RATE NOTES

	Issued	Bid	Offer	C.cpn
Abbey Natl Treasury −1/16 99	1000	99.74	99.81	5.81
Bankamerica 1/8 99	750	99.76	99.85	6.00
Belgium 1/16 97 DM	500	100.11	100.21	4.43
BFCE −0.02 96	350	100.00	100.09	6.04
Canada −1/4 99	2000	99.43	99.51	5.62
CCCE 0 06 Ecu	200	99.44	99.58	5.67
COMMERZBK O/S FIN −1/8 98	750	99.60	99.68	5.75
Credit Lyonnais 1/16 00	300	97.79	98.18	5.87
Denmark −1/8 97	1000	99.95	100.02	5.75
Dresdner Finance 1/32 98 DM	1000	100.04	100.13	4.57
Ferro del Stat 0.10 97	420	100.06	100.21	6.12
Finland 0 97	1000	100.06	100.12	5.75
FINLAND −1/8 99	1500	99.71	99.78	5.75
IMI Bank Intl 1/4 99	500	100.03	100.14	6.14
Italy 1/16 99	1500	99.76	99.84	6.00
Italy 1/4 98	2000	100.09	100.17	6.12
LKB Baden-Wuert Fin −1/8 98	1000	99.92	99.98	6.25
Lloyds Bank Perp S 0.10	600	82.88	83.81	5.98
Malaysia 1/16 05	650	99.55	99.77	6.00
New Zealand −1/8 99	1000	99.82	99.91	5.81
Nova Scotia 3/16 99	500	99.92	100.01	6.06
Ontario 0 99	2000	99.68	99.77	5.93
Renfe 0 98	500	99.63	99.78	6.06
State Bk Victoria 0.05 99	125	99.99	100.13	5.94
Sweden 0 98	1500	100.03	100.10	5.87
Sweden −1/8 01	2000	99.40	99.48	5.75

CONVERTIBLE BONDS

	Issued	Conv. Price	Bid	Offer	Prem
Browning-Ferris 6 3/4 05	400	52 1/2	98 3/4	99 7/8	+69.9
Chubb Capital 6 98	250	86	110 1/4	111 1/8	+1.
Gold Kalgoorlie 7 1/2 00	65	1.0554	107 5/8	109 1/8	+28.9
Hanson 9 1/2 06 £	500	2.48	101	101 5/8	+24.7
Hanson America 2.39 01	420	29.6375	80 3/4	81 1/2	+53.1
Hong Kong Land 4 01	410	31.05	83 1/2	84 1/4	−16.2
Land Secs 6 3/4 02 £	84	6.72	95 3/4	97 3/4	+8.6
Lasmo 7 3/4 05 £	90	5.64	89	90 1/2	
Mitsui Bank 2 5/8 03	200	2332.6	79 7/8	81 5/8	+41.3
Mount Isa Fin 6 1/2 97	100	2.283	98 1/4	99 1/4	+68.8
Natl Power 6 1/4 08 £	250	4.33	111 1/4	112 1/4	−0.8
Ogden 6 02	85	39.077	93	94 1/4	+52.2
Pennzoil 4 3/4 03	500	58.8097	95 1/4	96 1/4	+14.3
Sumitomo Bank 3 1/8 04	300	3606.9	82 1/2	83 1/2	+26.
Sun Alliance 7 1/4 08 £	155	3.9	102 3/4	103 3/4	+10.
Texas Instruments 2 3/4 02	300	41 7/16	173 1/2	174 3/4	−0.
Transatlantic Hldgs 5 1/2 09 £	250	5.05	79	80	+13.

* No information available - previous day's price
‡ Only one market maker supplied a price

STRAIGHT BONDS: The yield is the yield to redemption of the bid-price; the amount issued is in millions of currency units. Chg. day=Change on day.
FLOATING RATE NOTES: Denominated in dollars unless otherwise indicated. Coupon shown is minimum. Spread=Margin above six-month offered rate (‡three-month §above mean rate) for US dollars. C.cpn=The current coupon.
CONVERTIBLE BONDS: Denominated in dollars unless otherwise indicated. Cnv. price=Nominal amount of bond per share expressed in currency of share at conversion rate fixed at issue. Prem=Percentage premium of the current effective price of acquiring shares via the bond over the most recent price of the shares.

© The Financial Times Ltd., 1995. Reproduction in whole or in part in any form not permitted without written consent. Data supplied by International Securities Market Association.

Fig. 9.8 FT/ISMA international bond service

- **Convertible bonds:** bonds that can be converted into shares of the issuing company at a price set at the time of issue. These are often discounted, meaning the issuing company pays a relatively low rate of interest. Investors gamble on the future success of the company by accepting a lower return in the short term in the expectation that the company will be successful. If it is, the investor will convert the bond into equity providing an income stream in dividend payments and capital growth.

- **Currency:** borrowers choose the currency that they wish to borrow in. There are dangers of currency risk: borrowers typically choose a country with a lower rate of interest so that the rate paid is less. But if the currency rises, the debt becomes more expensive to repay.

Using the information

This market offers an alternative method of raising money for companies who do not want to issue stock or accept the conditions of a bank loan. It grew up because of the restraints of government regulations in traditional equity and money markets.

It also offers opportunities for interest rate and currency swaps. When a company which can, for instance, easily raise money in sterling because of local reputation needs dollars to fund an acquisition or expansion, it may find an American company in the opposite position and swap debt.

For investors the markets are international and anonymous – there is no register of creditors – and tax efficient. They offer the chance to play the markets for currencies, debt, equity and interest rates simultaneously but because of their complexity they are generally restricted to large investment banks.

Half-yearly, the newspaper assesses the state of the Eurobond market with tables ranking lead managers of Eurobond issues by billions of dollars worth of business, and the amount of business conducted in each currency. Eurodollars are by far the most popular currency of issue.

"Britain was facing a Financial Crisis. Very simply, They – whoever They are, perhaps the international branch of They – took a look at Britain's trade balances and balance sheets and decided to sell sterling. Then all the currency speculators began to sell sterling, and pretty soon nobody was buying sterling, except the Bank of England, which has to."

GEORGE J W GOODMAN

(*"ADAM SMITH'*), 1967

"Money is a good servant, but a bad master. Money made it easier for earlier societies to escape from slavery or serfdom. But money, though essential, is only a means, not an end. You cannot eat it, drink it, wear it, or live in it."

DOUGLAS JAY

10

CASH AND CURRENCY
The foreign exchange and money markets

- **The currency markets** – determining the rates of exchange for sterling, the dollar and other leading currencies: reading the figures and using the information on exchange rates for the pound, spot and forward; the dollar, spot and forward; and other currencies of the world

- **The money markets** – determining the price of money and short-term financial instruments: UK interest rates; world interest rates; interbank fixing; Eurocurrency interest rates; US interest rates

The currency markets are global markets for foreign exchange. Their primary purposes are to allow companies and other organisations to purchase goods from abroad, and for foreign investment or speculation. Hence they are markets largely of concern to companies and financial institutions or investors in stocks that are particularly sensitive to currency or interest rate movements.

The money markets include the foreign exchange markets but also cover the domestic UK market for short-term loans essentially between the major institutions of the City: banks, accepting houses, discount houses and the Bank of England.

One page of the *Financial Times*, the Currencies and Money page, is given over largely to recording dealing rates and brief reports of trading in the foreign exchange (forex) and money markets. It is headed by a brief report describing the major events in the foreign exchange markets during the previous day's trading. In addition, there are more detailed descriptions of the experiences of individual major currencies, both on the previous day and over a rather longer time-span. These items generally discuss the main factors affecting exchange rates.

With the exception of the domestic money market in its various forms, these are international markets in which business is conducted twenty-four hours a day by telephone and computer screen. As the London markets close in the evening, business is handed over to New York, which overlaps with Tokyo for a couple of hours each afternoon. Thus, there are no official closing rates in these international markets. The newspaper takes a representative sample of rates from major participants in the London markets at around 5pm local time each trading day.

THE CURRENCY MARKETS

Foreign exchange markets exist to facilitate international trade, and allow companies involved in international trade to hedge transactions through the forward purchase or sale of relevant currencies at a

fixed rate, designed to counteract any potential losses through future rises or falls in their values. In practice however, the bulk of turnover in these markets is attributable to speculation, and while speculation provides the markets with necessary liquidity, it can also destabilise those markets, hence creating a further need for hedging.

As in all markets the value of currencies in the international market is determined by supply and demand. The main players are the foreign exchange dealers of commercial banks and foreign exchange brokers. However, the market is often significantly affected by the intervention of central banks on behalf of governments. So, in this marketplace there is considerable interaction between the authorities and market professionals.

The ten biggest financial centres have seen trading volumes of forex grow by an average of 47 per cent since April 1992, considerably faster than the 42 per cent growth of the previous three year period. Total net daily currency trading has jumped to about $1.3 trillion from $880 billion in 1992, from $60 billion in 1983, and from $10–20 billion in 1973. London has increased its lead as world's top forex market with turnover leaping 60 per cent over the three years to 1995 to $464 billion a day, double the turnover of New York, the second biggest market.

Much of this vast expansion reflects growth in world trade, foreign direct investment and cross border portfolio investment, but it has also been spurred by a variety of new financial instruments and by increasingly powerful computers and telecommunications. The growth of trade and cross border investment creates a need for firms and fund managers to hedge their currency risk, but only 7 per cent of London transactions in forex and 17 per cent of New York transactions involve non-financial companies.

Speculation provides liquidity but makes the markets volatile and prediction difficult. Currency swings can be vast and often not very attached to fundamentals. They are particularly damaging for companies which rely heavily on exports or imported raw materials.

The core determining factor of a currency's value is the health of the real national economy, especially the balance of payments current account. If there is a surplus on the current account, that is, a country sells more goods than it buys, then buyers have to acquire that currency to purchase goods. This adds to foreign reserves and bids up the price of that currency. As it rises, exports rise in price, fall in quantity and the currency falls again.

The currency's value is also affected by the level of inflation and the domestic rate of interest. High rates of interest and low inflation make a currency attractive for those holding assets denominated in it or lending it to borrowers. So typically one country raising interest rates while others remain the same will raise the value of that currency as money flows into the country. This will have a limited effect if the fundamentals are wrong, that is, if there is a persistent deficit on the current account.

A significant factor determining short-term currency values is market sentiment. There is a self-fuelling process in which enthusiasm for a currency, or the lack of it, drives the rate. Speculators might decide, as they did with the pound sterling on Black Wednesday in September 1992, that a currency is overvalued or simply that there are speculative gains to be made. Short selling will then cause it to fall, often in spite of government intervention.

Currencies are measured in terms of one another or a trade-weighted index, a basket of currencies. The value of a currency in a trade-weighted index is assessed on a basis which gives a value appropriate to the volume of trade conducted in that currency. The *Financial Times* provides detailed information on two primary currencies in the world: the pound and the dollar. A large number of international contracts are struck in these currencies and the dollar particularly is used globally as a reserve currency.

The pound spot and forward

Figure 10.1(a) lists spot and forward prices for the pound against the currencies of the other major industrialised countries.

Reading the figures

- **Closing mid-point, change on day and day's mid high and low:** yesterday's closing price for immediate delivery of pounds, the mid-point between the prices at which they can be bought and sold; the change on the previous day's price; and the day's high and low for mid-point prices, the highest and lowest prices at which dealings have taken place during the European trading day. Since sterling is the largest currency unit, all prices are given in so many D-Marks, francs, dollars, etc. to the pound.

POUND SPOT FORWARD AGAINST THE POUND

ct 12		Closing mid-point	Change on day	Bid/offer spread	Day's Mid high	low	One month Rate	%PA	Three months Rate	%PA	One year Rate	%PA	Bank of Eng. Index
rope													
stria	(Sch)	15.7376	−0.0353	287 - 465	15.7989	15.7066	15.7072	2.3	15.6486	2.3	-	-	107.0
lgium	(BFr)	45.9849	−0.1455	624 - 073	46.2010	45.9110	45.8899	2.5	45.6999	2.5	44.9649	2.2	109.6
nmark	(DKr)	8.6718	−0.022	667 - 769	8.7117	8.6564	8.6641	1.1	8.6476	1.1	8.5851	1.0	110.3
land	(FM)	6.7465	−0.0266	384 - 545	6.7900	'6.7440	6.7421	0.8	6.734	0.7	-	-	88.1
ance	(FFr)	7.7870	−0.0306	833 - 906	7.8155	7.7805	7.7939	−1.1	7.7995	−0.6	7.7941	−0.1	109.4
rmany	(DM)	2.2364	−0.0051	352 - 376	2.2469	2.2310	2.2313	2.8	2.2219	2.6	2.1809	2.5	112.2
eece	(Dr)	366.920	−2.066	724 - 115	369.703	366.584	-	-	-	-	-	-	67.3
land	(I£)	0.9776	+0.0005	767 - 785	0.9788	0.9767	0.9768	1.0	0.9755	0.9	0.9723	0.5	97.5
y	(L)	2517.65	−10.99	583 - 947	2529.49	2515.17	2524.9	−3.5	2539.8	−3.5	2607.95	−3.6	70.2
xembourg	(LFr)	45.9849	−0.1455	624 - 073	46.2010	45.9110	45.8899	2.5	45.6999	2.5	44.9649	2.2	109.6
therlands	(Fl)	2.5038	−0.0076	025 - 050	2.5165	2.4993	2.4973	3.1	2.4864	2.8	2.4402	2.5	109.6
rway	(NKr)	9.8232	−0.0449	173 - 291	9.8769	9.8012	9.8108	1.5	9.7889	1.4	9.7134	1.1	99.8
rtugal	(Es)	235.074	−0.278	921 - 227	235.726	233.070	235.614	−2.8	236.834	−3.0	-	-	95.5
ain	(Pta)	192.446	−1.879	291 - 602	193.619	192.291	192.946	−3.1	193.886	−3.0	198.286	−3.0	81.4
veden	(SKr)	10.9209	−0.0237	099 - 318	10.9528	10.8958	10.9231	−0.2	10.9276	−0.2	10.951	−0.3	82.6
itzerland	(SFr)	1.8146	−0.0028	133 - 159	1.8260	1.8109	1.8075	4.7	1.7956	4.2	1.7427	4.0	115.7
ʞ	(£)	-	-	-	-	-	-	-	-	-	-	-	84.2
u	-	1.2150	−0.007	143 - 157	1.2213	1.2141	1.2139	1.1	1.2117	1.1	1.2023	1.0	-
R	-	1.055600	-	-	-	-	-	-	-	-	-	-	-
nericas													
gentina	(Peso)	1.5722	−0.0007	716 - 727	1.5745	1.5685	-	-	-	-	-	-	-
azil	(R$)	1.5061	−0.0016	054 - 068	1.5083	1.5028	-	-	-	-	-	-	-
nada	(C$)	2.1051	+0.003	040 - 061	2.1107	2.1004	2.1042	0.5	2.104	0.2	2.1091	−0.2	85.4
xico	(New Peso)	10.5744	−0.0205	553 - 935	10.5989	10.5346	-	-	-	-	-	-	-
A	($)	1.5724	−0.0007	719 - 729	1.5748	1.5687	1.5712	0.9	1.569	0.9	1.5574	1.0	92.7
cific/Middle East/Africa													
stralia	(A$)	2.0725	+0.012	705 - 745	2.0747	2.0705	2.0738	−0.8	2.0766	−0.8	2.0914	−0.9	86.7
ng Kong	(HK$)	12.1567	−0.0053	520 - 613	12.1748	12.1290	12.1532	0.3	12.1408	0.5	12.1072	0.4	-
lia	(Rs)	53.3908	+0.1256	581 - 235	53.4580	53.1870	-	-	-	-	-	-	-
ael	(Shk)	4.7142	−0.0085	091 - 193	4.7260	4.7073	-	-	-	-	-	-	-
pan	(Y)	157.625	−1.03	504 - 746	159.150	157.270	156.71	7.0	155.1	6.4	148.175	6.0	143.4
laysia	(M$)	3.9998	+0.0049	977 - 018	4.0042	3.9908	-	-	-	-	-	-	-
w Zealand	(NZ$)	2.3762	−0.0068	745 - 778	2.3800	2.3745	2.3821	−3.0	2.3914	−2.6	2.417	−1.7	101.4
lippines	(Peso)	40.7724	−0.0575	122 - 325	40.8325	40.7122	-	-	-	-	-	-	-
udi Arabia	(SR)	5.8975	−0.0024	954 - 995	5.9060	5.8836	-	-	-	-	-	-	-
gapore	(S$)	2.2383	−0.0013	368 - 398	2.2449	2.2341	-	-	-	-	-	-	-
uth Africa	(R)	5.7475	+0.0021	445 - 505	5.7607	5.7380	-	-	-	-	-	-	-
uth Korea	(Won)	1208.00	−0.06	753 - 846	1209.76	1205.23	-	-	-	-	-	-	-
wan	(T$)	42.2992	−0.0243	747 - 236	42.3983	42.2063	-	-	-	-	-	-	-
ailand	(Bt)	39.4673	−0.049	390 - 955	39.5680	39.3820	-	-	-	-	-	-	-

ates for Oct 11. Bid/offer spreads in the Pound Spot table show only the last three decimal places. Forward rates are not directly quoted to the market but implied by current interest rates. Sterling index calculated by the Bank of England. Base average 1990 = 100. Index rebased 1/2/95. Bid, Offer and d-rates in both this and the Dollar Spot tables derived from THE WM/REUTERS CLOSING SPOT RATES. Some values are rounded by the F.T.

Fig. 10.1(a) Pound spot and forward against the pound

■ Pound in New York		
Oct 16	⋯⋯Close ⋯⋯	⋯ Prev. close ⋯
£ spot	1.5727	1.5742
1 mth	1.5715	1.5730
3 mth	1.5693	1.5709
1 yr	1.5570	1.5587

Fig. 10.1(b) Pound in New York

- **Bid/offer spread:** a representative spread on the price at the close. Different banks may quote slightly different rates at the same time, particularly if the market is moving in a very volatile fashion. As with shares, marketmakers buy currencies at a lower price than they sell them in order to make a profit. The spreads are shown only to the last three decimal places.

- **Forward rates:** prices on contracts struck for settlement one month, three months or one year ahead, or prices implied by current interest rates; and the annualised interest rate differential between the two countries that implies. Forward currency rates and interest rates are intimately connected. A bank given an order to supply dollars against pounds in three months' time will in theory (out of simple prudence) purchase the dollars at once and leave them on deposit for three months. If dollars are yielding less than pounds, it will lose interest by switching from pounds to dollars. It naturally passes this cost on to the customer by charging more for three months dollars than it would for spot dollars. The forward dollars are sold at a premium: the buyer receives fewer dollars per pound. The curve of forward rates, at a premium (the currency units cost more forward, that is, the buyer receives fewer per pound the longer forward they are purchased) or a discount, is essentially determined by the interest rates available for deposit of these currencies relative to sterling. The lower the interest rate available, the higher the effective cost of buying that currency in advance, and this is reflected in the forward rates.

- **Bank of England index:** the relative trade-weighted position of currencies against the pound compared to a base value of 1990=100. So a figure of 112 for the D-Mark would indicate that it has strengthened by 12 per cent against the pound, weighted by volume of trade since 1990. Calculated by the Bank of England, the index is not a monetary value, but a measure of the strength or weakness of the pound against other currencies.

- **SDRs and ecus:** two international currency substitutes, the Special Drawing Right (SDR) of the International Monetary Fund (IMF) and the European currency unit (ecu). Both of these are currency baskets made up of a predetermined amount of a number of different currencies: five in the case of the SDR, the unit in which the IMF accounts

are denominated; rather more for the ecu which comprises currencies in which transactions concerning the European Monetary System (EMS) are administered. Their composite character means that these currency substitutes are less volatile than the individual units, and they are being used to an increasing extent for commercial purposes.

- **Pound in New York:** Figure 10.1(b) details the rates for the pound in the New York market on a spot basis and one, three and twelve months ahead, plus the close on the previous trading day.

Using the information

The global foreign exchange market, the huge size of which dwarfs every other international financial market, has always presented technical difficulties for institutions seeking end-of-day rates that are authoritative and consistent. The market functions around the clock in virtually every country and knows no limitations such as fixed trading hours or any obligation to report "closing" rates. Until 1992, no single, consistent, set of forex rates had gained universal acceptance, with the result that the various reference sources used by the investment industry and the wider business community sometimes varied widely. This problem was compounded when market conditions were volatile.

The rates shown in this and other FT currency tables use data drawn from the WM/Reuters Closing Spot Rates. Developed by the two companies in consultation with leading London financial market practitioners, these now set a daily global standard for the rates required for index calculation, investment management and portfolio valuation. A single suite of rates allows accurate comparisons between competing indices and competing funds. Users of rates for commercial contracts and transactions also benefit from access to a consistent set of data, drawn from the market at a precisely fixed time and rigorously screened to exclude anomalous quotes.

The WM Company calculates and publishes a daily fixing based on market rates derived from Reuters' forex reporting system, and covering around seventy currencies. At short intervals before and after 4pm London time, representative bid, offer and mid rates against the US dollar are selected from a wide range of contributing banks and forex dealers. Spot rates for all currencies against sterling are then calculated as cross rates from the dollar parities, reflecting forex market practice. The

choice of 4pm as the reference point results from research that suggests that this time not only captures a far larger selection of timely quotes from continental European contributors, but also reflects more accurately the peak trading period for the London and New York markets.

It is possible that by the time the rates are consulted, the markets may have moved quite sharply. The rates in the newspaper cannot guarantee to be up to the minute; what they do provide is a daily record of the market's activities for reference purposes. The rates are frequently used by exporters and importers striking contracts in more than one currency at an agreed published rate.

Businesses frequently need to hedge against currency risk. Typically, a UK business with significant dollar income might sell dollars forward at a particular rate. This protects it against the pound weakening (though it also means gains from it strengthening would be missed), but more importantly makes the exchange rate predictable for that company to aid planning.

International investors too are exposed to currency risk. While investing in foreign equities naturally exposes an investor to the currencies in which they are denominated, exposure can also be achieved by investing in those currencies as assets in their own right. The markets for exchanging sterling, dollars, D-Marks and yen need not only be a means of switching between different national equity markets. They can also be a way to enhance total portfolio returns, to speculate on future shifts in exchange rates or, for the more risk-averse investor, to hedge bets through interest rate and currency diversification.

For the global investor balancing an overall portfolio of equities, bonds and cash, it may be wise to explore the opportunities for holding the cash portion in alternatives to savings accounts or money market funds denominated in the base currency. Interest rate differentials between countries mean that banks and fund managers elsewhere might be offering better returns. And if differentials get wider, there may be currency appreciation benefits as well: on the whole, higher rates in one place will attract more buyers of the currency driving up its value.

An alternative way to get currency exposure is through managed currency funds. These are generally run by international fund management companies, are often located in the Channel Islands for obvious tax advantages, and operate in a similar way to unit and

investment trusts: investors buy units in the fund and its managers pursue the best returns they can by investing in the appropriate cash and currency markets. Currency fund data form part of the FT managed funds service discussed in chapter 8.

Just like trusts, the precise markets in which the funds invest vary considerably and most companies have a good selection from which to choose. Some might be focused on a single currency, investing in short-term money market deposits in its country of origin. Others are multi-currency accounts, perhaps using sterling or the dollar as the point of reference, and moving in and out of other currencies in anticipation of advantageous exchange rate movements. Typically, decisions will be made on the basis of assessing the relevant fundamental economic data; sometimes, they might be based on technical analysis of the past patterns of currency fluctuations.

The dollar, spot and forward

The dollar has long been the dominant currency in world trade and the United States has often been able to pay for its imports with dollars. Given that fact and the persistent twin deficits of the US current account and government budget, the country is consistently exporting dollars which then move around world markets and economies. Hence the importance of the dollar spot and forward rates published in the *Financial Times* (see Figure 10.2).

- **Prices for the dollar spot and forward:** the equivalent range of information as the pound spot and forward.

- **Pounds and ecus:** all prices, except for sterling, the Irish pound and the ecu, are quoted in terms of francs, guilders, etc. to the dollar. Sterling, the Irish pound and the ecu are quoted in dollars rather than in so many units to the dollar. It is important to bear this in mind when comparing forward rates and the direction of movement of the dollar against these currencies.

- **JP Morgan index:** like the Bank of England index, these figures show the relative trade-weighted position of currencies, in this case against the dollar. The base is 1990=100.

DOLLAR SPOT FORWARD AGAINST THE DOLLAR

Oct 12		Closing mid-point	Change on day	Bid/offer spread	Day's mid high	low	One month Rate	%PA	Three months Rate	%PA	One year Rate	%PA	J.P Morgan index
Europe													
Austria	(Sch)	10.0087	−0.0179	062 - 111	10.0400	9.9975	9.9936	1.8	9.9634	1.8	9.8542	1.5	107.0
Belgium	(BFr)	29.2450	−0.0795	400 - 500	29.3800	29.2220	29.204	1.7	29.125	1.6	28.825	1.4	109.1
Denmark	(DKr)	5.5150	−0.0115	135 - 165	5.5415	5.5095	5.5157	−0.2	5.5115	0.3	5.521	−0.1	109.4
Finland	(FM)	4.2906	−0.015	868 - 943	4.3254	4.2868	4.2902	0.1	4.2891	0.1	4.2846	0.1	87.0
France	(FFr)	4.9523	−0.0172	515 - 530	4.9700	4.9501	4.9608	−2.1	4.9708	−1.5	4.9923	−0.8	108.9
Germany	(DM)	1.4223	−0.0026	220 - 226	1.4287	1.4205	1.4201	1.9	1.4157	1.8	1.3972	1.8	111.5
Greece	(Dr)	233.350	−1.21	300 - 400	235.180	233.150	235.075	−8.9	238.275	−8.4	251.75	−7.9	66.5
Ireland	(I£)	1.6084	−0.0016	074 - 094	1.6105	1.6035	1.6086	−0.1	1.6087	−0.1	1.6152	−0.4	-
Italy	(L)	1601.15	−6.28	050 - 180	1607.50	1599.25	1607.9	−5.1	1619.95	−4.7	1677.15	−4.7	69.4
Luxembourg	(LFr)	29.2450	−0.0795	400 - 500	29.3800	29.2220	29.204	1.7	29.125	1.6	28.825	1.4	109.1
Netherlands	(Fl)	1.5923	−0.0042	920 - 926	1.5996	1.5907	1.5897	2.0	1.5846	1.9	1.5646	1.7	108.9
Norway	(NKr)	6.2473	−0.0257	455 - 490	6.2825	6.2405	6.2435	0.7	6.2373	0.6	6.2273	0.3	98.6
Portugal	(Es)	149.500	−0.11	450 - 550	149.910	148.000	149.965	−3.7	150.975	−3.9	155.6	−4.1	95.8
Spain	(Pta)	122.390	−1.14	330 - 450	123.050	122.330	122.77	−3.7	123.54	−3.8	127.035	−3.8	80.6
Sweden	(SKr)	6.9454	−0.0119	406 - 501	6.9673	6.9250	6.9629	−3.0	6.9994	−3.1	7.1679	−3.2	82.3
Switzerland	(SFr)	1.1541	−0.0012	536 - 545	1.1605	1.1525	1.1505	3.7	1.1444	3.4	1.1166	3.2	115.2
UK	(£)	1.5724	−0.0007	719 - 729	1.5748	1.5687	1.5712	0.9	1.569	0.9	1.5574	1.0	83.9
Ecu	–	1.2942	+0.0068	938 - 945	1.2954	1.2880	1.2946	−0.4	1.2953	−0.3	1.2976	−0.3	-
SDR†	–	0.66880	-	-	-	-	-	-	-	-	-	-	-
Americas													
Argentina	(Peso)	0.9999	-	998 - 999	0.9999	0.9995	-	-	-	-	-	-	-
Brazil	(R$)	0.9579	−0.0005	577 - 580	0.9580	0.9577	--	-	-	-	-	-	-
Canada	(C$)	1.3388	+0.0025	385 - 390	1.3415	1.3353	1.3393	−0.4	1.3406	−0.5	1.3508	−0.9	84.5
Mexico	(New Peso)	6.7250	−0.01	150 - 350	6.7350	6.6900	6.7272	−0.4	6.7304	−0.3	6.7353	−0.2	-
USA	($)	-	-	-	-	-	-	-	-	-	-	-	93.9
Pacific/Middle East/Africa													
Australia	(A$)	1.3180	+0.0082	172 - 189	1.3211	1.3172	1.3198	−1.6	1.3234	−1.6	1.3431	−1.9	88.3
Hong Kong	(HK$)	7.7313	+0.0001	308 - 318	7.7318	7.7308	7.7329	−0.2	7.7348	−0.2	7.755	−0.3	-
India	(Rs)	33.9550	+0.095	450 - 650	33.9650	33.8500	34.105	−5.3	34.41	−5.4	35.88	−5.7	-
Israel	(Shk)	2.9981	−0.0041	958 - 004	3.0040	2.9958	-	-	-	-	-	-	-
Japan	(Y)	100.245	−0.61	200 - 290	101.230	99.9800	99.75	5.9	98.83	5.6	94.955	5.3	143.0
Malaysia	(M$)	2.5437	+0.0042	432 - 442	2.5446	2.5398	2.5437	0.0	2.544	−0.1	2.5517	−0.3	-
New Zealand	(NZ$)	1.5110	−0.0037	106 - 117	1.5149	1.5106	1.5151	−3.3	1.5226	−3.1	1.5473	−2.4	-
Philippines	(Peso)	25.9300	−0.025	000 - 600	25.9600	25.9000	-	-	-	-	-	-	-
Saudi Arabia	(SR)	3.7506	+0.0001	505 - 507	3.7507	3.7505	3.7511	−0.2	3.752	−0.1	3.7551	−0.1	-
Singapore	(S$)	1.4235	−0.0002	230 - 240	1.4270	1.4213	1.4201	2.9	1.4138	2.7	1.389	2.4	-
South Africa	(R)	3.6553	+0.003	545 - 560	3.6635	3.6530	3.6806	−8.3	3.7306	−8.2	3.9618	−8.4	-
South Korea	(Won)	768.250	+0.3	200 - 300	768.900	767.800	771.25	−4.7	774.75	−3.4	793.25	−3.3	-
Taiwan	(T$)	26.9010	−0.0035	940 - 080	26.9300	26.8870	26.921	−0.9	26.961	−0.9	-	-	-
Thailand	(Bt)	25.1000	−0.02	900 - 100	25.1340	25.0900	25.1875	−4.2	24.835	4.2	26.055	−3.8	-

† SDR rate per $ for Oct 11. Bid/offer spreads in the Dollar Spot table show only the last three decimal places. Forward rates are not directly quoted to the market but are implied by current interest rates. UK, Ireland & ECU are quoted in US currency. J.P. Morgan nominal indices Oct 11. Base average 1990=100

Fig. 10.2 Dollar spot and forward against the dollar

Other currencies of the world

Monday's newspaper carries a table of virtually every currency of the world, showing its value in terms of four key currencies: sterling, the dollar, the D-Mark and the yen (see Figure 10.3). The rates given are usually the average of the latest buying and selling rates. Many of these currencies are pretty obscure in terms of their role outside their countries of origin; many of them are fixed against the dollar or tied

The table below gives the latest available rates of exchange (rounded) against four key currencies on Friday, October 6, 1995. In some cases the rate is nominal. Market rates are the average of buying and selling rates except where they are shown to be otherwise. In some cases market rates have been calculated from those of foreign currencies to which they are tied.

		£ STG	US $	D-MARK	YEN (X 100)
Afghanistan	(Afghani)	7022.36	4442.00	3112.82	1408.93
Albania	(Lek)	148.051	93.6500	65.6272	92.9529
Algeria	(Dinar)	79.8513	50.5100	35.3959	50.1340
Andorra	(French Fr)	7.9278	5.0149	3.5143	4.9776
	(Sp Peseta)	195.630	123.750	86.7204	122.829
Angola	(Kwanza)	8998.48	5692.00	3988.79	5649.63
Antigua	(E Carr $)	4.2684	2.7000	1.8921	2.6799
Argentina	(Peso)	1.5800	0.9995	0.7004	0.9921
Armenia	(Dram)	632.360o	400.000	280.308	397.022
Aruba	(Florin)	2.8298	1.7900	1.2544	1.7767
Australia	(Aus $)	2.0767	1.3136	0.9205	1.3038
Austria	(Schilling)	15.8723	10.0404	7.0360	9.9657
Azerbaijan	(Manat)	6948.06o	4395.00	3079.89	4362.28
Azores	(Port Escudo)	237.333	150.130	105.207	149.012
Bahamas	(Bahama $)	1.5809	1	0.7008	0.9926
Bahrain	(Dinar)	0.5960	0.3770	0.2642	0.3742
Balearic Is	(Sp Peseta)	195.630	123.750	86.7204	122.829
Bangladesh	(Taka)	63.5502	40.2000	28.1710	39.9007
Barbados	(Barb $)	3.1797	2.0113	1.4095	1.9963
Belarus	(Rouble)	18180.4o	11500.0	8058.86	11414.4
Belgium	(Belg Fr)	46.4612	29.3900	20.5957	29.1712
Belize	(B $)	3.1618	2.0000	1.4015	1.9851
Benin	(CFA Fr)	792.780	501.490	351.430	497.757
Bermuda	(Bermudian $)	1.5809	1	0.7008	0.9926
Bhutan	(Ngultrum)	53.5908	33.9000	23.7561	33.6476
Bolivia	(Boliviano)	7.6988	4.8700	3.4128	4.8337
Botswana	(Pula)	4.4284	2.8011	1.9629	2.7803
Brazil	(Real)	1.5150	0.9584	0.6716	0.9513
Brunei	(Brunei $)	2.2583	1.4285	1.0011	1.4179
Bulgaria	(Lev)	107.770	68.1700	47.7716	67.6625
Burkino Faso	(CFA Fr)	792.780	501.490	351.430	497.757
Burma	(Kyat)	8.9424	5.6565	3.9639	5.6144
Burundi	(Burundi Fr)	391.115	247.400	173.371	245.558
Cambodia	(Riel)	3636.07	2300.00	1611.77	2282.88
Cameroon	(CFA Fr)	792.780	501.490	351.430	497.757
Canada	(Canadian $)	2.1056	1.3320	0.9334	1.3221
Canary Is	(Sp Peseta)	195.630	123.750	86.7204	122.829
Cp. Verde	(CV Escudo)	131.167	82.9700	58.1430	82.3524
Cayman Is	(CI $)	1.3093	0.8282	0.5804	0.8220
Cent. Afr. Rep	(CFA Fr)	792.780	501.490	351.430	497.757
Chad	(CFA Fr)	792.780	501.490	351.430	497.757
Chile	(Chilean Peso)	634.079	401.100	281.079	398.114
China	(Yuan)	13.1486	8.3174	5.8286	8.2555
Colombia	(Col Peso)	1547.65	979.000	686.055	971.712
Comoros	(Fr)	587.466	371.602	260.408	368.836
Congo	(CFA Fr)	792.780	501.490	351.430	497.757
Costa Rica	(Colon)	296.419	187.500	131.395	186.104
Côte d'Ivoire	(CFA Fr)	792.780	501.490	351.430	497.757
Croatia	(Kuna)	8.4326	5.3341	3.7380	5.2944
Cuba	(Cuban Peso)	1.5809	1	0.7008	0.9926
Cyprus	(Cyprus £)	0.7206	0.4558	0.3194	0.4524
Czech Rep.	(Koruna)	41.6048	26.3180	18.4429	26.1221
Denmark	(Danish Krone)	8.7753	5.5510	3.8900	5.5097
Djibouti Rep	(Djib Fr)	276.658	175.000	122.635	173.697
Dominica	(E Carrib $)	4.2684	2.7000	1.8921	2.6799
Dominican Rep	(D Peso)	21.7216	13.7400	9.6286	13.6377
Ecuador	(Sucre)	4191.76o	2651.50	1858.09	2631.76
	(Sucre)	4151.44a	2626.00	1840.22	2606.45
Egypt	(Egyptian £)	5.3727	3.3985	2.3816	3.3732
El Salvador	(Colon)	13.8487	8.7600	6.1388	8.6948
Equat'l Guinea	(CFA Fr)	792.780	501.490	351.430	497.757
Estonia	(Kroon)	18.0444	11.4140	7.9986	11.3290
Ethiopia	(Ethiopian Birr)	9.1692	5.8000	4.0645	5.7568
Falkland Is	(Falk £)	1	0.6326	0.4433	0.6278
Faroe Is	(Danish Krone)	8.7753	5.5510	3.8900	5.5097
Fiji Is	(Fiji $)	2.2235	1.4065	0.9856	1.3960
Finland	(Markka)	6.8170	4.3122	3.0219	4.2801
France	(Fr)	7.9278	5.0149	3.5143	4.9776
Fr. Cty/Africa	(CFA Fr)	792.780	501.490	351.430	497.757
Fr. Guiana	(Local Fr)	7.9278	5.0149	3.5143	4.9776
Fr. Pacific Is	(CFP Fr)	142.416	90.0854	63.1292	89.4148
Gabon	(CFA Fr)	792.780	501.490	351.430	497.757
Gambia	(Dalasi)	15.2557	9.6500	6.7624	9.5782
Germany	(D-Mark)	2.2559	1.4270	1	1.4164
Ghana	(Cedi)	2078.88	1315.00	921.514	1305.21
Gibraltar	(Gib £)	1	0.6326	0.4433	0.6278
Greece	(Drachma)	370.970	234.665	164.446	232.918
Greenland	(Danish Krone)	8.7753	5.5510	3.8900	5.5097
Grenada	(E Carr $)	4.2684	2.7000	1.8921	2.6799
Guadaloupe	(Local Fr)	7.9278	5.0149	3.5143	4.9776
Guam	(US $)	1.5809	1	0.7008	0.9926
Guatemala	(Quetzal)	9.3556	5.9179	4.1471	5.8739
Guinea	(Fr)	1569.36	992.700	695.655	985.310
Guinea-Bissau	(Peso)	28513.1	18036.0	12639.1	17901.7
Guyana	(Guyanese $)	227.334	143.800	100.771	142.730
Haiti	(Goude)	30.0371	19.0000	13.3147	18.8586
Honduras	(Lempira)	15.3980	9.7400	6.8255	9.6675
Hong Kong	(HK $)	12.2239	7.7325	5.4187	7.6749
Hungary	(Forint)	207.858	131.485	92.1409	130.506
Iceland	(Icelandic Krona)	102.379	64.7600	45.3819	64.2779
India	(Indian Rupee)	53.5908	33.9000	23.7561	33.6476
Indonesia	(Rupiah)	3585.37	2268.00	1589.35	2251.12
Iran	(Rial)	4742.70u(2)	3000.00	2102.31	2977.67
Iraq	(Iraqi Dinar)	0.9486	0.6000	0.4205	0.5955
Irish Rep	(Punt)	0.9816	0.6209	0.4351	0.6163
Israel	(Shekel)	4.7556	3.0083	2.1081	2.9859
Italy	(Lira)	2556.79	1617.35	1133.39	1605.31
Jamaica	(Jamaican $)	56.5172	35.7500	25.0526	35.4839
Japan	(Yen)	159.271	100.750	70.6027	100
Jordan	(Jordanian Dinar)	1.1272	0.7130	0.4996	0.7077
Kazakhstan	(Tenge)	97.0120	61.3650	43.0028	60.9082
Kenya	(Kenya Shilling)	87.8585	55.5750	38.9453	55.1613
Kiribati	(Australian $)	2.0767	1.3136	0.9205	1.3038
Korea North	(Won)	3.3990	2.1500	1.5067	2.1340
Korea South	(Won)	1215.04	768.600	538.613	762.878
Kuwait	(Kuwaiti Dinar)	0.4735	0.2995	0.2099	0.2973
Laos	(New Kip)	1454.43	920.000	644.709	913.151
Latvia	(Lats)	0.8529	0.5395	0.3781	0.5355
Lebanon	(Lebanese £)	2544.38	1609.50	1127.89	1597.52
Lesotho	(Maluti)	5.7879	3.6613	2.5657	3.6340
Liberia	(Liberian $)	1.5809	1	0.7008	0.9926
Libya	(Libyan Dinar)	0.5620	0.3555	0.2491	0.3529
Liechtenstein	(Swiss Fr)	1.8156	1.1485	0.8048	1.1400
Lithuania	(Litas)	6.3236	4.0000	2.8031	3.9702
Luxembourg	(Lux Fr)	46.4612	29.3900	20.5957	29.1712
Macao	(Pataca)	12.6260	7.9866	5.5968	7.9272
Macedonia	(Denar)	62.1300	39.3004	27.5406	39.0079
Madagascar	(MG Fr)	5216.97	3300.00	2312.54	3275.43
Madeira	(Port Escudo)	237.333	150.130	105.207	149.012
Malawi	(Kwacha)	24.1310	15.2641	10.6966	15.1505
Malaysia	(Ringgit)	4.0099	2.5365	1.7775	2.5176
Maldive Is	(Rufiya)	18.6072	11.7700	8.2481	11.6824
Mali Rep	(CFA Fr)	792.780	501.490	351.430	497.757
Malta	(Maltese Lira)	0.5556	0.3515	0.2463	0.3488
Martinique	(Local Fr)	7.9278	5.0149	3.5143	4.9776
Mauritania	(Ouguiya)	209.556	132.555	92.8907	131.568
Mauritius	(Maur Rupee)	28.4325	17.9850	12.6034	17.8511
Mexico	(Mexican Peso)	10.3309	6.5350	4.5795	6.4864
Miquelon	(Local Fr)	7.9278	5.0149	3.5143	4.9776
Moldova	(Leu)	7.1852	4.5450	3.1850	4.5112
Monaco	(French Fr)	7.9278	5.0149	3.5143	4.9776
Mongolia	(Tugrik)	709.982	449.100	314.716	445.757
Montserrat	(E Carr $)	4.2684	2.7000	1.8921	2.6799
Morocco	(Dirham)	13.3597	8.4507	5.9220	8.3878
Mozambique	(Metical)	15767.9	9974.00	6989.49	9899.75
Namibia	(S A Rand)	5.7879	3.6613	2.5657	3.6340
Nauru Is	(Australian $)	2.0767	1.3136	0.9205	1.3038
Nepal	(Nepalese Rupee)	79.6616	50.3900	35.3119	50.0149
Netherlands	(Guilder)	2.5304	1.6007	1.1217	1.5888
N'nd Antilles	(A/Guilder)	2.8298	1.7900	1.2544	1.7767
New Zealand	(NZ $)	2.3871	1.5099	1.0581	1.4987
Nicaragua	(Gold Cordoba)	12.2564	7.7528	5.4329	7.6951
Niger Rep	(CFA Fr)	792.780	501.490	351.430	497.757
Nigeria	(Naira)	34.7798o	22.0000	15.4170	21.8362
	(Naira)	136.111m	86.1000	60.3364	85.4591
Norway	(Nor. Krone)	9.9697	6.3065	4.4194	6.2596
Oman	(Rial Omani)	0.6086	0.3850	0.2698	0.3821
Pakistan	(Pak. Rupee)	49.9365	31.5884	22.1362	31.3533
Panama	(Balboa)	1.5809	1	0.7008	0.9926
Papua New Guinea	(Kina)	2.0939	1.3245	0.9282	1.3146
Paraguay	(Guarani)	3102.52	1962.50	1375.26	1947.89
Peru	(New Sol)	3.5625	2.2535	1.5792	2.2367
Philippines	(Peso)	40.9282	25.8900	18.1430	25.6973
Pitcairn Is	(£ Sterling)	1	0.6326	0.4433	0.6278
	(NZ $)	2.3871	1.5099	1.0581	1.4987
Poland	(Zloty)	3.8644	2.4445	1.7130	2.4263
Portugal	(Escudo)	237.333	150.130	105.207	149.012
Puerto Rico	(US $)	1.5809	1	0.7008	0.9926
Qatar	(Riyal)	5.7561	3.6410	2.5515	3.6139
Reunion Is. de la	(F/Fr)	7.9278	5.0149	3.5143	4.9776
Romania	(Leu)	3466.12	2192.50	1536.44	2176.18
Russia ‡	(Rouble)	0.9895o	0.6259	0.4386	0.6213
	(Rouble)	7106.94m	4495.50	3150.32	4462.03
Rwanda	(Fr)	477.764	302.210	211.780	299.960
St Christopher	(E Carr $)	4.2684	2.7000	1.8921	2.6799
St Helena	(£)	1	0.6326	0.4433	0.6278
St Lucia	(E Carr $)	4.2684	2.7000	1.8921	2.6799
St Pierre	(French Fr)	7.9278	5.0149	3.5143	4.9776
St Vincent	(E Carr $)	4.2684	2.7000	1.8921	2.6799
San Marino	(Italian Lira)	2556.79	1617.35	1133.39	1605.31
Sao Tome	(Dobra)	2285.60	1445.76	1013.15	1435.00
Saudi Arabia	(Riyal)	5.9290	3.7505	2.6282	3.7226
Senegal	(CFA Fr)	792.780	501.490	351.430	497.757
Seychelles	(Rupee)	7.6547	4.8420	3.3931	4.8060
Sierra Leone	(Leone)	1195.16	756.000	529.783	750.372
Singapore	($)	2.2583	1.4285	1.0011	1.4179
Slovakia	(Koruna)	46.7994	29.6030	20.7449	29.3826
Slovenia	(Tolar)	194.343	122.932	86.1470	122.017
Solomon Is	($)	5.3773	3.4014	2.3836	3.3761
Somali Rep	(Shilling)	4141.96	2620.00	1836.02	2600.50
South Africa	(Rand)	5.7879	3.6613	2.5657	3.6340
Spain	(Peseta)	195.630	123.750	86.7204	122.829
Spanish Ports In N Africa	(Sp Peseta)	195.630	123.750	86.7204	122.829
Sri Lanka	(Rupee)	82.3623	52.1000	36.5102	51.7122
Sudan Rep	(Dinar)	118.568	75.0000	52.5578	74.4417
Surinam	(Guilder)	777.803	492.000	344.779	488.338
Swaziland	(Lilangeni)	5.7879	3.6613	2.5657	3.6340
Sweden	(Krona)	11.1122	7.0293	4.9259	6.9770
Switzerland	(Fr)	1.8156	1.1485	0.8048	1.1400
Syria	(£)	66.2397	41.9000	29.3623	41.5881
Taiwan	($)	42.5233	26.8990	18.8500	26.6988
Tanzania	(Shilling)	948.540	600.000	420.463	595.534
Thailand	(Baht)	39.7031	25.1150	17.5999	24.9280
Togo Rep	(CFA Fr)	792.780	501.490	351.430	497.757
Tonga Is	(Pa'anga)	2.0767	1.3136	0.9205	1.3038
Trinidad/Tobago	($)	9.0151	5.7025	3.9962	5.6601
Tunisia	(Dinar)	1.4932	0.9445	0.6619	0.9375
Turkey	(Lira)	79188.8	50092.5	35103.4	49719.6
Turks & Caicos	(US $)	1.5809	1	0.7008	0.9926
Tuvalu	(Australian $)	2.0767	1.3136	0.9205	1.3038
Uganda	(New Shilling)	1573.00	995.000	697.267	987.593
Ukraine	(Karbovanets)	271914.8	172000.0	120532.6	170719.6
U A E	(Dirham)	5.8061	3.6728	2.5738	3.6455
United Kingdom	(£)	1	0.6326	0.4433	0.6278
United States	(US $)	1.5809	1	0.7008	0.9926
Uruguay	(Peso Uruguayo)	10.4340	6.6000	4.6251	6.5509
Vanuatu	(Vatu)	177.530	112.300	78.6966	111.464
Vatican	(Lira)	2556.79	1617.35	1133.39	1605.31
Venezuela	(Bolivar)	268.405	169.785	118.980	168.521
Vietnam	(Dong)	17412.0	11014.0	7718.29	10932.0
Virgin Is-British	(US $)	1.5809	1	0.7008	0.9926
Virgin Is-US	(US $)	1.5809	1	0.7008	0.9926
Western Samoa	(Tala)	3.9493	2.4981	1.7506	2.4795
Yemen (Rep of)	(Rial)	79.0450o	50.0000	35.0385	49.6278
Yemen (Rep of)	(Rial)	221.326r	140.000	98.1079	138.958
Yugoslavia	(New Dinar) (1)	-	-	-	-
Zaire Rep	(Zaire)	8572.16	5422.33	3799.81	5381.97
Zambia	(Kwacha)	1488.87	941.785	659.976	934.774
Zimbabwe	($)	13.9969	8.8538	6.2045	8.7879

Fig. 10.3 FT guide to world currencies

CROSS RATES AND DERIVATIVES

EXCHANGE CROSS RATES

Number of French francs per D-Mark

Number of D-Marks per ten French francs

Number of D-Marks per French francs

Number of Irish pounds per dollar

Number of ecus per hundred yen

Oct 12		BFr	DKr	FFr	DM	I£	L	FI	NKr	Es	Pta	SKr	SFr	£	C$	$	Y	Ecu
Belgium	(BFr)	100	18.86	16.94	4.863	2.125	5474	5.446	21.36	511.3	418.4	23.75	3.947	2.175	4.578	3.419	342.8	2.642
Denmark	(DKr)	53.02	10	8.979	2.578	1.127	2902	2.887	11.33	271.1	221.9	12.59	2.093	1.153	2.427	1.813	181.7	1.401
France	(FFr)	59.05	11.14	10	2.871	1.255	3232	3.216	12.61	301.9	247.1	14.02	2.331	1.284	2.703	2.019	202.4	1.560
Germany	(DM)	20.56	3.878	3.483	1	0.437	1126	1.120	4.393	105.1	86.05	4.884	0.812	0.447	0.941	0.703	70.48	0.543
Ireland	(I£)	47.06	8.876	7.970	2.289	1	2576	2.563	10.05	240.6	196.9	11.18	1.858	1.024	2.155	1.609	161.3	1.244
Italy	(L)	1.827	0.345	0.309	0.089	0.039	100.	0.099	0.390	9.340	7.644	0.434	0.072	0.040	0.084	0.062	6.261	0.048
Netherlands	(FI)	18.36	3.463	3.110	0.893	0.390	1005	1	3.923	93.89	76.84	4.361	0.725	0.399	0.841	0.628	62.94	0.485
Norway	(NKr)	46.81	8.828	7.927	2.276	0.995	2562	2.549	10	239.3	195.9	11.12	1.848	1.018	2.143	1.600	160.4	1.237
Portugal	(Es)	19.56	3.689	3.312	0.951	0.416	1071	1.065	4.178	100.	81.84	4.645	0.772	0.425	0.895	0.669	67.04	0.517
Spain	(Pta)	23.90	4.507	4.047	1.162	0.508	1308	1.301	5.106	122.2	100.	5.676	0.943	0.520	1.094	0.817	81.91	0.631
Sweden	(SKr)	42.11	7.941	7.131	2.048	0.895	2305	2.293	8.995	215.3	176.2	10	1.662	0.916	1.928	1.440	144.3	1.113
Switzerland	(SFr)	25.33	4.778	4.290	1.232	0.538	1387	1.380	5.412	129.5	106.0	6.017	1	0.551	1.160	0.866	86.83	0.669
UK	(£)	45.98	8.672	7.787	2.236	0.977	2517	2.504	9.823	235.1	192.4	10.92	1.815	1	2.105	1.572	157.6	1.215
Canada	(C$)	21.84	4.120	3.699	1.062	0.464	1196	1.190	4.667	111.7	91.40	5.188	0.862	0.475	1	0.747	74.87	0.577
US	($)	29.25	5.517	4.954	1.422	0.622	1601	1.593	6.249	149.6	122.4	6.947	1.155	0.636	1.339	1	100.3	0.773
Japan	(Y)	29.18	5.503	4.941	1.419	0.620	1597	1.589	6.233	149.2	122.1	6.929	1.152	0.635	1.336	0.997	100.	0.771
Ecu		37.84	7.137	6.409	1.840	0.804	2072	2.061	8.085	193.5	158.4	8.988	1.494	0.823	1.733	1.294	129.7	1

Danish Kroner, French Franc, Norwegian Franc, and Swedish Kronor per 10; Belgian Franc, Yen, Escudo, Lira and Peseta per 100.

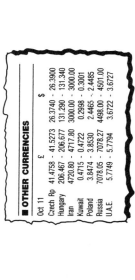

■ OTHER CURRENCIES		
Oct 11	£	$
Czech Rp	41.4758 - 41.5273	26.3740 - 26.3900
Hungary	206.467 - 206.677	131.290 - 131.340
Iran	4720.80 - 4717.80	3000.00 - 3000.00
Kuwait	0.4715 - 0.4722	0.2998 - 0.3001
Poland	3.8474 - 3.8530	2.4465 - 2.4485
Russia	7078.05 - 7078.27	4498.00 - 4501.00
U.A.E.	5.7749 - 5.7794	3.6722 - 3.6727

Fig. 10.4 (a) Exchange cross rates (b) Other currencies

to important international or regional currencies; and many of them are very strictly controlled by the local monetary authorities, and are not openly dealt on world foreign exchange markets.

For the major currencies of the world, a daily table shows exchange cross rates (see Figure 10.4(a)). This provides the reciprocal values for sixteen of the world's principal trading currencies plus the ecu, quoted in a grid displaying each currency's value in terms of the others. Half-yearly, the newspaper shows current and six months earlier values for sixteen currencies in terms of dollars, D-Marks and yen as well as charts tracking the past six months' movements of the dollar against the yen and the D-Mark and trade-weighted indices for the dollar, the yen and sterling.

One last daily table headed "Other currencies" gives sterling and dollar buy and sell rates for a handful of second-rank currencies in which some sort of free market exists (see Figure 10.4(b)) or which are politically sensitive. In some of these cases, there may be a considerably higher degree of official exchange rate control than with front rank currencies.

Saturday's newspaper adds a table of over thirty tourist rates against the pound in its Weekend Money section. These are the rates at which individuals can buy the currencies.

THE MONEY MARKETS

The money markets are the markets in deposits and short-term financial instruments, places for money that is available for short periods and where money can be converted into longer period loans. It is a wholesale market for professionals only, though its operations have an impact on the price of money and liquidity generally. Its main functions are:

- those banks temporarily short of funds can borrow while those with a surplus can put it to work;

- a source of liquidity;

- banks can borrow wholesale funds as can companies and governments;

- to correct imbalances between the banking system as a whole and the government.

FT reports describe monetary conditions and central bank money market intervention in a number of countries, focusing especially on

the United Kingdom. The choice of market centres will depend on the amount of activity in each on the preceding day.

UK interest rates

The UK money market report is designed to be read in conjunction with the London money rates table (see Figure 10.5). It describes the flows of funds between the government and the banks on the previous day, the resulting state of credit (whether it is abundant or in short supply) and the actions of the Bank of England in the market. When, as is usual, the market is short of credit, the way in which and the price at which the Bank chooses to supply it can sometimes be a significant pointer to the direction in which monetary policy is moving. The Bank can influence both monetary conditions and the relationship between the interest rates of loans of different maturities.

The London money rates table in Figure 10.5 provides details of interest rates for overnight deposits and other short-term instruments. These are representative interest rates taken by the newspaper from major market participants near the end of the London trading day.

UK INTEREST RATES

LONDON MONEY RATES

Oct 11	Over-night	7 days notice	One month	Three months	Six months	One year
Interbank Sterling	$7\frac{5}{8} - 6\frac{1}{4}$	$6\frac{3}{4} - 6\frac{1}{16}$	$6\frac{3}{4} - 6\frac{5}{8}$	$6\frac{13}{32} - 6\frac{11}{16}$	$6\frac{13}{32} - 6\frac{11}{16}$	$6\frac{7}{8} - 6\frac{3}{4}$
Sterling CDs	-	-	$6\frac{33}{32} - 6\frac{31}{32}$	$6\frac{33}{32} - 6\frac{31}{32}$	$6\frac{3}{4} - 6\frac{11}{16}$	$6\frac{3}{4} - 6\frac{11}{16}$
Treasury Bills	-	-	$6\frac{21}{32} - 6\frac{13}{32}$	$6\frac{5}{8} - 6\frac{9}{16}$	-	-
Bank Bills	-	-	$6\frac{21}{32} - 6\frac{5}{8}$	$6\frac{5}{8} - 6\frac{13}{32}$	$6\frac{9}{16} - 6\frac{1}{2}$	-
Local authority deps.	$6\frac{5}{8} - 6\frac{1}{2}$	$6\frac{5}{8} - 6\frac{1}{2}$	$6\frac{11}{16} - 6\frac{5}{8}$	$6\frac{3}{4} - 6\frac{11}{16}$	$6\frac{3}{4} - 6\frac{11}{16}$	$6\frac{3}{4} - 6\frac{5}{8}$
Discount Market deps	$7\frac{1}{4} - 6\frac{1}{2}$	$6\frac{11}{16} - 6\frac{9}{16}$	-	-	-	-

Fig. 10.5 London money rates

- **Loan period:** rates are given for a number of maturities, varying from overnight to one year, for a number of different instruments.

- **Interbank sterling:** this is a measure of short-term swings in rates; a constantly changing indicator of the cost of money in large amounts for banks themselves. For each maturity date, the first figure is the offer or lending rate, and the second figure the bid or

borrowing rate. The interbank market exists to allow banks to lend and borrow surplus liquidity in substantial amounts; in practice, very large company depositors should be able to deal at or near interbank rates when they are placing money in the market. Rates for different maturities produce the yield curve; when interest rates might drop, the yield curve will be negative.

- **Sterling CDs:** certificates of deposit issued in sterling by UK banks and in which a secondary market exists. These carry a slightly lower rate than interbank loans.

- **Treasury and Bank bills:** the rates at which various bills of exchange are discounted. Bills of exchange are securities issued by companies, banks or governments (in this case, the Treasury and banks) with a fixed maturity value. Discounting them means buying them at a discount from face value with the discount rate being the difference between purchase price and face value as a percentage of the face value.

- **Deposits:** money lent to local authorities (offered rate for deposits), as well as the rates at which discount houses (the institutions with which the Bank of England carries out the bulk of its operations in the money market) accept the secured money from banks. Banks are required to maintain a certain amount of cash with the discount market, and these rates are generally below interbank levels.

World interest rates

The money rates table in Figure 10.6 lists representative interest rates from nine major domestic markets outside London.

- **Loan period:** current overnight and one, three, six and twelve month rates in Germany, France, Switzerland, the Netherlands, Japan, Italy, Belgium, Ireland and the United States; and the same rates one week ago.

- **Lombard intervention:** traditionally, the rate at which the central bank in Germany intervenes in the interbank market to manage day-to-day liquidity lending to German commercial banks. France, Belgium and Switzerland also have an official intervention rate of this kind.

WORLD INTEREST RATES

MONEY RATES

October 12	Over night	One month	Three mths	Six mths	One year	Lomb. inter.	Dis. rate	Repo rate
Belgium	4 1/8	4 1/8	4 3/16	4 5/16	4 1/2	8.00	3.50	–
week ago	4 1/16	4 1/8	4 1/8	4 1/4	4 3/8	8.00	3.50	–
France	6 1/4	6 15/16	7	6 15/16	6 7/8	5.00	–	7.25
week ago	5 5/8	6 15/16	6 3/16	6 1/4	6 1/4	5.00	–	6.15
Germany	4 1/8	4 1/8	4	4	4	5.50	3.50	4.03
week ago	4 1/8	4 1/8	4	4	4	5.50	3.50	4.05
Ireland	5 7/16	5 11/16	5 29/32	6 1/8	6 13/32	–	–	6.25
week ago	5 11/16	5 11/16	5 13/16	5 7/8	6 1/4	–	–	6.25
Italy	10 3/8	10 5/16	10 1/2	10 5/8	10 5/8	–	9.00	10.36
week ago	10 7/32	10 5/16	10 9/16	10 5/8	10 5/8	–	9.00	10.36
Netherlands	3 15/16	3 7/8	3 15/16	3 15/16	4 1/16	–	3.50	3.80
week ago	3 15/16	3 7/8	3 7/8	3 7/8	4 3/32	–	3.50	3.80
Switzerland	1 3/4	2 1/8	2 1/4	2 5/16	2 3/16	5.00	2.00	–
week ago	2 1/16	2 1/8	2 3/8	2 3/8	2 3/8	5.00	2.00	–
US	5 13/16	5 13/16	5 7/8	5 13/16	5 13/16	–	5.25	–
week ago	5 3/4	5 13/16	5 13/16	5 13/16	5 13/16	–	5.25	–
Japan	1/2	5/16	1/4	1/4	1/4	–	0.50	–
week ago	15/32	5/16	1/4	1/4	17/32	–	0.50	–

■ **$ LIBOR FT London**

	Over night	One month	Three mths	Six mths	One year			
Interbank Fixing	–	5 7/8	5 15/16	5 29/32	5 7/8	–	–	–
week ago	–	5 7/8	5 15/16	5 29/32	5 7/8	–	–	–
US Dollar CDs	–	5.61	5.60	5.60	5.64	–	–	–
week ago	–	5.61	5.60	5.60	5.65	–	–	–
ECU Linked Ds	–	5 25/32	5 25/32	5 25/32	5 3/4	–	–	–
week ago	–	5 25/32	5 9/16	5 13/16	5 5/8	–	–	–
SDR Linked Ds	–	3 25/32	3 21/32	3 21/32	3 11/16	–	–	–
week ago	–	3 25/32	3 21/32	3 21/32	3 11/16	–	–	–

$ LIBOR Interbank fixing rates are offered rates for $10m quoted to the market by four reference banks at 11am each working day. The banks are: Bankers Trust, Bank of Tokyo, Barclays and National Westminster.
Mid rates are shown for the domestic Money Rates, US$ CDs, ECU & SDR Linked Deposits (Ds).

EURO CURRENCY INTEREST RATES

Oct 12	Short term	7 days notice	One month	Three months	Six months	One year
Belgian Franc	4 3/16 - 4 1/16	4 3/16 - 4 1/16	4 5/16 - 4 3/16	4 3/8 - 4 1/4	4 7/16 - 4 5/16	4 1/2 - 4 3/8
Danish Krone	6 1/2 - 6 1/4	5 5/8 - 5 1/8	5 11/16 - 5 1/2	5 3/4 - 5 5/8	5 7/8 - 5 5/8	5 15/16 - 5 11/16
D-Mark	4 1/8 - 4	4 1/8 - 4	4 1/16 - 3 15/16	4 1/16 - 3 15/16	4 1/16 - 3 15/16	4 1/16 - 3 15/16
Dutch Guilder	3 13/16 - 3 1/8	3 13/16 - 3 1/8	3 1/2 - 3 13/32	3 31/32 - 3 31/32	4 1/32 - 3 31/32	4 1/16 - 3 31/32
French Franc	6 - 5 1/2	6 5/8 - 6 3/8	7 1/8 - 6 7/8	7 1/8 - 6 7/8	7 1/8 - 6 7/8	6 9/16 - 6 7/16
Portuguese Esc.	8 15/16 - 8 13/16	8 7/8 - 8 3/4	9 1/8 - 9	9 1/4 - 9 1/8	9 7/16 - 9 5/16	9 3/4 - 9 1/2
Spanish Peseta	9 1/2 - 9 3/8	9 1/2 - 9 3/8	9 1/2 - 9 13/32	9 1/2 - 9 13/32	9 5/8 - 9 1/2	9 1/16 - 9 9/16
Sterling	6 11/16 - 6 9/16	6 11/16 - 6 9/16	6 23/32 - 6 23/32	6 13/16 - 6 3/4	6 7/8 - 6 13/16	6 31/32 - 6 29/32
Swiss Franc	2 - 1 7/8	2 1/16 - 1 15/16	2 1/16 - 2 1/16	2 1/16 - 2 1/16	2 3/8 - 2 1/4	2 3/8 - 2 1/4
Can. Dollar	6 7/16 - 6 1/4	6 3/16 - 6	6 1/4 - 6 1/8	6 7/16 - 6 1/8	6 9/16 - 6 7/16	6 5/8 - 6 1/2
US Dollar	5 13/16 - 5 11/16	5 13/16 - 5 11/16	5 3/4 - 5 5/8	5 7/8 - 5 3/4	5 13/16 - 5 11/16	5 13/16 - 5 5/8
Italian Lira	8 1/16 - 8 1/16	10 5/16 - 10 1/16	10 5/16 - 10 3/16	10 13/32 - 10 13/32	10 5/8 - 10 1/2	10 11/16 - 10 9/16
Yen	9/16 - 1/2	7/16 - 5/16	3/8 - 1/4	5/16 - 3/16	5/16 - 3/16	3/8 - 1/4
Asian $Sing	2 1/4 - 2 1/8	2 3/4 - 2 5/8	2 13/16 - 2 11/16	2 13/16 - 2 11/16	2 7/8 - 2 3/4	3 1/8 - 3

Short term rates are call for the US Dollar and Yen, others: two days' notice.

Fig. 10.6 World interest rates

● **Discount rate:** the rate at which central banks are prepared to buy bills of exchange from the discount houses, often known as the bank rate (or occasionally in the United Kingdom, the base lending or minimum lending rate). Although often the most significant interest

rate in domestic economies, they are not all strictly comparable: in some countries other market rates set by the central bank have more influence on the level of market interest rates than the bank rate itself.

- **Repo rate:** another rate at which central banks intervene in the market, this is the rate at which they will repurchase bills having sold them. It is an important rate in certain countries, notably Germany where it is taken to be a key indicator of the central bank's intentions for monetary policy.

Interbank fixing

Also as part of Figure 10.6, the *Financial Times* publishes the FT London Interbank Fixing. These are one, three, six and twelve month Eurodollar deposit rates representing the average of rates collected from four leading banks (Bankers Trust, Bank of Tokyo, Barclays and National Westminister) at 11am London time every trading day.

- **LIBOR:** the rates are intended to be used as a reference point by borrowers or lenders of floating rate money when the rate of interest is linked to Eurodollar LIBOR (London Inter-Bank Offered Rate). LIBOR, a major reference point for the international financial markets, is not calculated in any universal way or at a universally recognised time. These figures, published daily by the *Financial Times* since June 1980, are intended to fill this gap by providing an internationally acceptable standard rate. Rates are given for the last fixing and a week ago.

- **CDs:** rates are also quoted for US-dollar, ecu-linked and SDR-linked certificates of deposit. These are, in essence, marketable bank deposits: a depositor who buys a three-month CD from a bank may sell it to a third party if liquidity is needed before the maturity date. Because CDs can be sold on, unlike ordinary deposits, they carry slightly lower interest rates.

While the LIBOR represents the rate at which banks in London lend wholesale to each other, the equivalent rate for deposits is covered by the London Interbank Bid Rate (LIBID). Different LIBORs apply to different key currencies, and similar sets of interbank rates exist in

certain other financial centres, for example, the Paris Inter-Bank Offered Rate (PIBOR) in France.

Eurocurrency interest rates

The Currencies and Money page gives a fairly full list of interest rates on deposits in various currencies in markets outside their countries of origin, the so-called Euromarket rates (see Figure 10.6). Outside the United States, for example, banks are not bound by any considerations of reserve requirements on their holding of dollars, and outside France, French francs are not affected by French controls. These then are free market rates at which banks lend and borrow money to and from each other.

- **Eurocurrencies:** interest rates are quoted for thirteen currencies and the so-called "Asian" dollar, that is, offshore dollars traded in the Far East before the European market opens. A short-term rate is given (generally referring to the day after next), and also rates for one week, and one, three, six and twelve months ahead.

The Eurocurrency interest rates follow but do not necessarily match domestic rates. The rates are lowest for the strongest currencies. The key rate is the LIBOR, the heart of the interbank market, which is in turn the core of the money markets.

US interest rates

Another table relevant to both the money markets and the bond markets, and actually listed on the International Capital Markets pages, covers US interest rates (see Figure 10.7):

US INTEREST RATES

Close		Treasury Bills and Bond Yields			
Prime rate	$8\frac{3}{4}$	One month	5.63	Two year	5.75
Broker loan rate	$7\frac{1}{2}$	Two month	5.56	Three year	5.81
Fed.funds	$5\frac{5}{8}$	Three month	5.47	Five year	5.91
Fed.funds at intervention	$5\frac{1}{2}$	Six month	5.57	10-year	6.09
		One year	5.60	30-year	6.44

Fig. 10.7 US interest rates

- **Rates:** the prime rate, the rate at which US banks lend to highly creditworthy customers, and the equivalent of the United Kingdom's base lending rate; and the Federal Funds rate, which is the overnight rate paid on funds lent between the member banks of the US Federal Reserve System. The latter is highly volatile and the most sensitive reflection of the day-to-day cost of money in the United States.

- **Treasury bills and bond yields:** these are yields on US government securities, the equivalent of UK Treasury bills and gilts. They range in maturity term from one month to the 30 years of the benchmark long bond, and in this case have a positive yield curve indicating that investors expect a premium for holding investments over the longer term.

The tight interconnections between the bond markets and the money markets are indicated further in one last weekly table that appears in Monday's newspaper on the World Bond Markets page (see Figure 10.8). This table charts the year's movements of yields on ten year benchmark bonds in the United States, the United Kingdom, France, Germany, Italy and Spain. It also lists discount rates and overnight, three month, one, five and ten year interest rates in the United States, Japan, Germany, France, Italy and the United Kingdom. The ten year rates naturally correspond with the ten year benchmark bond yields. Half-yearly, the newspaper publishes a table comparing current and six months earlier figures for interest rates on three-month money in fifteen countries as well as inflation rates in those countries at the same points.

Interest rates obviously play a critical role binding together the world's many financial markets, and strongly influencing companies' costs of borrowing and investors' likely returns. For the investor, the direction and relative importance of their effects on a given equity portfolio vary considerably. The immediate effect of a rise in interest rates in one country is that the dividend yield of a share will be relatively less attractive than the interest rate on a local deposit account. The yield will also be less appealing than that of a government bond in the same country, the price of which will have fallen so that its fixed coupon's yield corresponds to the interest rate. Investors with a portion of their assets in cash or other alternatives to equity should note these relative return movements.

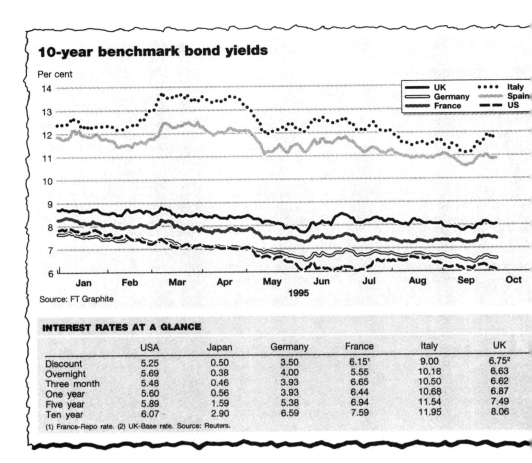

Fig. 10.8 Benchmark bond yields

A share's dividend yield may become even less desirable since the rate rise will probably increase the company's interest costs, reducing its profitability and perhaps leading it to cut dividends. The extent of the increased costs will hinge on the company's level of borrowing, and its skills at locking into fixed rate funding prior to the rate rise. Higher leverage and larger floating rate loans suggest greater potential damage to dividend yields from rising interest rates.

On the other hand, much of the return sought on shares is from their potential for capital growth, and rate movements need not affect that. Interest rates tend to rise and fall in line with the level of economic activity. In a recession and the early stages of a recovery, they will gen-

erally be low and falling to encourage borrowing; while in the subsequent expansion and boom, they will rise as the demand for money exceeds the supply. As countries emerge from recession and move into boom, interest rates tend to rise, increasing capital costs. But, at the same time, growing economies should offer numerous opportunities for enhanced profitability. Over the longer term, the prospects for corporate profitability tend to have far more of an influence on share prices than interest rates. And those prospects are in turn powerfully affected by the growth potential and stability of the local economy.

Of course, rising interest rates may not necessarily signal the expansive phase of the business cycle. They could, for example, indicate excessive government budget deficits which drive up the cost of borrowing. In that case, rate increases are unlikely to be promising for share values. Rate rises might also be a reflection of the need to restrain high or impending inflation. In a national context, this need not be disastrous since low inflation will benefit long-term corporate profitability, while high inflation at least implies low real interest rates. Within a global portfolio, however, company shares in relatively high inflation countries are eventually going to diminish in value when the currency in which they are priced devalues.

Equity returns are particularly affected by interest rates in firms and sectors where business revenues and costs are especially sensitive to rate changes, such as banks and life assurance companies. Even firms in industries dependent on household expenditure, such as the retail sector and breweries, may experience important changes in profits, as consumers shift their spending in response to the cost of credit. In addition, it is, as always, essential to note that as a result of investor expectations, the effects of changed interest rates could conceivably come before the change actually occurs. Financial markets often discount the future in this way, building into the prices of the assets traded on them all past, present and prospective information on their future values.

Interest rates also interact closely with currency rates: they are two of the most volatile features of world financial markets. To protect against their fluctuations and other price movements, many investors and companies employ a variety of risk management techniques which in turn offer speculative opportunities. This leads to the subject of the next chapter, the market for futures, options and other derivative assets.

"A derivative is like a razor. You can use it to shave yourself and make yourself attractive for your girlfriend. You can slit her throat with it. Or you can use it to commit suicide."
FINANCIAL TIMES, 4 MARCH 1995

"Essentially local events may now have disruptive implications for the international financial system as a whole."
BANK FOR INTERNATIONAL SETTLEMENTS

11

FUTURES AND OPTIONS
The derivatives markets

- **The international markets for derivatives** – futures and options become an integral part of the international capital markets

- **Options** – the right to buy or sell an underlying asset: reading the figures and using the information on LIFFE equity options; traditional options

- **Financial futures** – agreements to buy or sell a standard quantity of an underlying asset at a future date: bond derivatives; interest rate derivatives; currency derivatives; stock index futures and options

The market for futures and options is concerned with the management and transfer of risk. Like the currency market, the market for derivatives, as futures, options and their variants are collectively known, is valuable for those wishing to hedge transactions as well as being a source of speculative opportunity, for risk mitigation or risk-taking.

Until the collapse of Barings Bank in February 1995, derivative instruments were rarely mentioned beyond narrow professional financial circles. Now labelled "the wild card of international finance", and behind the financial disasters of not only Barings but also Metallgesellschaft, Procter & Gamble, Orange County, California, and Hammersmith and Fulham Local Authority, they are widely discussed and feared. At the same time, their purpose and the functioning of the various markets on which they are traded remain shrouded in mystery.

A derivative instrument is an asset the performance of which is based on (derived from) the behaviour of the price of an underlying asset (often simply known as the "underlying"). Underlying assets (traded in what is known as the cash market) may be shares, bonds, currencies, interest rates or commodities, but in each case, the assets themselves do not need to be bought or sold.

A derivative product can be either "exchange-traded" where a contract is bought or sold on a recognised exchange, or it can be "over the counter" (OTC). An OTC instrument is "written" (sold) by a financial institution and tailored to suit the requirements of the client. Swaps where borrowers exchange the type of funds most easily raised for the type of funds which are required (based either on currency or interest rate considerations), usually through the medium of a bank intermediary, are a key OTC instrument.

THE INTERNATIONAL MARKETS FOR DERIVATIVES

Over the past fifteen years or so, financial futures and options have established themselves as an integral part of the international capital markets. While futures and options originated in the commodities business, the concept was applied to financial securities in the United States in the early 1970s. Currency futures grew out of the collapse of the Bretton Woods fixed exchange rate system, and heralded the growth of a wide variety of financial instruments designed to capture the advantages or minimise the risks of an increasingly volatile financial environment. Now these products are traded around the world by a wide variety of institutions.

Financial Times' coverage of the derivatives markets focuses primarily on those products traded on exchanges such as the London International Financial Futures Exchange (LIFFE, pronounced "life") and the two oldest and biggest exchanges, the Chicago Mercantile Exchange (CME) and the Chicago Board of Trade (CBT). There are over forty recognised, regulated exchanges worldwide.

The underlying cash instruments, be they bonds, equities, indices, interest rates or foreign exchange, are becoming ever more closely linked in price and trading patterns to the derivative instruments. In some markets, the turnover in derivatives is many times greater than turnover in the underlying products.

Essentially, futures and options provide alternative vehicles both for trading and for the management of a diverse set of financial risks. They are thus of benefit to financial market participants ranging from securities houses that are trading shares and government bonds for their own accounts, to multinational companies that wish to manage their foreign exchange or interest rate exposure.

Investment managers, for example, tend to use derivatives in two ways. One is in deciding on the appropriate allocation of assets within their portfolios. In this case, exposure to a particular market can be changed for a time at perhaps 5 or 10 per cent of the cost of dealing in the underlying cash market, making it economically viable to change exposure for short periods. The second role is in fund

management where futures and options can be used to modify risk/ return profiles, a form of insurance against a downturn in the market.

Other financial institutions tend to use derivatives as sources of income. In the Barings' incident, for example, it was apparently Nick Leeson's job to exploit small differences in prices by buying financial instruments on one Far East exchange and selling those same instruments on another exchange, the process of arbitrage. In fact, it appears he became involved in one-way speculation. In January and February 1995, he effectively took a one-way bet on Japanese equities through increasingly heavy purchases of Nikkei 225 futures contracts on both the Osaka and Tokyo exchanges. The bet became horribly unstuck due to a sustained period of weakness in the Japanese equity market.

The rest of this chapter examines the various futures and options contracts on which data and analysis are published in the *Financial Times*. Readers seeking greater detail on the full range of derivative instruments, as well as examples of how they work in practice, are referred to Francesca Taylor's *Mastering Derivatives Markets* (*Financial Times* Pitman Publishing, 1996) and to Lawrence Galitz's *Financial Engineering: Tools and Techniques to Manage Financial Risk* (*Financial Times* Pitman Publishing, 1995).

OPTIONS

Options are derivative securities: they derive their value from the value of underlying assets. In the case of financial options, these underlying assets may be bonds, interest rates, currencies, individual stocks or stock groupings or indices such as the FT-SE 100. An option on an asset represents the right to buy or sell that asset at a predetermined price (the striking, strike or exercise price) at a predetermined future date (in the case of a European-style option) or by a predetermined future date (in the case of an American-style option). It is important to note that an option conveys the right, but not the requirement, to buy or sell.

The seller (generally known as the writer) of a put (an option to sell) or a call (an option to buy) receives a premium upfront from the option buyer. Other than this premium, there is no further exchange

of money until and unless the option is exercised, either at or before expiration. If, say, over the life of a European-style call option, the price of the underlying asset rises above the striking price of the option, the option is said to be "in the money": the buyer can exercise the option at expiration and receive a profit equal to the difference between the option striking price and the actual price of the underlying assets, less the premium paid to the option writer. An in the money option is said to have intrinsic value.

If the call is "out of the money" or "at the money", that is, the underlying asset price is below or at the striking price, the option buyer will generally choose not to exercise the option. Nothing will be earned from the option position, and a loss will be incurred equal to the premium paid to the option writer. Before expiry, any option still has time value, the possibility that it will be worth exercising; at expiry it only has intrinsic value left and if it is out of the money it has no intrinsic value.

On the other side of the transaction, the option writer receives the premium paid by the buyer. This represents clear profit if the option remains unexercised. On the other hand, the option writer also assumes the risk of having to sell the underlying asset at a striking price significantly below actual market price or to buy the underlying asset at a striking price significantly above the actual market price. In either of these cases, the loss suffered by the option writer at the exercise of the option can overwhelm any premium received for writing the option. It is potentially limitless.

LIFFE equity options

The LIFFE is the primary market for options and futures in the United Kingdom. It provides facilities for trading in derivatives contracts on stocks, stock indices, bonds, currencies and interest rates. Until 1992, the London Traded Option Market was a separate entity that dealt in equity option contracts, but it is now a part of the LIFFE. Nevertheless, the *Financial Times* continues to list price and trading data on equity and other financial derivatives separately. LIFFE equity options (traded options) are shown in Figure 11.1.

Closing price of the share in the stock market

Striking price for this line of options

Premiums for call options with a February exercise date

Premiums for call options with a February exercise date

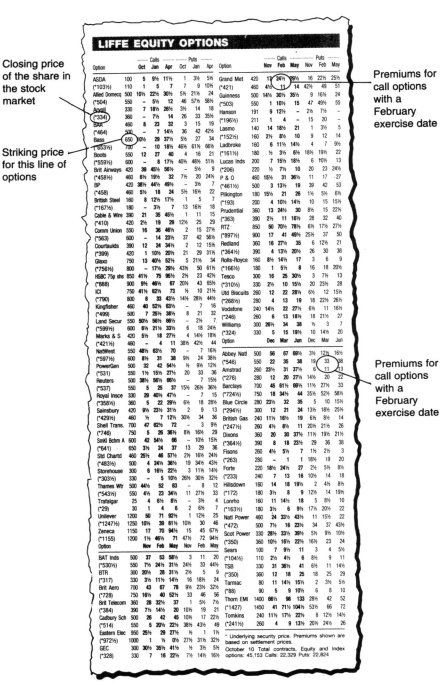

Fig. 11.1 LIFFE equity options

Reading the figures

- **Option:** the first column lists the security from which the options are derived and its closing price in the cash market on the previous day. For example, in this table, the Hanson stock closed at 196½ pence.

- **Striking price:** the second column gives the option series quoted. For Hanson, there are two series, one with a striking price of 191 pence, the other with a striking price of 211 pence. Thus, one is lower than the current cash market price, the other higher.

- **Calls:** the third, fourth and fifth columns give the price or premiums payable for call options that can be exercised on three different dates. For Hanson, the price of a 191 pence call option that expires in February is 12½ pence, while a 211 option that expires in the same month costs 4 pence.

- **Puts:** the last three columns give the premiums payable for put options that can again be exercised on three dates in the future.

Using the information

The buyer of an option is willing to risk a limited amount (the premium) in exchange for an uncertain reward (the possibility of buying at some level below or selling at some level above the market price), whereas the option writer is willing to accept an offsetting, uncertain risk (having to sell at some level below or buy at some level above the market price) in return for a certain reward (the option premium).

Option contracts, like insurance policies, are used to protect the investor, whether writer or buyer, from unacceptable risk. The option buyer is in a position analogous to that of the owner of an insurance policy; the uncovered option writer is like the insurance underwriter who accepts risk in return for premium income.

For most investors and companies, options are protection against wide price fluctuations. For dealers and speculators they are an opportunity for big profits.

As an investment, call options are highly geared so that a small change in the underlying asset value has a significant effect on the option value. Put options on the other hand are more of a hedging

strategy protecting against the fall of stock or portfolio value by establishing a floor price below which they cannot fall.

As in the currency markets, it is important in the options markets to have liquidity and so the *Financial Times'* reports often focus on the turnover in the option markets as in this example:

> Traded options lacked the strong activity seen in futures and volume fell to 23,905 lots. BP was the busiest stock option with a day's total of 1,326. It was followed by Glaxo at 1,238 lots and Argyll Group at 1,010.
>
> (*Financial Times*, 12 July 1994)

Traditional options

Whereas traded options are a standardised product that may be bought and sold and are transferable within the confines of the exchange, traditional options are bargains struck between two parties that are not readily transferable. Unlike traded options, however, they are available on any security on which the brokers involved care to make a price.

As with shares, transactions in traditional options used to be made within two-week account dealing periods but have now moved to five day rolling settlement. Details of the current period for standard three-month options are listed in a chart that appears in the *Financial Times* from Tuesday to Saturday (see Figure 11.2):

TRADITIONAL OPTIONS

First Dealings	Oct 9	Expiry	Jan 11
Last Dealings	Oct 20	Settlement	Jan 18

Calls: **Eurotunnel, Hanson Wts, Sterling Publishing.** Puts: **Brit Aerospace, Close Bros, Eurotunnel, Hollas.**

Fig. 11.2 Traditional options

- **First and last dealings:** the beginning and end dates for the latest beginning period of issuing or buying three-month call, put or double options. Double options give the right, but not the obligation, to buy or sell the underlying stock.

- **Last declarations and settlement:** the last day but one on which traditional options bought in the three-month period beginning the previous day must be declared. Declaration means that the option is on the point of expiring and the owner must state whether or not the option to buy or sell the underlying security will be exercised. Under the new settlement system (see chapter 5), the last declarations date has been replaced by the expiry date. The actual settlement day is then five business days after the expiry date.

- **Calls and puts:** a list of some of the traditional options available in this account period.

FINANCIAL FUTURES

A financial futures contract is an agreement to buy or sell a standard quantity of a certain financial instrument or foreign currency at a future date and at a price agreed between two parties. Trades are usually executed on an exchange floor with buyers and sellers grouped together in a pit shouting at each other in what is termed "open outcry". Some exchanges have developed automated systems which allow trading to take place on computer screens. The financial guarantee is generally provided by a central clearing house which stands between buyer and seller and guarantees the trade.

Futures and options are leveraged instruments. This means that for a relatively small down payment (margin for futures, premium for options), participants gain a disproportionately large exposure to price movements in the underlying cash market, hence their appeal as a trading vehicle. They are also used to a large extent as a hedging mechanism. For example, if a US multinational company incurs a significant exposure to the D-Mark through the nature of its export markets, but also believes that the dollar will appreciate against the German currency over coming months, the treasurer might wish to sell D-Mark futures to cover the company's risk. Losses incurred by lower revenues should then be at least partially offset by gains from selling the future.

An investor might also use futures to hedge a portfolio, most commonly using index futures, which are futures on major market

indices. For example, if the market is expected to fall, selling stock index futures can protect portfolio value: if the market does fall, the loss on the actual stocks is compensated by the profits of buying back the futures at a reduced price.

The relationship between the futures and cash markets is kept stable by the arbitragers who seek out discrepancies between the prices. Generally, futures trade a little above the cash price, reflecting the time and risk premiums. If, for example, there are expectations of a market rise and the future and cash prices are equivalent, money goes into the futures, driving up its price relative to the cash price.

Bond derivatives

The International Capital Markets and Currencies and Money pages of the *Financial Times* feature details of a wide range of commonly traded financial derivatives. For example, under World Bond Prices, there are prices for futures and options on French, German, Italian, Spanish, UK, US, Japanese and ecu-denominated bonds (see Figure 11.3). For the most part, these are traded on the LIFFE, its French and Spanish equivalents (the MATIF and the MEFF) and the Chicago Board of Trade.

- **Bond and date:** the name of the future indicates the underlying bond on which it is based, in the case of the UK bond future a notional UK gilt worth £50,000; the date in the first column of the bond futures is when the contract will be finally settled.

- **Face value and calibration:** for most bond futures, there is a nominal face value, in the case of the US Treasury bond future, $100,000. That price is a notional one, the owner paying (or receiving if the future price is below 100 per cent) only the difference between that and the futures contract price. The price on this future is calibrated in thirty-seconds, that is, the price can move by a minimum of one 32nd of one per cent.

- **Opening, settlement price, change, high and low:** for bond futures, information on the price at which contracts began trading in the morning (not necessarily the same as the previous day's clos-

ing price); the current settlement price (yesterday's closing price, the price at which the contract would currently be settled); the change on the previous day's closing price; and highs and lows reached during the day's trading.

OND FUTURES AND OPTIONS

rance

NOTIONAL FRENCH BOND FUTURES (MATIF) FFr500,000

	Open	Sett price	Change	High	Low	Est. vol.	Open int.
ıc	115.58	115.40	-0.12	115.64	115.23	96,689	99,542
ır	114.92	114.72	-0.12	114.92	114.62	324	2,709
ı	115.10	114.90	-0.12	115.10	115.00	296	1,245

LONG TERM FRENCH BOND OPTIONS (MATIF)

| ike | ·········· CALLS ·········· | | | ·········· PUTS ·········· | | |
ce	Nov	Dec	Mar	Nov	Dec	Mar
₄	-	-	-	0.20	0.55	-
5	0.82	-	-	0.49	0.90	-
3	0.36	0.76	-	0.95	1.36	-
₇	0.10	0.41	-	-	-	-
3	-	0.17	0.04	-	-	-

vol. total, Calls 9,938 Puts 13,808 . Previous day's open int., Calls 114,269 Puts 133,303.

ermany

NOTIONAL GERMAN BUND FUTURES (LIFFE)* DM250,000 100ths of 100%

	Open	Sett price	Change	High	Low	Est. vol	Open int.
c	95.59	95.75	+0.16	95.82	95.57	98913	183448
r	95.15	95.18	+0.16	95.20	95.10	500	3530

BUND FUTURES OPTIONS (LIFFE) DM250,000 points of 100%

| Strike | ·········· CALLS ·········· | | | ·········· PUTS ·········· | | |
Price	Nov	Dec	Jan	Mar	Nov	Dec	Jan	Mar
9550	0.58	0.87	0.76	1.08	0.33	0.62	1.08	1.40
9600	0.33	0.61	0.56	0.86	0.58	0.86	1.38	1.68
9650	0.17	0.41	0.40	0.68	0.92	1.16	1.72	2.00

Est. vol. total, Calls 17745 Puts 9731. Previous day's open int., Calls 190984 Puts 152148

Italy

■ **NOTIONAL ITALIAN GOVT. BOND (BTP) FUTURES** (LIFFE)* Lira 200m 100ths of 100%

	Open	Sett price	Change	High	Low	Est. vol	Open int.
Dec	102.00	102.03	+0.24	102.31	101.52	49646	44945

■ **ITALIAN GOVT. BOND (BTP) FUTURES OPTIONS** (LIFFE) Lira200m 100ths of 100%

| Strike | ·········· CALLS ·········· | | ·········· PUTS ·········· | |
Price	Dec	Mar	Dec	Mar
10200	1.62	2.53	1.59	2.80
10250	1.39	2.30	1.86	3.07
10300	1.18	2.09	2.15	3.36

Est. vol. total, Calls 1020 Puts 3897. Previous day's open int., Calls 36031 Puts 36486

Spain

■ **NOTIONAL SPANISH BOND FUTURES** (MEFF)

	Open	Sett price	Change	High	Low	Est. vol.	Open int.
Dec	89.12	88.94	-0.06	89.15	88.74	43,393	31,926
Mar	-	88.88	-	-	-	-	8

UK

■ **NOTIONAL UK GILT FUTURES** (LIFFE)* £50,000 32nds of 100%

	Open	Sett price	Change	High	Low	Est. vol	Open int.
Dec	106-10	106-09	+0-04	106-11	106-01	31054	101573
Mar	105-25	105-25	+0-03	105-25	105-25	32	69

■ **LONG GILT FUTURES OPTIONS** (LIFFE) £50,000 64ths of 100%

| Strike | ·········· CALLS ·········· | | | | ·········· PUTS ·········· | | | |
Price	Nov	Dec	Jan	Mar	Nov	Dec	Jan	Mar
106	0-58	1-23	1-26	1-60	0-40	1-05	1-40	2-10
107	0-28	0-56	0-63	1-32	1-10	1-38	2-13	2-46
108	0-11	0-33	0-42	1-08	1-57	2-15	2-56	3-22

Est. vol. total, Calls 2335 Puts 400. Previous day's open int., Calls 32139 Puts 25273

Ecu

■ **ECU BOND FUTURES** (MATIF) ECU100,000

	Open	Sett price	Change	High	Low	Est. vol.	Open int.
Dec	86.74	86.70	+0.16	86.76	86.58	1,070	7,351

US

■ **US TREASURY BOND FUTURES** (CBT) $100,000 32nds of 100%

	Open	Sett price	Change	High	Low	Est. vol.	Open int.
Dec	114-26	115-05	+0-12	115-05	114-19	247,671	318,401
Mar	114-14	114-26	+0-14	114-26	114-10	1,360	12,633
Jun	-	114-04	+0-05	114-04	114-00	153	2,505

Japan

■ **NOTIONAL LONG TERM JAPANESE GOVT. BOND FUTURES** (LIFFE) Y100m 100ths of 100%

	Open	Close	Change	High	Low	Est. vol	Open int.
Dec	122.28	-	-	122.43	122.20	2208	0

* LIFFE futures also traded on APT. All Open interest figs. are for previous day.

Fig. 11.3 Bond futures and options

- **Estimated volume and open interest:** the estimated number of contracts actually exchanged during the day, and the number in which traders have expressed interest in buying or selling on the previous day. Not all contracts in which there is open interest are actually traded: they do not become part of estimated volume.

- **Options:** as with equity options, premiums for call and put options with a range of different striking prices and maturities, plus estimated volume and open interest details. Some of these options, like the UK long gilt futures option, are options to buy futures.

Interest rate derivatives

The Currencies and Money page carries similar tables for interest rate futures and options (see Figure 11.4), including futures on three month PIBOR, Euromarks, Eurolira, Euro-Swiss francs and ecus, Eurolira options, as well as the ones shown. Interest rate derivatives can be used to cover any interest rate risk from an overnight exposure to one lasting twenty-five years. Interest rate risk is either of increased funding costs for borrowers or of reduced yields for investors.

An example of how these contracts work, and one of particular interest to companies and financial institutions in the United Kingdom is the short sterling futures market. The short sterling futures contract is based on a notional three-month deposit transaction. Its price is equal to 100 minus whatever interest rate is expected by the market when the three-month contract expires. Hence the price of the contract rises when interest rates fall. The market also gives an indication of interest rate expectations, which is valuable for policy-makers and other forecasters.

Short sterling traders can use the market to protect themselves against possible interest rate movements, effectively fixing the interest rate at which they borrow or lend. For example, a lender who fears rate falls can buy short sterling contracts expiring in three months: if by then rates have not fallen the lender has lost nothing; if they have fallen, the lower return on the investment is offset by a rise in the price of the futures contract. Similarly, a borrower fearing a rate rise

could hedge the risk by selling short sterling futures: if rates do rise, the contracts can be bought back at a lower price, offsetting the higher interest costs. Speculators can use the markets for gambles on future rate movements.

■ **THREE MONTH STERLING FUTURES** (LIFFE) £500,000 points of 100%

	Open	Sett price	Change	High	Low	Est. vol	Open int.
Dec	93.37	93.38	–	93.39	93.35	7034	82983
Mar	93.48	93.50	+0.01	93.52	93.47	16783	71287
Jun	93.46	93.49	+0.02	93.50	93.45	7166	48175
Sep	93.30	93.36	+0.04	93.39	93.30	7043	37238
Dec	93.09	93.16	+0.06	93.16	93.08	2173	25898

Also traded on APT. All Open interest figs. are for previous day.

■ **SHORT STERLING OPTIONS** (LIFFE) £500,000 points of 100%

Strike		CALLS			PUTS	
Price	Dec	Mar	Jun	Dec	Mar	Jun
9325	0.18	0.40	0.53	0.05	0.15	0.29
9350	0.05	0.25	0.39	0.17	0.25	0.40
9375	0.01	0.14	0.27	0.38	0.39	0.53

Est. vol. total, Calls 4259 Puts 2150. Previous day's open int., Calls 142180 Puts 140209

■ **THREE MONTH EURODOLLAR** (IMM) $1m points of 100%

	Open	Sett price	Change	High	Low	Est. vol	Open int.
Dec	94.22	94.27	+0.01	94.29	94.25	94,890	367,002
Mar	94.50	94.65	+0.06	94.69	94.58	177,600	407,284
Jun	94.50	94.69	+0.07	94.73	94.60	110,652	283,088

■ **US TREASURY BILL FUTURES** (IMM) $1m per 100%

	Open	Sett price	Change	High	Low	Est. vol	Open int.
Dec	94.80	94.79	–	94.82	94.79	3,786	9,884
Mar	95.01	95.08	+0.06	95.13	95.01	850	6,239
Jun	95.07	95.13	+0.06	95.13	95.07	52	386

All Open Interest figs. are for previous day

■ **EUROMARK OPTIONS** (LIFFE) DM1m points of 100%

Strike			CALLS				PUTS	
Price	Nov	Dec	Jan	Mar	Nov	Dec	Jan	Mar
9575	0.22	0.24	0.44	0.47	0.01	0.03	0.02	0.05
9600	0.02	0.07	0.23	0.28	0.06	0.11	0.06	0.11
9625	0	0.02	0.09	0.14	0.29	0.31	0.17	0.22

Est. vol. total, Calls 7392 Puts 4607. Previous day's open int., Calls 242058 Puts 227440

■ **EURO SWISS FRANC OPTIONS** (LIFFE) SFr 1m points of 100%

Strike		CALLS			PUTS	
Price	Dec	Mar	Jun	Dec	Mar	Jun
9775	0.24	0.40	0.43	0.06	0.09	0.16
9800	0.06	0.22	0.27	0.13	0.16	0.25
9825	0.02	0.11	0.15	0.34	0.30	0.38

Est. vol. total, Calls 1630 Puts 100. Previous day's open int., Calls 6727 Puts 2175

Fig. 11.4 Interest rate futures and options

Currency derivatives

The Currencies and Money page also contains listings for currency futures on D-Marks, Swiss francs, yen and sterling and an option on the sterling/dollar exchange rate listed on the Philadelphia Stock Exchange (see Figure 11.5). These can be used for managing currency risk, the danger of receiving a smaller amount of the base currency than expected, or paying out more of the base currency to purchase a required amount of foreign currency. Alternatively, they may be used by speculators aiming to buy and sell currencies for profit.

■ **D-MARK FUTURES** (IMM) DM 125,000 per DM

	Open	Sett price	Change	High	Low	Est.vol	Open int.
Dec	0.7092	0.7054	−0.0055	0.7109	0.7052	15,077	51,639
Mar	0.7108	0.7087	−0.0055	0.7115	0.7082	344	4,472
Jun	–	0.7117	−0.0055	–	0.7345	4	567

■ **SWISS FRANC FUTURES** (IMM) SFr 125,000 per SFr

	Open	Sett price	Change	High	Low	Est.vol	Open int.
Dec	0.8797	0.8756	−0.0064	0.8790	0.8754	7,580	34,878
Mar	0.8868	0.8837	−0.0065	0.8868	0.8834	148	2,344
Jun	–	0.8917	−0.0065	–	0.8925	6	505

■ **JAPANESE YEN FUTURES** (IMM) Yen 12.5 per Yen 100

	Open	Sett price	Change	High	Low	Est.vol	Open int.
Dec	0.9971	0.9881	·−0.0079	0.9907	0.9875	13,884	61,568
Mar	1.0028	1.0017	−0.0080	1.0035	1.0014	337	9,727
Jun	–	1.0144	−0.0082	–	1.0150	4	435

■ **STERLING FUTURES** (IMM) £62,500 per £

	Open	Sett price	Change	High	Low	Est.vol	Open int.
Dec	1.5622	1.5588	−0.0032	1.5638	1.5580	4,578	47,264
Mar	1.5580	1.5564	−0.0028	1.5606	1.5554	2,709	891
Jun	–	1.5532	−0.0024	–	1.5530	2	10

■ **PHILADELPHIA SE £/$ OPTIONS** £31,250 (cents per pound) (Nov 22)

Strike Price	CALLS Dec	CALLS Jan	CALLS Feb	PUTS Dec	PUTS Jan	PUTS Feb
1.540	2.51	3.15	3.74	0.30	1.04	1.81
1.550	1.81	2.53	3.16	0.57	1.41	2.13
1.560	1.21	2.02	2.63	0.97	1.85	2.55
1.570	0.75	1.56	2.22	1.52	2.40	3.09
1.580	0.43	1.18	1.81	2.19	2.96	3.68
1.590	0.22	0.86	1.46	2.92	3.64	4.32

Previous day's vol., Calls 4,533 Puts 5,423 . Prev. day's open int., Calls 245,170 Puts 290,664

Fig. 11.5 Currency futures and options

Stock index futures and options

Stock index futures and options began to be traded on the LIFFE in 1984. A stock index future is an agreement between two parties to

compensate each other for movements in the value of a stock index over the contract period. The value of the stock index is defined as being the value of the index multiplied by a specific monetary amount, the index multiplier or amount per full index point.

A stock index option gives the holder the right but not the obligation to buy or sell an agreed amount of an equity index at a specified price on or before a specified date. A premium is paid for this right. One of the key principles behind stock index futures and options is cash settlement. This is the process used at expiry (or exercise) whereby a cash difference reflecting a price change is transferred, rather than a physical delivery of the underlying basket of shares.

As all derivatives, both index options and futures can be used for either hedging or speculation. For example, a fund manager wishing to hedge the value of a portfolio when the stock market may fall will sell index futures. Being long in the cash market and short in the futures market will mean that if the market does fall, a nominal loss on the portfolio is compensated by a gain on the futures which can be bought back at a lower price. A speculator expecting a market fall may sell futures without any underlying exposure, or sell call options on the index, profiting from the premium if the market does fall and the options expire out of the money.

The back page of the *Financial Times* second section carries a daily round-up of equity futures and options trading, focusing particularly on derivatives based on the FT-SE 100 and FT-SE Mid 250 indices (see Figure 11.6):

- **Index futures:** as with bond futures, the table includes opening prices, settlement prices, price changes, daily highs and lows, estimated volume and open interest.

- **Index points:** pounds per full index point are a measure of the trading unit, for example, the FT-SE 100 index future unit is £25 per index point. This means that when the index is at 3,600, a futures buyer is covering the equivalent of £90,000 of equities. If the index rises 200 points, the buyer can sell a matching contract and make a profit of £5,000.

■ **FT-SE 100 INDEX FUTURES** (LIFFE) £25 per full index point (APT)

	Open	Sett price	Change	High	Low	Est. vol	Open int.
Dec	3637.0	3629.0	+6.0	3651.0	3625.0	10451	63005
Mar	3666.0	3652.0	+6.0	3671.5	3652.5	2706	8217
Jun	-	3659.0	+6.0	-	-	0	134

■ **FT-SE MID 250 INDEX FUTURES** (LIFFE) £10 per full index point

	Open	Sett price	Change	High	Low	Est. vol	Open int.
Dec	3985.0	3970.0	-10.0	3985.0	3973.0	205	3318
Mar	-	4015.0	-10.0	-	-	0	300

■ **FT-SE 100 INDEX OPTION** (LIFFE) (*3624) £10 per full index point

	3450		3500		3550		3600		3650		3700		3750		3800	
	C	P	C	P	C	P	C	P	C	P	C	P	C	P	C	P
Dec	190	$8\frac{1}{2}$	$145\frac{1}{2}$	15	102	$23\frac{1}{2}$	66	39	38	$62\frac{1}{2}$	20	$96\frac{1}{2}$	8	141	2	191
Jan	$205\frac{1}{2}$	$21\frac{1}{2}$	$165\frac{1}{2}$	$31\frac{1}{2}$	$128\frac{1}{2}$	44	98	63	$70\frac{1}{2}$	87	$48\frac{1}{2}$	116	$32\frac{1}{2}$	$152\frac{1}{2}$	$19\frac{1}{2}$	194
Feb	226	31	189	$43\frac{1}{2}$	153	58	$122\frac{1}{2}$	78	$94\frac{1}{2}$	101	72	$129\frac{1}{2}$	$52\frac{1}{2}$	163	38	201
Mar	238	43	$201\frac{1}{2}$	56	170	$73\frac{1}{2}$	$140\frac{1}{2}$	$93\frac{1}{2}$	$113\frac{1}{2}$	$117\frac{1}{2}$	91	$145\frac{1}{2}$	69	$175\frac{1}{2}$	53	$210\frac{1}{2}$
Jun†			$244\frac{1}{2}$	96			180	$129\frac{1}{2}$			129	178			88	238

Calls 4,403 Puts 3,062

■ **EURO STYLE FT-SE 100 INDEX OPTION** (LIFFE) £10 per full index point

	3475		3525		3575		3625		3675		3725		3775		3825	
Dec	$163\frac{1}{2}$	$10\frac{1}{2}$	$120\frac{1}{2}$	17	82	$28\frac{1}{2}$	$50\frac{1}{2}$	$46\frac{1}{2}$	$27\frac{1}{2}$	73	$12\frac{1}{2}$	$108\frac{1}{2}$	$5\frac{1}{2}$	$150\frac{1}{2}$	2	197
Jan	$187\frac{1}{2}$	27	149	38	$114\frac{1}{2}$	$52\frac{1}{2}$	84	$71\frac{1}{2}$	$58\frac{1}{2}$	96	39	$125\frac{1}{2}$	$24\frac{1}{2}$	$160\frac{1}{2}$	$14\frac{1}{2}$	200
Feb	$202\frac{1}{2}$	$31\frac{1}{2}$	$166\frac{1}{2}$	$44\frac{1}{2}$	134	61	$105\frac{1}{2}$	82	$81\frac{1}{2}$	107	$61\frac{1}{2}$	136	$45\frac{1}{2}$	$169\frac{1}{2}$	33	206
Mar			$184\frac{1}{2}$	$60\frac{1}{2}$			120	$93\frac{1}{2}$			72	$143\frac{1}{2}$			40	209
Jun†			228	$99\frac{1}{2}$			170	137			$119\frac{1}{2}$	183			80	$239\frac{1}{2}$

Calls 1,222 Puts 4,353 * Underlying index value. Premiums shown are based on settlement prices.
† Long dated expiry months.

Fig. 11.6 FT-SE index futures and options

- **Index options:** as with equity options, the table includes the current value of the underlying index, as well as the premiums for put and call options with a range of different striking prices and maturities.

- **European-style:** this option can only be exercised at the maturity date. Since this date is fixed, the premiums are typically a little lower than for more standard (American-style) options which can be exercised at any point prior to maturity.

The UK market for index futures and options can be used in its own right for speculation, or as an overlay on a portfolio of UK securities in order to hedge its value or to expose it to greater risk and the potential for greater gain. Similarly, derivatives based on foreign market indices can be used to hedge an international portfolio or to gain exposure to those markets. One of the most important is of course the US market, and below the daily table of US indices are prices for futures contracts on the S&P 500 index, a series of futures very widely used for hedging and speculative purposes. The S&P 500

prices are accompanied by listings for five other leading index futures contracts (see Figure 11.7).

INDEX FUTURES

	Open	Sett Price	Change	High	Low	Est. vol.	Open int.
■ CAC-40 (200 x Index)							
Oct	1845.0	1839.0	+14.0	1852.0	1826.5	17,350	26,118
Nov	1853.0	1849.0	+13.5	1861.5	1837.0	1,096	26,118
■ DAX							
Dec	2198.5	2191.0	-2.5	2201.0	2175.0	20,776	100,801
Mar	2220.0	2212.0	-6.0	2221.0	2198.0	108	6,681

	Open	Sett Price	Change	High	Low	Est. vol.	Open int.
■ OMX							
Nov	1348.05	–	–	1356.00	1342.50	3,103	15,883
■ SOFFEX							
Oct	3100.0	3134.8	+22.8	3135.0	3092.0	6,757	16,842
Nov	3149.0	3132.5	-1.3	3155.0	3122.0	4,849	1,696

	Open	Sett price	Change	High	Low	Est. vol.	Open int.
■ S&P 500							
Dec	588.15	592.35	+4.10	592.50	587.50	82,084	201,007
Mar	592.90	597.25	+4.15	597.40	592.65	977	12,777

	Open	Sett price	Change	High	Low	Est. vol.	Open int.
■ Nikkei 225							
Dec	17630.0	18100.0	+610.0	18100.0	17610.0	27,739	152,646
Mar	17640.0	17640.0	+580.0	18060.0	17630.0	2,272	7,173

Open interest figures for previous day.

Fig. 11.7 Index futures

- **CAC-40:** a futures contract on the Compagnie des Agents de Change 40, a weighted index of forty of the one hundred companies with the highest market capitalisation listed on the "forward" section of the Paris Bourse. This contract is traded on the MATIF (Marché à Terme des Instruments Financières).

- **DAX:** the Deutsche Aktien Index, an indicator based on the shares of the thirty top blue chip German companies, forms the basis for a futures contract traded on the Deutsche Terminborse (DTB).

- **OMX:** a futures contract traded on the Stockholm Options Exchange, based on the OMX index of the Swedish equity market. This contract is also traded in London.

- **SOFFEX:** a contract traded on the Swiss Options and Financial Futures Exchange based on a Swiss market index. The SOFFEX is a completely automated screen-based exchange.

- **S&P 500:** this contract is traded on the CME.

- **Nikkei 225:** the index of the shares of the 225 blue chip companies listed on the Tokyo Stock Exchange forms the basis for the notorious contract that brought down Barings. It is also traded on the Osaka Stock Exchange.

Stock index futures of this kind offer a number of advantages to investors and fund managers. First, they permit investment in these markets without the trouble and expense involved in buying the shares themselves. Second, operating under a margin system, like all futures, they allow full participation in market moves without significant commitment of capital. Third, transactions costs are typically many times lower than those for share transactions. Fourth, it is much easier to take a short position. Lastly, fund managers responsible for large share portfolios can hedge their value against bear moves without having to sell the shares themselves.

A typical report on the UK equity futures and options market looks like this, an analysis of a key index future and its relationship with other markets:

A squeeze pushed stock index futures above the 3,000 level for the first time in more than three weeks, but the contract closed below the day's best as London was unsettled by a faltering Wall Street. Having opened at 2,962, the September futures contract on the FT-SE 100 moved steadily ahead with UK economic data on output prices for June taken to indicate inflation remained under control. However, the poor opening in New York in the afternoon checked a further advance and September finished the day at 2,997, up 38 on its previous close and 9 points above its estimated fair value premium to cash of about 5 points. Volume was 15,720 lots.
(*Financial Times*, 12 July 1994)

This demonstrates how an index future price is determined. In this case, it has risen because of positive economic news and fallen back slightly because of the impact of Wall Street. The extract indicates the impact of the underlying cash markets and the performance of the overall economy as reflected in inflationary expectations. The extract also illustrates the direct relationship between the FT-SE 100

future and the cash instrument, the index itself. A future is generally assumed to be at a fair value premium, the correct reflection of its value as determined by the time to maturity and the risk. Here it is above fair value suggesting it might go down, perhaps as arbitragers sell it and buy the index.

As the extract makes clear, economic news and other financial markets are crucial in determining futures market behaviour. Similarly, their ability to spread risk and deliver exceptional profits makes the derivatives markets increasingly central to financial activity and a major influence on the world economy.

"Gold, the barbarous relic."
JOHN F KENNEDY

"I have this working arrangement with the Gnome of Zurich, and the Gnome's job is to keep me posted on gold so I can get out of the market before the price of money goes through the roof. Gnomes, of course, are the original gold-bugs."
GEORGE J W GOODMAN ("*ADAM SMITH*")

12

PRIMARY PRODUCTS
The commodities markets

- **London spot markets** – commodities available for immediate delivery

- **Commodity futures markets** – opportunities for hedging and speculation in the markets for "softs": cocoa, coffee and sugar; other commodities

- **Metals** – precious and base metals: the London Metal Exchange; reading the figures and using the information on gold and the London bullion market; other metals

- **Other key commodity markets** – London traded options; the markets in New York and Chicago; commodity price indices

Commodities are basic raw materials, primary products and foodstuffs that are homogeneous and generally traded on a free market. Commodity contracts may represent cash transactions for immediate delivery, or, more commonly, forward contracts for delivery at a specified time in the future. The bulk of such contracts are bought and sold on a commodities exchange by dealers and commodity brokers or traders. Their homogeneity, coupled with fast communications and an efficient system of quality grading and control, means that they can be traded without an actual transfer of the goods. This allows enormous scope for hedging and speculative activity as traders buy and sell rights of ownership in spot and futures markets. Commodities were in fact the origin of the derivative markets discussed in the previous chapter.

As in all free markets, the prices of commodities are determined by the forces of demand and supply. And because of the nature of the conditions of demand and supply for commodities, their prices tend to swing more violently than prices of manufactured goods. A small but persistent surplus of the supply of, say, tin, over demand can cause a dramatic slump in prices; similarly, disastrous weather conditions and a poor harvest can drive up a crop price.

Commodities are primarily of interest to industrial users. Oil is the one with the most widespread potential impact since almost all businesses have some energy needs, but there are plenty of other examples. Prospective cocoa prices, for instance, are critical to chocolate makers, while certain metal prices will affect such companies as producers of cars, ships and manufactured goods, as well as the construction industry.

Companies whose profitability is partly dependent on the cost of their raw materials will naturally seek protection from potential surges in primary commodity prices. It is this need to hedge that gives rise to the futures markets.

For investors, commodities offer the potential for exceptionally high returns but a very high degree of risk. In addition, investing in

physical commodities is rarely possible given the problem and costs of storage. Indeed, few private investors play even the commodities futures markets except through various managed funds, which diversify their risks across a variety of commodities, or by investing in companies in oil, gold mining and other extractive and exploratory industries. The majority of the players in the primary commodity markets are professional speculators who take the opposite side of hedgers' positions. For this small group, the commodity sector is ultimately high risk for high reward.

The *Financial Times'* Commodities and Agriculture page appears from Tuesday to Friday with the upper section devoted to reports on the markets and the lower section to a presentation of the previous day's trading and price data from markets in London, New York and Chicago. The lower section also appears on Saturday with a review of the week in the markets.

Monday's newspaper has a commodities column in its Markets: This Week section, examining prospects for the coming week and other longer term issues. The commodities markets are dominated by a limited range of players but are important to all markets and the wider economy particularly as a leading indicator of trends and expectations in inflation and equity and bond prices.

LONDON SPOT MARKETS

Price coverage begins with the London markets for spot goods – commodities available for delivery within two days. Generally, these figures represent the cost of actual physical material, exceptions being the London daily sugar prices and the cotton index which are guide prices based on a selection of physical price indications. An example of spot markets is shown in Figure 12.1.

- **Prices and changes in price from the previous trading day:** figures are given for the principal crude oils, oil products, metals, meat, sugar, grains, rubber, vegetable oils and oilseeds, cotton and wool.

LONDON SPOT MARKETS

■ CRUDE OIL FOB (per barrel/Nov)   +or-

Dubai	$14.58-4.68w	-0.120
Brent Blend (dated)	$15.85-5.87	-0.190
Brent Blend (Nov)	$15.90-5.92	-0.160
W.T.I. (1pm est)	$17.14-7.17w	-0.270

■ OIL PRODUCTS NWE prompt delivery CIF (tonne)

Premium Gasoline	$172-173	
Gas Oil	$150-151	
Heavy Fuel Oil	$84-86	
Naphtha	$149-150	
Jet fuel	$176-178	-1
Diesel	$151-152	-1

Petroleum Argus. Tel. London (0171) 359 8792

■ OTHER

Gold (per troy oz)♣	$383.50	-0.35
Silver (per troy oz)♣	540.5c ·	-4.0
Platinum (per troy oz.)	$414.75	
Palladium (per troy oz.)	$138.00	-0.25
Copper (US prod.)	Unq.	
Lead (US prod.)	41.75c	
Tin (Kuala Lumpur)	15.43m	-0.04
Tin (New York)	298.5c	+6.0
Cattle (live weight)†	125.82p	+1.19*
Sheep (live weight)†♠	99.40p	-1.67*
Pigs (live weight)†	97.21p	-1.80*
Lon. day sugar (raw)	$303.6	+7.8
Lon. day sugar (wte)	$396.0	+13.0
Barley (Eng. feed)	£114.50x	
Maize (US No3 Yellow)	£104.0w	
Wheat (US Dark North)	Unq.	
Rubber (Nov)♥	91.50p	+0.50
Rubber (Dec)♥	91.50p	+0.50
Rubber (KL RSS No1)	349.5m	+3.0
Coconut Oil (Phil)§	$715.0u	-10.0
Palm Oil (Malay.)§	$650.0	+10.0
Copra (Phil)§	464.0y	-6.0
Soyabeans (US)	186.0	
Cotton Outlook'A' index	90.95c	-1.35
Wooltops (64s Super)	451p	-14

£ per tonne unless otherwise stated. p pence/kg. c cents/lb. r ringgit/kg. m Malaysian cents/kg. u Nov/Dec.♥ w Nov. y Oct/Nov. x Oct/Dec London Physical. § CIF Rotterdam. ♣ Bullion market close. ♠ Sheep (Live weight prices). * Change on week † Prices are for previous day.

Fig. 12.1 London spot markets

- **Weekly price changes:** Saturday's newspaper adds figures on prices at the close of trading for the week, the change on the previous week, prices one year ago and the highs and lows for the year to date (see Figure 12.2). Half-yearly the newspaper summarises current prices in key commodity markets as well as prices six months and a year previously.

WEEKLY PRICE CHANGES

	Latest prices	Change on week	Year ago	·········· 1995 ·········· High	Low
Gold per troy oz.	$382.00	-2.20	$390.70	$394	$373
Silver per troy oz	338.50p	-3.40	329.50p	375.50p	267.90p
Aluminium 99.7% (cash)	$1609.5	-62.5	$1734.50	$2149.50	$1609.50
Copper Grade A (cash)	$2762.5	-60.0	$2552.50	$3216.00	$2702.50
Lead (cash)	$650.5	+6.0	$651.00	$692.50	$536.50
Nickel (cash)	$7865.0	+25.0	$6877.5	$10160	$6947.5
Zinc SHG (cash)	$958.0	-16.5	$1067.5	$1208.5	$958.0
Tin (cash) ˙	$6170.0	-80.0	$5520.0	$7175.0	$5095.0
Cocoa Futures Dec	$916	+19	$981	$1050	$830
Coffee Futures Nov	$2383	+29	$3663	$3297	$2354
Sugar (LDP Raw)	$308.6	+1.5	$317.3	$378.1	$289.2
Barley Futures Nov	$110.75	+3.00	$104.25	$113.00	$102.00
Wheat Futures Nov	$120.25	+4.05	$107.25	$120.25	$111.00
Cotton Outlook A Index	89.80c	-0.25	73.80c	116.80c	85.05c
Wool (64s Super)	445p	-6	440p	532p	475p
Oil (Brent Blend)	$15.795	-0.205	$16.25	$19.01	$15.05

Per tonne unless otherwise stated. p Pence/kg. c Cents lb. x Dec.

Fig. 12.2 Weekly price changes

COMMODITY FUTURES MARKETS

As indicated, futures markets are chiefly used by consumers of physical commodities to avoid the risks of adverse price movements during the periods between contracting purchases and receiving deliveries. This hedging involves the opening of parallel but opposite futures contracts when physical orders are made, so that physical 'profits' or "losses" made by the time the commodity is delivered will be cancelled out by losses or profits on the futures markets.

The futures markets are basically paper markets, not to be confused with forward physical prices, which are simply quotations for physical material for delivery some time in the future. Speculators take on the risk consumers wish to avoid in the hope of accruing the potential profits that the consumer has relinquished.

Coffee, cocoa and sugar

The main UK futures market for "soft" commodities (foodstuffs) is the London Commodity Exchange (LCE, formerly the London Futures and Options Exchange, FOX, and, in 1996, to be merged with LIFFE). Its core contracts are in coffee, cocoa and sugar, but it also

features other agricultural products (wheat, barley and potatoes), a freight futures contract previously traded on the Baltic Exchange, and some traded options (see below). LCE prices for coffee, cocoa and sugar are shown in Figure 12.3:

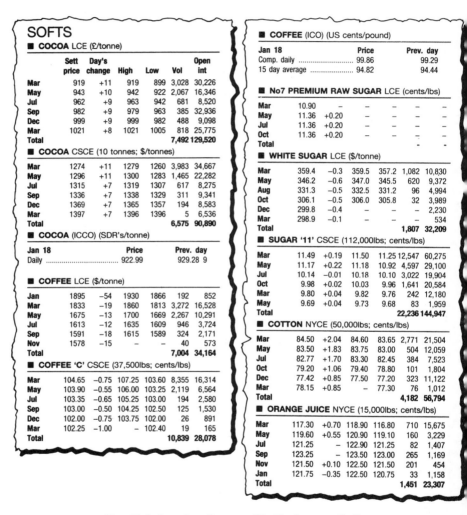

SOFTS

■ COCOA LCE (£/tonne)

	Sett price	Day's change	High	Low	Vol	Open int
Mar	919	+11	919	899	3,028	30,226
May	943	+10	942	922	2,067	16,346
Jul	962	+9	963	942	681	8,520
Sep	982	+9	979	963	385	32,936
Dec	999	+9	999	982	488	9,098
Mar	1021	+8	1021	1005	818	25,775
Total					7,492	129,520

■ COCOA CSCE (10 tonnes; $/tonnes)

Mar	1274	+11	1279	1260	3,983	34,667
May	1296	+11	1300	1283	1,465	22,282
Jul	1315	+7	1319	1307	617	8,275
Sep	1336	+7	1338	1329	311	9,341
Dec	1369	+7	1365	1357	194	8,583
Mar	1397	+7	1396	1396	5	6,536
Total					6,575	90,890

■ COCOA (ICCO) (SDR's/tonne)

Jan 18	Price	Prev. day
Daily	922.99	929.28 9

■ COFFEE LCE ($/tonne)

Jan	1895	−54	1930	1866	192	852
Mar	1833	−19	1860	1813	3,272	16,528
May	1675	−13	1700	1669	2,267	10,291
Jul	1613	−12	1635	1609	946	3,724
Sep	1591	−18	1615	1589	324	2,171
Nov	1578	−15	–	–	40	573
Total					7,004	34,164

■ COFFEE 'C' CSCE (37,500lbs; cents/lbs)

Mar	104.65	−0.75	107.25	103.60	8,355	16,314
May	103.90	−0.55	106.00	103.25	2,119	6,564
Jul	103.35	−0.65	105.25	103.00	194	2,580
Sep	103.00	−0.50	104.25	102.50	125	1,530
Dec	102.00	−0.75	103.75	102.00	26	891
Mar	102.25	−1.00	–	102.40	19	165
Total					10,839	28,078

■ COFFEE (ICO) (US cents/pound)

Jan 18	Price	Prev. day
Comp. daily	99.86	99.29
15 day average	94.82	94.44

■ No7 PREMIUM RAW SUGAR LCE (cents/lbs)

Mar	10.90	–	–	–	–	–
May	11.36	+0.20	–	–	–	–
Jul	11.36	+0.20	–	–	–	–
Oct	11.36	+0.20	–	–	–	–
Total					-	-

■ WHITE SUGAR LCE ($/tonne)

Mar	359.4	−0.3	359.5	357.2	1,082	10,830
May	346.2	−0.6	347.0	345.5	620	9,372
Aug	331.3	−0.5	332.5	331.2	96	4,994
Oct	306.1	−0.5	306.0	305.8	32	3,989
Dec	299.8	−0.4	–	–	–	2,230
Mar	298.9	−0.1	–	–	–	534
Total					1,807	32,209

■ SUGAR '11' CSCE (112,000lbs; cents/lbs)

Mar	11.49	+0.19	11.50	11.25	12,547	60,275
May	11.17	+0.22	11.18	10.92	4,597	29,100
Jul	10.14	−0.01	10.18	10.10	3,022	19,904
Oct	9.98	+0.02	10.03	9.96	1,641	20,584
Mar	9.80	+0.04	9.82	9.76	242	12,180
May	9.69	+0.04	9.73	9.68	83	1,959
Total					22,236	144,947

■ COTTON NYCE (50,000lbs; cents/lbs)

Mar	84.50	+2.04	84.60	83.65	2,771	21,504
May	83.50	+1.83	83.75	83.00	504	12,059
Jul	82.77	+1.70	83.30	82.45	384	7,523
Oct	79.20	+1.06	79.40	78.80	101	1,804
Dec	77.42	+0.85	77.50	77.20	323	11,122
Mar	78.15	+0.85	–	77.30	76	1,012
Total					4,182	56,794

■ ORANGE JUICE NYCE (15,000lbs; cents/lbs)

Mar	117.30	+0.70	118.90	116.80	710	15,675
May	119.60	+0.55	120.90	119.10	160	3,229
Jul	121.25	–	122.90	121.25	82	1,407
Sep	123.25	–	123.50	123.00	265	1,169
Nov	121.50	+0.10	122.50	121.50	201	454
Jan	121.75	−0.35	122.50	120.75	33	1,158
Total					1,451	23,307

Fig. 12.3 London Commodity Exchange: Softs

- **Contract size and pricing:** after the name of the commodity and the exchange on which it is traded is the size of the contract (how many tonnes, pounds, gallons or bushels of the commodity in a

single contract) and the manner of pricing (for example, dollars, pounds or SDRs per tonne).

- **Date:** the first column lists the expiry dates for the futures contracts currently in issue.

- **Settlement price:** the second column indicates the closing offer prices in the brokers' bid/offer spreads, the price at which they are prepared to sell a specific futures contract in these commodities. As usual with a spread, the bid prices will have been somewhat lower.

- **Day's change:** the third column indicates the change over closing offer prices on the preceding trading day.

- **High/low:** the fourth and fifth columns show the highest and lowest levels at which trades were executed during the day. It is possible for prices to close outside these ranges because they may move further near the end of the day without any business actually being done.

- **Volume:** the sixth column shows the actual number of lots or trading units that changed hands during the day.

- **Open interest:** the last column shows the number of lots of trading units up for sale or purchase during the day, not all of which will have actually been bought or sold.

- **ICCO and ICO:** indicator prices calculated by the International Cocoa Organisation and the International Coffee Organisation. These are related to price support systems, affecting changes in export quotas and buffer stock sales or purchases. Cocoa indicator prices are denominated in Special Drawing Rights (see chapter 10) to prevent them from being too susceptible to currency movements.

- **Sugar futures:** the market for white (refined) sugar operates on an automated trading system, in which dealers operate from their offices via screens linked to a central computer. This contrasts with the open outcry "ring-dealing" system of most other commodity markets.

A typical report on these soft commodity markets looks like this:

Coffee futures prices yesterday leapt by 30 per cent to their highest level in more than eight years, after a second severe frost in Brazil in as many weeks raised fears of a severe shortage of beans in the next couple of years. The surge in futures

prices, which have climbed by 220 per cent this year, increases the likelihood of further rises in retail coffee prices of at least 15 per cent.

(*Financial Times*, 12 July 1994)

In this case, the futures prices for coffee have benefited from the likelihood of future scarcity of this commodity. The prices are following the simple laws of supply and demand: as supply falls, the price rises.

Other commodities

The *Financial Times* also carries information on the International Petroleum Exchange (IPE) and its futures contracts in crude oil and gas oil. Indeed the North Sea oil price features daily on the front page of the newspaper in its key market summary. The Commodities and Agriculture page also provides coverage of certain minor markets: tea on Tuesdays, nuts and seeds on Thursdays, wool on Fridays and spices on Saturdays.

METALS

The London Metal Exchange

The main non-ferrous metals (aluminum, copper, lead, nickel, tin and zinc) are traded on the London Metal Exchange (LME). Although it has always operated as a futures market, the LME has traditionally had a closer relationship with the physical trade than other London markets. It is claimed to account for 70 to 80 per cent of its turnover. Only in 1987 did new investor protection legislation force the LME to abandon its cherished principal trading system in favour of the central clearing system used by the other commodity futures markets. Figure 12.4 shows the LME listing from the commodity prices section of the *Financial Times*. Saturday's newspaper adds a table of LME warehouse stocks of the metals.

● **Close and previous, high and low:** these are price indicators as on the LCE, except that for close and previous, both bid and offer prices are shown. The prices are for immediate delivery and for delivery in three months. The futures price is for a standard

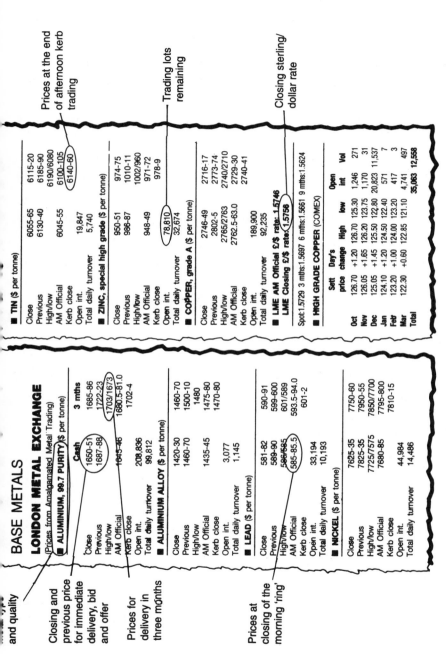

Fig. 12.4 London Metal Exchange

contract of metal of a defined grade. It is generally higher than the spot price, a phenomenon known as "contango" or "forwardation". The reverse, where the spot price stands at a premium over the futures price, is called "backwardation".

- **AM Official:** these are the values of the metals at the end of the morning "ring". The ring opens at 11.50am and closes at 1pm with a ten minute interval starting at 12.20pm. It is followed by twenty-five minutes of after hours dealing, known as the kerb session because it used to be conducted on the street outside the exchange. Prices at the close of the official ring are widely used for industrial supply contract pricing.

- **Kerb close:** the afternoon "unofficial" ring begins at 3.20pm and ends at 4.30pm. Kerb trading continues until 5pm with each metal phasing out from 4.45pm. This column carries the final prices from this session.

- **Open interest:** the number of trading lots that remain to be covered by opposite transactions or physical delivery. Lot sizes are twenty-five tonnes except for nickel which is six tonnes.

- **Total daily turnover:** the number of trading lots traded that day.

- **Closing:** the last line of the LME table gives the sterling/dollar rates published by the exchange at the unofficial close. This can be used to translate LME prices for contract purposes.

Gold

Twice a day at 10.30am and 3pm, representatives of the major bullion dealers meet at the offices of NM Rothschild to set the fixing price of a troy ounce of gold, and a substantial number of transactions tends to take place at the fixing sessions. Figure 12.5 shows the London bullion market listing.

Reading the figures

- **Gold:** morning and afternoon fixing prices in dollars per troy ounce (with sterling and Swiss franc conversions), as well as early and late prices for the London market. As with currency markets, there is no official close although the word is used to describe the late price.

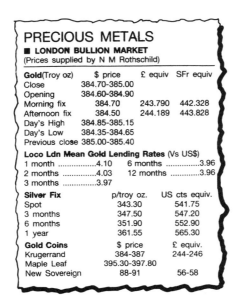

Fig. 12.5 London bullion market

- **Loco London Mean Gold Lending Rates:** familiarly known as "Gold Libor", these are the interest rates at which large gold holders, principally central banks, will lend gold held in their reserves to approved borrowers, principally miners, who repay the loans from future production. The low rates on offer reflect the highly secure nature of the loans and the extra cost to the borrower of the spread between the bid and offer price on the gold market, usually about $2.50 an ounce.

- **Silver fix:** prices at the morning silver fix in pence per troy ounce, with US cents equivalents.

- **Gold coins:** prices for a representative selection of gold coins. Gold coin prices are for large quantities and are exclusive of value added tax.

Using the information

The gold market can be attractive for investors and speculators. The price of gold is affected by a wide range of factors, moving up and down with bond yields, interest rates and exchange rates. Gold does not pay interest, and so its price is likely to be higher with lower interest rates.

Gold is often a safer asset when there is upward pressure on inflation. But it is also a currency risk for non-US investors since its price is always denominated in dollars. Given the relatively small number of players in the gold markets, the price can be significantly influenced by individuals.

Other metals

On Wednesday, the *Financial Times* lists minor metals prices, covering what are known as the strategic metals (because of their importance in high technology and military applications). The metals are antimony, bismuth, cadmium, cobalt, mercury, molybdenum, selenium, tungsten ore, vanadium and uranium. There are also regular price listings for gold and silver on the US market, and for two other precious metals: platinum and palladium.

A typical report on the metals markets looks like this, an indication of the effects of the markets on the actual users of commodities as inputs in their production processes, as well as on the broader economy:

> Recent rises in raw material prices, combined with fierce price competition in retail markets is threatening a profit squeeze in some manufacturing sectors. A surge in the price of metals and other imported commodities pushed the cost of raw materials and fuel for manufacturers up by a seasonally adjusted 0.8 per cent in June.
> (*Financial Times*, 12 July 1994)

OTHER KEY COMMODITY MARKETS

London traded options

Traded options appear in a number of commodity futures contracts. Options confer on holders the right, but not the obligation, to trade at a predetermined price, the striking price, within a pre-set timespan. For this, they pay a non-returnable premium. Since the premium is the only money the investor can lose, options represent a relatively low-risk way of speculating in commodities.

Traded options differ from straight options only in that they can be bought and sold rather than just operated by the original buyer. Figure 12.6 gives the FT traded options listing:

```
LONDON TRADED OPTIONS
Strike price $ tonne    ····· Calls ·····   ····· Puts ·····

■ ALUMINIUM
(99.7%) LME          Dec   Feb   Dec   Feb
1600 ..............   121   158    24    42
1650 ..............    62   100    64    82
1700 ..............    26    59   127   139
■ COPPER
(Grade A) LME        Dec   Feb   Dec   Feb
2700 ..............   113   112    57    95
2800 ..............    64    70   106   150
2900 ..............    32     -   174     -
■ COFFEE LCE        ·Nov   Jan   Nov   Jan
2050 ..............   273   259     -    39
2100 ..............   224   226     -    52
2150 ..............   177   197     -    67
■ COCOA LCE          Dec   Mar   Dec   Mar
875 ...............    36    72    20    27
900 ...............    23    57    32    37
925 ...............    15    45    49    50
■ BRENT CRUDE IPE    Nov   Dec   Nov   Dec
1550 ..............    43    53     -    22
1600 ..............     2    29     3    43
1650 ..............     -    11    50    78
```

Fig. 12.6 London traded options

- **Puts and calls:** current call (buy) and put (sell) premiums (prices) for options maturing in December and February with three different striking prices for each commodity.

The markets in New York and Chicago

The *Financial Times* also covers commodities futures markets in the United States since many of them are of interest to European readers, including traders in the commodities and outside speculators following the markets on both sides of the Atlantic. These markets are also, of course, the original futures markets and are still very influential because of that. Extracts from the New York and Chicago exchanges are shown in Figure 12.7.

In New York, the exchanges covered are:

- **The Commodity Exchange (Comex):** for copper, silver and gold. The price of gold on the Comex is a widespread reference, and is noted daily on the front page of the newspaper.

- **The New York Mercantile Exchange (Nymex):** for platinum, palladium, crude oil, natural gas, unleaded gasoline and heating oil.

GRAINS AND OIL SEEDS

■ WHEAT LCE (£ per tonne)

	Sett price	Day's change	High	Low	Open int	Vol
Nov	116.85	+0.65	116.85	116.05	1,558	353
Jan	119.25	+0.85	119.25	118.75	1,887	57
Mar	121.25	+0.85	121.25	120.50	1,313	41
May	123.15	+0.70	123.25	122.50	2,052	36
Jul	124.50	+0.60	-	-	74	-
Sep	106.40	-0.10	-	-	6	-
Total					6,921	487

■ WHEAT CBT (5,000bu min; cents/60lb bushel)

	Sett price	Day's change	High	Low	Open int	Vol
Dec	497½	+11¾	498	488½	57,572	11,194
Mar	504¼	+10½	505½	497	28,490	4,829
May	475	+9¼	476	467	3,123	251
Jul	428	+7½	428½	421½	10,531	1,317
Sep	429¼	+7¼	429½	425	837	116
Dec	438½	+8½	439	431	445	92
Total					101,001	17,799

■ MAIZE CBT (5,000 bu min; cents/56lb bushel)

	Sett price	Day's change	High	Low	Open int	Vol
Dec	327/6	+2/4	329/6	326/0	228,481	38,191
Mar	334/0	+2/0	336/4	332/6	153,325	14,610
May	335/0	+1/4	338/0	334/4	25,283	2,972
Jul	332/6	+1/4	335/4	332/2	43,676	3,388
Sep	297/0	+0/2	298/2	295/6	5,500	612
Dec	279/0	+0/2	280/6	278/4	18,905	1,664
Total					475,821	61,597

■ BARLEY LCE (£ per tonne)

	Sett price	Day's change	High	Low	Open int	Vol
Nov	107.65	-0.10	107.75	107.60	574	26
Jan	110.40	-0.25	-	-	710	-
Mar	113.40	+0.65	-	-	576	-
May	115.20	-0.10	-	-	146	-
Sep	104.00	-	-	-	-	-
Nov	107.00	-	-	-	-	-
Total					2,006	26

■ SOYABEANS CBT (5,000bu min; cents/60lb bushel)

	Sett price	Day's change	High	Low	Open int	Vol
Nov	656/4	+3/2	662/0	654/6	75,983	26,709
Jan	667/0	+3/4	672/6	665/0	38,777	9,100
Mar	676/4	+3/4	681/6	674/4	18,472	4,356
May	681/6	+3/2	687/0	680/4	8,474	1,598
Jul	686/6	+3/0	691/4	686/0	9,795	935
Aug	686/4	+4/0	687/0	683/4	163	4
Total					162,803	43,534

■ SOYABEAN OIL CBT (60,000lbs; cents/lb)

	Sett price	Day's change	High	Low	Open int	Vol
Oct	26.57	-	26.70	26.55	1,328	1,075
Dec	26.70	+0.09	26.87	26.66	41,696	17,527
Jan	26.84	+0.10	27.05	26.80	12,833	2,430
Mar	27.06	+0.13	27.28	26.98	10,591	1,702
May	27.25	+0.11	27.40	27.20	5,229	502
Jul	27.37	+0.15	27.45	27.35	3,355	230
Total					78,478	23,553

ENERGY

■ CRUDE OIL NYMEX (42,000 US galls. $/barrel)

	Sett price	Day's change	High	Low	Open int	Vol
Nov	17.59	+0.18	17.60	17.35	54,270	36,847
Dec	17.37	+0.10	17.38	17.20	81,959	29,323
Jan	17.21	+0.06	17.23	17.12	45,892	9,248
Feb	17.15	+0.05	17.15	17.07	20,911	2,860
Mar	17.11	+0.05	17.07	17.06	16,784	627
Apr	17.07	+0.05	17.03	17.02	12,690	1,499
Total					348,050	84,755

■ CRUDE OIL IPE ($/barrel)

	Sett price	Day's change	High	Low	Open int	Vol
Nov	16.31	+0.08	16.40	16.25	20,752	8,216
Dec	16.13	+0.13	16.15	16.03	76,659	22,851
Jan	16.00	+0.12	16.01	15.92	28,787	3,596
Feb	15.95	+0.10		15.82	9,647	1,121
Mar	15.90	+0.10	15.90	15.74	6,440	378
Apr	15.78	+0.10	15.78	15.49	3,418	624
Total					159,346	37,292

■ HEATING OIL NYMEX (42,000 US galls.; c/US galls.)

	Sett price	Day's change	High	Low	Open int	Vol
Nov	48.85	-0.07	49.15	48.45	36,563	8,380
Dec	49.42	-0.10	49.70	49.05	41,744	6,008
Jan	49.87	-0.10	50.15	49.65	35,717	2,194
Feb	49.62	-0.05	49.85	49.55	16,503	556
Mar	48.62	-	48.85	48.70	6,562	131
Apr	47.57	+0.05	47.70	47.70	4,076	77
Total					158,128	18,040

Precious Metals continue

■ GOLD COMEX (100 Troy oz.; $/troy oz.)

	Sett price	Day's change	High	low	Open int
Oct	383.9	-0.3	-	-	320
Dec	386.1	-0.3	387.0	386.0	98,357
Feb	388.3	-0.3	388.9	388.1	23,467
Apr	390.7	-0.3	391.2	390.6	9,970
Jun	393.4	-0.3	394.0	393.3	12,330
Aug	395.9	-0.3	-	-	2,880
Total					181,223

■ PLATINUM NYMEX (50 Troy oz.; $/troy o...)

	Sett price	Day's change	High	low	Open int
Oct	412.0	-1.5	411.5	411.5	555
Jan	412.0	-0.5	414.0	411.5	20,974
Apr	412.5	-0.4	414.5	413.5	1,577
Jul	413.7	-0.4	414.5	414.5	1,499
Oct	413.9	-0.4	-	-	31
Total				-	24,636

■ PALLADIUM NYMEX (100 Troy oz.; $/tro...)

	Sett price	Day's change	High	low	Open int
Dec	139.45	+0.50	139.50	138.20	4,916
Mar	140.95	+0.50	141.50	140.25	1,003
Jun	142.20	+0.50	-	-	75
Total					5,994

■ SILVER COMEX (100 Troy oz.; Cents/tro...)

	Sett price	Day's change	High	low	Open int
Oct	532.2	-3.5	-	-	57
Dec	536.0	-3.7	542.0	535.0	60,185
Jan	537.7	-3.7	541.0	537.7	26
Mar	542.6	-3.7	547.5	542.0	12,291
May	546.8	-3.7	548.5	546.8	6,665
Jul	550.7	-3.7	-	-	6,466
Total					99,880

MEAT AND LIVESTOCK

■ LIVE CATTLE CME (40,000lbs; cents/lbs)

	Sett price	Day's change	High	Low	Open int	Vol
Oct	65.950	-0.200	66.325	65.900	5,830	2,120
Dec	67.825	-0.125	68.200	67.775	29,495	5,821
Feb	67.000	+0.250	67.175	66.750	14,753	1,173
Apr	67.050	+0.275	67.175	66.775	8,324	786
Jun	63.025	+0.175	63.175	62.850	3,603	1,235
Aug	61.650	+0.150	61.725	61.450	1,310	876
Total					63,642	12,011

■ LIVE HOGS CME (40,000lbs; cents/lbs)

	Sett price	Day's change	High	Low	Open int	Vol
Oct	46.450	+0.725	46.500	45.700	4,456	1,278
Dec	46.050	+0.775	46.300	45.400	13,215	5,472
Feb	48.650	+0.625	48.825	48.125	7,312	1,165
Apr	48.175	+0.525	48.225	47.600	2,541	465
Jun	53.150	+0.900	53.150	52.300	2,853	276
Aug	51.725	+0.800	51.800	50.900	1,307	44
Total					32,432	8,741

■ PORK BELLIES CME (40,000lbs; cents/lbs)

	Sett price	Day's change	High	Low	Open int	Vol
Feb	63.325	+2.000	63.325	62.450	5,758	1,589
Mar	62.950	+2.000	62.950	62.000	555	193
May	64.150	+1.950	64.150	62.000	137	21
Jul	64.425	+1.625	64.500	63.500	463	64
Aug	61.900	+1.900	61.900	61.300	38	5
Total					6,951	1,867

Fig. 12.7 Commodity prices on New York and Chicago exchanges: Precious Metals, Meat and Livestock, Grains and Oil Seeds, and Energy

- **The Cocoa, Sugar and Coffee Exchange (CSCE).**

- **The Cotton Exchange (NYCE):** this also trades frozen concentrated orange juice.

In Chicago, prices are quoted from:

- **The Chicago Mercantile Exchange (CME or Merc):** for live cattle, live hogs and pork bellies.

- **The Chicago Board of Trade (CBT):** for maize, wheat, soyabeans, soyabean meal and soyabean oil.

The many other US markets are not covered because they are too small or primarily of interest to domestic US consumers.

Commodity indices

The last item in the commodities section of the newspaper is a record of three indices (see Figure 12.8):

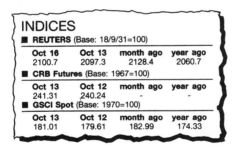

Fig. 12.8 Commodity price indices

- **Reuters:** this index is calculated from sterling prices for seventeen primary commodities, weighted by their relative importance in international trade. Values are given for the last two days, a month ago and a year ago.

- **CRB Futures:** an index of twenty-one commodity futures prices compiled by the New York-based Commodities Research Bureau. Each commodity gets equal weight; and the index is dominated by food prices with a weight of 57 per cent.

- **GSCI Spot:** a commodity spot price index produced by Goldman, Sachs.

Part III

UNDERSTANDING THE ECONOMIES

"A few suggestions for getting the headline figures into some sort of perspective: never trust a single month's figures; be suspicious of seasonal adjustment; remember the broad context of all the numbers you read."

ANTHONY HARRIS, *FINANCIAL TIMES*, 1987

"An economist is an expert who will know tomorrow why the things he predicted yesterday didn't happen today."

LAURENCE J PETER

13

UK ECONOMIC INDICATORS

- **Gross domestic product** – the country's national accounts: consumption and investment; government policy and the business cycle; output by market sector

- **Production and employment** – key indicators of real economic performance: industrial production and manufacturing output; retail sales; and the labour market

- **Inflation** – rates of price changes: the retail prices index; inflation versus unemployment; competitiveness

- **Money and finance** – the money supply, lending and interest rates

- **External trade** – the balance of payments, terms of trade and official reserves

In addition to the regular coverage of the financial markets, the *Financial Times* also reports on the progress of other key markets. These include the product and labour markets, as well as the overall economies of the United Kingdom, Europe and the world. Almost every day sees publication of new facts and figures for one economic indicator or another: consumer credit, industrial production, retail sales, the public sector borrowing requirement, unemployment, inflation, the balance of payments, and so on. These indicators all interact with, and have effects on, the financial markets and, as a result, it is vital to understand their implications when making key business and investment decisions.

For the UK economy, FT coverage is particularly intense. Each month a wealth of figures is produced by the Central Statistical Office (CSO), the government department responsible for compiling economic statistics. These official figures, many with track records that go back decades, together throw light on the state of the economy, indicating to businesses, consumers and the government whether the economy is in recession, growing or at a turning point. The *Financial Times* tracks much of this monthly and quarterly data, together with unofficial but longstanding and widely regarded economic surveys produced by bodies such as the Confederation of British Industry (CBI).

The data compiled by the CSO usually refer to the previous month's economic activity. They are collected through nationwide surveys with the results analysed by teams of statisticians at the CSO's centre in Newport, Gwent. By the time the figures are announced to the public, they have generally been "smoothed" to take account of seasonal patterns and to give a clearer picture of the underlying trend. For example, average earnings figures are "seasonally adjusted" for the extra hours worked in retailing and postal services in the period before Christmas.

Many of the figures are presented as indices, assuming constant prices from a given date, usually 1990=100. The reference date is arbi-

trary and merely provides a convenient landmark for comparison. What matters is not the index numbers themselves but the change from one period to the next. Figures for such key economic indicators as unemployment, inflation, output and gross domestic product (GDP) are especially likely to make the headlines, particularly when the monthly or quarterly changes are sharp.

Economic Trends is the CSO publication that brings together all the main economic indicators, while *Financial Statistics* provides data on a wide range of financial topics. These include financial accounts for various sectors of the economy, government income and expenditure, public sector borrowing, banking statistics, monetary aggregates, institutional investment, company finance and liquidity, security prices and exchange and interest rates.

Economic news reports appear in the first section of the *Financial Times* the day after they are released by the CSO. For easy reference, a table of UK economic figures appears on Thursday. The UK Economic Indicators table gathers together a range of key economic statistics to give an instant overview of activity in the UK economy. The figures are broken down into five principal sets of values, indices and rates of change: Output, Economic Activity, Inflation, Financial and External Trade. The following are the indicators, detailed in these tables and elsewhere, that are most likely to be reported in the press as well as to provoke public interest. More detailed explanations of the economic indicators discussed in this chapter can be found in my companion volume to this book, *The Financial Times Guide to Using Economics and Economic Indicators* (*Financial Times* Pitman Publishing 1994).

GROSS DOMESTIC PRODUCT

Each quarter, the newspaper presents figures on the National Accounts of the six biggest economies in the Organisation for Economic Cooperation and Development (OECD), the club that comprises twenty-six industrialised countries of the world. The economies covered are those of the United States, Japan, Germany, France, Italy and, the United Kingdom (see Figure 13.1):

INTERNATIONAL ECONOMIC INDICATORS: **NATIONAL ACCOUNTS**

Figures for GDP/GNP are in billions of European currency units (Ecu). The first breakdown is in current prices and the second shows growth rates in the constant price seri

■ UNITED STATES

CURRENT PRICES	Gross Domestic Product	Private Cons.	Private Invest.	Govt. Spend.	Net Exports
			as a % of GDP		
1985	5,298.1	66.0	17.7	19.1	-2.9
1986	4,339.9	66.8	16.8	19.5	-3.1
1987	3,933.8	67.2	16.5	19.4	-3.2
1988	4,141.1	67.3	16.2	18.7	-2.2
1989	4,766.1	67.1	15.8	18.6	-1.5
1990	4,351.6	67.8	14.6	18.9	-1.3
1991	4,620.1	68.2	13.0	19.2	-0.3
1992	4,646.3	68.7	13.1	18.7	-0.5
1993	5,419.3	69.0	13.9	18.1	-1.0
1994	5,683.1	68.7	15.3	17.4	-1.5
4th qtr.1994	5,586.5	68.6	15.6	17.2	-1.4
1st qtr.1995	5,529.1	68.5	15.9	17.2	-1.6
2nd qtr.1995	5,335.8	69.0	15.6	17.2	-1.8
3rd qtr.1995	5,463.1	68.9	15.7	17.2	-1.7

CONSTANT PRICES	% growth in				
	GDP	Cons.	Invest.	Govt.	Exports
1985	3.2	4.4	-1.5	6.1	1.2
1986	2.9	3.6	-1.5	5.2	6.6
1987	3.1	2.8	1.9	3.0	10.5
1988	3.9	3.6	3.2	0.6	15.8
1989	2.5	1.9	1.4	2.0	11.9
1990	1.2	1.5	-4.7	3.1	8.2
1991	-0.6	-0.4	-8.4	1.2	6.3
1992	2.3	2.8	6.1	-0.7	6.7
1993	3.1	3.3	13.0	-0.8	4.1
1994	4.1	3.5	16.1	-0.8	9.0
4th qtr.1994	4.1	3.5	14.7	-1.0	11.6
1st qtr.1995	4.0	2.8	13.9	-0.1	14.0
2nd qtr.1995	3.3	3.3	7.2	0.4	11.4
3rd qtr.1995	3.3	3.2	7.7	-0.4	10.4

■ JAPAN

CURRENT PRICES	Gross National Product	Private Cons.	Total Invest.	Govt. Cons.	Net Exports
			as a % of GNP		
1985	1,780.2	58.7	28.0	9.5	3.7
1986	2,033.6	58.3	27.7	9.7	4.3
1987	2,102.2	58.4	28.4	9.4	3.8
1988	2,466.0	57.6	30.4	9.2	2.9
1989	2,625.4	57.3	31.5	9.1	2.2
1990	2,321.9	57.0	32.5	9.1	1.4
1991	2,729.4	56.1	32.3	9.1	2.5
1992	2,848.8	56.7	30.8	9.2	3.3
1993	3,609.2	57.6	29.7	9.5	3.2
1994	3,911.0	58.7	28.6	9.8	3.0
4th qtr.1994	3,849.1	59.1	28.3	9.7	2.8
1st qtr.1995	3,875.6	59.0	28.4	10.2	2.4
2nd qtr.1995	4,228.5	59.2	28.5	10.1	2.3
3rd qtr.1995					

CONSTANT PRICES	% growth in				
	GNP	Cons.	Invest.	Govt.	Exports
1985	4.5	3.3	6.5	0.3	6.6
1986	3.0	3.5	4.2	5.2	-6.1
1987	4.3	4.2	8.4	1.6	5.1
1988	6.3	5.3	14.2	2.3	10.6
1989	4.9	4.7	9.3	2.0	16.4
1990	5.1	4.4	8.2	1.5	10.8
1991	4.0	2.5	4.5	2.0	5.0
1992	1.3	2.1	-2.5	2.0	2.0
1993	0.1	1.1	-2.2	2.4	-1.6
1994	0.5	1.8	-3.0	2.2	2.6
4th qtr.1994	0.3	1.1	-1.3	0.6	6.7
1st qtr.1995	0.0	0.7	0.4	3.5	5.6
2nd qtr.1995	0.1	1.8	1.3	0.5	5.6
3rd qtr.1995	0.1	1.4		0.9	9.1

■ GERMANY

CURRENT PRICES	Gross Domestic Product	Private Cons.	Total Invest.	Govt. Cons.	E
			as a % of GNP		
1985	820.4	56.8	19.6	20.0	
1986	906.0	55.4	19.6	19.8	
1987	961.5	55.7	19.3	20.0	
1988	1,009.8	55.0	20.1	19.7	
1989	1,075.2	55.0	20.8	18.8	
1990	1,182.9	54.4	21.5	18.3	
1991	1,396.1	57.0	23.6	19.5	
1992	1,520.9	57.1	22.9	20.1	
1993	1,628.1	58.2	21.4	20.1	
1994	1,727.7	57.3	22.6	19.6	
4th qtr.1994	1,772.2	56.9	23.4	19.3	
1st qtr.1995	1,827.2	57.0	22.7	19.7	
2nd qtr.1995	1,882.2	56.7	22.5	19.5	
3rd qtr.1995					

CONSTANT PRICES	% growth in				
	GDP	Cons.	Invest.	Govt.	E
1985	2.3	1.8	-1.2	2.1	
1986	2.3	3.5	3.8	2.5	
1987	1.4	3.5	0.3	1.6	
1988	3.6	2.4	7.6	2.1	
1989	3.7	3.2	6.5	-1.6	
1990	5.9	5.2	8.7	2.2	
1991	4.9	5.7	6.7	0.3	
1992	1.8	2.6	0.1	5.0	
1993	-1.2	0.5	-6.5	-0.5	
1994	3.0	0.9	9.7	1.2	
4th qtr.1994	3.7	0.3	15.9	1.7	
1st qtr.1995	2.7	0.9	8.2	1.4	
2nd qtr.1995	2.5	2.3	3.8	1.8	
3rd qtr.1995					

■ FRANCE

CURRENT PRICES	Gross Domestic Product	Private Cons.	Total Invest.	Govt. Cons.	Net Exports
			as a % of GDP		
1985	691.8	60.8	18.9	19.6	0.7
1986	746.1	60.2	19.6	19.2	1.0
1987	770.5	60.6	20.2	19.1	0.1
1988	815.2	59.8	21.4	18.7	0.1
1989	877.8	59.4	22.3	18.2	0.1
1990	940.6	59.3	22.5	18.2	0.0
1991	973.0	59.6	21.5	18.6	0.3
1992	1,024.6	59.8	19.8	19.1	1.3
1993	1,068.6	60.6	17.1	20.1	2.2
1994	1,124.5	60.1	18.0	19.8	2.1
4th qtr.1994	1,151.0	59.6	18.5	19.7	2.2
1st qtr.1995	1,172.5	59.3	18.5	19.7	2.5
2nd qtr.1995	1,190.5	59.8	17.8	19.8	2.6
3rd qtr.1995					

CONSTANT PRICES	% growth in				
	GDP	Cons.	Invest.	Govt.	Exports
1985	1.9	2.4	2.8	2.3	1.9
1986	2.5	3.9	8.8	1.7	-1.4
1987	2.3	2.9	5.1	2.8	3.1
1988	4.5	3.3	9.8	3.4	8.1
1989	4.3	3.1	8.8	0.5	10.2
1990	2.5	2.7	3.4	2.1	5.4
1991	0.8	1.4	-3.1	2.8	4.1
1992	1.3	1.4	-4.7	3.4	4.9
1993	-1.5	0.2	-14.0	3.3	-0.4
1994	2.9	1.5	10.5	1.1	5.8
4th qtr.1994	4.1	1.6	19.8	0.9	7.7
1st qtr.1995	4.0	1.8	7.5	1.6	10.8
2nd qtr.1995	2.9	2.7	1.2	2.0	6.8
3rd qtr.1995					

■ ITALY

CURRENT PRICES	Gross Domestic Product	Private Cons.	Total Invest.	Govt. Cons.	Net Exports
			as a % of GDP		
1985	561.8	62.6	22.5	16.7	-1.9
1986	615.7	62.2	20.9	16.5	0.4
1987	658.4	62.4	21.0	16.9	-0.3
1988	710.5	61.9	21.5	17.1	-0.5
1989	790.8	62.4	21.3	16.9	-0.6
1990	861.4	61.8	21.0	17.7	-0.4
1991	933.5	62.2	20.4	17.7	-0.4
1992	945.0	63.0	19.4	17.8	-0.3
1993	844.0	62.5	16.8	17.9	2.9
1994	859.9	62.8	17.0	17.3	2.9
4th qtr.1994	859.9	62.5	18.0	17.1	2.4
1st qtr.1995	838.2	61.5	18.7	16.8	3.0
2nd qtr.1995	798.6	62.0	17.9	16.6	3.5
3rd qtr.1995					

CONSTANT PRICES	% growth in				
	GDP	Cons.	Invest.	Govt.	Exports
1985	2.6	3.0	1.7	3.4	3.2
1986	2.9	3.7	1.4	2.6	2.5
1987	3.1	4.2	4.6	3.4	4.7
1988	4.1	4.2	6.3	2.8	5.4
1989	2.9	3.5	2.3	0.8	8.8
1990	2.1	2.5	3.7	1.2	7.0
1991	1.2	2.7	-0.1	1.6	0.5
1992	0.7	1.1	-0.1	1.0	5.0
1993	-1.2	-2.5	-18.3	0.7	9.4
1994	2.2	1.6	4.4	0.0	10.9
4th qtr.1994	3.1	2.0	14.2	0.5	10.8
1st qtr.1995	4.1	1.4	13.9	0.0	13.9
2nd qtr.1995	2.9	1.1	2.7	-0.7	17.6
3rd qtr.1995					

■ UNITED KINGDOM

CURRENT PRICES	Gross Domestic Product	Private Cons.	Total Invest.	Govt. Cons.	Ex
			as a % of GDP		
1985	606.6	60.9	17.2	21.1	
1986	573.7	62.8	17.1	21.0	-
1987	600.8	62.7	18.0	20.6	-
1988	709.6	63.5	20.3	19.9	-
1989	766.9	63.4	21.0	19.7	-
1990	770.8	63.1	19.2	20.5	-
1991	821.6	63.4	16.1	21.6	-
1992	811.6	63.9	15.4	22.1	-
1993	810.7	64.3	15.1	21.9	-
1994	864.9	63.9	15.5	21.6	-
4th qtr.1994	877.4	63.8	15.9	21.4	-
1st qtr.1995	866.2	63.7	15.3	21.3	-
2nd qtr.1995	847.4	63.8	15.8	21.3	-
3rd qtr.1995	852.5	64.0	15.6	21.3	-

CONSTANT PRICES	% growth in				
	GDP	Cons.	Invest.	Govt.	Ex
1985	3.9	3.8	3.8	-0.1	
1986	4.3	6.8	2.8	1.6	
1987	4.8	5.3	10.7	1.0	
1988	5.0	7.5	17.3	0.7	
1989	2.2	3.2	3.6	1.4	
1990	0.4	0.6	-7.4	2.5	
1991	-2.0	-2.2	-12.3	2.6	
1992	-0.5	-0.1	1.6	-0.1	
1993	2.3	2.6	2.7	0.3	
1994	4.0	2.8	5.4	1.9	
4th qtr.1994	4.2	2.4	8.6	1.5	
1st qtr.1995	3.5	1.9	1.8	0.3	
2nd qtr.1995	2.6	2.4	5.7	0.7	
3rd qtr.1995	2.1	2.6	3.4	0.9	

Seasonally adjusted data used in all cases. GDP/GNP is broken down into private consumption expenditure, investment (the sum of gross fixed capital formation and t change in stocks), general government final consumption, and net exports (exports of goods and services minus imports of goods and services). The US includ investment by government in the government series rather than under investment. Quarterly GDP/GNP totals are annualised. The growth rates are the percentage char over the corresponding period in the previous year, and are positive unless otherwise stated. The figures in the fifth column of each set of growth rates refer only exports, rather than to net exports. Data supplied by Datastream and WEFA from national government sources.

Fig. 13.1 International economic indicators: National accounts

- **Gross domestic product:** this measures overall economic activity in a country and is calculated by adding together the total value of annual output of goods and services. The first breakdown is in current prices with quarterly figures annualised. The second breakdown shows growth rates in constant prices, adjusting for the effects of inflation: the growth rate is the percentage change over the corresponding point in the previous year. GDP can also be measured by income to the factors producing the output (essentially capital and labour) or expenditure by individuals, businesses and the government on that output.

- **Private consumption:** the percentage of GDP expenditure made up of consumer spending on goods and services. These figures typically include imputed rents on owner occupied housing, but not interest payments, purchases of buildings or land, transfers abroad, business expenditure, buying of second-hand goods or government consumption.

- **Total investment:** the percentage of GDP expenditure made up of capital investment (as opposed to financial investment) by both the private and public sectors. This is spending on new factories, machinery, equipment, buildings, roads, accommodation, raw materials, etc. "Gross domestic fixed capital formation", as investment is sometimes termed, is a key component of current growth of GDP as well as a critical foundation for future expansion. Obviously, investment in machines has greater potential for future output than that of houses, though the contribution of infrastructure such as roads may be harder to assess.

- **Government consumption:** the percentage of GDP made up of consumer spending by the public sector. Government spending on such items as infrastructure is accounted in these figures under total investment, though in some presentations of GDP, government spending encompasses both consumption and investment.

- **Net exports:** the percentage of GDP made up of the difference between the value of national exports of goods and services and that of imports. In current prices, this balance of trade in goods and services (the current account of the balance of payments) in

the United Kingdom is typically negative with the value of imports exceeding that of exports.

A month after the end of each quarter the CSO produces a provisional estimate of GDP based on output data, such as industrial production and retail sales (see below). A month later the CSO provides a further estimate taking account of income and expenditure data. Finally, one month after that, the full national accounts are produced based on complete information. As well as revisions to the provisional GDP figures, the national accounts show a full breakdown of economic activity during the previous quarter by sector, and identify trends in such key GDP components as personal disposable income, personal consumption and savings, and fixed investment and stock building. The CSO publication that contains the annual UK national accounts is known as the *Blue Book*.

When the level of GDP falls compared with the previous quarter, the economy is said to be contracting. Two consecutive quarterly falls, and it is said to be in recession. When GDP rises quarter to quarter, the economy is expanding. The movement of GDP from slump to recovery to boom to recession to slump again is known as the business cycle. Government macroeconomic policy is often aimed at smoothing this cycle, easing the pain of recession and applying restraint when the economy is in danger of overheating. This would typically be done through fiscal policy (boosting public expenditure and cutting taxes, or the reverse) or monetary policy (loosening or tightening the money supply, perhaps through lowering or raising interest rates).

Private consumption is a function of personal disposable income, the amount of income available to households after payment of income taxes and national insurance contributions. The other side of this coin is personal savings, the difference between consumer income and consumer spending. This can be either actual savings held in a deposit account or repayments of debt. The savings ratio is the proportion of income that is saved expressed as a percentage of personal disposable income.

Investment is also the twin of savings. By definition, investment equals savings: leaving exports and imports out of the picture, if

consumption plus savings equals total income, income equals expenditure, and consumption (household and government) plus investment (private and public) equals expenditure, then investment and savings are equivalent. What happens is that income saved rather than consumed is available for investment: savings and investment are both about deferring current consumption for future prospects of consumption.

The fourth element of total GDP arises from the fact that the economy is open to international trade and financial flows. Exports contribute to growth; in contrast, imports can stifle it, reducing increases in national output relative to growth in demand. For example, increasing imports might suggest that demand is outstripping what can be provided by domestic output. Longer term increases in imports might imply declining competitiveness on the part of national industries. If the level of imports is consistently and substantially higher than that of exports, and the deficit is not balanced by net inflows of interest, profits, dividends, rents and transfer payments, the current account balance stays in deficit. This can be financed in the capital account temporarily, but longer term a deficit leads to exchange rate problems, as discussed in chapter 10.

In terms of the state of the economy, growth in personal consumption often leads a general recovery from recession, encouraging manufacturers to invest. Accounting for around 60 per cent of total GDP in most industrialised countries, it is clearly a critical target of government macroeconomic policy. But if consumption grows faster than productive capacity, imports are sucked into the national economy. This can have adverse implications both for the balance of payments and for domestic inflation where prices of imported goods drive up the general price level.

Government policy and the business cycle

Clearly a vital component of GDP is government spending on both consumption and investment. As shown in chapter 4, this is financed by taxation of individuals and corporations. The difference between government revenues and income is known as the public sector borrowing requirement (PSBR). Forecasts for this and other key

elements of the economy are published by the Treasury at the time of the annual government budget in November in what is known as the *Red Book*.

Monthly figures for the PSBR show how much the government has borrowed or paid back in one month. When tax revenues are weak and government spending high, for example in a recession, the PSBR is likely to grow. It will narrow once the economy picks up and tax revenues rise again as more people find jobs. Thus, the state of public sector finances is, in part, dependent on the state of economic activity: this part of the deficit is referred to as the "cyclical" deficit. However, governments also incur persistent debts by systematically spending more than they collect in tax revenues: this part of the deficit, which exists regardless of economic activity, is referred to as the "structural" deficit.

Government policy on the PSBR has two basic effects on the economy. The first is through fiscal policy: if the PSBR is increased in times of stagnant or falling output and high unemployment, the directly higher spending of the government and/or the indirectly higher spending of consumers resulting from their lower taxes and greater disposable incomes stimulate demand. Through various multiplier effects, this can lead to recovery, increased output, reduced unemployment and growth. However, the second effect may temper this: high, persistent and/or growing annual PSBRs may drive up the cost of borrowing, discouraging both consumption and investment. Governments are frequently torn between the conflicting effects of the macroeconomic policies at their disposal.

The pattern of the business cycle, whether influenced by government policy or not, is shown by cyclical indicators, produced once a month by the CSO. These monitor and predict changes in the UK economy: based on series that are good leading indicators of turning points in GDP, such as business and consumer confidence surveys, they provide early indications of cyclical turning points in economic activity. In addition to these and the Treasury's predictions for the UK economy, hundreds of other private and public bodies produce their own forecasts, ranging from City analysts to independent think-tanks to the Treasury's panel of independent forecasters, the "wise men". The OECD also produces a forecast for the UK economy.

Output by market sector

In addition to the breakdown of GDP by consumption, investment, government activity and international trade, the CSO produces a breakdown by output of various market sectors. The *Financial Times* presents the essentials of this data in the Output section of the weekly UK economic indicators table (see Figure 13.2). All of these except housing starts are indices based on 1990=100.

The key sectors can be analysed by comparing their percentage change over a period with the percentage change in overall GDP: relatively faster growing sectors, for example, are making a more substantial contribution to overall growth. A given percentage change in a dominant sector naturally has a larger effect on total activity than that of a less important sector. This point is particularly important to bear in mind when comparing the relative importance of certain sectors in different countries, and the changes of those sectors' importance. For example, a shifting balance from the manufacturing sector to the services sector is often noted in mature economies. Developing countries in contrast are more likely to be starting with agriculture and shifting to manufacturing.

UK ECONOMIC INDICATORS

OUTPUT- By market sector; non-durable goods, investment goods, intermediate goods (materials and fuels), engineering output, metal manufacture, textiles, clothing and footwear (1990=100); housing starts (000s, monthly average).

	Non-drble. goods	Invest. goods	Intmd. goods	Eng. output	Metal mnfg.	Textiles etc.	Housg. starts·
1994							
1st qtr.	100.5	93.1	104.5	95.2	84.6	90.2	16.7
2nd qtr.	101.3	94.0	107.9	96.5	86.0	90.8	18.8
3rd qtr.	101.6	96.7	109.2	99.8	86.7	89.3	17.3
4th qtr.	102.2	96.8	108.5	100.6	89.5	91.5	13.9
July	100.9	95.8	108.2	98.4	85.4	89.6	18.2
August	101.8	97.3	109.2	100.1	88.1	88.8	16.8
September	102.1	97.1	110.2	101.0	86.7	89.6	17.0
October	101.5	97.7	109.2	101.3	87.4	89.6	16.1
November	102.6	97.0	107.2	100.8	88.8	92.2	14.8
December	102.3	95.9	109.1	99.7	92.3	92.6	10.8
1995							
1st qtr.	103.6	96.2	109.7	99.8	87.3	90.0	14.7
2nd qtr.	104.4	96.0	109.5	99.6	87.1	91.0	16.4
3rd qtr.	103.9	96.2	110.7	100.1	87.3	89.0	14.3
January	103.3	95.5	108.9	98.6	87.6	89.9	13.5
February	103.6	96.7	109.1	100.5	87.4	90.0	14.4
March	103.9	96.4	111.1	100.2	87.0	90.1	16.3
April	103.9	95.9	109.7	99.2	87.0	91.0	14.8
May	104.7	96.3	109.7	99.8	86.7	90.9	16.4
June	104.7	95.9	109.0	99.8	87.6	91.1	18.1
July	104.0	96.1	110.5	100.1	87.8	89.9	14.7
August	104.2	96.4	109.9	100.7	87.1	88.7	14.6
September	103.4	96.0	111.6	99.4	86.9	88.4	13.6

Fig. 13.2 UK economic indicators: Output

- **Consumer goods:** an index of output of finished goods bought directly for use by individuals and households, for example, television sets. This index is indicative of trends in the consumer sector and its important role in the economy as a whole. Key components of it are often reported separately, such as output of motor vehicles and consumer durables: up or downturns in either of these are a good leading indicator of the stage of the business cycle.

- **Investment goods:** an index of output of capital goods bought by industry and the government for the production of other goods, for example, printing presses. Again, this index is a leading indicator of the state of the economy.

- **Intermediate goods:** an index of the output of goods that require further stages of processing (materials or fuels) or which will become parts of other finished consumer or investment goods, for example, computer microchips.

- **Engineering output, metal manufacture, textiles, clothing and footwear:** indices of output in these sectors, all important in the UK economy.

- **Housing starts:** a monthly average of the thousands of new houses on which construction has begun in the period. Housing starts are another key leading indicator of economic activity, responding quickly to increases in earnings, employment and interest rates. For example, cuts in interest rates often prompt an upturn in construction, perhaps signalling that recovery is on the way.

PRODUCTION AND EMPLOYMENT

The overall national accounts figures give a broad historic picture of the state of the economy while the output figures break it down by market sector. Figures for Economic Activity included in the weekly UK economic indicators table (see Figure 13.3) focus on key indicators of national economic performance that generally appear in advance of detailed GDP figures. These too are often leading indicators of the prospects for the economy. They cover various indices of

manufacturing and retail performance, together with unemployment and unfilled vacancies over two years on a monthly or quarterly basis. All except engineering orders, unemployment and vacancies are indices based on 1990=100.

Comparative figures for retail sales volume, industrial production, the unemployment and vacancy rates, as well as a composite leading indicator for the six leading economies of the OECD are published monthly in the international economic indicators table under Production and Employment.

UK ECONOMIC INDICATORS

ECONOMIC ACTIVITY- Indices of industrial production, manufacturing output (1990=100); engineering orders (£ billion); retail sales volume and retail sales value (1990=100); registered unemployment (excluding school leavers) and unfilled vacancies (000s).

	Indl. prod.	Mfg. output	Eng. order*	Retail vol.	Retail value*	Unem- ployed	Vacs.
1994							
1st qtr.	100.7	97.1	25.1	104.9	109.7	2,750	141.2
2nd qtr.	103.0	98.7	25.5	105.8	113.7	2,665	149.3
3rd qtr.	104.4	100.0	26.7	106.9	115.6	2,595	162.4
4th qtr.	104.2	100.7	27.0	107.1	137.4	2,468	178.7
July	103.4	99.4	26.4	106.6	116.3	2,630	157.0
August	104.6	100.3	26.6	106.7	114.9	2,593	163.7
September	105.1	100.3	26.7	107.4	115.6	2,562	166.6
October	104.6	100.3	26.5	107.1	119.9	2,515	177.3
November	103.7	101.0	26.4	107.0	129.5	2,470	180.0
December	104.4	100.8	27.0	107.2	162.7	2,419	178.8
1995							
1st qtr.	105.0	100.7	26.7	106.4	112.2	2,369	174.3
2nd qtr.	105.1	101.0	26.7	107.3	118.8	2,320	180.3
3rd qtr.	105.6	101.2		107.4	119.9	2,290	185.0
January	104.3	100.0	26.5	105.5	109.2	2,392	175.5
February	104.9	100.9	27.0	106.7	112.7	2,367	173.4
March	105.9	101.2	26.7	106.9	114.7	2,347	174.0
April	105.0	100.7	26.4	107.3	119.3	2,328	181.7
May	105.3	101.1	26.0	107.1	118.7	2,317	179.6
June	104.9	101.2	26.7	107.5	118.5	2,314	179.7
July	105.5	101.2	26.9	107.9	121.6	2,313	179.8
August	105.4	101.5	26.3	107.0	118.4	2,292	182.4
September	105.9	100.9		107.3	119.8	2,265	192.8
October				107.1	124.2	2,266	191.0

Fig. 13.3 UK economic indicators: Economic activity

● **Industrial production:** an index of the value-added output of the production industries. This index excludes services, agriculture, trade and finance.

● **Manufacturing output:** an index of the value-added output of the production industries, excluding the production of the oil and gas industries. The index for manufacturing output can be broken

down to show the performance of various sectors such as engineering, chemicals, textiles, and food and drink, as shown above.

- **Engineering orders:** outstanding orders for output from the engineering industries in billions of pounds. Increases in orders, adjusted for inflation, are an indicator of future increases in economic activity, particularly if, as in this case, the demand is for capital goods.

- **Retail volume and value:** figures from the CSO that show the volume and value of retail sales over the previous month and over the previous quarter. The CSO breaks down the total by category of shops, such as food retailers or clothing and footwear.

Each month the CSO estimates the output of UK manufacturing industry and the level of energy production in the previous month. These come together as the index of output of the production industries. The two components are usually quoted separately because oil and gas output is often erratic and can easily distort the underlying performance of manufacturing industry. Repairs to oil installations in the North Sea, for example, can bring energy production sharply down in one month.

As well as monthly rises in output, the CSO compares output with the levels of a year ago and output in the latest three months (compared with the previous three months) to give a better idea of underlying trends. Industrial production is strongly indicative of the state of the economic cycle, since the output of industries producing capital goods and consumer durables is most reduced during a recession. While the monthly net output of physical goods in the United Kingdom represents only a third of total output, industrial production is the principal monthly indicator of the overall level of activity in the economy. Retail sales is also a leading indicator, functioning as a proxy for consumer spending in the eventual GDP figures.

A number of surveys, produced by bodies such as the CBI, supplement the regular FT reporting of UK economic statistics. One of the most important is the CBI's quarterly industrial trends survey of manufacturers. This gives a strong indication of future trends in manufacturing output by asking industrialists about the state of their order books.

The British Chamber of Commerce also carries out a quarterly economic survey of its members: unlike the CBI industrial trends survey, this includes the service sector. The CBI also does a monthly inquiry into the state of the distributive trades sector (mainly wholesalers and retailers) that supplements official information on retail sales.

Retail sales

The level of retail sales is another important leading indicator, and one that receives considerable media attention. Encompassing up to a half of all consumer spending in the eventual figures for GDP (most of the rest is spent in the service sector and on accommodation), the volume and value of retail sales are key indicators of consumer confidence and demand (see Figure 13.4). For example, a significant upturn in retail sales will typically lead to higher wholesale sales, to more factory orders and eventually to increased production. Figures for retail stocks and retail orders will also give some indication of the pace of demand.

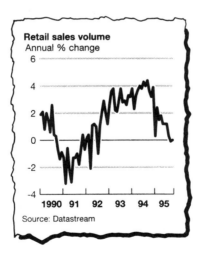

Fig. 13.4 Retail sales volume

The pattern of retail sales is influenced by a wide range of factors, many of which affect different sectors in different ways, according to

the characteristics of the products. For example, seasonality is very important with some goods: off licences will expect to see sales volume jump at Christmas or during a long hot summer; grocers, on the other hand, can expect fairly consistent demand throughout the year.

Figures on retail sales should be examined very carefully by the companies that support and supply retailers. For example, the results of the CBI's distributive trades survey of over 500 retailers, wholesalers and motor traders will indicate whether consumer demand for their products is growing or declining. Since the data are available relatively quickly, supplying companies are able to adjust their output quite flexibly.

The labour market

The Economic Activity table (see Figure 13.3) also includes two important indicators of the state of the labour market:

- **Registered unemployment:** the total number of people (in thousands, and excluding school leavers) who were out of work and claiming unemployment benefit in the previous period. The figure is seasonally adjusted to take account of annual fluctuations, such as at the end of the academic year when school leavers flood the jobs market.

- **Unfilled vacancies:** vacancies (in thousands) notified to Department of Education and Employment Job Centres, about one-third of the total vacancies in the economy. The change in the number of vacancies is seen as an important indicator of future employment trends.

Figures for unemployment and vacancies, as well as average earnings and unit wage costs, are provided by the Department of Education and Employment. The measure of unemployment, known as the claimant count, is often criticised for excluding large numbers of people who cannot find jobs but who are not eligible for unemployment benefit. Thus women seeking to return to work, the self-employed and 16 and 17 year old school leavers do not show up in the official count. Furthermore, the 1980s witnessed thirty changes to the definition of unemployment, all but one of which reduced the jobless total.

There are clearly more people unemployed than the official figures suggest. Every quarter, the Department of Education and Employment carries out a survey of the labour force, designed to capture those unemployed people who are left out of the claimant count. The Labour Force Survey (LFS) uses the International Labour Office measure of unemployment, an internationally recognised definition. It refers to people who were available to start work in the two weeks following their LFS interview and had either looked for work in the four weeks prior to interview or were waiting to start a job they had already obtained.

There is often a difference between the unemployment total revealed by the claimant count measure and the total arrived at by the LFS. The discrepancy between the two measures is usually greatest at a time of economic expansion when people feel encouraged to go out and look for work.

Department of Education and Employment statistics cover very detailed aspects of the labour market, including breakdown of unemployment by age, sex and region of the country. One example of the implications of such breakdowns is that a drop in the number of young unemployed men is usually regarded as a sign of economic recovery. Figure 13.5 illustrates changes in UK unemployment:

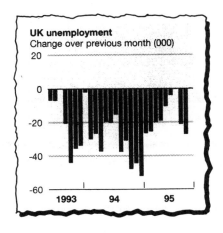

Fig. 13.5 Unemployment

INFLATION

Rates of change of prices in the UK economy feature in the Inflation section of the weekly UK economic indicators table (see Figure 13.6). A number of different measures of UK inflation are published by the CSO, but by far the most popular and widely covered is the retail prices index (RPI). In addition to the RPI, indices are provided for inflation in earnings, consumer and manufacturing goods, and commodities, as well as for the value of sterling. For earnings, materials and manufactured products, the indices are based on 1990=100; for retail and food indices, January 1987=100; for the Reuters index, 18 September 1931=100; and for sterling, 1990=100.

UK ECONOMIC INDICATORS

INFLATION-Indices of earnings (1990=100); basic materials and fuels; wholesale prices of manufactured products (1990=100); retail prices and food prices (Jan 1987=100); Reuters commodity index (Sept 18th 1931 =100); trade weighted value of sterling (1990=100)

	Earn-ings	Basic matls.*	Whsale. mnfg.*	RPI*	Foods*	Reuters cmdty.*	Sterling*
1994							
1st qtr.	121.7	101.0	114.9	142.0	130.8	1,765	90.7
2nd qtr.	122.7	103.3	115.6	144.5	132.7	1,919	89.0
3rd qtr.	123.7	104.7	116.0	144.6	132.2	2,100	87.9
4th qtr.	124.9	108.6	116.8	145.5	132.0	2,134	89.1
July	123.2	104.4	115.7	144.0	132.3	2,119	87.9
August	123.7	104.4	116.0	144.7	132.7	2,079	87.8
September	124.1	105.2	116.2	145.0	131.6	2,102	88.1
October	124.4	105.8	116.3	145.2	131.4	2,078	89.1
November	124.6	108.9	116.6	145.3	131.8	2,129	89.1
December	125.7	111.0	117.5	146.0	132.7	2,193	89.0
1995							
1st qtr.	126.3	112.8	119.1	146.8	135.0	2,286	87.2
2nd qtr.	126.7	114.8	120.4	149.5	137.0	2,309	84.3
3rd qtr.	127.5	114.3	121.1	149.9	137.9	2,200	84.3
January	125.7	112.7	118.7	146.0	134.1	2,263	88.6
February	126.0	112.7	119.0	146.9	135.0	2,268	87.4
March	127.1	112.9	119.5	147.5	135.9	2,324	85.6
April	126.7	114.2	120.2	149.0	135.8	2,318	84.4
May	126.6	114.8	120.5	149.6	138.1	2,317	84.3
June	126.7	115.4	120.6	149.8	137.0	2,293	84.1
July	127.0	114.2	120.9	149.1	135.9	2,245	83.6
August	127.6	113.9	121.1	149.9	138.7	2,212	84.4
September	127.8	114.9	121.4	150.6	139.1	2,142	84.8
October		114.1	121.6			2,098	84.3

Fig. 13.6 UK economic indicators: Inflation

- **Earnings:** an index that measures the monthly level of earnings of employees in the United Kingdom. The index is compiled from a monthly sample survey of the gross wages and salaries paid to the

employees of over 8,000 companies and organisations in the private and public sectors.

- **Basic materials and fuels:** an index that tracks the prices of raw materials and fuels used by UK industries. These indicators are often referred to as producer input prices.

- **Wholesale prices of manufactured products:** an index that tracks the prices of manufactured goods as they leave factories. These indicators are often referred to as producer output prices or "prices at the factory gate".

- **Retail prices index:** an index of the average change in the prices of millions of consumer purchases represented by a "basket" of goods. This is the most widely quoted index of inflation, sometimes referred to as the headline rate of inflation. The essential element to note is the change in the RPI year to year: if inflation is 4 per cent, this means that the RPI has risen by 4 per cent since the same month of the previous year; the average basket of goods is 4 per cent more expensive.

- **Food prices:** an index that tracks the prices of foods.

- **Reuters commodity index:** the same index listed in the commodities section of the newspaper and described in chapter 12. Here it is intended to be less a guide for investors in commodities, and more indicative of the prices of raw materials for businesses using them in their production processes.

- **Trade-weighted value of sterling:** like the Bank of England and JP Morgan indices discussed in chapter 10, a measure of the strength or weakness of the pound against the currencies of the United Kingdom's trading partners weighted by the volume of trade with each of those partners. A particularly decisive shift in the value of this indicator was in the last quarter of 1992 when the pound left the European Monetary System (EMS) and devalued against the currencies of most UK trading partners in the European Union (EU).

The monthly labour market statistics for growth in average earnings cover the whole economy, including both the service and manufactur-

ing sectors. In addition to basic wages, earnings also include overtime payments, grading increments, bonuses and other incentive payments. For this reason, earnings increases usually exceed settlement increases and wage claims.

Because the earnings figures are affected by special factors such as back pay and changes in the timing of pay settlements, the Department of Education and Employment also publishes its estimate of the underlying trend in earnings. Other figures published on the same day include hours of work and employment; hours of overtime worked; productivity (output per head); days lost through industrial disputes; and unit wage costs (wages per unit of output). Unit wage costs are an important indicator of inflationary pressures in an economy. If wages increase faster than productivity, then unit wage costs rise (see below).

Both producer input and output prices are expressed in terms of an index and are regarded as important forward indicators of retail price inflation. For example, a big leap in raw material prices may be absorbed by manufacturers for a while, but they are likely, at some stage, to raise prices to restore their profit margins. When they do, retailers will eventually respond by raising shop prices.

During the recession of the early 1990s, prices of raw materials and fuels used by UK manufacturers began to fall, reflecting depressed economic conditions abroad and domestically, as well as the strength of sterling. But this trend was reversed suddenly in September 1992 when sterling left the EMS and devalued. Input price inflation leapt from being flat in September to a year to year growth rate of over 4 per cent in November, reflecting the higher cost of imported raw materials as a result of the weaker pound.

The retail prices index

The CSO says it gets more queries from the public about the RPI than any other statistic, a reflection of the influence inflation has on everyone's life. For example, inflation determines the real value of savings, affects increases in pensions and other state benefits and plays an important part in wage bargaining.

The index is compiled by tracking the prices of a "basket" of goods, which represents spending by the typical UK family. All types

of household spending are represented by the basket apart from a handful of exceptions, including savings and investments, charges for credit, betting and cash gifts. Indirect taxes such as value-added tax (VAT) are included, but income tax and national insurance payments are not: direct taxes are sometimes accounted for in a separate index, the tax and price index.

The average change in the price of the RPI basket is calculated from the findings of government price collectors. Each month, they visit or telephone a variety of shops, gathering about 130,000 prices for different goods and services. They go to the same places and note the prices of the same things each month so that over time they compare like with like. Information on charges for gas, water, newspapers, council rents and rail fares are obtained from central sources. Some big chain stores, which charge the same prices at their various branches, help by sending information direct from their headquarters to the CSO.

The components of the RPI are weighted to ensure that the index reflects average household spending. Thus housing expenditure has a much greater weighting than cinema tickets; the biggest weightings currently go to housing, food and motoring. The weights are obtained from a number of sources but mainly from the CSO's Family Expenditure Survey. For this, a sample of 7,000 households across the country keep records of what they spend over a fortnight plus details of big purchases over a longer period. The spending of two groups of people is excluded on the grounds that their pattern of spending is significantly different from most people's: families with the top 4 per cent of incomes and low income pensioners who mainly depend on state benefits.

Every year the components and the weightings of the RPI are reviewed to take account of changing spending habits. Over the past few years, microwave ovens, video recorders and compact discs have been introduced, while black and white televisions were dropped when sales declined.

In addition to the "all items" index, the CSO publishes the RPI excluding mortgage interest payments (RPIX), an underlying measure of inflation favoured by the Treasury. It does this because a cut or rise in interest rates automatically influences mortgage interest

payments. These have a higher weighting than any other component of the RPI and, as a result, have a strong bearing on the direction of the index. Excluding mortgage interest payments from the standard index prevents interest rate changes obscuring the underlying pattern of price changes as Figure 13.7 illustrates:

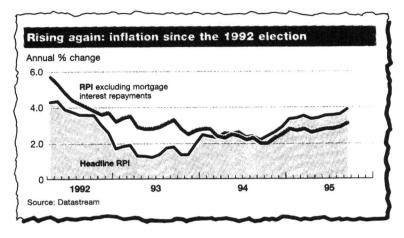

Fig. 13.7 Retail prices index

Inflation versus unemployment

A key economic debate is over the causes of, and relationship between inflation and unemployment, in particular, whether there is a trade-off between them. This trade-off begins with the questions of which is worse, economically, socially and politically, and which therefore should be the primary goal of economic policy. Over the past decade, western governments have tended to argue that it is the control of inflation that should come first, traditionally the viewpoint of the political centre-right. Inflation makes it hard to distinguish between changes in relative price rises and general price rises, distorting the behaviour of individuals and firms and reducing efficiency; since it is unpredictable, it causes uncertainty and discourages investment; and it redistributes wealth unjustly, from creditors to borrowers, from those on fixed incomes to those on wages, and from everyone to the government.

Certainly inflation is damaging to the performance of the real economy, but so is high unemployment. It is an incredible waste of productive resources, it is expensive in terms of government benefits, and it is miserable for all the individuals who experience it. Along with substantial earnings differentials, and tax policies that favour the better off, it can cause drastic disparities in the distribution of income and potentially disastrous social disruption. Concerns about the consequences of high global unemployment in the early 1990s have seen a resurgence of interest in the pursuit of full employment, traditionally a key policy goal of the center-left. This raises the central issue of how unemployment and inflation are connected, and what full employment might mean.

It used to be believed that there was a simple trade-off between the two variables: what is called the Phillips curve, after its progenitor, suggested that in order to reduce inflation, society had to tolerate higher unemployment, and *vice versa*. This inverse relationship did in fact exist in the US economy amongst others through the 1960s; it subsequently broke down irretrievably as later years witnessed both high inflation and high unemployment, what became known as stagflation. Such times led to the coining of a new economic indicator, the misery index, the combination of the rates of consumer price inflation and unemployment (an alternative misery index adds together inflation and interest rates).

Nowadays, the consensus of economic opinion seems to be that there is some level of output and employment beyond which inflation rises. For example, there is always a gap between the actual level of output and the potential level, a measure of the amount of slack in the economy called the output gap. If this gap is closed too far, supply cannot rise to meet any increased demand, thus forcing up prices; there exist what economic reports often call bottlenecks or supply constraints. This might be called a situation of excess demand: spending power, perhaps arising from tax cuts, increased consumer borrowing or a bigger money supply, exceeds the availability of goods and services, bidding up their prices.

Similarly, it is argued that beyond a certain unemployment rate, what has been called the natural or non-accelerating inflation rate of unemployment, higher demand becomes inflationary. At such a

point, the supply and demand for labour are in balance; beyond it, higher demand for labour supposedly drives up wage costs, which feeds through to retail price inflation, which in turn encourages demands for higher wages, and so on in an inflationary spiral.

Estimates vary of what that rate of unemployment really is and arguments continue about whether it should be regarded as the "full employment" unemployment rate. It is assumed to depend on such factors as the level of minimum wages, benefits, employment taxes, unionisation, the age structure of the labour force and other demographic factors, and these are now the issues of much economic and political debate.

Financial markets' perception of the natural rate is reflected when news of an increase in the jobless figures is greeted enthusiastically by the markets with stock and bond prices surging in response to lengthening dole queues. On the other hand, the impact of falling unemployment can be bad for share prices, especially if the economy is "overheating". Falling unemployment is, after all, characteristically a lagging indicator of the business cycle. But longer term, depending on the sectors and regions in which a portfolio is invested, more jobs and lower unemployment should mean better returns.

Competitiveness

A monthly table of international economic indicators for Prices and Competitiveness (see Figure 13.8) gives details of indices for consumer prices, producer prices, earnings, unit labour costs and the real exchange rate for six leading OECD countries. Yearly figures are shown in index form with the common base year of 1985=100. The real exchange rate is an index throughout; the other quarterly and monthly figures show the percentage change over the corresponding period in the previous year.

- **Consumer prices:** indices of consumer prices that are not seasonally adjusted. These are equivalents of the UK RPI.

- **Producer prices:** indices of producer prices that again are not seasonally adjusted, and use varying measures of output.

	Consumer prices	Producer prices	Earnings	Unit labour costs	Real exchange rate
■ FRANCE					
1985	100.0	100.0	100.0	100.0	100.0
1986	102.5	97.2	104.5	101.6	103.4
1987	105.9	97.8	107.8	103.0	104.8
1988	108.8	102.8	111.1	104.1	102.1
1989	112.6	108.4	115.4	105.2	100.1
1990	116.5	107.1	120.6	109.6	103.4
1991	120.2	105.8	125.8	113.4	101.1
1992	123.1	104.0	130.3	115.6	104.7
1993	125.6	101.1	133.7	118.1	107.0
1994	127.7	102.5	136.7		106.5
3rd qtr.1994	1.6	1.9	n.a.	n.a.	107.2
4th qtr.1994	1.6	5.3	n.a.	n.a.	106.8
1st qtr.1995	1.7	1.0	n.a.	n.a.	106.4
2nd qtr.1995	1.6	1.9	n.a.	n.a.	106.7
September 1994	1.6	n.a.	-	n.a.	107.4
October 1994	1.7	n.a.	2.1	n.a.	107.4
November	1.6	n.a.	-	n.a.	106.7
December	1.6	n.a.	-	n.a.	106.2
January 1995	1.7	n.a.	2.0	n.a.	105.7
February	1.7	n.a.	-	n.a.	105.9
March	1.8	n.a.	-	n.a.	107.5
April	1.6	n.a.	2.0	n.a.	108.2
May	1.6	n.a.	-	n.a.	105.7
June	1.6	n.a.	-	n.a.	106.3
July	1.5	n.a.		n.a.	106.7
August	1.9	n.a.		n.a.	106.2

Fig. 13.8 International economic indicators: Prices and competitiveness (France)

- **Earnings:** indices of non-seasonally adjusted earnings.

- **Unit labour costs:** seasonally adjusted indices of labour costs per unit of output, measured in domestic currencies. Unit labour costs reflect labour costs and productivity.

- **Real exchange rate:** calculated by JP Morgan as indices of relative national costs or prices expressed in a common currency. These real effective exchange rates are calculated against a composite of fifteen industrial countries' currencies, adjusted for changes in the relative wholesale prices of domestic manufactures (a measure of inflation). A fall in the index indicates improved international competitiveness.

National competitiveness is a difficult and controversial concept to define. One attempt is that it is the degree to which a country can produce goods and services that meet the tests of international markets while simultaneously maintaining and expanding the real incomes of its people over the long term. This depends on changes in costs and prices relative to comparable changes in countries with which trade is conducted, adjusting for movements of the exchange rate. It is generally accepted that greater competitiveness of a country's output can be achieved through some combination of reasonable productivity growth and an appropriately valued exchange rate.

Each of these indicators gives some guide to national competitiveness. The first two are measures of domestic rates of inflation: for each country, they can be used to assess changes in the general price level and inflationary prospects. In effect, they can be interpreted in the same way as all the above figures for inflation in the United Kingdom. However, when they are compared internationally, they become indicative of countries' ability to sell their exports abroad; they show relative consumer and producer prices. For example, if UK consumer prices are rising faster than French ones, without compensating movements in the franc-sterling exchange rate, UK exports to France are more expensive than they were, and hence less competitive.

Earnings and unit labour costs focus on the relative costs side of comparisons of international competitiveness. Earnings measure total labour costs; unit labour costs measure labour costs divided by output, and are therefore a function of productivity. Earnings and unit labour costs are an important indicator of inflationary pressures in an economy: if labour costs increase faster than productivity, then unit labour costs rise. Used to compare countries, they reveal cost competitiveness: higher unit labour costs, without compensating movements in the exchange rate, make it harder for companies to price their goods competitively on the international market and maintain their profit margins.

Real exchange rates are effective exchange rates between countries' currencies that have been adjusted to take account of differential rates of inflation. The inflation indicator might be wholesale prices as in the table or unit labour costs. Either way, the real exchange rate is an excellent indicator of national competitiveness, incorporating

changes in the exchange rate, the relative rates of inflation and the relative growth of productivity. Its importance was illustrated by the particularly decisive shift in the value of this indicator for the United Kingdom in the last quarter of 1992 when the pound left the EMS.

The combination of devaluation and productivity growth gave the United Kingdom a strong low cost advantage over other EU countries, though not against North America or Japan. For companies exporting to the EU, competing with EU imports, or considering either of these options, this was good news. They were able to price their goods very competitively, and still earn quite attractive profits. Thus competitiveness on a national scale and as a corporate concern become intertwined.

MONEY AND FINANCE

One or two of the financial indicators discussed earlier in this book, as well as monetary indicators such as the money supply, appear in the Financial section of the weekly UK economic indicators table (see Figure 13.9). In addition, the *Financial Times* provides monthly figures for Money and Finance in international economic indicators of the six leading economies of the OECD. These focus on measures of narrow and broad money, short- and long-term interest rates and equity market yield.

Every month the Bank of England publishes figures showing the amount of money in circulation in the UK economy, and the year to year percentage changes. The total value of money in circulation depends on the definition of the money supply. In the United Kingdom there are two main measures, one broad and one narrow. Sometimes monetary authorities choose to target growth in the money supply as part of an anti-inflationary strategy. Rapid growth in the amount of money circulating in the economy is often taken to be a sign that inflationary pressures are building up.

- **M0:** also known as "narrow money" or the monetary base, this measure consists almost entirely of notes and coins in circulation. Growth in Mo indicates that consumer spending is buoyant; a contraction in Mo suggests consumers are behaving more cautiously.

UK ECONOMIC INDICATORS

FINANCIAL-Money supply (annual percentage change), M0, new M2 (retail deposits and cash), M4; bank sterling lending to private sector; building societies' net inflow; consumer credit†; Clearing Bank base rate (end period).

	M0 %	M2 %	M4 %	Bank lending £m	BS inflow* £m	Cnsmer. credit† £m	Base rate %
1994							
1st qtr.	5.4	5.6	5.3	+ 4,261	-1,322	+888	5.25
2nd qtr.	6.4	4.7	5.4	+ 5,761	651	+1,539	5.25
3rd qtr.	6.6	4.6	4.8	+ 9,317	699	+1,613	5.75
4th qtr.	7.1	4.2	4.4	+12,012	1,520	+1,954	6.25
July	6.5	4.7	4.7	+ 2,566	286	+400	5.25
August	6.2	4.6	4.7	+ 3,311	91	+722	5.25
September	7.2	4.5	4.9	+ 3,440	322	+491	5.75
October	7.4	4.1	4.1	+ 1,949	526	+533	5.75
November	7.2	4.0	4.5	+ 5,972	301	+590	5.75
December	6.8	4.5	4.6	+ 4,091	693	+831	6.25
1995							
1st qtr.	6.6	4.2	4.9	+16,518	1,615	+1,719	6.75
2nd qtr.	6.0	5.3	6.3	+10,793	2,074	+1,697	6.75
3rd qtr.	5.8	6.1	8.2	+13,594	2,471	+1,821	6.75
January	6.6	4.4	4.6	+ 4,660	576	+562	6.25
February	6.2	4.1	4.7	+ 3,796	519	+619	6.75
March	7.0	4.1	5.5	+ 8,062	520	+538	6.75
April	6.3	4.9	5.6	+ 4,318	868	+513	6.75
May	5.9	5.3	6.4	+ 5,157	860	+590	6.75
June	5.7	5.7	6.8	+ 1,317	346	+594	6.75
July	5.7	5.4	8.0	+ 7,530	956	+895	6.75
August	6.1	6.3	8.4	+ 2,105	612	+518	6.75
September	5.5	6.5	8.2	+ 3,959	903	+608	6.75
October	5.2						6.75

Fig. 13.9 UK economic indicators: Financial

- **M2:** a broader and more recently introduced measure of the money supply, covering Mo plus sterling retail deposits in banks and cash. By UK definitions, this is a narrower measure than M4 (see below), though the definition of M2 in some other countries is broader, and their M2 is "broad money".

- **M4:** known in the United Kingdom as "broad money", this measure comprises Mo plus bank and building society retail and wholesale deposits.

- **Bank lending:** bank and building society lending to the private and corporate sectors in millions of pounds, also known as M4 lending. Sluggish growth in M4 lending indicates that consumers and companies are reluctant to borrow, while strong M4 growth is indicative of a stronger economy. On the same day that the Bank of England publishes the M4 lending figures, the British Bankers Association puts out its own monthly statement about lending by the main retail banks.

- **Building societies' net inflow:** the difference between the amount building societies have deposited with them and the amount they have lent in millions of pounds. The lower or more negative this figure, the more encouraging the signs for the housing market.

- **Consumer credit:** a useful snapshot of consumer behaviour, measuring net changes in how much consumers have borrowed from retailers, finance houses, building societies and on the main bank credit cards in millions of pounds. It does not cover mortgages or bank loans and thus accounts for only around 15 per cent of total private sector debt.

- **Clearing bank base rate:** the lowest interest rate at which high street banks will lend money at the end of the period. This is close to the rate paid by a floating rate mortgage payer.

EXTERNAL TRADE

Each month the CSO publishes figures showing how much the United Kingdom imported and exported in the previous month and consequently how much the country is in deficit or surplus with the rest of the world. These are reported in the External Trade section of the weekly UK economic indicators table (see Figure 13.10). A monthly table of international economic indicators covers Balance of Payments for the six main economies of the OECD. The figures it provides for exports, visible trade and current account balances, and ecu and effective exchange rates are examined in chapter 15.

The CSO's monthly figures are mainly concerned with trade in visible items or merchandise goods. Trade in visible items is presented both in current values and in volume terms with adjustments made for erratic components, such as aircraft and precious stones, that are likely to distort the underlying trend. Visible trade is simpler to measure than invisible trade in services, and financial transactions such as transfer payments, interest payments, profits and dividends. Indices are also provided for other components of the balance of payments plus the terms of trade and domestic reserves.

UK ECONOMIC INDICATORS

EXTERNAL TRADE- Indices of export and import volume (1990=100); visible balance (£m); current balance (£m); oil balance (£m); terms of trade (1990=100); official reserves (end period)

	Export volume	Import volume	Visible balance	Current balance	Oil balance	Terms of trade*	Reserves US$bn
1994							
1st qtr.	112.8	109.8	-3,137	-1,038	+952	104.5	42.92
2nd qtr.	117.1	108.0	-2,383	- 578	+1,184	102.1	43.37
3rd qtr.	119.5	107.5	-2,165	+ 493	+888	101.3	43.48
4th qtr.	123.9	114.2	-3,053	- 567	+1,046	100.9	43.90
July	117.5	107.8	- 760		+259	101.3	43.58
August	119.8	109.7	- 623		+273	102.8	43.54
September	121.5	109.3	- 782		+356	100.1	43.48
October	122.3	111.7	- 806		+323	102.0	43.97
November	125.5	114.5	- 767		+368	101.0	44.00
December	120.7	116.7	-1,480		+355	100.2	43.90
1995							
1st qtr.	124.2	109.8	-1,896	-1,193	+1,281	99.7	46.12
2nd qtr.	123.3	112.5	-3,207	-2,333	+1,124	100.1	46.64
January	121.0	109.1	- 716		+400	101.6	42.78
February	123.3	110.3	- 691		+424	100.1	42.75
March	126.7	110.1	- 489		+494	98.2	46.12
April	120.5	113.7	-1,381		+455	99.6	46.47
May	125.1	111.9	- 935		+385	100.0	46.63
June	124.2	111.9	- 891		+284	100.6	46.64
July	124.3	115.3	-1,145		+204	101.6	47.00
August	126.0	117.1	-1,265		+287	101.2	47.06
September							47.06
October							47.18

Fig. 13.10 UK economic indicators: External trade

- **Export volume:** a volume index of the level of exports of goods from the United Kingdom based on 1990=100. The volume of exports is determined by the demand from overseas which in turn depends on the state of the importing economies, the price of the exports (a function of relative inflation levels and the exchange rate) and, of course, the quality of the products.

- **Import volume:** a volume index of UK purchases of goods from abroad based on 1990=100. Like export volume, import volume depends on relative prices arising from relative inflation and exchange rates, as well as the state of the UK economy. When the economy is growing, imports generally increase.

- **Visible balance:** also known as the (merchandise) trade balance, this is the net balance in the value of exports and imports of goods in millions of pounds. When the United Kingdom imports more visible items than it exports, a perennial national problem, it is said to have a "trade gap". This may be of no particular concern provided it is offset by surpluses elsewhere on the balance of payments, such as in invisible items.

- **Current balance:** the balance of trade in both goods and services plus net interest, profits, dividends, rents and transfer payments flowing into the United Kingdom from countries overseas in millions of pounds. A deficit on the current account balance must be made up in the capital account of the overall balance of payments through net investment into the country, loans from abroad or depletion of the official reserves. A persistent deficit puts pressure on the currency (as discussed in chapter 10), encouraging devaluation to increase the price competitiveness of exports and decrease that of imports.

- **Oil balance:** the balance in the value of trade in oil in millions of pounds. The positive balance for the United Kingdom reflects the continuing production of North Sea oil.

- **Terms of trade:** a price index (based on 1990=100) that shows UK export prices in relation to import prices. An improvement in the terms of trade occurs when export prices rise at a faster rate than import prices. The fall in the terms of trade indicated by the table in the fourth quarter of 1992 was a result of the ejection of sterling from the EMS. The fall in the value of the pound against the currencies of many trading partners meant that UK exports were relatively lower priced while imports were higher priced.

- **Official reserves:** Treasury figures for the United Kingdom's official gold and foreign currency reserves held by the Bank of England. The data show the total reserves in billions of US dollars at the end of the period, and act as a guide to the extent of Bank of England intervention on the foreign currency markets to support or undermine the value of the pound during that period. It is difficult to get an exact picture of this intervention because of other Bank transactions, including new borrowing and repayment of debt by the public sector, and official transactions for government departments and foreign central banks.

By bringing together the balances in visible and invisible trade, the CSO provides the current account. Adding in the capital account provides a complete statement of the United Kingdom's trade and

financial transactions with the rest of the world. This full picture is known as the balance of payments and is published every quarter. A publication known as the *Pink Book* gives detailed balance of payments data including the City of London's contributions to the United Kingdom's overseas earnings, total transactions with the rest of the European Union and details of the UK's overseas assets and liabilities.

*"Grounded in Sydney, could it take off
from Brussels."*

THE ECONOMIST CROSSWORD, 1995

*"The path to European monetary union will not be
a stroll; it will be hard and thorny."*

KARL BLESSING,

BUNDESBANK PRESIDENT, 1963

14

THE EUROPEAN ECONOMY
Market integration and monetary union

- **The European economy** – exchange rates and the European Monetary System (EMS); currency market volatility in 1992 and 1993

- **Prospects for economic and monetary union (EMU)** – the exchange rate mechanism (ERM), the ecu and the euro

National economies like that of the United Kingdom can no longer be examined in isolation. Increasingly international flows of goods, services and capital are making economies more and more interdependent and, with an almost global consensus on the positive effects of free trade, this movement can only go further. Countries' economies interact in a number of ways, generally facilitating each other's progress, and certainly having important effects upon and being in turn affected by the national and international financial markets. Nowhere is this more evident than in the European Union (EU). This chapter explores the basics of the European economy. More detailed explanations of much of this information can be found in my companion volume to this book, *The Financial Times Guide to Using Economics and Economic Indicators*.

THE EUROPEAN ECONOMY

The European Union is on its way to representing one-third of world output, compared with one-quarter for the United States and one-sixth for Japan. As a market comprising fifteen countries, the Union accommodates over a quarter of all world commerce within its frontiers. Furthermore, it is the world's most substantial source of foreign direct investment, its most important provider and consumer of services and the largest global supplier of aid.

The European Union has been through a number of transformations in its history, the most economically significant of which, to date, is the "1992" project, the creation of a single market. On 1 January 1993, that single market came into effect: in principle and to a large extent in practice, the remaining obstacles to the free flow of goods, services, capital and labour between the then twelve member states of the EU were removed, and the Union moved significantly closer to its goal of becoming a genuine "common market".

In the face of serious upheavals in European currency markets, notably in the latter halves of 1992 and 1993, the EU's long-term goal is to establish a full economic union, involving a close harmonisation

of member countries' general economic policies, the centralisation of fiscal and monetary control procedures and a single currency. The single market has already produced a number of benefits for European consumers and businesses, and it is anticipated that there are many more to be reaped from the process of "ever closer union".

One of the most important steps towards that full economic and monetary union (EMU) was taken in 1979, when the then European Community set about creating a "zone of currency stability" known as the European Monetary System (EMS). Since then, the Treaty on European Union, agreed at Maastricht in 1991 and signed the following year, has established a timetable for further advancement of the EMU goal.

Exchange rates and the European Monetary System

The idea behind the European Monetary System was to achieve currency stability through coordinated exchange rate management. This would facilitate intra-Union trade and set the stage for a single currency towards the end of the 1990s. The exchange rate mechanism (ERM), a system of fixed but flexible exchange rates, was the central plank of the EMS. Countries participating in the ERM would keep the value of their currencies within margins of 2.25 per cent either side of agreed central rates against the other currencies in the mechanism. Sterling, the peseta and the escudo, all of which joined the ERM several years after its inception, were allowed to move within margins of 6 per cent.

The ERM worked by requiring members to intervene in the foreign exchange markets in unlimited amounts to prevent currencies breaching their ceilings or floors against the other currencies. For example, if the peseta fell to its floor against the D-Mark, the Bank of Spain was required to buy pesetas and sell D-Marks. Other members could help by intervening on behalf of the weak currency. This, in theory, would prop up the peseta before it fell through its floor.

Second, the country whose currency was under fire could raise its short-term interest rates to make its currency more attractive to investors. If intervention on the foreign exchanges and adjustment of short-term rates failed to stop a currency from sliding too low or rising too high, an absolute last resort was a realignment of the central rates to relieve the tensions in the system.

In the early years of the ERM there were several realignments but from 1987 until 1993, when the ERM was effectively suspended,

there were none. Many economists argue that it was the failure of the mechanism to realign in response to the strength of the D-Mark that led to the tensions of the autumn of 1992 and the summer of 1993.

Currency market volatility in 1992 and 1993

After five years of relative calm, the currency markets of Europe erupted in a sequence of dramatic market events. The explanation for these events lies in German reunification at the end of the 1980s. To pay for unification the German government had to borrow substantial amounts of money, which forced up the cost of borrowing in Germany. High German interest rates coincided with low US interest rates and the result was strong international demand for D-Marks, forcing German rates even higher.

This happened just as the rest of Europe, heading into recession, needed lower interest rates to stimulate economic activity. However, since all the other currencies were committed to maintaining their central rates against the D-Mark, they were forced to keep their interest rates at levels that were damaging their economies. So long as Germany's rates were high, countries like the United Kingdom and France were unable to lower their lending rates without causing a run on the pound and the franc.

In the case of the United Kingdom, the tensions became too much for the system in September 1992. The country was suffering its longest recession since the 1950s yet had interest rates of 10 per cent. With inflation low, the real cost of borrowing was exceptionally high. The markets took the view that such high lending rates at a time of recession were unsustainable. Pressure on the pound mounted over August, but the UK government, mindful of the hardship being caused by the high cost of borrowing, was unwilling to raise rates further in order to protect the pound. Its only weapons were intervention on the foreign exchanges and repeated assurances by ministers that there would be no devaluation.

Events came to a head on 16 September 1992, Black Wednesday (or White Wednesday to "Eurosceptics", delighting at its negative implications for future European union), when sterling and the Italian lira were forced out of the mechanism. Speculative investors, losing confidence in the currencies and seeing the opportunity for significant profits, shifted vast funds out of sterling and the lira into the D-Mark. Many, for example, sold the pound short, expecting to be able to buy it back at a much reduced rate.

The effect of all this selling was to drive the pound down. On the day, the UK government tried to save it by buying large quantities of pounds, and by announcing an increase in interest rates to 15 per cent. But this was not enough to stem the flow against sterling: effectively, the Bank was transferring its reserves to the short selling speculators. After a steady drain on reserves, the government pulled out. Both sterling and the lira sank well below their ERM floors as soon as the authorities gave up the struggle to keep them within their old bands.

For the next eleven months, relative calm returned to what was left of the mechanism. However, in August 1993, tensions arose once more, this time centred on the French franc. The problems were familiar: France was in a recession with high unemployment yet was unable to cut its very high interest rates. One solution would have been for Germany to ease its lending rates, but the Bundesbank, the German central bank, would not contemplate such a move for fear of encouraging inflation at home. According to the German constitution, the prime duty of the Bundesbank is to monitor domestic monetary policy. Thus it was required by law to put the need for low German inflation before the travails of the ERM.

As pressure mounted, EU finance ministers met to find a solution. The answer was to widen the currency bands for all except the D-Mark and the Dutch guilder to 15 per cent. The bands were so wide that although the ERM survived in name, the currencies were effectively floating. With the new bands a currency could theoretically devalue by 30 per cent (from its ceiling to its floor) against another member without falling out of the system. That has been the system of the ERM since then.

The ERM and the ecu

The state of the European Monetary System is published in grid form on the front page of Monday's *Financial Times* (see Figure 14.1).

- **EMS grid:** the member currencies of the ERM measured against the weakest currency in the system. The currencies are in descending order of relative strength. Most of the currencies can fluctuate within 15 per cent of agreed central rates against the other members of the mechanism. The exceptions are the D-Mark and the guilder, which move in a narrow 2.25 per cent band.

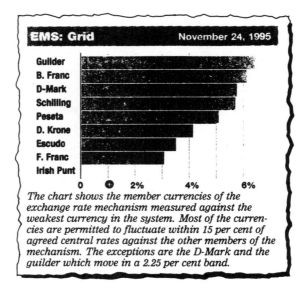

Fig. 14.1 EMS grid

The daily Currencies and Money page of the newspaper includes a further table of figures for the European Monetary System, particularly in relation to the European currency unit or ecu (see Figure 14.2). The value of the ecu is calculated as a weighted average of a basket of specified amounts of EU currencies. The ecu is not the single currency, which will be called the euro.

EMS EUROPEAN CURRENCY UNIT RATES

Nov 14	Ecu cen. rates	Rate against Ecu	Change on day	% +/- from cen. rate	% spread v weakest	Div. ind.
Netherlands	2.15214	2.10036	+0.00326	−2.41	6.81	18
Belgium	39.3960	38.5507	+0.0507	−2.15	6.52	16
Germany	1.91007	1.87539	+0.00262	−1.82	6.16	18
Austria	13.4383	13.1970	+0.019	−1.80	6.14	13
Spain	162.493	161.380	−0.222	−0.68	4.95	5
Denmark	7.28580	7.26865	+0.00588	−0.24	4.48	2
Portugal	195.792	197.016	−0.188	0.63	3.59	−4
France	6.40608	6.46498	−0.01038	0.92	3.29	−8
Ireland	0.792214	0.825771	−0.000491	4.24	0.00	−29
NON ERM MEMBERS						
Greece	292.867	309.925	−0.387	5.82	−1.50	−
Italy	2106.15	2108.24	−12.09	0.10	4.13	−
UK	0.786652	0.848240	+0.000418	7.83	−3.33	−

Fig. 14.2 EMS European currency unit rates

- **Ecu central rates:** the basic rates of national currencies against the ecu around which they may fluctuate. These rates are set by the European Commission. As with the EMS grid, the currencies are in descending order of relative strength.

- **Rate against ecu and change on day:** the current market rates of the national currencies against the ecu, and the changes in those rates from the day's starting rates.

- **Percentage deviation from the central rate:** percentages by which the current market rates are above or below the central rates. The percentage differences are for the ecu against the national currencies: a positive difference indicates that the currency has weakened against the ecu.

- **Percentage spread over the weakest currencies:** percentages by which currencies are spread against the weakest currency in the system, numerical equivalents of the graphic display of the EMS grid.

- **Divergence index:** ratios between two spreads, the percentage deviation of actual market rates from ecu central rates, and the maximum permitted percentage deviation of currencies' market rates from their ecu central rates. This is an indicator of how close to their new permitted floors currencies have fallen. In this example, since the Dutch and German currencies are tied closer together than the rest, their divergence indices are the same.

- **Non-ERM members:** the Italian and UK currencies have still not sought re-entry to the ERM and the Greek currency has never been involved as yet, but for the purpose of tracking convergence between all countries of the EU, the newspaper calculates their currency rates against the ecu.

PROSPECTS FOR ECONOMIC AND MONETARY UNION

Following the upheavals of the ERM, plans to introduce a single currency in Europe by 1999 at the latest, as agreed at Maastricht, look somewhat optimistic. It was after all agreed that EMU would only be possible after participating countries had achieved a broadly similar economic performance. It was anticipated that the discipline of the former version of the ERM would help European economies to converge but, without it, countries are freer to pursue their own monetary and fiscal policies.

For EMU to take place, convergence is required in a number of key areas, including interest rates, which should be at broadly similar levels across countries; and inflation, which should be at comparably low and sustainable levels. With a system of irrevocably fixed exchange rates, or a single currency, persistent differences in inflation could lead to certain countries experiencing significant competitiveness problems and, as a result, serious employment losses.

Government deficits and national debts are also an important feature of convergence: high fiscal deficits and/or high public debt as a proportion of GDP would have to be avoided by all member states, both to counter inflation and to guard against the emergence of excessive real interest rates for the EU as a whole.

During the 1980s while the ERM was in place, EU inflation rates converged to a large extent. Big divergences remain, however, in the spheres of fiscal balances and unemployment. There is considerable scepticism about the EU's abilities to bring the different economies into line by the end of the decade. Figure 14.3 illustrates the contrasting economic performance of the United Kingdom, Germany and France.

Alongside the process of "deepening" the Union (not only through EMU, but also through plans for political union as well as the social dimension of Europe) is one of "widening", extending the membership to other countries in Europe. The EU currently has fifteen members, with the most recent countries to join being Austria, Finland and Sweden. Poland, Hungary, Slovakia and the Czech Republic are all keen to join in the not too distant future. Some EU governments, notably that of the United Kingdom, believe enlargement of the EU should be given priority over rapid moves towards economic and monetary union.

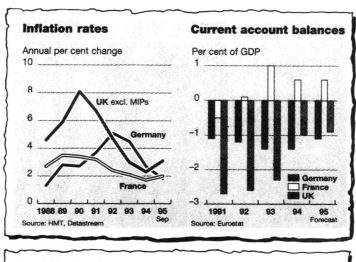

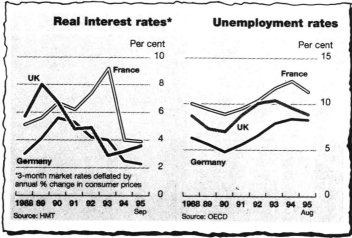

Fig. 14.3 Economic performance (UK, Germany and France)

"No nation was ever ruined by trade."

BENJAMIN FRANKLIN

"When your neighbour loses his job, it's a slowdown; when you lose your job, it's a recession; when an economist loses his job, it's a depression."

ANON

15

THE WORLD ECONOMY
Trade, growth and international institutions

- **The world economy** – the main regional groupings: North America, the European Union, and east Asia; and the rest of the world

- **Global economic institutions** – the key international forums: the IMF; World Bank; G7; OECD; and EBRD

- **Economic growth and development** – export orientation, sequencing, aid and debt; migration, the environment and economic transition

- **International trade** – comparative advantage and the gains from trade; trade liberalisation and the Uruguay Round; the role of exchange rates and international finance

Business and investment decisions are increasingly made in an international context. Global flows of goods, services and capital are making national economies more and more interdependent, and this trend appears unlikely to be reversed. First, there seems to be a consensus on the positive effects of liberal trade policies whereby barriers to trade between nations are reduced and removed. Second, national product markets are increasingly dominated by powerful multinational corporations, companies that cut across national boundaries and are eager to produce and sell their output wherever they can do so profitably. And third, as the second part of this book discussed, there are the international financial markets (for debt and equity capital, for cash and currencies, and for commodities and derivative products), in which borrowers seek the cheapest funds available, and investors and speculators chase the highest possible returns.

Economic globalisation is having increasingly important effects on national economies, on local financial markets and on individual companies. In making business and investment decisions, it is no longer advisable simply to take account of the domestic economy, either with regard to particular markets or at the aggregate level. Even if a business tends to rely on domestic suppliers or sell primarily to the home market, or if investors restrict their portfolios to the local exchanges, it is still useful to consider international trade and financial flows, and economic developments elsewhere in the world. These can affect any business, adding an international dimension to economic considerations.

Alongside the process of globalisation are the processes of market integration and regionalisation, pursued by national governments. The countries of western Europe are well advanced on the path to integrating their trade and currencies, as well as coordinating their economic policies, and many other regions of the world are following their example. These processes too interact with the business of exporting and importing, with running a business more generally, and with national and international asset markets. It is valuable to

understand them and their coverage in the *Financial Times* in order to make more informed business and investment decisions.

THE WORLD ECONOMY

The world economy breaks down into a number of key regional or other economic groupings based on standards of living, levels of output and trade, and historical or geographical connection. The three most powerful blocs are North America (the United States and its partners in the North American Free Trade Agreement or NAFTA, Canada and Mexico), the fifteen member states of the European Union (EU) and east Asia centred on Japan. While the United States remains the world's dominant economy, representing a quarter of global output and a third of the industrialised countries' output, the other two blocs are certainly threatening its position. This post-communist balance is sometimes described as the tripolar world.

Japan and the NAFTA and EU countries, plus seven other industrialised countries, primarily located in western Europe, form the Organisation for Economic Cooperation and Development (OECD), the "rich countries' club". The leading countries of the OECD (the United States, Japan, Germany, France, Italy, the United Kingdom and Canada) make up the Group of Seven (G7), which as a whole accounts for two-thirds of world output. Then there are the "newly industrialised countries" (NICs) of south-east Asia, the mainly Middle Eastern nations of the Organisation of Petroleum Exporting Countries (OPEC), the ex-communist countries of eastern Europe and the former Soviet Union, and the developing countries of Latin America, Africa and the rest of the world.

1973 is often seen as the turning point of the post-war period, marking the end of the high growth, low inflation, full employment, and fixed exchange rate years, and the beginning of the more uncertain times since. The problems of the latter period were launched by the floating of the dollar and the consequent chaos in the international financial markets; and by the oil crises, when the price of oil quadrupled within the space of three months.

The collapse of communism at the end of the 1980s was expected to usher in a new era of prosperity for the 1990s, but so far this decade global growth has proved disappointing. For example, unemployment in the twenty-six industrialised nations of the OECD has jumped from less than 25 million in 1990 to nearly 35 million today.

The good news on the global scene is that Latin America appears to be resolving its economic problems after a decade of low growth and falling living standards, triggered by the Mexican debt crisis of 1982. The dynamic economies of south-east Asia continue to notch up more growth this decade although at a slower pace than in the boom years of the 1980s.

Meanwhile, the countries of eastern Europe are finding that the struggle to make the transition from a command economy to a market economy is far more difficult than expected. Worse still is the position of the former Soviet Union: Russia's economic reform efforts have run into ever greater problems, while the disintegration of the Comecon trading bloc has greatly increased the adjustment problems of all the former communist states. Africa continues to lag economically behind the rest of the globe.

Although economic statistics from outside the United Kingdom are reported by the *Financial Times* on a less systematic basis than the UK figures, a broad range of figures are published throughout the year. For the world, the most regular and reliable statistics are collated by the IMF in its monthly publication *International Financial Statistics* and its annual *World Economic Outlook*. Another useful source of statistical information is the OECD, in particular its annual country reports and the twice yearly *Economic Outlook*.

On Tuesday, the newspaper includes a table of international economic indicators comparing key variables for the six main economies of the OECD: the United Kingdom, the United States, Japan, Germany, France and Italy. In rotation, these cover monthly figures for Production and Employment, Prices and Competitiveness (see Figure 13.8 in chapter 13), Money and Finance, and Balance of Payments (see Figure 15.2), plus a quarterly presentation of figures for National Accounts (see Figure 13.1 in chapter 13). For countries outside the OECD, especially in Latin America, Africa and Asia, the most detailed economic coverage, in addition to IMF statistics, is

often the FT special survey of the country, published once a year. Figure 15.1 features an example, the key facts on South Africa.

KEY FACTS

Area .... 1,221,037 sq km
Population .... 41.24m (1995 estimate)
Head of state ....President Nelson Mandela
Currency .... Rand (R)
Average exchange rates . 1994 $1=R3.549; 13/11/95 $1=R3.635
.................................1994 £1=R5.442; 13/11/95 £1=R5.669

ECONOMY

	1994	1995[1]
Total GDP ($bn)	121.9	133.3
Real GDP growth (%)	2.3	3.0
GDP per capita ($)	3,004	3,217
Components of GDP (%)		
Private consumption	57.7	
Total investment	19.7	
Government consumption	20.8	n.a.
Exports	27.5	
Imports	−25.8	
Consumer prices (% pa)	9.0	10.2
Real ind. output (% pa)	1.3	2.9
Reserves minus gold ($bn)	1.7	1.7
3 month TB rate (%)	11.0	13.8
Long bond yield (%)	14.7	14.9
FT-A index (% change over year)	+19.7	−0.2
Current account balance ($bn)	−0.6	−1.6
Exports ($bn)	25.1	26.2
Imports ($bn)	21.4	23.5
Trade balance ($bn)	3.7	2.7
Export volume of goods (% pa)	0.8	4.0
Import volume of goods (% pa)	15.2	12.0
Total foreign debt ($bn)	27.9	n.a.
Main trading partners (1994 %)	Exports	Imports
US	4.9	16.2
Japan	4.6	10.2
Asia excluding Japan	9.8	10.2
Africa	9.5	2.8
EU	21.2	46.7

[1] = EIU estimates for 1995 except reserves (end-September), interest rates (end-October), stock market (% change from 31/12/94 to 13/11/95)

Source: Department of Finance, Economist Intelligence Unit, IMF, Datastream

Fig. 15.1 Key facts (South Africa)

GLOBAL ECONOMIC INSTITUTIONS

A number of international forums exist to discuss global economic issues, and the newspaper reports on most of their activities. The main ones are:

- **The International Monetary Fund:** set up by the Bretton Woods agreement of 1944 and coming into operation in March 1947, this institution was established to encourage international cooperation on monetary issues. The aim of the Fund is to tide members over temporary balance of payments difficulties. It does this by making hard currency loans to members while trying to enforce structural adjustment of their economies. The Fund has more than 140 members who pay subscriptions according to the size of their economies. They pay 75 per cent of the quota in their own currency and 25 per cent in international reserve assets. Members are then given borrowing rights with the Fund, which they can use to help finance a balance of payments deficit. Countries in difficulty can also negotiate standby credit on which they can draw as necessary. Members are required to repay their drawings over a three to five year period.

- **The World Bank:** established at the same time as the IMF, and originally intended to finance Europe's post-war reconstruction, this institution has subsequently concentrated on loans to poor countries to become one of the largest single sources of development aid. The Bank has traditionally supported a wide range of long-term investments, including infrastructure projects such as roads, telecommunications and electricity supply. Its funds come mainly from the industrialised nations, but it also raises money on international capital markets. The Bank operates according to business principles, lending at commercial rates of interest only to those governments it feels are capable of servicing and repaying their debts.

- **Group of Seven (G7):** a grouping that dates back to 1975 when the French president, Valéry Giscard d'Estaing, invited the leaders of the United States, West Germany, Japan and the United Kingdom to discuss economic problems following the first oil price shock. Since then, the summits have grown to include political and foreign

issues which form the subject of a political declaration issued on the penultimate day of talks. The sixth and seventh members are Italy and Canada. Since the disintegration of the Soviet Union, Russia has also participated in many of the discussions.

- **Organisation for Economic Cooperation and Development:** sometimes referred to as the rich countries' club, this organisation's membership consists of the twenty-six industrialised nations of the world (the Czech Republic being the most recent new member) with a secretariat based in Paris. It too goes back to the end of the war when it was set up to organise Europe's recovery. It is now more of a think-tank to discuss economic issues of mutual interest, but it is a particularly valuable source of publications. Its annual surveys of the member countries and twice yearly *Economic Outlook* provide a useful overview of prospects for the industrialised world.

- **European Bank for Reconstruction and Development (EBRD):** a development bank set up in 1990 to help the countries of eastern Europe develop market economies. An EU initiative, it resembles existing multinational regional development banks, such as the African Development Bank, and was the first institution specifically designed to coordinate western economic help for eastern Europe in the wake of the collapse of their communist regimes. EU states and institutions have a 53.7 per cent stake; most other European countries are also shareholders and the United States has the biggest single stake of 10 per cent. Japan's 8.5 per cent shareholding matches those of the United Kingdom, Germany, France and Italy.

ECONOMIC GROWTH AND DEVELOPMENT

All countries pursue economic growth, an increase in their output of goods and services, and in their incomes to purchase those goods and services as well as those produced abroad. For countries outside the industrialised world, this is generally termed development. Numerous different policies have been tried since the war to achieve this goal, but nowadays, it is typically pursued through a combination of encouraging production of goods for export, attracting

foreign direct investment, borrowing from banks and international institutions, aid from overseas, macroeconomic stabilisation policy, and market liberalisation. Much debate centres on the appropriate "sequencing" of economic policies for development, meaning which ones should come first.

The economies of south-east Asia have been the most successful at development, becoming the "newly industrialised countries", or NICs. Much of that success may have resulted from high export orientation as measured by exports as a proportion of GDP, what is known as export-led growth. Many of the countries of eastern Europe, Latin America, Africa, and elsewhere in Asia (notably India and China), are eager to follow the progress of the NICs, and, as a consequence, it is important for the markets of the developed world to be open to their products.

Part of such development can be funded by foreign aid: in 1992, for example, the rich industrial countries gave $60 billion in aid to poor countries, 0.33 per cent of their total GDP. Two-thirds was in the form of bilateral grants and loans, as opposed to contributions to multilateral institutions. An average of 28 per cent is tied to the purchase of goods and services from donor countries. This kind of aid is less beneficial to poor countries since it forces recipients to pay higher prices for imports, encourages them to invest in vast capital projects, and does little for the relief of poverty, one of the most pressing problems of the developing world.

Another notable problem for developing countries has been the debt crisis, when numerous governments defaulted on their loans from western banks. Until early 1995, this had eased considerably since the late 1980s when Latin American countries particularly had very high debt service ratios, the proportion of export revenues taken up by debt repayment. It was re-ignited at that point when Mexico was plunged into a deep financial crisis with implications for the rest of the continent and other emerging markets.

The World Bank discerns five major development challenges for the future. These are the promotion of economic reforms likely to help the poor, perhaps in contrast to the inequitable "structural adjustment" (somewhat extreme free market) programmes of the past; increased investment in people, particularly through education, health care and family planning; protection of the environment; stim-

ulation of private sector development; and public sector reform that provides the conditions in which private enterprise might flourish.

Migration, the environment and economic transition

Alongside the long standing issues of economic development in the "third world" are the more recent development problems of the formerly planned economies of eastern Europe and the ex-Soviet Union. The transition of these countries to democratic market economies has thrown up many new questions about the appropriate sequencing of economic policies and the extent to which market reforms (including price liberalisation, trade liberalisation, privatisation, establishment of capital markets and the institution of a legal and regulatory framework) should be implemented suddenly as "shock therapy". There is also concern in the traditional developing world about the diversion of industrialised nations' attention, aid, trade preferences and capital.

A major issue in both developing and ex-communist countries is the environment, and whether the goals of expanded trade and development, and protection and preservation of the environment, are compatible. For example, should developing countries adopt less strict regulations on pollution by "dirty" industries than the developed world in order to attract investment by firms in those industries? At the heart of this debate is the concept of "sustainable development", whether there are policies that promote both economic growth and an improved environment. This is a highly contentious issue: many developing countries ask why environmental concerns should hinder their progress when the industrialised countries had ignored such concerns in their own development.

Another issue high on the international agenda is also very contentious, that of migration. Flows of goods, services and capital are well covered by the institutions of global capitalism, but there is little policy on the treatment of international flows of people. Indeed, there is much hypocrisy among believers in the free market system, demanding "free markets, free trade and free enterprise", but at the same time, strict immigration controls. If trade and finance can flow freely, why not labour, some ask. Such considerations have stressed the importance of free trade and foreign investment to discourage mass migration: by investing directly in the poorer parts of the world and

providing open markets to their products, the industrialised countries will not experience so much migratory pressure from those places.

INTERNATIONAL TRADE

International trade is a central driving force of global economic growth and development, and the general trend since the war has been for it to increase. Today, the United States is the biggest exporter at 12.6 per cent of world exports, while Germany and Japan are neck and neck for second place. The trade figures for these and three other leading European countries (France, Italy and the United Kingdom) are published monthly in the *Financial Times* (see Figure 15.2).

- **Exports:** the level of exports of merchandise (that is, trade in physical goods, not services) in billions of ecus.

- **Visible trade balance:** the difference between the value of merchandise exports and imports in billions of ecus. The value of imports can be derived by subtracting the visible trade balance from exports.

- **Current account balance:** the balance of trade in goods and services in billions of ecus.

- **Ecu exchange rate:** the number of national currency units per ecu.

- **Effective exchange rate:** a nominal average exchange rate against a trade-weighted basket of currencies presented as an index based on 1985=100 (in fact, period averages of the Bank of England trade-weighted indices discussed in chapter 10). Effective exchange rates do not take account of differential rates of inflation, and are therefore not a useful guide to national competitiveness. They are, though, a valuable way of expressing the equivalent of a currency's movements against all other key currencies in one figure.

The interaction of national economies through international trade increases world output by allowing countries to specialise in the production of those goods and services which they can produce most efficiently. Countries could cut themselves off from the rest of the

INTERNATIONAL ECONOMIC INDICATORS: BALANCE OF PAYMENTS

Trade figures are given in billions of European currency units (Ecu). The Ecu exchange rate shows the number of national currency units per Ecu. The nominal effective exchange rate is an index with 1985=100.

	UNITED STATES					JAPAN					GERMANY				
	Exports	Visible trade balance	Current account balance	Ecu exchange rate	Effective exchange rate	Exports	Visible trade balance	Current account balance	Ecu exchange rate	Effective exchange rate	Exports	Visible trade balance	Current account balance	Ecu exchange rate	Effective exchange rate
1985	279.8	−174.2	−163.0	0.7623	100.0	228.2	73.5	64.5	180.50	100.0	242.7	33.2	22.5	2.2260	100.0
1986	231.0	−140.6	−153.4	0.9836	81.4	208.9	94.2	87.2	165.11	127.7	248.5	53.5	41.3	2.1279	108.6
1987	220.2	−131.8	−144.1	1.1541	71.9	194.7	83.7	75.5	166.58	138.8	254.4	56.7	40.0	2.0710	114.9
1988	272.5	−100.2	−107.4	1.1833	67.0	218.7	79.8	67.0	151.51	153.7	272.6	61.4	41.9	2.0739	114.1
1989	330.2	−99.3	−94.3	1.1017	70.0	245.5	70.6	53.4	151.87	147.0	310.1	65.2	52.0	2.0681	113.3
1990	309.0	−79.3	−72.7	1.2745	66.7	220.0	50.0	28.5	183.94	132.5	324.3	51.7	38.5	2.0537	118.1
1991	340.5	−53.5	−6.0	1.2391	65.7	247.6	83.3	62.4	166.44	143.7	327.3	11.0	−15.6	2.0480	117.1
1992	345.9	−65.2	−47.5	1.2957	64.4	254.8	102.1	90.4	164.05	150.7	330.5	16.6	−16.7	2.0187	120.6
1993	397.3	−98.7	−85.4	1.1705	66.3	300.0	120.8	111.1	130.31	181.0	323.0	31.4	−13.4	1.9337	125.3
1994	432.3	−127.0	−127.6	1.1857	65.1	323.5	122.5	108.8	120.99	194.9	358.8	37.9	−17.4	1.9198	125.6
4th qtr.1994	110.8	−32.3	−35.1	1.2346	63.3	81.1	28.5	24.4	122.03	197.6	93.2	9.3	−4.4	1.9056	127.3
1st qtr.1995	111.4	−32.6	−30.9	1.2619	62.7	81.9	28.2	23.4	121.16	202.1	94.4	11.8	−2.0	1.8645	131.1
2nd qtr.1995	110.1	−33.1	−33.1	1.3175	59.0	87.5	29.4	23.6	111.31	225.3	98.9*	12.6	−1.4	1.8402	133.4
3rd qtr.1995					61.0					203.7					131.7
October 1994	35.3	−10.9	n.a.	1.2544	62.6	25.7	8.4	7.2	123.44	197.1	30.7	3.4	−2.9	1.9072	127.3
November	36.6	−11.5	n.a.	1.2369	63.0	27.5	10.2	8.6	121.21	199.1	31.0	3.9	0.6	1.9044	127.3
December	38.9	−9.9	n.a.	1.2126	64.4	27.9	9.9	8.6	121.44	196.6	31.5	2.0	−2.1	1.9054	127.3
January 1995	36.8	−12.0	n.a.	1.2374	64.0	25.8	8.7	7.8	123.32	196.1	30.8	5.0	−0.4	1.8929	128.7
February	37.2	−10.7	n.a.	1.2455	63.3	28.7	9.8	8.4	122.27	198.1	32.0	3.8	−1.5	1.8698	130.0
March	37.4	−9.9	n.a.	1.3029	60.8	27.4	9.7	7.2	117.89	211.3	31.6	2.9	−0.1	1.8308	134.4
April	36.0	−11.1	n.a.	1.3279	58.7	29.0	8.8	6.2	111.24	226.8	32.9	4.6	−0.9	1.8320	134.5
May	37.6	−10.8	n.a.	1.3055	59.1	29.1	10.0	8.1	111.17	224.4	32.1	4.1	−0.1	1.8420	132.9
June	36.6	−11.2	n.a.	1.3192	59.0	29.4	10.5	9.3	111.51	225.1	34.0	3.9	−0.5	1.8465	132.7
July	35.1	−11.7	n.a.	1.3335	59.2	26.8	7.9	7.2	116.38	217.2				1.8511	133.0
August				1.2954	61.3				122.52	202.6				1.8705	131.1
September					62.5					191.6					131.1

**Fig. 15.2 International economic indicators: Balance of payments
(US, Japan and Germany)**

world, and seek to provide for all their needs domestically. However, if, for example, their industries are particularly good at making high quality, low cost computers, and not so efficient at growing rice, it makes sense to focus their energies on the manufacture of computers, and, in effect, trade them for rice with other countries. Even if those other countries are not more efficient at rice-growing, but agriculture is still their most effective industry, specialisation in production followed by free trade should still be beneficial to all parties.

It is generally accepted that specialisation (to some degree) and free trade allow all countries to develop more rapidly, and expand global output and incomes. However, there are many obstacles to their working out in practice. These arise from the interests of particular groups within countries (including managers, investors and employees), and play out in governments' trade and commercial policies, in recurrent trade disputes between countries and trading blocs, and in the great debate between free trade and protectionism.

A number of arguments for protection are advanced. For example, companies in declining or internationally uncompetitive industries sometimes demand protection in order to avoid going out of business. Their managers might argue for the "national interest", the importance of producing their goods domestically, the unemployment their failure would cause (here they would be backed by their workforce), and the "cheating" strategies their foreign competitors adopt.

Similarly, firms in "infant industries" (often new, high technology, sectors) might claim they need protection because they are as yet too young, small and weak to compete effectively at the international level. Governments themselves might pursue strategic protection of industries they believe it might be dangerous for foreigners to control.

The trade policies of the EU, for example, are the outcome of three conflicting compulsions: the liberal commitment to the idea of free trade, as reflected in multiple global trading initiatives; the protectionist desire to shield some domestic producers from foreign suppliers; and what is known as a "pyramid of preferences" which ranks various trading partners, often on the basis of historical connection. The protectionist element of these policies has predominantly been directed at manufactured imports from other industrialised countries, but, increasingly, they also affect goods produced by competitive suppliers in less developed countries.

Trade liberalisation and the Uruguay Round

The growth of international trade is frequently hampered by barriers erected to keep out imports and protect domestic industries. These might take the form of tariffs, quotas, duties, limits, "voluntary export restraints" and a host of other schemes. Since the end of the war, big advances have been made in reducing these barriers to the free flow of goods and services, but there is still a long way to go. The world recession of the early 1990s threatened a renewed bout of protectionism as countries looked inwards to deal with their own problems.

The main forum for addressing trade issues was the General Agreement on Tariffs and Trade (GATT), a multinational institution set up in 1947 to promote the expansion of international trade through a coordinated programme of trade liberalisation. The GATT's primary two-pronged approach was to eliminate quotas and reduce tariffs. It supervised several conferences (or "rounds") on tariff reductions and the removal of other barriers to trade, and, in late 1993, brought to completion the Uruguay Round of trade discussions. Part of the final agreement was that it should become the World Trade Organisation.

The Uruguay Round (1986–93) was an attempt by the international community to renegotiate the world trading system. With the participation of over one hundred countries, it aimed both to repair the old GATT and to extend it to many new areas: it was the first negotiating round in which developing countries pledged themselves to substantive obligations; it was the first application of liberal trading principles to the services sector, foreign direct investment, and intellectual property rights; and it re-integrated into the GATT system two important sectors, textiles and agriculture.

The success of the Uruguay Round centres on, among other things, an enormous cut in tariffs. This, coupled with more transparent and orderly trading rules, should give a powerful boost to the world economy, stimulating competition and offering developing countries new opportunities for integration into international markets. The accords of the Final Act, agreed on 15 December 1993, came into force in 1995 following ratification by all member countries.

The Uruguay Round introduced a series of institutional innovations to back up the new rules: a semi-judicial dispute settlement

system, a trade policy review mechanism and the new World Trade Organisation. The principal change is that the old GATT has lapsed: the new system as it results from the Final Act of the Uruguay Round is a very different and legally distinct institution. It should create a considerably more stable and more open framework for international trade relations.

Alongside the process of trade liberalisation across the globe is that of market integration. This process typically begins with a free trade agreement, an arrangement between countries (usually in the same geographical region of the world) to eliminate all trade barriers between themselves on goods and services, but in which each continues to operate its own particular barriers against trade with the rest of the world. It may develop into a customs union or common market where arrangements for trade with the rest of the world are harmonised, subsequently into a single market like the EU, and perhaps on to full economic and monetary union.

A number of regional free trade agreements exist, most notably the NAFTA and the Association of South East Asian Nations (ASEAN), which includes Brunei, Indonesia, Malaysia, the Philippines, Singapore, Thailand and Vietnam. Such initial efforts at market integration are spreading rapidly, including, for example, the Mercosur in Latin America incorporating Brazil, Argentina, Uruguay and Paraguay. At least one hundred such groupings had been formed by the end of 1995.

Exchange rates and international finance

The cross border exchange of goods and services is made possible by the fact that it is possible to convert one national currency into another. Thus, a UK company wishing to buy a US product (priced naturally in the local currency, dollars) can make the transaction by buying dollars with its pounds. The price it pays for those dollars in sterling is the exchange rate, and the markets on which it buys them are the international currency markets.

When these markets are allowed to work freely, with the price of currencies in terms of other currencies fluctuating according to demand and supply, it is known as a floating exchange rate system. That, for example, is the kind of system currently in place between

the dollar and the yen. The opposite is to have rates set by governments with occasional devaluations and revaluations, a fixed rate system, such as the one that operated in the post-war world up to 1973. In practice, systems are typically somewhere in between, with rates allowed to fluctuate to some extent, but managed by national monetary authorities.

As well as providing the means for companies and countries to conduct trade across borders, exchange rates also allow various forms of international investment and speculation. Broadly characterised, there are three types: first, there is speculation by owners of large quantities of "hot money", constantly moving their funds around the world in pursuit of the best return, and going in and out of money market accounts in response to minuscule shifts in relative interest rates. "Hot money" flows in and out of countries in response to the pursuit of short-term gain and without any considerations of longer term issues of economic development of product markets or national economies. It moves simply on the basis of movements or expected movements of exchange rates and relative interest rates.

Second, there is portfolio investment in international asset markets by investors. This flow of cross border financial investment is growing substantially as investors place larger portions of their portfolios in international equities and bonds. As with all portfolio investment, this might be short- or long-term investment, depending on the goals of the investors, immediate profit or longer term financial goals. It is reflected particularly in the increasing enthusiasm for the emerging markets (see chapter 7).

Third, there is international capital investment by companies, seeking low cost production facilities and/or access to new markets, and by governments and financial institutions. In the case of the private sector, this is called foreign direct investment (FDI); from governments, it might be in the form of loans, or conditional or unconditional aid. Such investment might also come from major global organisations such as the World Bank. Given the difficulties of planning such investments, they typically have long-term ambitions in mind.

Part IV

BEYOND THE FINANCIAL PAGES

"I am a better investor because I am a businessman, and a better businessman because I am an investor."

WARREN BUFFETT

"Because there is so much noise in the world, people adopt rules of thumb."

FISCHER BLACK

16

COMPANY AND INVESTOR LIVES
The key performance ratios

by Ken Langdon

- **Key financial ratios** – what to look for in annual reports: gearing; income gearing; return on capital employed; and pre-tax profit margin

- **Key shareholder ratios** – what to look for in the financial pages: yield; price/earnings ratio; and dividend cover

- **The life of a growth stock** – four stages in the history of a telecommunications company: the annual report; and changes in the key financial and shareholder ratios

Any person in business has two, three or at most four financial ratios by which he or she measures performance. These ratios are very specific to each individual. The head of a consultancy will be concerned with the ratio of days billed to days available. A sales manager will be worried about orders taken to date as a proportion of the budget or target for that period of time. And a self-employed one-man company in the building trade will probably focus simply on what money is owed to him, what money he owes to his suppliers, what his bank balance is, and the amount and timing of his next tax bill. These financial ratios are by no means the only indicators of the health of a business, but they are chosen by their owners because of their crucial importance to achieving success.

Investors are never in the position of a manager in a business of knowing intimately how it is doing, but there are some ratios available which allow them to make well informed assessments. Two of the most crucial ratios are reported daily in the *Financial Times* (**dividend yield** and the **price/earnings ratio**), and a third on a weekly basis: **dividend cover**, which is published in the London share service in Monday's newspaper.

The next source of information available to investors is the company's annual report. This offers some consistency of key indicators since they are regulated by law and accountancy standards. Using these, investors can make relevant comparisons of one company with another, particularly if the companies are in the same industry sector. Company reports are notorious for what they hide as well as what they reveal. It is possible, at least in the short term, for creative accountants and their board room employers to produce figures that more accurately reflect their aspirations for the company rather than its actual performance. However, this does tend to disappear with time: as the business continues to perform in a certain way, so the accountants will eventually force the board to be more frank with the shareholders.

Despite this caveat, the annual report does give some very useful information. For the small private investor, generally the most usable of these ratios are **return on capital employed, gearing, income gearing**

(or interest cover) and **pre-tax profit margin**. Armed with these seven ratios, investors are in a better position to make decisions. The problem is that for many private investors this is too time consuming and they either take decisions based on less information than this, or trust their money to the professionals who charge royally for the privilege.

This chapter endeavours to describe a quick method of getting to these figures, and then, by the example of a company going through a thirty year life cycle, to show how the mix of investor or shareholder ratios and the company's key financial or management ratios paint a picture of the health and prospects of potential investments. If investors add a judicious reading of the chairman's statement to discover the board's intentions for the future, they are as well prepared as is possible without becoming a full time company watcher.

KEY FINANCIAL RATIOS

The four company ratios provide an effective check on progress and are reasonably easy to calculate. They should always be done for the two years in the report so that changes over time are reflected. The chairman's statements can then be checked to see if they comment on changes which an investor may regard as significant. Frequently, the report will include "Facts for Shareholders" or "Five year Record", which include some calculated ratios. The advantage of these is that they remove the need to do any extrapolation or calculation. Unfortunately, there are two disadvantages that make them much less useful. The first is that the published ratios are calculated in a way that suits each company: they will tend to use figures that are not misleading or inaccurate, but which give a gloss on performance that the truly objective investor wishes to avoid.

The second problem is connected: since companies use ratios which suit themselves, they do not use the same ones. So, for the sake of consistency, it is better for an investor to become very familiar with four ratios and to work them out for him or herself. An investor can also build a personal database of examples, offering various benchmarks for examining and comparing any company. This is particularly true if studying only one or a limited number of business sectors.

The rules of thumb quoted below are useful to an investor as he or she learns to appreciate the significance of the ratios. They are only guides, however, and as the company history below suggests, their significance varies depending on the business the company is in and the stage of its life cycle it has reached.

Gearing

Gearing (or balance sheet gearing, as it is often called to distinguish it from other forms of gearing) compares the amount of money in shareholders' funds with the amount of external liabilities which the company has. High gearing is more risky than low gearing, but could mean that the company is pushing hard for expansion and needs high levels of debt to finance that growth. It is possible to calculate gearing in a number of ways, but one of the easiest is also one of the harshest measures of a company's exposure to the perils of high levels of debt and creditor dependence.

The ratio is a comparison between the total debt liabilities of a company with its shareholders' funds. The higher the ratio, the more likely it is that debt will become a burden. The more debt, the more interest, the lower the profits and therefore the worse the potential for paying dividends.

The calculation is as follows: find the current liabilities in the annual report, often called "liabilities: amounts falling due within one year". Add "creditors: amounts falling due after more than one year", ensuring that everything is included, to find total debt liabilities. Find the figure for total shareholders' funds, but do not include minority interests. Divide total debt liabilities by total shareholders' funds and multiply by 100 to arrive at a percentage figure. The figures for Eurotunnel in 1994 provide a good example of a highly geared company: its gearing was 466 per cent and getting worse:

Eurotunrel in £'000

Provisions 141
Current and long-term debt liabilities..8,113,322
Total debt liabilities 8,113,463
Total shareholders' funds 1,739,833

> **Gearing ratio rule of thumb**
>
> **Low gearing** ....below 100 per cent
> **Medium gearing** ....100–200 per cent
> **High gearing** ....above 200 per cent

Income gearing

The total debt liabilities to shareholders' funds ratio has the limitation that it includes all current liabilities as well as all debt. It is often valuable therefore to have another ratio which indicates the company's ability to service its debt. Income gearing (and its reciprocal, interest cover – see chapter 2) provides this information. It is the ratio of interest payable to the profits out of which interest is paid. It takes a little more calculation than the other ratios, but has the merit of being impossible to fudge. Many investors regard it as the key gearing ratio.

To calculate income gearing: find the interest payable for the year, often a detail in the notes. The figure on the balance sheet is "net interest", which is interest payable minus interest receivable, not the figure needed here. Find the earnings, or profit, before interest and tax. Often this must be calculated by adding interest payable to the pre-tax profit shown on the profit and loss account. Divide interest payable by profit before interest and tax and multiply by 100 to express it as a percentage. As an example, in 1994, British Telecom's income gearing by this calculation was 12.4 per cent, reflecting its low level of debt.

British Telecom in £ million

Interest payable 389
Profit before tax 2,756
Profit before interest and tax ... 3,145

> **Income gearing ratio rule of thumb**
>
> **Low income gearing** ....below 25 per cent
> **Medium income gearing** ....26–75 per cent
> **High income gearing** ....above 75 per cent

Return on capital employed

This measure is a key indicator of managerial performance, relating pre-tax profit to the long-term capital invested in the business. It is a good guide as to whether sufficient return is being generated to maintain and grow dividends and avoid problems of liquidity. Unfortunately, it is prone to being misrepresented: there are a number of areas where boards can make this simple measure lead an investor away from the company's problems rather than towards them. Nevertheless, over time it does reveal what is necessary to know about the health of a company measured by profits. Many investors regard it as the key profitability ratio.

To calculate ROCE: capital employed is equivalent to total assets minus current liabilities and this figure is often given on the balance sheet. If not, calculate it as long-term debt, plus provisions for liabilities and charges, plus any other long-term liabilities, plus shareholders' funds, plus minority interests. Divide pre-tax profit by capital employed and multiply by 100 to express it as a percentage. As examples, in 1994, Hewlett Packard's profitability by this calculation was 21.37 per cent, while Land Securities' was 4.79 per cent. It should be noted that for relevant comparisons, it is best to use companies in the same business.

Hewlett Packard in $ million

Earnings before taxes 2,423
Long-term debt 547
Other long-term liabilities 864
Shareholders' funds 9,926
Capital employed....................... 11,337

Land Securities in £ million

Profit on ordinary activities before tax ...245
Total assets minus current liabilities.....5,120

> **Return on capital employed rule of thumb**
>
> **Low profitability** ....below 10 per cent
> **Medium profitability** ....10–20 per cent
> **High profitability** ....above 20 per cent

Pre-tax profit margin

This indicator reveals the profits earned per pound of sales and therefore measures the efficiency of the operation. This ratio is an indicator of the company's ability to withstand adverse conditions such as falling prices, rising costs or declining sales.

To calculate pre-tax profit margin: take the pre-tax profit figure on the profit and loss account. Divide it by the total sales revenues often known in UK reports as "Sales turnover" and multiply by 100 for a percentage. As examples, in 1995, Seeboard's pre-tax margin was 11.88 per cent and Pilkington's 5.38 per cent. Again, for relevant comparisons, it is best to use companies in the same business.

Seeboard in £ million

Profit on ordinary activities before taxation ... 142
Turnover 1,195

Pilkington in £ million

Profit on ordinary activities before taxation ... 144
Turnover 2,676

Pre-tax profit margin rule of thumb

Low margin ....below 2 per cent
Medium margin ....4–8 per cent
High margin ....above 8 per cent

KEY SHAREHOLDER RATIOS

Chapter 5 explains the following indicators of company and share performance and where they can be found in the *Financial Times* listings of share price information. The following is a brief refresher before examining how these ratios, along with the financial ratios explored above, may change over the life of a company.

Yield

This is the percentage return on investment that a shareholder receives in dividend compared to the current share price. It is listed daily in the newspaper, along with the average for all the industry sectors. Generally, investors looking for income will pick shares with an above average yield. However, long-term investors will also look for yield, particularly when they are investing in a tax efficient way as for example with a PEP. Here the tax advantage magnifies the growth available in a high yielding share.

Price/earnings ratio

Also known as the multiple, the p/e ratio reflects the market's valuation of a company expressed as a multiple of past earnings (profits). It is listed daily in the newspaper, along with the average for all the industry sectors. Investors looking for capital growth will look for shares which have a high p/e. If the market has made a correct prediction, an investor in such a share should expect to see growth of sales and profits in the company.

Dividend cover

This ratio of the profits to gross dividends is another useful indicator for investors. Many private investors recognise the long-term benefits of a growing income stream from dividends. If they are investing for the long term, therefore, they may very well look for shares that are out of favour with the market and which, as a result, have a high yield. It is quite likely that the capital growth of such a share may be very limited in the short or even medium term. But this slow growth at the early stage is less important if the dividend payments are worth having.

The problem arises where a high yielding share has insufficient profits to continue to increase or even maintain its dividend. The chances of its being able to keep the payments up are indicated by the number of times the dividend is covered by the profits.

THE LIFE OF A GROWTH STOCK

There is no such thing as a typical company. Their different products, markets and management styles make each enterprise unique. It is possible, however, to use the following example as a benchmark of the characteristics and ratios of a company over a long period of time. For each of the four stages, there is an indication of the kind of information the annual report may provide, and the likely financial and shareholder ratios.

Stage One: inception to ten years old

Turn back the clock to the time when telecommunications was in its meteoric growth phase. The imaginary sample company, Phoneco, was created by a flotation from its parent where it had been a non-core business. The newly floated company in the early stages has the ability to generate very rapid growth of sales. The market is eager for the new service and sales are there for the taking for any company that can lay down a telecommunications network.

Phoneco is very aggressive at this stage. It needs volume to cover its voracious appetite for cash as it invests millions of pounds in infrastructure. This makes its competitiveness very sharp. To a considerable extent, it will sacrifice profit for market share. It hires a salesforce of "hunters", salespeople who enjoy the challenge of getting new business quickly. These salespeople are good at closing business and handling objections. If they do not close business fast, they go elsewhere. It is to be expected that there is high morale in the company as the business and consumer markets flock to the upstart.

The annual report

The chairman's statement will reflect this growth. Extracts may include such comments as the following: "May saw another milestone when the new connections rate for residential customers signing up with Phoneco reached 30,000 per month"; and "our sales growth last year exceeded 50 per cent, and although this is likely to prove exceptional, Phoneco is confident of its ability to take further

advantage of the expanding market over the next few years." The report's tone will reflect the excitement and enthusiasm of the fledgling, which is discovering success for the first time.

The financial ratios

The board is running Phoneco by its cash flows rather than by its profit and loss account. It needs huge amounts of cash for capital investment and will probably have very high levels of borrowing. This high gearing will show itself in both of the gearing ratios, with a high percentage of debt and very little profit left over once interest is deducted. Profitability will be relatively low measured by both return on capital employed and the profit margin.

Phoneco's financial ratios at Stage One:

Gearing......................500 per cent
Income gearing..........95 per cent
ROCE...........................1 per cent
Pre-tax profit margin...1 per cent

The shareholder ratios

Investors will find that the market only sees Phoneco as long-term potential, resting in the high risk part of their portfolios. It is undesirable for the company to pay large amounts in dividend, since it needs all its cash to fund its expansion. Hence, the yield will be low. The p/e will be very high as the market calculates future profit streams for the company as it gets into a position to exploit its assets. The dividend cover may very well be high, not because the profits are huge but because the dividend is low.

Phoneco's shareholder ratios at Stage One

Yield..0.3
Price/earnings 35
Dividend cover 13

Stage Two: ten to twenty years old

Phoneco has come of age. It has survived the heady days of 30 per cent year on year growth and shown itself to be competitive. The company is

now well into the FT-SE 250 list of companies. It has a viable market share in the areas where it already operates and is looking for new opportunities to make further investment either in new markets, such as overseas, or in new product areas, such as telephone equipment.

This diversified growth will still cost a great deal of money, but the business now generates a healthy cash flow and is profitable. There is still a fair amount of risk in the company. It is vulnerable to making mistakes as it moves into new activities. No matter how good the prospects, it is always more risky to take old products into new markets or new products into old markets than to keep doing more of the same.

The annual report

The chairman's statement may now see more talk of consolidation of the company's current affairs, although the emphasis of the report will still be on growth, and possibly on new initiatives. Extracts from the statement for a Stage Two company may include such remarks as "our earnings per share before exceptional items grew by 22 per cent"; and "our strengthening financial position allows us to explore new areas seeking basic telephone services, while at the same time consolidating our strategy to focus on those parts of the world where we are already strong and where our returns will be the greatest'.

The financial ratios

The debt ratios are still high. Almost certainly by this time, Phoneco will have been back to its investors for more cash through a rights issue. This, of course, radically reduces the debt to equity ratio, but it will rise again to reflect continued investment. Profitability has improved to what could be described as fairly safe levels. This means that the current business will produce reliable profits, and it is only in the new areas of activity that there is still high risk.

Phoneco's financial ratios at Stage Two

Gearing.......................200 per cent
Income gearing ....75 per cent
ROCE............................10 per cent
Pre-tax profit margin......4 per cent

The shareholder ratios

Phoneco wants to pay out some dividend of real worth. It probably had to make promises in this area when it made its cash call and it sees dividend as a sign of impending "respectability". Nevertheless, the yield is still well below the sector average, as the price of the share is buoyed by the market's expectation of further growth. The p/e is also still very high. It is probably less than other new entrants in Stage One of their life cycles, but it will be well above the industry average. The dividend is stretching cover much more than in the first phase. Investors are starting to ask when the return to their money will start to come through, and there is no room for the very high dividend cover of the earlier stage.

Phoneco's shareholder ratios at Stage Two

Yield......................................1.6
Price/earnings 25
Dividend cover....................3.5

Stage Three: twenty to thirty years old

The company has achieved respectability. It is now at the bottom end of the FT-SE 100 companies. It is a complex company and the analysts are looking for good statements of strategy, which prove that the current management can run a cruiser, having been very successful in managing fast patrol boats and destroyers. The company's share price will vary with the changes in the industry. A bad regulatory change, for example, could endanger profit growth significantly. Long-term planning is no longer a luxury, but a vital responsibility of the board and its advisers.

The company will have some "big names" on its board with the possibility of an ex-cabinet minister amongst its numbers. Risk has changed in its nature. The company could now afford to make some mistakes without threatening its actual life. The market sees the risk as comparative with other stocks in the sector. Investors will see reports of sell-offs of one share in the sector and swaps into other companies in the same sector being recommended.

The annual report

It is unlikely that the annual report will claim that everything is rosy. Shareholders expect more circumspect statements with admissions of error and promises of remedy. A careful look at the ratios on which the chairman reports can be revealing. For example, if he produces a graph showing that the past twenty-five years of share price appreciation has consistently outperformed the market index, he is probably trying to reassure the market that there is still plenty of growth potential there. He does not want the growth in share price to stall, although it will certainly have slowed.

Like the professionals, the private investor should look for a confident statement of comprehensive and long-term goals and strategies. Extracts from the chairman's statement for a Stage Three company may say: "we see alliances with other companies as an important contributor to our vision to be the supplier of choice for people seeking high levels of features combined with international coverage"; "new technologies offer enormous opportunities to broaden the services available to our current customers. The convergence of voice, music, graphics, video and data will radically alter the way we conduct our lives"; and "the reorganisation, which we completed during the year, has ensured that we can carry through our promises of presenting a global image and relationship with our key accounts worldwide.'

The financial ratios

The ratios have now reached the mature end of industry averages. Gearing is at the low risk end and less than a third of profits are required to pay the interest bill. The measure of return on capital employed is as meaningful and reliable as any other large company's, and reflects the kind of return expected from the whole sector as opposed to the rapid growth part of the sector. The relatively high pre-tax profit margin shows the built-in profitability of the telecommunications sector, which can exploit its expensive investments in infrastructure for many, many years.

Phoneco's financial ratios at Stage Three

Gearing.........................100 per cent
Income gearing ....30 per cent
ROCE.............................20 per cent
Pre-tax profit margin......8 per cent

The shareholder ratios

The dividend is an important part of large investors' portfolio plans. The yield will therefore tend to be around the average for the sector and even for the whole market. The p/e is similarly near the average for the sector. The dividend cover has gone sharply down as investors start to make the returns they were expecting at this stage in Phoneco's life cycle.

Phoneco's shareholder ratios at Stage Three

Yield 4.0
Price/earnings...............................18
Dividend cover 1.9

Stage Four: over thirty years old

The board is now commanding a battleship or a stately galleon. Shareholders have stopped looking for excitement in the share and want long-term promises on dividends and the delivery of these promises. The company is in the top twenty of the FT-SE 100 and has a high profile chairman and non-executive directors. The chairman will be frequently heard on the television and radio talking about the company's performance, the economic situation, the regulatory environment and other current affairs.

Representatives of the company now have a lot of power over standards bodies and supplier policies. Someone from Phoneco will be one of the panel in any debate with a telecommunications context from virtual reality shopping to home working. The sales force now comprises more "farmers' than 'hunters". The company has well founded key account management techniques in place to develop and protect market share.

The chairman will probably be found complaining about the view that the stock market takes of Phoneco's shares. The company likes to think it is a growth and innovation enterprise, while the market sees it as primarily a utility, with limited opportunities for the sort of growth which will make a significant difference to its profit stream.

The annual report

The chairman's statement will include an emphasis on benefits to customers. The company takes very seriously its dominant place in a number of markets, and is anxious to show that it is not exploiting this. Phoneco will boast of new offerings to its customers, lower prices and generally better service. Extracts from the chairman's statement for a Stage Four company may include: "steady growth of sales at 4 per cent and earnings at 5.5 per cent demonstrate our progress towards meeting the expectations of both our shareholders and our customers"; and "against this economic and competitive background, Phoneco's strategy remains clear. We will develop vigorously in our traditional markets and at the same time establish ourselves in new markets for advanced services both in our traditional and new parts of the world".

The financial ratios

The ratios are all safer than the industry average and are at the top end of the benchmark. There is no question in the short term that the company can maintain its market and profit growth, limited though that is. Investors will be wary for any signs of decline. Regulations and new competitors represent the biggest risk. Phoneco has already shown good control of costs, but this needs to be a continuing phenomenon and reflected in the profit margin.

Phoneco's financial ratios at Stage Four

Gearing..........................60 per cent
Income gearing ....20 per cent
ROCE..............................25 per cent
Pre-tax profit margin....10 per cent

The shareholder ratios

The share is now in almost all pension and private portfolios. The expectation is for dividend progress rather than capital growth, and the yield and dividend cover show it. The yield is well above the average and cover is at a low level. Dividend cover probably wants to stay around here except if there is an exceptional item affecting profits. The p/e is the sign of the stately galleon.

> **Phoneco's shareholder ratios at Stage Four**
>
> **Yield** 5.9
> **Price/earnings** 13.8
> **Dividend cover** 1.5

Ken Langdon is a contributor to *The Financial Times Handbook of Management*, and works with businesses and investors to improve understanding of financial information. For further details, contact (01628) 782193.

"The new sound of finance is the machine-gun clatter of fingers on a keyboard."

SAUL HANSELL,

INSTITUTIONAL INVESTOR, 1989

"The arrival of a global free market and the new information technologies drive away power and authority from the institutions that ran the old world."

ANDREW MARR, *RULING BRITANNIA*

17

FINANCE ON THE SUPERHIGHWAY
Electronic information and markets

- **Reading the electronic pages** – using online financial information: Reuters, Bloomberg, Dow Jones Telerate and FT Extel

- **The electronic marketplace** – threats to the London Stock Exchange: continental European exchanges; electronic exchanges; EASDAQ; Tradepoint

- **Dealing with the internet** – financial uses for the new technology: Electronic Share Information; financial information on the net; "umbrella" sites, markets and financial services

The *Financial Times* provides a globally used reference point for financial data, but the newspaper medium obviously has the limitation of only being published once a day. For readers needing to supplement the newspaper's overview of the news and markets with more sophisticated real-time data, there are other media, notably the computer. The growing versatility of computers, their increased power, larger memories, faster modems and interconnectedness all mean that the options for accessing information on financial markets have never been greater than they are today. A brief introduction to a variety of electronic markets and information sources is the subject of this chapter.

READING THE ELECTRONIC PAGES

The electronic counterpart of the financial pages of a newspaper are provided by such information product suppliers as Reuters, Bloomberg, Dow Jones Telerate and FT Extel. These companies deliver news services, markets reports and price quotations to customer screens in most financial institutions. They provide constant real-time datafeeds on currencies, stocks, bonds, futures, options and other instruments across a range of countries and markets. The services also provide software to analyse the data, graphical displays and asset price analysis, allowing the user to retrieve historic news and price quotations.

Some of these companies also offer transaction products which enable traders to deal from their keyboards. Reuters, for example, have an equity trading mechanism called Instinet which allows traders to negotiate deals directly but anonymously via a computerised "bulletin board" where traders place their bids and offers of shares, and deals are matched automatically. The company also operates the Globex after hours trading system for futures and options on behalf of the Chicago Mercantile Exchange and the MATIF.

Indeed, Reuters provides a very complete financial information service and is probably the dominant player in Europe and outside North America. Its coverage of equity and foreign exchange markets is particularly good. Meanwhile, Dow Jones Telerate offers high quality data on fixed income securities, and FT Extel, through its acquisition of Interactive Data in the United States, also now has one of the most complete databases on fixed income securities, covering most sectors of the US domestic and international bond market.

The relatively recent entry of Bloomberg into the market for electronic financial information has encouraged a great expansion in what these services offer. Rather than just providing share and bond prices, Bloomberg's software made it possible to manipulate information, for example, comparing the characteristics of different bonds or testing an investment's performance under different projections, Such products are now commonplace. FT Extel, for example, offers "Company Analysis", a software product for analysing financial statement information.

Electronic sources of financial information have been around for some time, but never has the market been so competitive, the quality of what is provided so high nor the range of products so varied. For market participants, the difficult decision is over how to make the trade-off between data quality and cost. Most of the databases are essential tools of investing for professionals dealing in equities and other instruments. The needs of the individual investor, unless a very active trader with an extremely large personal portfolio probably run to something less complete and less expensive.

Using online financial information

As an example of how to make sense of the electronic pages, Reuters screens for equities provide a good introduction. One of the system's big advantages is that a single screen can be divided into smaller windows, enabling the user to view several pieces of information simultaneously. The following three figures, however, focus on one window at a time to give the reader a clear view of the kind of information that is available. Figure 17.1, for example, provides basic price information on the FT-SE 100 companies, similar to the trading volume table on the back page of the *Financial Times*.

```
                              Reuters: Quotes :.FTS3
Function . Edit  Screens  Format  View  Setup  Help

.DJI   ↓5173.84   +14.45        GBP=X 1.5205      GBPDEM=X 2.2119      14:36
                                                                      REUTER
.FTS3    FT-SE 100   ↑3645.1  +5.9      at 14:35        H3645.4   L3618.2
Up 38      Down 51     Unchanged 11                SEAQ Vol 415.9m  at 14:35
 ABF   725  -2*  BT   352½ +6½* GUS  667  +35  PSON 661 +16* SEL  933    -2*
 ALLD  496  +4   BTR  322  +1½* HNSN 191½ +4½  PWG  526  -1* SHEL 829½  +0½*
 ANL   627  -7*  CBRY 547  +6*  HSBA 1001 +10  RBOS 569  .+3 SN   192   +0½
 ASSD 103¼  -0¼  CCM  982 -19*  ICI  744   -7  RCOL 660 -10* SPW  369     0*
 AWA   163  +4½  CKSN 312   0*  III  424   -1* RDLD 373  +9  STAN 564    -2*
 AYL   309  -2   CTLD 383½ +3½  INCH 202   -9  REED 982 -17* SUN  380    -7*
 BA    795  -5   CUAC 638   0*  KGF  510   +2  REX  330   0  SVT  668     0
 BAA   485  +1*  CW   441  -3*  LADB 155    0  RMC  997 -17  TATE 466    +9
 BARC  776   0   DLAR 684 +32*  LAND 604    0  RNK  414  -1  THN  1592   -4
 BASS  719  +7   ETP  359  -5   LGEN 672   -6* ROYL 384  +3  TI   435    -5
 BATS  552  -5*  FTE  338   0*  LLOY 882   -6  RR   175  +3  TOMK 261    -2
 BAY   469  +2*  GAA  635 -10*  LON  891   +2* RTO  329  +6  TSB  411½  -1½
 BCI   331  +1   GACC 655 -15   LSMR 167   -1  RTR  607  -6  TSCO 289    -1*
 BMAH  934 -26   GARD 270  -5   MEB  979   +4* RTZ  936  -7* TW   559    -1
 BOC  896½ +13½* GAS  228½ -0½  MKS  439   +3  SBa  696  -7  ULVR 1329  +24*
 BOOT  580  +3   GEC  315  +1*  NPR  460    0* SBRY 371   0  VOD  221½  +4½
 BP   527½ +0½   GKN  799  -9   NWB  662   -2* SCTN 598  -3  WLMS 325    +2*
 BS    166 -1½*  GLXO 889½ +3½* NWW  588   -1  SDR  1330 -5  WLY  440     0*
 BSCT  274  -4*  GMET 448  +2   PO   476   -2* SEAR 96½  -1  WTB  651    -8
 BSY   421 +19   GUIN 454  +2   PRU  435   -5* SEBE 765  -3  ZEN 1299½ -16½
```

Fig. 17.1 Electronic FT-SE 100 price information

The top line of the screen gives the current time and data on three other indicators: the level of the Dow Jones Industrial Average and its movement so far today, and the exchange rate of sterling against the dollar and the D-Mark. The next line gives the level of the FT-SE 100 index, its movement so far today and its high and low for the day. The arrow by the side of the Dow and Footsie indicate whether their last moves were up or down. The third line indicates how many of the FT-SE 100 company share prices are up, down and unchanged for the day, plus the total volume of FT-SE 100 shares traded. The remainder of the screen lists the current middle prices for the one hundred companies and the day's price change so far. Each stock is known by a code: BT, for example, is British Telecom, GUIN is Guinness and PSON is Pearson.

Figure 17.2 shows a screen that goes into greater depth on a company's price information, in some ways similar to the information carried in the FT London share service. Here, the top line gives the stock code, the full name of the company and the market on which it trades

```
BT.L         BRITISH TELECOM   00140843 LSE GBp NMS75000       /    /       11DEC95 10:11
Last         Bid           Ask           Mid+2         Mid Close     Volume       Sector
↓350         350           352           351           349           1444669      O#.FTTN
 350         Open          High          Low           Rtr.News      N.Time       Headlines
 352         349           353           349                         :            BTY1
 350         LT:08DEC95    Yr.High       Yr.Low        High.Jan87    Low.Jan87
 350         349           421⅛          334.75
Div:12FEB96  Yield         Ex.Date       P.E           Earnings      Background
17.70        6.34 %        27DEC95       12.55         27.80         BT.LB1
```

Fig. 17.2 Electronic share price information

(LSE is the London Stock Exchange). The next two lines give the price at which the stock traded, the current bid, ask and middle prices, the closing price on the previous day and the volume of shares traded. The next four lines give the price at which the stock opened today and its high and low for the day and for the year. The last two lines show the net dividend for the year and the date on which the latest installment of it will be paid; and the gross dividend yield, the date the stock went ex-dividend, the price/earnings ratio, earnings per share and the code for getting the company's most recent accounts (see Figure 17.3).

```
                                           Reuters: Quotes: BT.LB2
Function  Edit  Screens  Format  View  Setup  Help
|
BRITISH TELECOM <BT.L>       News [BT.L]      LSE Back <BT.LB1>                      BT.LB2
AUDITED PROFIT/LOSS  (GBP) 31MAR95    31MAR94    31MAR93    31MAR92    31MAR91
Turnover                    13893m     13675m     13242m     13337m     13154m
Operating Result             2693m      3015m      2449m      3415m      3531m
Pre-Tax Profit/Loss          2662m      2756m      1972m      3073m      3075m
Net Attributable             1731m      1767m      1220m      2044m      2080m
BALANCE SHEET
Fixed Assets                17092m     16896m     16471m     16445m     16119m
Current Assets               4367m      5669m      4763m      5037m      4412m
Cash                          138m        60m        51m       175m       127m
Total Assets                21459m     22565m     21234m     21482m     20531m
Current Liabilities          5090m      5544m      4441m      5187m      4797m
Long-Term Debt               3361m      3199m      3386m      3768m      4468m
Total Liabilities            9330m      9444m      8944m      9620m      9867m
Shareholders Equity         11997m     13026m     12218m     11754m     10572m
Preferred Stock                  0          0          0          0          0
Minority Interests            132m        95m        72m       108m        92m
Description      (22MAY94):The supply of telecommunication services and
equipment. In the year, 98% of Group turnover arose from operations in the
United Kingdom.
```

Fig. 17.3 Electronic company accounts

Figure 17.2 shows the kind of shareholder ratios covered by the newspaper but which electronically are available real-time. Figure 17.3 goes to the kind of information for which there is no room in a newspaper and which can only otherwise be obtained by reference to company annual reports as discussed in the last chapter. From these data on the company's profit and loss account and balance sheet over five years, the key financial ratios of pre-tax profit margin, return on capital employed (ROCE), gearing and income gearing can be calculated. A second screen is available that breaks down the profit and loss account into half year statements and adds figures for such ratios as dividend cover, ROCE and gearing. Other individual company screens include a rolling list of news headlines that relate to the company, and a rolling list of the spreads offered by marketmakers and the last prices and volumes at which they traded.

THE ELECTRONIC MARKETPLACE

Since the dramatic changes of Big Bang in 1986 (see chapter 3), the London Stock Exchange has relied heavily on a computer screen-based information and dealing system. Marketmakers and dealers operate from trading floors in their own offices, feeding details of the prices at which they are prepared to trade into a computerised system called SEAQ (Stock Exchange Automated Quotation). This was originally designed to be a price information system, but it evolved into an automated dealing system. Dealers use the SEAQ screen to assess who is offering the best price, and telephone the marketmaker to arrange the deal. They can also deal in international equities through SEAQ International, which quotes prices for shares in any company listed on an exchange approved by London.

For many years, London has dominated cross border share trading through the SEAQ International system, but the growing muscle of its rival European exchanges is raising questions about whether it can remain the centre of international share trading. London's competitive advantage was that it offered greater liquidity and lower costs for traders. But increasingly its rivals are modernising their trading and

settlement systems to allow low cost trading, and local firms are becoming more willing to invest capital in buying and selling for their own account, raising exchange turnover and liquidity. The migration of equity trading to such places as Paris and Frankfurt is currently not reflected in international dealing figures, which record that 90 per cent of all European cross border trades go through SEAQ International, but that is simply a result of regulations demanding that all deals are recorded on the system whether they take place there or not.

An example of the growing challenge to London's dominance of the European equity markets is a plan by the French and German equity and derivatives markets to build a joint trading system. The aim is to create a "double" platform, a common computerised network through which European equities, bonds and derivatives can all be traded via a single screen. Another challenge came in January 1996 with the "coming into force" of the European Union's (EU) Investment Services directive, which allows securities firms in member states to apply for remote membership of other EU exchanges without having to set up a local office. Firms can now execute their own trades without paying commission to a local broker, enabling them to offer more competitive prices.

There have been sporadic attempts over the years to create a Europe-wide stock exchange, pooling liquidity on a scale that matches the US markets. This looks like it may become a reality with the planned launch in 1996 of EASDAQ (European Association of Securities Dealers Automated Quotation), a market based on the huge US electronic market NASDAQ and planned for location in Brussels. Like NASDAQ, the aim is to attract young fast growing companies with international ambitions, and not simply to act as a nursery for other markets. In this way, it could become serious competition, first for the new junior London market, the Alternative Investment Market (AIM), but subsequently for the main market itself.

Tradepoint

Competition with the London Stock Exchange is not confined to continental Europe. In September 1995, the first direct local rival to the stock exchange in its two hundred year history opened for business.

Known as Tradepoint, this electronic exchange aims to offer a cheap and "user-friendly" alternative to the stock exchange's marketmakers. It provides trading facilities in shares of the 400 largest UK companies by market capitalisation, allowing investors to deal directly and anonymously via their personal computers linked into a central computer that automatically matches the buy and sell orders it receives.

A key factor behind the launch of Tradepoint is that the London exchange is one of the last major markets to have a quote-driven dealing system, based on marketmakers quoting guaranteed bid and offer prices at which they are willing to deal with prospective traders. In order-driven systems like Tradepoint, anonymous buyers and sellers are matched, considerably reducing the dealing costs implied by the spread between marketmakers' bid and offer prices.

Anyone linked into Tradepoint's central data system can enter the number of shares they want to buy or sell and at what price. A computerised order book then aggregates all the bids and offers of a particular share, and puts them up on screen. The most liquid shares can be traded by "instant auction": a counterparty can accept a deal simply by clicking a mouse or making a keystroke. Less liquid shares will be traded in weekly "periodic auctions", when the computer will calculate the "balance price" for all accumulated bids and offers, the price at which the maximum number of shares can be traded. To help users respond quickly to market shocks, such as a change in interest rates, the system will enable them to withdraw all outstanding bids and offers with a single keystroke.

An important feature of Tradepoint is that users are assured of anonymity even with their trading counterparties. This is crucial because it ensures that competitors of those trading cannot get access to commercially sensitive information. Deals are cleared through the London Clearing House which clears trades for a number of exchanges including the LIFFE.

Tradepoint has been designated by the Securities and Investment Board (SIB) as a "recognised investment exchange", an equivalent status to the London Stock Exchange. At its launch, the market aimed to capture 2 per cent of turnover in UK shares within eighteen months, rising to 10 per cent within five years. It also plans to expand the list of traded securities to include shares in smaller companies, international equities and Eurobonds.

The London Stock Exchange

The new markets in London and Europe offer investors and companies a number of opportunities that the London Stock Exchange does not as yet provide, notably cheaper dealing in existing shares and access to companies that are not currently traded in London. To retain its dominance of European equity trading, the traditional market is fighting back on a number of fronts. Domestically, it has created the AIM to attract new firms, and it also runs the Stock Exchange Alternative Tracking Service (SEATS), an order-driven bulletin board for smaller or infrequently traded companies. Internationally, it is trying to coax emerging markets to list their shares in London, especially in the form of Global Depositary Receipts, tradeable certificates representing overseas equity listed on another exchange.

There is also considerable talk of launching a new electronic market for trading in the companies of the FT-SE-A 350. This would be a hybrid market, mixing features of the order- and quote-driven systems (even in the most liquid stocks) via the new Sequence trading platform. This replacement for SEAQ and SEAQ International is planned for launch in August 1996. It will compete directly with Tradepoint, and may be particularly popular with marketmakers and investment banks who want an order-driven system that is used exclusively by intermediaries, and not, like Tradepoint, accessible to institutional investors as well.

Company listings and providing a trading platform are two key roles for the exchange, and regulation is a third. Its settlement role, though, is expected to disappear. Currently, the system for transferring stock and money between buyers and sellers involves the considerable paperwork of share registration, certificate delivery, and the like. The exchange had been developing an electronic alternative called Taurus, but this failed, and electronic transfer of stocks and shares will now be implemented with the launch of a system called CREST, developed under the aegis of the Bank of England.

DEALING WITH THE INTERNET

Revolutionary changes in the constellation of the world's stock exchanges are important for many companies, institutional investors

and financial intermediaries, but the growth of computing power will have far more wide-reaching effects. Computers are bridging the divide between the large investing institutions, traditionally close to the markets, and individual investors, previously far from the action and at a considerable disadvantage. The primary force behind this development is the internet, the global network linking personal computers around the world. As a result of reaching a critical mass of public awareness in the mid-1990s and the evolution of the highly accessible and "multimedia" World Wide Web, the internet has become a major new means of communication, with a range of important implications for the financial markets.

Via the internet, a personal computer and modem offer relatively easy access to real-time prices and the ability to chart them with historical prices. They also provide the opportunity to research background information on companies, market and economies; to give trading orders directly, with the advantages of speed and savings on telephone charges; and to integrate all of these into a personal finance and/or portfolio management software package.

The United Kingdom's first share trading services on the internet were launched in the autumn of 1995 with a joint venture between discount stockbrokers ShareLink and Cambridge-based technology company Electronic Share Information (ESI). The latter provides online share information in the form of UK stock market prices updated six times a day, as well as real-time FT-SE 100 data and historic price information which can be printed off or displayed in charts; the former offers share dealing over the internet linked to the ESI service. A similar service, carried over a private network in order to protect traders' security, is provided by Infotrade. Both companies require investors to set up an account with the broker before dealing and allow no direct access to that account via the internet.

ESI is not an equity market, but it is bidding to launch one by the end of 1996 to compete with the London Stock Exchange and Tradepoint. The company is applying to the SIB to become a third recognised investment exchange, one which would offer dealing in shares of large companies already quoted on the London market, but which would also enable smaller companies, such as computer and biotechnology businesses, to raise finance and have a market where their

shares can be traded. By providing a lower cost route to going public than established exchanges, the ESI market would be in direct competition with the AIM. But in providing facilities for individual investors to buy and sell directly at only minimal brokerage costs, it would be a valuable new service. Neither the London exchange nor Tradepoint are accessible to small investors.

Financial information on the net

To access financial information over the internet, the place to start is with a commercial service provider. For broadly based news and information, the individual investor may wish to start with CompuServe, which contains a wealth of information and is relatively inexpensive. Prodigy and Dow Jones News Retrieval Services are good alternatives in the United States. There is a range of services providing real-time price information on US stocks, such as Quote.Com, Interquote and Pawws. A limited service is provided free, such as individual quotes on shares, but there are charges for a more flexible service. Each site connects to brokers offering online dealing. A site at the US university MIT also provides useful information on US stock prices.

A number of stock exchanges are on the internet, including the American Exchange, the Madrid stock exchange, the Australian Stock Exchange and the Johannesburg Stock Exchange. Another site provides a list of the range of stock exchanges on the internet as well as share price information services. Other financial markets are covered by companies like Numa Financial Services, which provides extensive information on futures and options, including details of courses, conferences, software and calculators for pricing various derivatives. The LIFFE, the Chicago Mercantile Exchange, Chicago Board of Trade and the Singapore International Monetary Exchange (Simex) are also on the net, as is a site with foreign exchange rate details.

Brokers have a number of sites on the World Wide Web, but at present primarily for information only. They include the InvestNet service from brokers Cheviot Capital; Charles Stanley broking services; Fidelity Investments; and in the United States, ETrade and Lombard. There are no full banking services on the net as yet because of

concerns about security, but a directory of banking sites is provided by the Chartered Institute of Banking and another by Bank Web. The UK Treasury also has a site with information on the government budget and other ministerial statements.

Lastly, there are a variety of publications that have been launched on the internet, including the *Financial Times*. Begun in May 1995, this carries leading editorial stories from the newspaper, with an emphasis on international news, as well as stock market and trade indices from around the world. Others include the *Wall Street Journal*; the *Electronic Telegraph; The Economist*; and "umbrella" sites like MoneyWeb and MoneyWorld UK, which offer general information on UK personal finance. The latter, for example, includes up-to-date information on the best savings and mortgage rates, performance information on investment funds as well as a directory of services on the internet. topics; Conde Nast is also establishing a magazine with personal finance information.

Key internet addresses:

Umbrella sites:

Financial Times: www.ft.com
Wall Street Journal: update.wsj.com
Electronic Telegraph: www.telegraph.com.uk
The Economist: www.economist.com
MoneyWorld UK: www.moneyworld.co.uk
MoneyWeb: www.demon.co.uk/moneyweb
Conde Nast: www.condenast.co.uk
FinWeb: www.finweb.com
Reuters (at Yahoo): www.yahoo.com
Teleshare: www.ws.pipex.com/tis/teleshare/teleshr.htm

Markets:

Quote.Com: www.quote.com
Interquote: www.interquote.com
Pawws: pawws.com
MIT: www.ai.mit.edu/stocks.html
American Exchange: www.amex.com

Madrid stock exchange: www.bolsamadrid.es
Australian Stock Exchange: www.asx.com.au
Johannesburg Stock Exchange: africa.com/pages/jse/page1.htm
Other stock exchanges: www.wiso.gwdg.de/ifbg/stock1.html
LIFFE: www.liffe.com
Chicago Mercantile Exchange: www.cme.com
Chicago Board of Trade: www.cbt.com
Foreign exchange rates: gnn.com/gnn/wic/trav.10.html
Simex: www. simex.com.sg

Financial services:

Numa Financial Services: www.num.com
Investnet: mkn.co.uk/invest
Charles Stanley: www.charles-stanley.co.uk
Etrade: www.etrade.com/etrade/html/ethome.htm
Lombard: www.lombard.com
Fidelity Investments: www.fid-intl.com/uk
Chartered Institute of Banking: www.qmw.ac.uk/~cib/supersite.html
Bank Web: www.bank-web.com
Infotrade: www.infotrade.co.uk
Electronic Share Information: www.esi.co.uk
ShareLink: www.esi.co.uk/sharelink/home.html
UK Treasury: www.hm-treasury.gov.uk

(most addresses preceded by http://)

> **"** *You may not get rich by using all the available information, but you surely will get poor if you don't.* **"**
> **JACK TREYNOR**

> **"** *Under the current system, a stock isn't truly attractive until a number of large institutions have recognised its suitability and an equal number of respected Wall Street analysts have put it on the recommended list. With so many people waiting for others to make the first move, it's amazing that anything gets bought. If you invest like an institution, you are doomed to perform like one.* **"**
> **PETER LYNCH**

18

SOURCES OF INFORMATION
A brief guide

- **Information sources** – newspapers; magazines; reference books; radio and television; institutional advice; annual reports, newsletters, tip sheets and City publications

- **Using the information** – reading between the lines of company and market commentary: BAA and Vodaphone as examples in Lex

- **Reading the *Financial Times*** – a brief reiteration of where to find the key information

The *Financial Times* is essential reading for anyone involved or interested in money and the financial markets. But there are plenty of other sources of information: not just the electronic datafeeds and internet services discussed in the previous chapter, but a variety of newspapers, magazines, newsletters and other publications as well as broadcast media. An information consumer requires three skills to avoid being overwhelmed by the deluge of information available: an ability to select the best sources; a filter to focus only on relevant information; and an understanding of how to read between the lines of financial reporting and comment, and carefully to distinguish it from sales promotion by interested parties. This chapter aims to be a rough guide to what is available and how to go about reading it. It closes by returning to the *Financial Times* itself with a brief reiteration of how to find your way through the newspaper and get to the information you need.

INFORMATION SOURCES

The US equivalent of the *Financial Times* is the *Wall Street Journal* which is available in European and Asian editions, though their international coverage is to some degree at the expense of the extremely detailed coverage of the US markets carried by its regular edition. Other good newspaper sources of business and financial information for the United States include the *New York Times* and *Investor's Business Daily*. In the United Kingdom, there is good coverage of the local, European and international markets in all the quality daily and Sunday newspapers, but nowhere near the depth of financial market data or company news carried by the *Financial Times*.

The key magazines for the investor are, in the United Kingdom, *Investors' Chronicle*, and in the United States, *Barron's*. *The Economist* also provides excellent broad coverage of international business and finance. Other magazines that cover financial issues include the

UK personal finance publications, such as *Moneywise, Inside Money* and *Money Observer*; US business magazines, such as *Forbes, Fortune* and *Business Week*; magazines for financial intermediaries, such as *Money Management*; the international banking magazine, *The Banker*; *International Financing Review* for corporate financiers; and *Euromoney* for those involved in the Euromarkets.

There are numerous reference publications on the markets, which can supplement the real-time information available electronically and the news coverage and data of papers and magazines. Good UK examples include the *Stock Exchange Yearbook*, which provides detailed history and financial information on all securities listed on the London exchange; the *Hambro Company Guide* which also provides data on all fully listed companies; the *Estimate Directory* which contains individual UK brokers' forecasts and composite forecasts for around 1,500 companies from around 40 brokers; and FT Extel's *Handbook of Market Leaders*, which includes data on contract details, share prices, up to five years of financial information, activity analysis, and graphic share price analysis.

In the United Kingdom, radio and television offer a limited number of programmes covering financial and business issues apart from the daily news. The notable ones are the weekly Radio 4 programme *Money Box* with its wide ranging discussions of personal finance, and BBC 2's business forum, *The Money Programme*. However, both television data services, CEEFAX and Teletext, provide share and option prices updated four times daily plus financial market headlines; and FT Cityline and Teleshare offer telephone services with real-time share prices, updated constantly. The United States is far better served by its broadcast media; indeed, at least one mainstream channel, CNBC, is devoted to business and finance.

For further details on the United Kingdom market for financial information, Proshare, an organisation committed to encouraging wider share ownership, publishes a useful guide to information sources for the private investor.

Institutional advice

On top of the generally objective information and analysis provided by the press, there is a host of rather less disinterested material from

the major players in the markets. Company reports are of course the single most important source of information on individual companies, containing all financial information and official statements from the company for the last financial year. All shareholders receive a copy of the annual report as of right and non-shareholders can apply to the company secretary for a free copy. The *Financial Times* also offers a free company report service for a wide selection of companies: the relevant companies are indicated in the London share service. How to start analysing the information provided by annual reports is discussed in chapter 16 of this book.

A secondary source of information for investors comes from newsletters or, as they are sometimes more disparagingly known, tip sheets. There are newsletters for every occasion and every investment style, particularly in the United States where estimates of the number published range from 800 to several thousand. In the United Kingdom, there are significantly fewer, perhaps only 20 of any substance, which is partly a result of the extensive coverage of the markets in the national press. It is also perhaps partly due to fear of their writers using the format to push stocks for their own advantage, and certainly investors should be aware of possible lack of objectivity. They should also examine a newsletter's track record before following its advice automatically.

The attraction of newsletters is that they offer ideas, data, analysis and a point of view which are not going to duplicate regular sources. Most are small operations centred on one individual, their editor-adviser, and their whole purpose is for investors to find information which others may not have, and to learn about opportunities both to sell and buy stocks before the mainstream investment community. Essentially, there are three main types of newsletter: company specific tip sheets, providing recommendations on specific stocks; market related newsletters, which cover the markets themselves and often involve sophisticated technical analysis; and political and/or socio-economic newsletters which, rather than focusing on specific investment advice, offer alternative views and analysis of what is happening in the world and how events may shape markets. The *Hulbert Financial Digest*, published in the United States, offers an objective source for the performance analysis of investment advisory newsletters.

Other subjective sources of information are the publications of major brokers and investment houses. Many financial institutions offer information sheets and/or newsletters of some kind to their clients, and these are frequently driven by the need for sales. The UK regulatory bodies, for example, demand that when brokers and tip sheet writers publish investment recommendations they must be researched and be able to be substantiated, but it is best to be sceptical.

With brokers' advice, it is vital to remember that their primary interest is in transactions rather than their clients' portfolio performance. This creates a bias towards activity or "churning" of the account. There is an additional bias towards encouraging purchases rather than sales. One reason for this is that the former have more commission-generating power since everyone is a potential buyer. The dominance of buy over sell recommendations may also be more likely because analysts can be reluctant to express pessimistic opinions: for effective research on their chosen industry sector, they need open lines of communication with companies' management. The outcome of this bias to the positive is that they frequently overestimate stocks' potential success.

Lastly, it is worth remembering that there is an awkward paradox at the heart of any published investment advice. If the advice is obvious, the markets will have already taken it into account. If it is not obvious, but still correct, the markets will react to it instantaneously so that most advisers will have already acted. The best kind of investment advice, therefore, is often general, not specific, and it is about spotting trends rather than discrete events.

USING THE INFORMATION

Newspapers like the *Financial Times* pride themselves on dealing in fact rather than speculation, and on the accuracy, authority and objectivity of their information and analysis. But even their reporting and comment must be interpreted: while the highly regarded FT Lex column, for example, does not make investment recommendations as such, it is still necessary to try to understand the underlying view and its implications. The following examples from the column, coverage

of the mobile telecommunications business Vodaphone and of the British Airports Authority published in late 1995, may provide some indication of how to "read between the lines" of any writing about companies and markets. They also show the kind of performance ratios that are seen as important by leading commentators on the market. The reader may still want to look at other hard facts of company and share price performance.

Vodaphone

The sharp drop in Vodaphone's share price yesterday, despite a 12 per cent year-on-year increase in earnings, suggests that US investors have lost some of their enthusiasm for the stock. It is a timely reminder that Vodaphone is a high-risk investment.

Although the results themselves were respectable, Vodaphone makes no bones of the fact that demand growth in the UK market, from which it still makes more than 100 per cent of its profits, is slowing. It is far from certain that this Christmas is going to be as good as the last. And almost all Vodaphone's new UK customers are individuals – bad news because they cost as much as businesses to attract, but tend to use their telephones much less. It is not surprising that revenues per subscriber are down. Moreover, the full effects of competition have yet to be felt. Tariffs, for instance, have not yet been seriously cut.

The shares have fallen recently but are still on a forward price/earnings multiple of 26 – a huge premium to the market. Some of that is justified by growth prospects overseas. But the shares still look far from cheap.

BAA

BAA's share price has underperformed the market over the last year, and yesterday's strong set of interim results did nothing to reverse the trend. Some adjustment in the company's previous extravagant rating was probably inevitable. But investors should start to ask whether the fall has gone too far.

Except for a slight Gulf War hiccup, BAA's growth record since privatisation has been consistently impressive. Yesterday's results suggest this will be sustained. Despite competition from Eurotunnel and a bad summer for charter flights, the company is still expecting growth of 5–6 per cent in passenger numbers this year. And net retail income per passenger is still growing, by a comfortable 3.4 per cent against last year. There is no sign that the company's ability to increase profits at around 10 per cent a year has been checked.

As an investment, BAA has its attractions. It offers a way into the strong growth of the airline sector, without the volatility which price wars bring. And it has the security of a utility but low regulatory risks. The company does face a regulatory review next year, but since UK landing charges are among the lowest in

the world, the outcome of this is unlikely to be severe. In any case, less than a
third of business is subject to price regulation.

The shares are still trading at a price/earnings premium to the market, but this
has shrunk to around 10 per cent. Given the security of the company's UK business, not to mention its long-term prospects overseas, this looks cheap.

Reading between the lines

A significant proportion of press coverage is about the profits companies earn and their prospective future profits. In these cases, both
companies have just published results and while both sets have been
good, neither have had a positive impact on the share price. Indeed,
Vodaphone's has fallen in response to the profits announcement.
This is quite a common phenomenon: the expectation of positive
results prior to their announcement often leads to buying pressure in
advance. Then when the results are actually announced, there is what
the press call "profit-taking" as speculators cash in on the earlier
price rise, causing the price to fall. Vodaphone also seems to have suffered from the views of overseas investors on its degree of riskiness as
an investment, indicating the importance of the global equity market.

The comments on BAA's share price refer to its performance relative to the market, either the FT-SE 100 of which both it and
Vodaphone are constituents or the wider All-Share index. The implication is that the company was previously "rated" too highly and its
subsequent "re-rating" downwards has naturally led to underperfor-
mance. Commentators are always trying to spot whether a share will
be re-rated upwards or downwards, though there tends to be a bias in
favour of predicting movement upwards. In this case, the suggestion
is that the re-rating was appropriate but will not continue.

The second paragraph in each story focuses on the markets
in which the two companies operate, and on the industry-specific
indicators that should be added to the all-purpose financial ratios
(of profitability, yield, etc.) when assessing their performances.
With Vodaphone, number of subscribers and revenues per subscriber
are the key measures, and the implication is that the fall in the
latter is bad news. With BAA, passenger numbers and net retail
income per passenger are the equivalent indicators, similarly reflecting

the overall size of the customer base and how much income is generated per customer.

The current and future prospects for the two markets and the degree of competition these two companies face are also very important considerations. Vodaphone is seeing a decline in demand growth in its key home market as well as increasing competition, both negative forces. BAA, on the other hand, is experiencing continuing buoyant domestic demand despite competition and occasionally difficult market conditions (war and a hot UK summer!). Both pieces' final paragraphs indicate that success in overseas markets holds the key for the two companies, but it is clearly being suggested that the strength of their current market positions will be an important determinant of that.

The third paragraph of the BAA commentary places the company not only in the context of the airline subset of its market sector, transport, but also relative to the utility sector. It also briefly explores the potential impact of regulation on the company, a factor that could equally be applied to Vodaphone and the telecommunications sector. All of these issues contribute valuable information on the company's market position and future prospects.

The final paragraphs of both pieces return to share valuations, commenting on price/earnings ratios relative to the market. Both are "at a premium" to the market (the All-Share ratio was 16.36), but the views taken are completely the opposite. Vodaphone shares are seen as being at a huge premium and "far from cheap", suggesting that their price will or should fall, that these shares are overrated; while BAA shares are seen as being at a reasonable premium and looking "cheap", suggesting that their price will, or should, rise, that they are underrated. Both comments could be taken by investors as indicating that they should get in or out of these stocks.

Comments in widely read publications, like these two examples, can easily have an impact on the markets as investors follow their implicit advice to buy or sell. They can also be seen as forecasting future price movements. There is no doubt that good financial reporting has a reasonable track record at predicting price movements of individual stocks, though they certainly are unable to forecast turning points for the market as a whole. Similarly, economic forecasters can often be read for their thoughts on the speed with

which a given indicator will continue to move in one direction, though they rarely spot the key turning points of the business cycle when slump turns into recovery or boom into recession.

READING THE *FINANCIAL TIMES*

The Lex column, carried on the back page of the *Financial Times'* first section (with additional Lex comments sometimes to be found close to the relevant news in different editions) is often the first item readers turn to. Where else in the newspaper can a reader find the information he or she needs? The following is a brief overview.

The main news and equity price information on companies and markets is to be found in the second section of the newspaper on Tuesday to Friday (and in the first section on Saturday). The first few pages focus on UK company news (results, key personnel, financing arrangements, takeovers, etc.) followed by similar news for overseas companies. The back page reports on the London Stock Exchange with a full market report, comments on individual stock movements and tables of market information. Inside the back page comes the London share service, price and key ratio details for all stocks for which there is a reasonably liquid market.

Moving back through the newspaper, there is a collection of commentaries on other leading international stock markets, more data on London equities and a page of data for individual shares and indices from a range of world stock markets. This is preceded by five pages of the FT managed funds service, details on a variety of unit trust and other pooled investments.

Since the second section of Monday's newspaper has rather less financial market news from the previous couple of days, it provides more of a survey of what has happened the previous week and what to look forward to. The London share service, for example, includes some longer term data on the listed shares, as well as dialling instructions for real-time share prices from FT Cityline. There are also pages on the week's prospects for the equity markets, bond markets and emerging markets, and reflective pieces on economics, global investing and investing in emerging markets.

On Saturday, the format is also a little different. The first section carries the company news and equity market data plus a table of dealings in less liquid London shares. Its Weekend Money section carries the managed fund service plus a wealth of articles, tables and charts relating to issues of personal finance and investment: the previous week in the markets, saving and borrowing rates, investing for growth and for income, pensions, financial planning, PEPs, annuities, and the performance of unit trusts and investment trusts.

Markets other than the equity markets receive daily coverage in the middle of the newspaper's second section. The International Capital Markets pages cover fixed income securities, including government bonds, corporate bonds and international bonds; the Commodities and Agriculture page covers the markets for gold and other metals, energy, "soft" food commodities, etc.; and the Currencies and Money page covers the money markets, the foreign exchange markets and the bond, currency and interest rate derivatives markets. Equity and equity index futures and options are listed under London equities or on the back page.

For the key data on the economy, Tuesday's first section carries one of five tables of international economic indicators for six leading OECD countries (France, Germany, Italy, Japan, the United Kingdom and the United States). Thursday's first section carries five tables of UK economic indicators. Monday's front page has the latest relative values of currencies within the European Monetary System, and on the back page of the second section, an economic diary of key international economic statistics due to be released in the coming week.

APPENDIX 1

The key ratios guide

KEY FINANCIAL RATIOS

PROFITABILITY

Pre-tax profit margin (per cent) = $\dfrac{\text{pre-tax profit} \times 100}{\text{turnover}}$

Return on capital employed (per cent) = $\dfrac{\text{pre-tax profit} \times 100}{\text{capital employed}}$

Earnings per share = $\dfrac{\text{after tax profit}}{\text{number of shares}}$

GEARING

Total liabilities = long-term debt + current or short-term liabilities

Balance sheet gearing or debt/equity ratio (per cent) = $\dfrac{\text{total liabilities} \times 100}{\text{ordinary funds}}$

Income gearing (per cent) = $\dfrac{\text{interest expense} \times 100}{\text{operating profit}}$

Interest cover = $\dfrac{\text{operating profit}}{\text{interest expense}}$

KEY SHAREHOLDER RATIOS

YIELD

$$\text{Dividend yield (per cent)} = \frac{\text{gross dividend per share} \times 100}{\text{share price}}$$

PRICE/EARNINGS

$$\text{Price/earnings ratio} = \frac{\text{share price}}{\text{earnings per share}}$$

DIVIDEND COVER

$$\text{Dividend cover} = \frac{\text{earnings per share}}{\text{gross dividend per share}}$$

APPENDIX 2

The key indices guide

THE FT ORDINARY SHARE INDEX (FT-30)

The original constituents in 1935

Associated Portland Cement
Austin Motor
Bass
Bolsover Colliery
Callenders Cables & Const.
Coats (J&P)
Courtaulds
Distillers
Dorman Long
Dunlop Rubber
Electrical & Musical Industries
Fine Spinners and Doublers
General Electric
Guest Keen & Nettlefolds
Harrods

Hawker Siddeley
Imperial Chemical Industries
Imperial Tobacco
International Tea Co's Stores
London Brick
Murex
Patons & Baldwins
Pinchin Johnson & Associates
Rolls Royce
Tate & Lyle
Turner & Newall
United Steel
Vickers
Watney Combe & Reid
Woolworth (FW)

The current constituents

Allied Domecq
ASDA Group
BICC
BOC Group
BTR
Blue Circle Industries
Boots
British Airways
British Gas
British Petroleum

British Telecom
Cadbury Schweppes
Courtaulds
Forte
General Electric
Glaxo Wellcome
GKN
Grand Metropolitan
Guinness
Hanson Trust

Imperial Chemical Industries
Lucas Industries
Marks & Spencer
National Westminster Bank
P&O Steam Navigation

Reuters
Royal Insurance
SmithKline Beecham
Tate & Lyle
Thorn EMI

THE FT-SE 'FOOTSIE' 100

The original constituents in 1984

Allied–Lyons
Associated British Foods
ASDA Group
Barclays Bank
Barratt Developments
Bass
BAT Industries
Beecham Group
Berisford
BICC
Blue Circle Industries
BOC Group
Boots
Bowater
BPB Industries
British & Commonwealth
British Aerospace
British Elect. Traction
British Home Stores
British Petroleum
Britoil
BTR
Burton Group
Cable & Wireless
Cadbury Schweppes
Commercial Union Assurance
Consolidated Gold Fields
Courtaulds
Dalgety
Distillers
Eagle Star

Edinburgh Investment Trust
English China Clays
Exco International
Ferranti
Fisons
General Accident
General Electric
Glaxo Holdings
Globe Investment Trust
Grand Metropolitan
Great Universal Stores
Guardian Royal Exchange
GKN
Hambro Life Assurance
Hammerson Prop. Inv. & Dev.
Hanson Trust
Harrisons & Crossfield
Hawker Siddeley
House of Fraser
Imperial Chemical Industries
Imperial Cont. Gas Association
Imperial Group
Johnson Matthey
Ladbroke
Land Securities
Legal & General
Lloyds Bank
Magnet & Southerns
MEPC
MFI Furniture Group
Marks & Spencer

Midland Bank
National Westminster Bank
Northern Foods
P&O Steam Navigation
Pearson
Pilkington
Plessey
Prudential Corporation
RMC
Racal Electronics
Rank Organisation
Reckitt & Colman
Redland
Reed International
Rowntree Mackintosh
Royal Bank of Scotland
Royal Insurance
RTZ Corporation
Sainsbury

Scottish & Newcastle
Sears Holdings
Sedgwick Group
Shell
Smith & Nephew
Standard Chartered
Standard Telephone & Cables
Sun Alliance
Sun Life Assurance Society
Thorn EMI
Tarmac
Tesco
Trafalgar House
Trusthouse Forte
Ultramar
Unilever
United Biscuits
Whitbread
Wimpey

The constituents as of January 1996

Abbey National
Allied Domecq
Argos
Argyll Group
ASDA Group
Associated British Foods
Bank of Scotland
BAA
Barclays Bank
Bass
BAT Industries
Blue Circle Industries
BOC Group
Boots
British Aerospace
British Airways
British Gas
British Petroleum
British Sky Broadcasting
British Steel

British Telecom
BTR
Burmah Castrol
Burton Group
Cable & Wireless
Cadbury Schweppes
Carlton Communications
Commercial Union
Cookson
Courtaulds
Enterprise Oil
Forte
Foreign & Colonial Investment Trust
General Accident
General Electric
GKN
Glaxo Wellcome
Granada
Grand Metropolitan
Great Universal Stores

Guardian Royal Exchange
Guinness
Hanson Trust
HSBC
Imperial Chemical Industries
Kingfisher
Ladbroke
Land Securities
Lasmo
Legal & General
Lloyds Bank
Marks & Spencer
National Grid
National Power
National Westminster Bank
North West Water
P&O Steam Navigation
Pearson
Pilkington
Powergen
Prudential Corporation
Rank Organisation
Reckitt & Colman
Redland
Reed International
Rentokil
Reuters
Rexam
RMC
Rolls Royce

Royal Bank of Scotland
Royal Insurance
RTZ Corporation
Sainsbury
Scottish & Newcastle
Scottish Power
Schroders
Severn Trent
Shell
Siebe
Smith & Nephew
Smithkline Beecham
Smiths Industries
Southern Electric
Standard Chartered
Sun Alliance
Tate & Lyle
Tesco
Thames Water
Thorn EMI
TI
Tomkins
TSB
Unilever
Vodaphone
Whitbread
Williams Holdings
Wolseley
Zeneca

THE DOW JONES INDUSTRIAL AVERAGE

The twelve constituents in 1897

American Cotton Oil

American Spirit

American Sugar

American Tobacco

Chicago Gas

General Electric

Laclede Gas

National Lead

Pacific Mail

Standard Rope & Twine

Tennessee Coal & Iron

US Leather

The thirty constituents in 1996

Allied-Signal

Aluminium Company of America

American Express

AT&T

Bethlehem Steel

Boeing

Caterpillar

Chevron

Coca Cola

Walt Disney

Du Pont

Eastman Kodak

Exxon

General Electric

General Motors

Goodyear

IBM

International Paper

McDonald's

Merck

Minnesota Mining

JP Morgan

Philip Morris

Procter & Gamble

Sears Roebuck

Texaco

Union Carbide

United Technologies

Westinghouse Electric

Woolworth

INDEX